Felicitous Space

Judith Fryer

Felicitous Space

*The Imaginative Structures
of Edith Wharton and
Willa Cather*

The University of North Carolina Press
Chapel Hill and London

© 1986 The University of North Carolina Press
All rights reserved
Manufactured in the United States of America

Library of Congress Cataloging in Publication Data

Fryer, Judith, 1939–
  Felicitous space.

Includes index.
    1. American fiction—20th century—History and
criticism. 2. Women in literature. 3. American fiction—
Women authors—History and criticism. 4. Feminism and
literature. 5. Wharton, Edith, 1862–1937—Criticism
and interpretation. 6. Cather, Willa, 1873–1947—
Criticism and interpretation. I. Title.
PS374.W6F73   1986   813'.52'09   85-8659
ISBN 0-8078-1655-8
ISBN 0-8078-4135-8 (pbk.)

The author is grateful for permission to reproduce passages from
the Edith Wharton Archives, Collection of American Literature,
the Beinecke Rare Book and Manuscript Library, Yale University,
New Haven, Connecticut, and from the Edith Wharton Manuscripts, Lilly Library, Indiana University, Bloomington, Indiana.

Poem #234 by Emily Dickinson is reprinted by permission of the
publishers and the Trustees of Amherst College from *The Poems of
Emily Dickinson*, edited by Thomas H. Johnson, Cambridge, Mass.:
The Belknap Press of Harvard University Press, Copyright 1951,
© 1955, 1979, 1983 by The President and Fellows of Harvard College.

for
these women
who have shared
their spaces
with me:

barbara
bettina
dorathea
liana
nina
ravina

CONTENTS

ILLUSTRATIONS

PREFACE

This book is set in a time and place historians—writing of "America's coming of age," "the search for order," "the incorporation of America," "the feminization of America," "the good years"—describe as the beginnings of modern America. The usual landmarks are Frederick Jackson Turner's address on the significance of the frontier in shaping the American character, Henry Adams's elegy to the Virgin as the world for which she stands succumbs, in the twentieth century, to the force of the Dynamo, the rise of the city, the bloodbath of World War I. This book, however, is a woman-centered inquiry; its focus is the experience of women, and its conceptual bounds are women's structures: the Woman's Building at the World's Columbian Exposition in Chicago in 1893 and the feminist utopian community, *Herland*, imagined in 1915 by Charlotte Perkins Gilman, who sought in restructuring the domestic environment to revolutionize the relationship between the sexes.

The first chapter is an investigation of women in terms of the spaces they inhabit, break free from, transform. Seeking to understand the interconnectedness between space and the female imagination, I turn to the fields of history, literature, environmental psychology, sociology and anthropology, geography, philosophy and the arts. All of this provides a context for my study of "Literature"—not as our critics have taught us to think of Literature, those "melodramas of beset manhood," as Nina Baym calls the canonical texts, that are particular expressions of being "American" in the dominant culture, but rather what Sarah Orne Jewett meant when she wrote to Willa Cather that "the Thing that teases the mind over and over for years, and at last gets itself put down rightly on paper—whether little or great, it belongs to Literature." During this period I define, two women writers depart from the canon to explore and inscribe their own experiences, those of a muted culture. Their imaginative structures are the focus of my inquiry in Chapters 2 through 11: Edith Wharton's meticulously conceived interiors, which include all that the eye can encompass; Willa Cather's unfurnished rooms and her landscapes that are physical and spiritual correlatives.

The structure of this book follows its own logic. Some readers will undoubtedly say what Jim Burden said of his manuscript "My Ántonia": it hasn't any form. Seventy years later, such a defense seems unnecessary: this book has form in the way that dreams do, in the way that certain modes of art do. Chapters 2 through 11 are a series of meditations; each is an invention spun upon a ground: a plan for a house, a room, a set of furnishings, a landscape, a story. Each of these meditations is concerned with the structures of fantasy.

Woman, in order to transform social and cultural structures, must write her self, Hélène Cixous insists in "The Laugh of the Medusa": "Woman must put herself into the text—as into the world and into history." And I have not been absent from this text, writing here a series of stories about the stories imaginative women, in the spaces they find felicitous, tell.

ACKNOWLEDGMENTS

This book has been a long time in the making. I began to think about women writers just after completing *The Faces of Eve*, a book that describes women characters imagined by American men. It was the summer of 1976: I was a participant in a National Endowment for the Humanities seminar at Yale and about to depart for a year as a Fulbright lecturer in Germany; my fellow seminar members and then the students in my graduate seminar at the University of Tübingen were my first audiences for the ideas that would eventually be developed here.

Another early audience was the community of women at the Bunting Institute in Cambridge, Massachusetts, where I spent a year in 1979–80: women with real interest in each other as persons and as scholars—the two were not separate—made for an unusual environment in which it was possible to work with great self-confidence and good feeling. In fact, one of the wonderful things about writing this book has been the network of women colleagues with which it has been associated, stretching out from Cambridge to Europe in one direction and to Ohio in the other. Liana Borghi, Bettina Friedl and other women too numerous to mention have listened to me and helped me to think more clearly; Elizabeth Wing and I have shared storytelling; harpsichordist Nina Sackett Key, in teaching me increasing grace and precision, has added a sustaining quality to my life and therefore to my writing.

Equally important in giving me a sense of connectedness has been the work of colleagues in American Studies: their ideas have influenced mine, and their lives have touched mine in important ways. There is the generosity, for example, of a fellow graduate student at Minnesota. Between 1976 and 1984 there was a stretch of time when I was unable to write, and in that period the book came apart. David Miller's gift to me was a careful reading of the pieces, and then of the entire manuscript as I wrote it; he offered insightful, penetrating commentary and constant support. I owe him an inexpressible debt of gratitude.

Others read the manuscript in various stages: Sacvan Bercovitch, Kathleen Foster and John Stilgoe read the first chapter, the most difficult one to write, and their responses helped me to say many complex things more clearly. Miami University colleagues Eugene Metcalf and Peter Williams were enthusiastic early readers, and Constance Pierce was a meticulous final reader. Edna Carter Southard and Thomas Hayes saved me from some mistakes in Chapter 2. Lynn Fryer's observations on Millet and Courbet enriched Chapter 8. Paul Alpers read a large part of the Cather section with great care; his insights were invaluable to my understanding of the pastoral tradition. My Minnesota teachers Mary Turpie and the late Bernard Bowron read the manuscript in first draft, and I thank them for their love and support.

In conceptualizing this work, I talked at length with Leo Marx; he was generous with his time, and he provided me with a hard problem to solve in the writing. Elizabeth Duvert and I took many walks in the environs of Oxford while I was thinking about the latter parts of the book; I learned much from her about space and landscape.

I owe too many intellectual debts to cite, but among the most important are those to Alan Trachtenberg, whose *The Incorporation of America* is a model of interdisciplinary scholarship; Lillian Schlissel, whose pioneering work on women's diaries and letters has influenced my own; Annette Kolodny for her sharply honed feminist re-readings of American literature; Dolores Hayden and Gwendolyn Wright for their feminist analyses of domestic spaces; John Brinckerhoff Jackson, John Stilgoe and Yi-Fu Tuan for their work on landscape; and Henry Glassie, who has taught me even more important things than how to read a floor plan, how to read culture from artifacts, and the importance of storytelling.

Staff at the Loeb Library of the Harvard University Graduate School of Design, Cambridge, Massachusetts; Beinecke Library, Yale University, New Haven, Connecticut; Lilly Library, Indiana University, Bloomington; the Harvard Center for Renaissance Studies, Villa I Tatti, Florence, Italy; Edith Wharton Restoration, Inc., Lenox, Massachusetts; the Willa Cather Pioneer Memorial Foundation, Red Cloud, Nebraska; Library, University of Nebraska, Lincoln; and Alderman Library, University of Virginia, Charlottesville, were helpful during the research stages of this work.

William Royall Tyler has graciously granted permission to reprint materials from the Edith Wharton manuscripts housed in the Beinecke and Lilly libraries.

Kathleen Marie Grondin meticulously typed various drafts of this manuscript with great patience; Sheila Kapur Fernandez carefully checked the endnotes; Doris Newton was a great help with the index. In the final stages, Deborah Fryer was a scrupulous and supportive proofreader, and my friend Herwig Friedl, in Germany, proved my only means, from Finland, of tracking down last-minute corrections.

Finally I would like to thank Iris Tillman Hill, editor-in-chief of the University of North Carolina Press, who has believed in this book from the beginning; Sandra Eisdorfer, editor; and designer Dariel Mayer.

The National Endowment for the Humanities provided support in the research stages—a summer grant in 1978 and a twelve-month grant in 1979–80. Miami University, Oxford, Ohio, awarded summer research grants in 1979 and 1982, and provided funds for research assistance and typing. The Rockefeller Foundation provided travel funds for the visits to the Southwest and Nebraska important to Chapter 10, a slightly different version of which appears in the forthcoming book, *Visions of Landscape: Women Artists of the American Southwest*, edited by Vera Norwood and Janice Monk. Chapter 1 was published separately in *Prospects: The Annual of American Cultural Studies* 9 (1985); earlier versions of Chapters 4, 5 and 10 were published, respectively, in *American Literary Realism* 17 (Autumn 1984); *Biography: An Interdisciplinary Quarterly* 6 (Spring 1983); and *Prairie Schooner* 55 (Spring 1981).

PROLOGUE

. . . in the central painting of a triptych [by the beautiful Spanish exile Remedios Varo], titled "Bordando el Manto Terrestre," were a number of frail girls with heart-shaped faces, huge eyes, spun-gold hair, prisoners in the top room of a circular tower, embroidering a kind of tapestry which spilled out the slit windows and into a void, seeking hopelessly to fill the void: for all the other buildings and creatures, all the waves, ships and forests of the earth were contained in this tapestry, and the tapestry was the world.

—Thomas Pynchon, *The Crying of Lot 49*

Thomas Pynchon's Oedipa Maas sees in the Varo triptych echoes of her own Rapunzel-like state, her world a tower from which Pierce Inverarity has ineffectually attempted to rescue her. Pynchon does not comment on the other two panels of the triptych: in the first the young women (more slender than frail) file away on bicycles from their convent-like towers—out for exercise or a trip to town; in the last, one of the maidens departs with her knight of deliverance. Nor does Pynchon observe that in the middle panel the young women, embroidering the tapestry of the world in their communal solitude, *create the world*. In which panel, one might ask, are the young women the most free?

The work of Remedios Varo is filled with women in towers, spinning, weaving, writing poetry, composing music—creating the world.[1] All of the women are the same woman. She frightens Pynchon. "Such a captive maiden," he writes, "soon realizes that her tower, its height and architecture, are like her ego only incidental: that what really keeps her where she is is magic, anonymous and malignant." Seeing no way "to understand how it works, . . . to measure its field strength, count its lines of force," he asks, "If the tower is everywhere and the knight of deliverance [is] no proof against its magic, what else?"[2]

BOOK I
Women and Space

The new space . . . has a kind of invisibility to those who have not entered it. It is therefore inviolable. At the same time it communicates power which, paradoxically, is experienced both as power of presence and power of absence.

—Mary Daly, *Beyond God the Father*

CHAPTER I

From White City to *Herland*

Behaviour and space are mutually dependent.
                              —Shirley Ardener, *Women and Space:*
                                   Ground Rules and Social Maps

I

Some fifty years ago Virginia Woolf made the discovery that women do not write when they have no spaces to themselves, no private places in which to retire and think their own thoughts. She was sitting on the banks of a river at the time, sifting the bits of her experience—the ejection of her person from piece after piece of male turf at "Oxbridge" college, the exclusion of her sex from the massive collections of the British Museum— and meditating on the subject of her lectures for this college, "women and fiction." Her conclusion, in what was to become "A Room of One's Own," seems less important than the *process* of her thought: watching the fish darting about in the water, she describes letting down a hook into the pool of her reflections and following the ripples as they flow out until she sees the pattern they make. As we follow Woolf's process here, and it is the process of her fiction as well, we see that as the repressiveness of the Oxbridge turf and the British Museum give way to the riverbank, anger gives way to reverie, an imaginative state in which she is at the center of a space rippling out to a seemingly infinite vastness, a space associated, in memory, with childhood freedom.

It was with the post-childhood identification with particular kinds of spaces, however, that Woolf would be concerned in her essay—one kind for Shakespeare, another for his sister, one kind for the men dining at Oxbridge College, another for the women at Fernham—and with the effects of these very different spatial determinations upon the imagination.

At Fernham, where not a penny could be spared for "amenities," for "partridges and wine, beadles and turf, books and cigars, libraries and leisure," she thinks of the men's college with its quiet rooms looking across quiet quadrangles, "of the urbanity, the geniality, the dignity which are the offspring of luxury and privacy and space," and she wonders "what effect poverty has on the mind; and what effect wealth has on the mind; . . . how unpleasant it is to be locked out; and . . . how it is worse perhaps to be locked in; and . . . of the safety and prosperity of the one sex and of the poverty and insecurity of the other and of the effect of tradition and of the lack of tradition upon the mind of a writer."[1]

At the root of Woolf's question—what conditions are necessary for the creation of works of art?—is the understanding that gender is a function of culture, and that culture, in prescribing social and economic norms according to gender, has a direct relationship to the imagination. Woolf argues that men and women imagine—and express—things differently because of economic and social conditions imposed upon them. This has not, until recently, been the majority view; others have inverted Woolf's contention arguing for an innate difference between women and men that predisposes them to imagine and desire certain kinds of space. So Erik H. Erikson concludes, for example, from his experiment of the late 1940s, the results of which later became the core of his essay, "Inner and Outer Space: Reflections on Womanhood." For this famous experiment, each of 150 boys and 150 girls, ages ten to twelve, was asked to construct an exciting movie scene from assembled toys and building blocks in Erikson's California office. Instructions given the young people are important, for although Erikson notes in passing that not one of his subjects constructed an "exciting scene from an imaginary moving picture,"[2] he was in fact "inviting" them to play roles. Erikson found that without exception the girls created not *moving* pictures, but static scenes: rooms, with elaborate doorways, which were images of domestic harmony, from the furniture arrangements to the figures grouped among the various pianos and chairs and stoves. The boys, on the other hand, all constructed high and elaborate towers or exterior scenes of movement. From this Erikson concluded that anatomy is indeed destiny, since even children reproduce their own bodies in play. He did not say that the experiment had props; he commented on neither the seeming class homogeneity nor the significance of the age group as precisely that when childhood freedom has given way to cultural conditioning which would shape the responses of young people to the "suggestions" of this figure of patriarchal authority; he failed to

*The right atmosphere for
the children's playroom*

Advertisement depicting suburban house as an ideal setting for children's play.
(*The House Beautiful*, 1928)

observe that these adolescents behaved *as they were expected to behave*, reproducing in their play the spaces traditionally occupied by role models.

As a matter of fact, Erikson's experiment comes on the heels of the "Better Homes in America" movement, a cooperative venture between government and private enterprise that sponsored conferences, classes and publications to demonstrate how "good homes build character." In towns, suburbs and rural areas, Better Homes enthusiasts came together to discuss zoning, construction standards, decoration and citizenship, mortgage financing, sanitation, racial strife and Communist threats to private enterprise: "Boys learned to erect 'boy-built' houses; girls learned to make them attractive."[3] Clearly, the boys and girls who came to Erikson's office were behaving appropriately, presenting themselves as having made successful adaptations to the demands of their middle-class society. Still, one might ask, why did none of these young people choose to express themselves otherwise?

Looking back to the beginning of this progressive belief in the relationship between the built environment and the national character, this parable, one of Edith Wharton's earliest stories called "The Valley of Childish Things," offers one kind of explanation. It begins:

> Once upon a time a number of children lived together in the Valley of Childish Things, playing all manner of delightful games, and studying the same lesson books. But one day a little girl, one of their number, decided that it was time to see something of the world about which the lesson books had taught her; and as none of the other children cared to leave their games, she set out alone to climb the pass which led out of the valley.
>
> It was a hard climb, but at length she reached a cold, bleak tableland beyond the mountains. Here she saw cities and men, and learned many useful arts, and in so doing grew to be a woman. But the tableland was bleak and cold, and when she had served her apprenticeship she decided to return to her old companions in the Valley of Childish Things, and work with them instead of with strangers.

On the way back she meets one of her old playmates, who has also been out in the world. They talk of building bridges and draining swamps and cutting roads, and she thinks to herself, "Since he has grown into such a fine fellow, what splendid men and women my other playmates must have become!" But she is disappointed. Instead of growing into men and women, her playmates have remained little children, playing the same old games. When she tries to tell them about the great things being done beyond the mountains, they pick up their toys and go farther down the valley to play. Turning to her fellow traveler, who is making a garden out of cockleshells and bits of glass and broken flowers for a little girl, she asks him if he wants to set to work building bridges, draining swamps and cutting roads. He replies that at the moment he is too busy; and as she turns to go, he adds, "Really, my dear, you ought to have taken better care of your complexion."[4]

This female version of Plato's allegory of the cave suggests the painful consequences of deviating from cultural patterns. By the ages of ten to twelve the young subjects of Erikson's experiment had learned to perform, to play roles that they were expected to play as social beings—in this case in twentieth-century America. If the option of rewriting the script occurred to them, they did not choose it; they walked onto a stage already set, and to have deviated from the expected pattern would have been to have risked the displeasure of the director. These were adolescents; they already knew that to be a successful adult, as sociologist Erving Goffman has pointed out, one learns to play a variety of roles by making smooth adjustments to the requirements of social scenes, performances that high-light official values like an ongoing ceremony that comes to be taken for reality itself. To choose *not* to play roles, then, is to refuse to participate in "reality"; or, "to stay in one's room away from the place where the party is given," as Goffman puts it, "is to stay away from where reality is being performed."[5]

It is this distinction between "one's room" and "the party," between the private space and the public place, that interests me here. In America there is a long-standing tradition that describes the tension between the two and that defines the private space as the realm of the imagination, the public place as the realm of behavior, a dichotomy Edith Wharton, among other writers, would exploit. Such a tradition posits a "silent language," some mode of consciousness that is not social, but creative.[6] This condition—the need to withdraw from the public place of performance to a private space where the imagination feels at home—is not, of course, particular to women. There is the classic example of Nathaniel Haw-thorne's sense of painful isolation in his self-chosen "owl's nest"[7] and, on the other hand, his sense of blocked creativity in the Custom House office when he was employed, like other males of his culture, in pursuit of "Uncle Sam's Gold." His immediate apprehension, when he holds the letter A to his breast, of the alienation of the deviant leads to the inspira-tion of *The Scarlet Letter* and to his own identification with his heroine. Yet women have stood, in our culture, for some space that is static and tranquil, and men have had the whole Territory to explore. While most of the men have been busy pursuing Uncle Sam's gold, women have been expected to create a space of respite, the "sivilizing" place, as Huck Finn called it. The separate spheres of the two sexes in America, those Tocque-ville had observed in 1830, had become so clearly marked by the end of the nineteenth century when Edith Wharton published "The Valley of Childish Things" as to suggest to American cultural critics "an abysmal fracture."[8]

The turn of the century, in fact, was seen as *the* moment of separa-tion between one era and another. The moment is marked in 1900 by Henry Adams as he contemplates the forty-foot dynamo engine in the Gallery of Machines at the Paris Exposition. Describing this moment in his autobiography, Adams would recall facing a wholly new force, one standing for "anarchical" energy and representing a disintegration of the cultural unity that had given the world meaning. Unity, up until this moment, had been represented by the force of the Virgin, by which Adams meant the spiritual energy that had inspired most of the world's great art; the new masculine force of the Dynamo, on the other hand, signaled a new era of "multiplicity." Henry Adams at this moment sees two modes of being in conflict, one residual, the other dominant; one artistic, the other technological; one female, the other male. His dismay stems from his inability either to understand the new era of multiplicity or to imagine a synthesis, an emergent mode, which might embody a new form of energy and passion.

Adams's moment is well chosen. It is as if he were frozen in time: looking backward, looking forward, the abysmal fracture he perceives between old and new modes of being, and the symbols he chooses to express that perception, express a widespread sense in turn-of-the-century America of sexual and cultural difference. His countrymen felt female energy only as reflected emotion, Adams observes; they felt "a railway train as power"—but "all the steam in the world could not, like the Virgin, build Chartres."[9]

While Henry Adams stood in front of the dynamo engine and thought about the Virgin, his contemporaries—American writers and reformers, cultural critics and philosophers—were preoccupied with theories about women and space; that is, they described the great change they sensed in this period in terms of shifts in gender roles and in terms of relationships to physical and built environments. Philosopher George Santayana, for example, used architecture as a metaphor to mark the demise of one era and the onset of another in America at the turn of the century, suggesting a new and unbridgeable division between the sexes in which women are the culture carriers: "The American Will inhabits the sky-scraper; the American Intellect inhabits the colonial mansion," Santayana wrote, mourning the passing of "the genteel tradition." The one, "all aggressive enterprise" is "the sphere of the American man; the other, at least predominantly, of the American woman."[10]

The structures Santayana used to represent two spheres of activity are not only symbols, however; they are actual constructions in turn-of-the-century America. Two such structures can stand as examples typical of the period; they are unique only in that they are described by well-known writers, one female, representative of the "genteel tradition," the other male, representative of that new aggressive force.

The drawing-room that figures prominently in the novels of Edith Wharton appeared earlier in her book called *The Decoration of Houses* in 1898. Co-authored with interior decorator Ogden Codman, Jr., it became a "practical handbook" for the "American Renaissance"—a time of high Victorian splendor in architecture, sculpture and the decorative arts when models of the Italian Renaissance and classical Rome, such as those designed by Beaux Arts architects Charles McKim, Stanford White and Richard Morris Hunt, represented the epitome of taste. An elaborate mapping of ideal domestic spaces, *The Decoration of Houses* emphasizes above all privacy and a sense of retreat: doors that lock and bolt mark the boundaries between public and private spaces. As can be seen from the description of the drawing-room, however, "privacy" has a particular meaning.

The American drawing-room, Wharton explains, has a twofold origin: one is the medieval English "with-drawing-room" to which "the lady and her maidens retired from the festivities of the hall"; the other is a

Examples of modern locksmith's work in the French style. (Edith Wharton and Ogden Codman, Jr., *The Decoration of Houses*, 1897)

Edith Wharton's parlor at 884 Park Avenue, New York City, decorated by Ogden Codman, Jr. (Edith Wharton and Ogden Codman, Jr., *The Decoration of Houses*, 1897, rev. ed. 1978; courtesy, W. W. Norton & Company)

combination of what in the Middle Ages and early Renaissance period of France were two rooms, the *salon de compagnie* and the *salon de famille*. "In houses of average size, where there are but two living rooms—the master's library, or 'den,' and the lady's drawing-room,—it is obvious that the latter ought to be used as a *salon de famille*, or meeting-place for the whole family," Wharton argued, its lighting soft and diffused, its furnishings and decoration simple and harmonious with "nothing . . . so striking or eccentric as to become tiresome when continually seen."[11] The lady's drawing-room, then, should be a symbol of American family life: too often it is a place of "exquisite discomfort" from which "the inmates of the house instinctively flee as soon as their social duties are discharged" when it should be the center of repose.[12] Feminine in origin and character, the drawing-room encloses the family, minimizing its contact with the outside world, setting the tone even for the articulation between inside and outside. Landscape, in *The Decoration of Houses*, exists in relation to the inside of the house; windows are designed to make landscape "what, *as seen from a room*, it logically ought to be: a part of the wall-decoration, in the sense of being subordinated to the same general lines."[13]

These very distinctions between public and private, between the world and the house, mark the book, of course, as one for leisure-class consumption. Although Wharton and Codman hoped that "a return to [the] architectural principles . . . of the past"[14] would by example filter down throughout American society, the elegantly furnished rooms they describe appealed to those whose primary concern was for the ornament and arrangement of abundant spaces. Two things, however, tie this book to other housing handbooks of the time. One is the recurrence of the keywords "taste" and "suitability," and the concurrent image of the house as an expression of the rituals of daily life, whose rooms suggest "a society which affirms a hierarchy of values." The other is the emphasis on "organicism"—a rejection of a superficial application of ornament independent of structure and an insistence upon architectural features that are integral parts of every house, inside and out, in the name of "reason, order and simplicity."[15]

That this "organicism" was also at the root of Louis Sullivan's architectural theory, divergent as his skyscrapers are from the drawing-rooms of Edith Wharton and from the whole Beaux Arts tradition, suggests the widespread belief in turn-of-the-century America in the relationship between the built environment and the national character. Between them, in fact, Wharton's drawing-room and Sullivan's skyscraper prefigure Erikson's experiment of a half-century later.

Describing himself both as a product and as a shaper of his culture, Louis Sullivan saw human structures as "the product and index of the thought of the people of the time and place."[16] By 1907, however, feeling like an abandoned prophet of democracy, he would characterize "the bulk of our architecture as rotten to the core," judging it, in *Kindergarten Chats*, by "its poverty of thought, its falsity in expression, its absence of manhood."[17] Sullivan had welcomed the new kingdom of force joyfully. Abandoning the East of the Beaux Arts architects for the more open and aggressive city of Chicago, he had begun in the late 1880s to build the sky-scrapers which, rooted in the ground and ornamented along their shafts with an elegance that emphasized their verticality and grew more elabo-rate at their skyward tips, were raw celebrations of phallic energy. "The need of the hour is for men!," Sullivan now urged, "men to the heart!" True architecture—as opposed to the false fronts that represent idealized forms from the past that have nothing to do with the function of a build-ing—bespeaks "the manliness of man." For Sullivan, *masculine* meant "that which is virile, forceful, direct, clear and straightforward, that which grasps and retains in thought"; *feminine* meant "intuitive sympathy, tact, suavity and grace—the qualities that soothe, elevate, ennoble and refine,"[18] qualities inappropriate, apparently, to public life, or, as Henry Adams would have said, to modern public life. American railway stations, for example, which according to *Building News* in 1875 were "to the nineteenth century what monasteries and cathedrals were to the thirteenth," were not felt as power, Sullivan said, but as so much "Stygian murk."[19] A building like the Illinois Central Railway Station was false because it was the *femi-nine* misplaced: a "droll and fantastical parody upon logic; [a] finical mass of difficulties; [a] web of contradictions; [a] blatant fallacy; [a] repellant and indurated mess; [a] canker on the tongue of the national speech." Only the architect—like Sullivan—who speaks the true American lan-guage could save the race: "A man that lives and breathes, that has red blood; a real man, a manly man; a virile force—broad, vigorous and with a whelm of energy—an entire male."[20]

Taking as his text Emerson, Whitman and Thoreau—the search for the American poet who would speak the language of democratic forms, the projection of the prophet of democracy, the urge to simplify into one rule that would admit of no exception: "form follows function"—Sullivan would see the tragedy of American culture as a disintegration of the or-ganic unity of the Transcendentalists. Like Sullivan, economist Thorstein Veblen, another Midwestern Progressive, found American architectural styles to be based on pretense and display. In his *Theory of the Leisure Class*, published just one year after Edith Wharton's *Decoration of Houses*, Veblen argued that architecture is a symbolic representation of a nation's material conditions and cultural expectations. He attributed the division between male and female, however, to a social Darwinist evolution of a leisure class, distinguished by "an ownership of the woman by the able-bodied

Louis Sullivan, Guaranty (Prudential) Building, Buffalo, New York, 1895. (Courtesy, Library of Congress)

Bradford Gilbert, Illinois Central Station, Chicago, 1892–93. (Courtesy, Illinois Central Gulf Railroad)

men of the community."[21] Women were an index to culture, Veblen argued: women like Edith Wharton, with their manners and breeding, decorum and formal ceremonial observances, represented a type in a certain stage of development. Since the woman's position in the scheme of life of any community is an expression of the socioeconomic development of that community, the disintegration or breakdown of cultural patterns is evidence of a progressive discontent on the part of the "new woman" with the discrepancy between her prescribed place in the accepted scheme of life and the exigencies of the economic situation.

Veblen's theories, founded in his observations of the relationship between behavior and environment, were based on widespread assumptions among Progressives like Louis Sullivan and Frank Lloyd Wright, Jane Addams and Charlotte Perkins Gilman, that changing the structure of the spaces in which men and women lived and worked would effect changes in behavior, altering the very relationships between the sexes.[22] It is in this period and in Veblen's and Sullivan's Chicago that the ferment about changing the built environment properly begins: with the World's Columbian Exposition of 1893, an idealized monumental version of America, White City on the shores of Lake Michigan.

II

Addressing the Association of American Historians at the World's Columbian Exposition of 1893 in Chicago, Frederick Jackson Turner announced that the first period of American history had come to an end with the closing—as officially reported by the U.S. census of 1890—of the frontier. "American social development has been continually beginning over again on the frontier," he said, developing an idea that would influence the next several generations of American historians. "This perennial rebirth, this fluidity of American life, this expansion westward with its new opportunities, its continuous touch with the simplicity of primitive society, furnish the forces dominating American character." Turner meant, of course, male Americans and male frontiers: "the fisherman, fur trader, miner, cattle-raiser, . . . and pioneer farmer . . . ; the trader's frontier, the rancher's frontier, . . . the miner's frontier, and the farmer's frontier." This frontier functioned like "a military training school, keeping alive the power of resistance to aggression, and developing the stalwart and rugged qualities of the frontiersman." To the frontier, he concluded, "the American intellect owes its striking characteristics. That coarseness and strength combined with acuteness and inquisitiveness; that practical, inventive turn of mind, quick to find expedients; that masterful grasp of material things, lacking in the artistic, but powerful to effect great ends; that restless, nervous energy; that dominant individualism, working for good and evil, and withal that buoyancy and exuberance which comes from freedom."[23]

In pointing out how Turner's description of American "character" refers to male Americans only, David Potter suggested that for women opportunity as individuals began where the frontier left off—in the city.[24] Although the typewriter he preferred to the plow turned out to be a less than liberating symbol for women, Potter was on the right track, for recent collections of women's letters and diaries of the frontier make clear the absence of mythologizing—or of any response to the land that was not direct and matter-of-fact—in the private writings of westering women.[25] Seldom involved in the decisions to go West, these women followed their men, often with a great deal of unhappiness, loneliness, privation and illness; for them place meant the reestablishment of domestic routines that gave order to their lives. Although there were women homesteaders, teachers and doctors among them, for the most part their private writings reflect their involvement with family, with the difficult and exhausting business of daily life, with illness and death. Roles in the city were not any less prescribed for women—most of them who were not housewives became domestic workers and factory laborers, secretaries, nurses and elementary school teachers; but collectively, women in an urbanizing America at the end of the nineteenth century were becoming a force increasingly prominent and disturbing.

If Turner described a world of force without women, Henry James posited a world of women without force. From the perspective of an expatriate, James in 1883, returning to America for a visit, noted his wish to write "a very American tale." Ignoring completely the milestones of technological achievement, he asked himself, in the year of the opening ceremonies of Brooklyn Bridge, what was "the most salient and peculiar point in our social life," and he found it to be "the situation of women." He perceived an "abyss of inequality, the like of which has never before been seen under the sun," which he attributed to "the growing divorce between the American woman (with her comparative leisure, culture, grace, social instincts, artistic ambitions) and the male American immersed in the ferocity of business, with no time for any but the most sordid interests, purely commercial, professional, democratic and political."[26] The novel that became *The Bostonians*, one of two in which James was concerned with the politics of the city, does indeed focus on women, but on women who in turning their backs on comparative leisure and social graces in order to pursue the ineffective measures of reform that James saw as profoundly antisocial, present collectively a picture of a society stunted and warped. *This* is what makes it so "very American."

Admittedly, Turner and James were concerned with different versions of America—different classes, geographies, ways of life, value systems. By "space" they meant opposite things: the American landscape for James took on the character of "a world created, a stage set." The " 'composed' felicity" of nature "suggested the furniture of a drawing-room"; "sweet old stones had the surface of grey velvet, and . . . scattered wild apples were like figures in the carpet." And the relationship of "space" to the American character meant, for James, not the invigorating, democratic effects of the frontier on American men, but the positive or negative effects of houses and urban neighborhoods on the imagination. Writing as "the restored absentee" on his last visit to America in 1903, James had grave reservations about the universal custom of the house with almost no one of its indoor parts distinguishable from any other. . . . This diffused vagueness of separation between apartments, between hall and room, between one room and another, between the one you are in and the one you are not in, between place of passage and place of privacy, is a provocation to despair which the public institution shares impartially with the luxurious "home." . . . Thus we have . . . every part of every house . . . visible, visitable, penetrable, not only from every other part, but from as many parts of as many other houses as possible. . . . Thus we see systematized the indefinite extension of all spaces and the definite merging of all functions; the enlargement of every opening, the exaggeration of every passage, the substitution of gaping arches and far perspectives and resounding voids for enclosing walls, for practicable doors, for controllable windows, for all the rest of the essence of the room-character, that room-suggestion which is so indispensable . . . to occupation and concentration.[27]

Approaching this problem of the relationship of space to the American character from opposite perspectives, then, Turner and James between them articulate the concerns of most historians, writers of imaginative literature and cultural critics at the turn of the century. Freedom and enclosure, male and female, force and culture, culture and nature—these terms figure as fact and symbol in all analyses of major shifts in cultural patterns in this time and place.

Two of the most imaginative recent histories of late nineteenth-century America, each attempting to create fresh structures for describing the tremendous change during this period, conceptualize again in terms of feminine and masculine. Not surprisingly, the gender of the historian informs the bias. Both Ann Douglas, in *The Feminization of American Culture*, and Alan Trachtenberg, in *The Incorporation of America*, see a disintegration of the promised organic wholeness that reached its peak during the Transcendental period. Both stress the strength of a Melville, who according to Douglas attempted to reeducate, defy and finally ignore a public addicted to sentimental fare, and who according to Trachtenberg writes the fable of America in an innocent and heroic Billy Budd condemned by a state that no longer grounds itself in natural reason, whose social laws are void of compassion and sympathy.

In the modernization of American culture that began in the Victorian period, according to Douglas, "some basic law of dialectical motion was disrupted, unfulfilled." She argues, somewhat like Henry Adams, that the demise of Calvinist patriarchal structures should have met with a

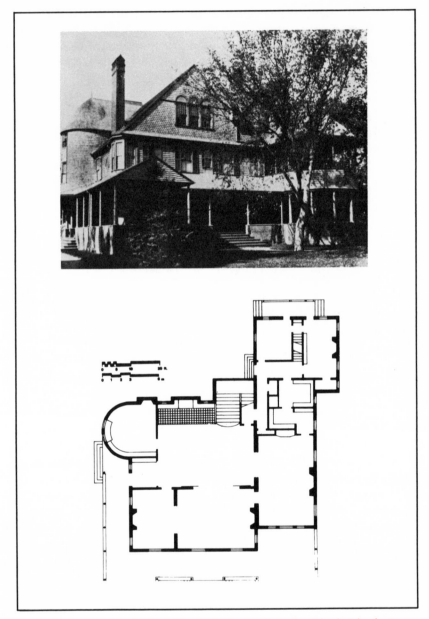

TOP: McKim, Mead and White, Isaac Bell house, Newport, Rhode Island, 1883. BOTTOM: Bell house, plan. (Arnold Lewis, *American Country Houses of the Gilded Age* [George W. Sheldon's *Artistic Country-Seats*, 1886–87], 1982; courtesy, Dover Publications)

viable, sexually diversified culture. Instead, the key to this period is Harriet Beecher Stowe's "Pink and White Tyranny"—the drive of nineteenth-century American women to gain power through the exploitation of their feminine identity as their society defined it. Increasingly freed from the responsibilities of domestic industry, these women comprised the vast majority of the churchgoing and reading public; they edited magazines and wrote books for other women like themselves; they became the prime consumers of American culture, and as such exerted an enormous influence on the chief male purveyors of that culture.[28]

Trachtenberg, on the other hand, focuses on the beginnings of modern corporate ownership, the directions of which became most clearly marked at the moment of greatest seeming harmony of all elements in American culture. An ironic gesture set in time between the financial panic of 1893 and the bloody Pullman strike of 1894, and in space separated from the world of misery and despair that lay outside its gates, White City, as the World's Columbian Exposition in Chicago came to be called, was quite literally the incorporation of the ideal. It was the fusion of two images of the city—Vanity Fair, the glittering marketplace, and the Celestial City, which dates in the American imagination to the very founding of our country.[29] White City, an imposition of a model city upon some seven hundred acres of once-swampy land dredged, filled and inlaid with canals, lagoons, plazas, promenades and a preserve of woods according to Frederick Law Olmsted's unifying ground plan, was "a lesson in the coordination of spaces and structures: . . . it taught the public utility of beauty, the coordination of art with the latest mechanical wonders."

The grounds of White City itself, organized hierarchically with the Court of Honor at its center, presented a set of contrasts, Trachtenberg suggests, the center representing America through its exhibitions, the outlying exotic Midway Plaisance standing for the rest of the world in subordinate relation, confirming by its carnival atmosphere the dignity of the center. All of the buildings of the Court of Honor were of steel-frame construction, coated with a composite plaster-like material called "staff," which the Chief of Construction, Daniel Burnham, applied everywhere throughout the court—"on sculpture, ornamentation of every kind, the construction of balustrades, vases, facing for docks," making possible an allusive facade, an illusion of marble and classic monumentality, a fusion of the mechanical and the artistic, the material and the spiritual.[30]

Henry Adams, with his usual cynicism, picking up on the rhetoric of the press in response to the Exposition, recognized the Fair for what it

Artist's rendering, bird's-eye view of World's Columbian Exposition, Chicago, 1893. (Courtesy, Judith Paine)

was—a performance, an elaborate stage set for a theatrical production. The artists and architects who had done the work offered little encouragement to hope for an improved public taste, he wrote: "to them the Northwest refused to look artistic. They talked as though they worked only for themselves; as though art, to the Western people, was a stage decoration; a diamond shirt-stud; a paper collar."[31] Even Adams, however, conceded that "Chicago was the first expression of American thought as a unity," but Edward Bellamy recognized the *semblance* of social wholeness that the Fair presented. "The underlying motive of the whole exhibition, under a sham pretense of patriotism," he wrote, "is business, advertising with a view to individual money-making."[32] Louis Sullivan, on the other hand, attacked the Fair on aesthetic grounds. In bitter protest against the authority of Eastern Beaux Arts architects over the design of the Exposition, he called it the worst possible event for the development of an indigenous American architecture. And architectural critic Montgomery Schuyler cautioned readers of the *Architectural Record* not to see White City, with its carefully regulated conformity, as real architecture pertinent to the needs of modern America.[33] Social critic Henry Demarest Lloyd, however, saw the Fair as revealing "to the people possibilities of social beauty, utility and harmony of which they had not even been able to dream." Even socialist Eugene V. Debs saw its "lofty ideal" as a "healthful influence . . . upon the national character"; and William Dean Howells exempted the Exposition from his assaults on selfishness and greed in the installments of his utopian novel running serially in *Cosmopolitan*, where his "Altrurian Traveler" perceives the very model for a better future in its "glorious capitals which will whiten the hills and shores of the east and the borderless plains of the west."[34]

If the Fair seemed a moment when contradictions were momentarily held in balance, so the Woman's Building, set at the exact junction between the Court of Honor and the Midway Plaisance, "just at the point of transition from the official view of reality to the world of exotic amusement,"[35] embodied the contradictions of women's self-presentation during this period. The only American building at the Fair whose design was open to competition, the Woman's Building was an ambiguous statement, reflecting the fundamental differences among the women assembled there. Sophia Hayden's Italian Renaissance palace was praised for qualities not usually ascribed to buildings: interior decorator Candace Wheeler called it "the most peaceably human of all the buildings . . . like a man's ideal of woman"; *Harper's Bazar* quoted an anonymous architect who called the

Sophia Hayden, Woman's Building, World's Columbian Exposition, Chicago, 1893. (Courtesy, Collection of the Hudson River Museum)

building "chaste and timid"; but Marie Thérèse Blanc, a French writer visiting the Fair, noted that the building had been "praised even to hyperbole for its feminine qualities of reserve, delicacy and distinction—wholly moral qualities which may not suffice when it is a question of striking from stone an idea, be it great or small."[36]

Inside were two large murals, Mary Fairchild MacMonnies's *Primitive Woman* and Mary Cassatt's *Modern Woman*. The first was an allegorical presentation of women of monumental proportions working at tasks of nurturance. The other, a triptych of young women in a garden, plucking the fruits of knowledge and the arts, with naked babies cavorting on the borders, outraged critics by its "radical" Impressionism and because men were completely absent from the representation. Both murals, however, were hung near the ceiling, too high to be seen clearly; they served as decorations. Displays ranged from the Queen of Italy's handmade lace and cigarettes rolled by Spanish women laborers to those showing increasing interest among middle-class women in technological invention and "scientific" approaches to philanthropy: portable sinks and dish-heaters, for example, portable bathtubs and mechanical dusters, all invented by women, women's patented transportation systems, typewriters and a city-wide waterworks project. Women also set up and staffed a model hospital and, in the Children's Building, a model kindergarten with the Froebel blocks Frank Lloyd Wright would later cite as a major inspiration.[37]

Women's activities at the Fair were administered by a Board of Lady Managers (a title chosen by the U.S. Congress and resented by board members), itself divided into two factions—one, wives of prominent businessmen, who in their own right had a network of social, cultural and financial connections, headed by Bertha Honore Palmer, wife of Chicago financier Potter Palmer; the other, the more radical representatives of women's groups across the country, identified with Isabella Beecher Hooker, Dr. Frances Dickinson and Phoebe Couzins, dubbed the "Isabellas" because of their interest in honoring Queen Isabella as the instigator of Columbus's voyage to the New World. The former group lobbied for a separate woman's building devoted to displays of the artistic and scientific achievements of women; the latter—which included sculptor Harriet Hosmer, who refused to display her statue of Queen Isabella in a woman's building—insisted upon women's equal participation with men in all activities and preferred an integration of examples of women's work with the rest of the displays. Mrs. Palmer proved omnipotent, not only as to the separate building, every detail of which she oversaw, but in the

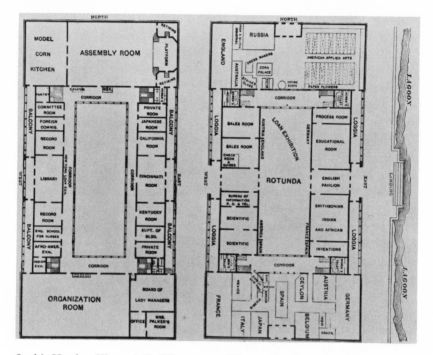

Sophia Hayden, Woman's Building, ground floor and gallery plans, World's Columbian Exposition, Chicago, 1893. (Courtesy, Chicago Historical Society)

construction of a women's dormitory, a children's building and in most aspects of women's participation in the Fair. The Board of Lady Managers so controlled the construction of the Woman's Building, in fact, that to the architect's horror, it became a kind of patchwork quilt of ornamentation by women.

As a symbol both of feminized and incorporated America, then, the Woman's Building, in its fusion of tradition with progressive energy, and of the spiritual with the technological, offered the same lesson as White City itself—a mode to be preached and practiced by reformers and builders in the decades to follow. White City had been the prototype, Gwendolyn Wright suggests in *Moralism and the Model Home*; "now the City Beautiful movement would provide the infrastructure for a perfect, planned society all over America."[38] Indeed, by the turn of the century, in small towns and suburbs with local improvement societies all over the country, plans were under way for civic construction projects undertaken by teams of architects, artists, business leaders and energetic women working together for the public good. The moral implications of the City Beautiful movement were made clear in religious publications like *The Congregationalist*, where Henry Demarest Lloyd in 1901 extolled the benefits advanced technology would bring to every American household. "Equal industrial power will be as invariable a function of citizenship as the equal franchise," Lloyd wrote. "Power will flow in every house and shop as freely as water. All men will become capitalists and all capitalists co-operators. . . . Women, released from the economic pressure which has forced them to deny their best nature and compete in unnatural history with men, will be re-sexed. . . . The new rapid transit, making it possible for cities to be four or five hundred miles in diameter and yet keep the farthest point within an hour of the center, will complete the suburbanization of every metropolis. Every house will be a center of sunshine and scenery."[39]

III

Lloyd's analysis—a worship of both Virgin and Dynamo—indulges in flights of flamboyant rhetoric divorced from the reality of turn-of-the-century America. Although there was indeed a widespread belief in the power of technology to cure the nation's ills, it does not follow that capitalists like Potter Palmer were likely to become models of cooperation, or co-operators in the various factories producing materials for grand structures like his Palmer House. When Lloyd says "all men will become capitalists," clearly he does not mean women (who had neither equal power nor the franchise), not even women like Mrs. Potter Palmer, who had proved in the organizational efforts of the Woman's Building to be as ruthless, competitive and powerful in her way as her husband was in his. Moreover, with the turn of the century, fewer women—re-sexed or otherwise—were choosing to remain in the center of sunshine and scenery. To the contrary, the increasing number of middle-class women working outside the home, participating in clubs and philanthropies, pursuing education, is clearly evidence of women's abandonment of the Victorian middle-class ideal of female seclusion. In 1870 less than 15 percent of American workers were women; by 1910 they made up almost a quarter of the work force. The figures from Lloyd's Chicago, where the female population exceeded the male, are even more striking: five times as many women were in the labor force by 1890 as had been in 1870; by 1903 one person in ten (one woman in four) was a working woman.[40] Nevertheless, both sexes, from a wide range of classes and with a wide range of skills, dwelling and working in buildings in country and city, perceiving great change and unrest in their America, shared with Lloyd notions that altering the built environment would change behavior and social relationships.

Women especially had long been concerned with housing: from conservative to radical, as they entered the public sphere, women turned their energies to using the forces of the new technology to domesticate American culture. As early as 1841 Catharine Beecher had been concerned with the design of healthful and efficient homes in her *Treatise on Domestic Economy*, expanded, with the help of her sister Harriet Beecher Stowe, into the more sophisticated *The American Woman's Home* in 1859. From the middle of the century on, model house plans appeared with increasing frequency in women's periodicals, whose readership increased greatly after 1879 when Congress lowered the postage rate for magazines. Between 1895 and 1917, Chicago reformers alone established sixty-eight settlement houses, the common aim of which was kindling the ideal of the middle-class home and community in the city's slum areas.[41] At the same time, however, experiments in "cooperative housekeeping," based on Charlotte Perkins Gilman's kitchenless houses, flourished throughout the United States between 1884 and 1925, including thirteen community dining clubs and twenty cooked-food delivery services, which lasted from six months to thirty-three years.[42]

Here we have a seeming paradox: exactly as women moved increasingly outside the home—becoming a cause of social disorder—the *model* home became a rigid construct imposed on a social situation as a means of establishing order and control, suggesting by the ordering of spaces that could be endlessly duplicated particular values, particular norms concerning family life, sex roles, community relations and social equality. Controlling aesthetic disorder, as Gwendolyn Wright points out, seemed a way of controlling society.[43] In this time in which the very fabric of society was tearing apart—for the liberation of women from traditional cultural patterns involves the social structures of home, family, work, leisure, sexual relationships—a similar solution was proposed by both traditionalists and reformers. Those who would preserve existing patterns and those who would restructure those patterns shared a belief in the relationship between the spaces that human beings inhabit and the behavior of those human beings. But none of these writers, philosophers, architects or social scientists, including those most concerned with the "situation of

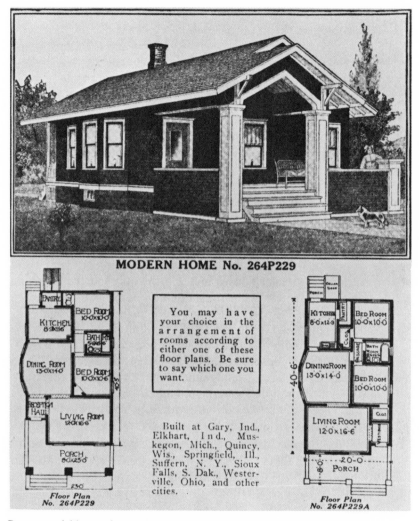

Precut model house from Sears, Roebuck & Co. (Courtesy, Chicago Historical Society)

women," was concerned with the design of spaces in which the female imagination might flourish. Perhaps all cultures in times of social upheaval take comfort in patterns that can be copied; yet there seems something particularly American about the campaign to define and publicize housing models and to connect these models to other, larger social goals.[44]

The American belief in the morality of architecture begins, of course, long before White City. Descendants of the Puritans, whose ordered townscape expressed clear ideas about religious and social values, were receptive ground, for example, for the ideas of John Ruskin, whose *Stones of Venice* and *Seven Lamps of Architecture*, originally published in England in 1849 and 1854, were available in America by mid-century and popular for more than four decades, with more than one hundred editions appearing by 1895. Books, articles and lectures for every kind of audience cited reverently Ruskin's ideas that architecture was the embodiment of Polity, Life, History and Religion, and that domestic architecture above all possessed the power to uplift and to reflect human development.[45] Thus President Timothy Dwight of Yale could stress the connection between the moral development of human beings and their modes of building,[46] while a Smith College publication proposed "an environment in which desirable conduct becomes a reflex response," in which improvements in the domestic environment are "so many props in the social framework so necessary to any ultimate solution."[47] The idea that one's environment was a crucial force in shaping personality was for different reasons attractive to men and women; both sexes subscribed to the idea that the quality of civilization depended upon the construction of a proper domestic national architecture.

Typical was the work of two New England architects, John Calvin Stevens and Albert Winslow Cobb, who published in 1889 a pattern book of their house designs entitled *Examples of American Domestic Architecture*. With Calvinist intensity, Stevens, the writer of the text, protested against the extravagance of the 1880s: the "degrading luxury" of mansions, "unwholesome hiving" in apartments and "painful contrasts of class." Stevens saw the profession of architecture "flourishing like some rank, luxurious weed"; his alternative to this decadence was a mission for the socially conscious architect. Homes of simple, unpretentious form, he wrote, available to the entire population, could become "a powerful helping agent in the process of sharing the fruits of labor equitably among all, and so promoting public health and happiness."[48]

The decade of the 1890s, with its rejection of "freakish" and "meaningless eccentricities," was the turning point for American suburban architecture, according to Herbert Croly, editor of *Architectural Record* from 1900 to 1909 and author of several books on domestic architecture. In *The Promise of American Life*, published in 1909, Croly extended his principles of architecture to a general philosophy of social reform, arguing that government, like architecture, was the responsibility of "true leaders." Looking forward rather than back as Santayana had done, Croly's aesthetic/political philosophy, based on a centralized organization, professional expertise and scientific planning, would offer a basis for Theodore Roosevelt's "New Nationalism" and Woodrow Wilson's "New Freedom" programs.[49]

Like Croly, Frank Lloyd Wright recognized, in later years, the turn of the century as a period of an important shift in residential design—specifically, the new dwellings that appeared upon the prairies from 1893 to 1910. Wright had drawn many of his ideas from the surge of general interest in housing reform during the 1890s, from the suggestions of domestic scientists, public health workers, arts and crafts enthusiasts and progressive reformers, incorporating their ideals for economical and efficient space planning, open areas, built-in furniture, large expanses of windows, natural "organic" materials and modern technology. He also responded to the more abstract desires for family stability, community life and the preservation of individuality, all symbolized in residential design. Gwendolyn Wright points out that although Frank Lloyd Wright's architectural expression of these concerns reached a remarkably high and innovative aesthetic level, his houses were not as bizarre, disliked or out of place as he often implied. Well before the third of his *Ladies Home Journal* houses appeared in 1907, the builders' press had recognized his work and his influence on suburban housing design. *The National Builder* published a photograph of his Fricke house in Oak Park in 1905 and of the Heath house in Buffalo the following year, calling such composition and practical interior space planning "happily . . . typical." Such widespread acceptance of Wright's Prairie house was due in large part to the exposure given model house designs in the *Ladies Home Journal*, with its circulation of over a million readers by the time his plans began to appear there.[50]

The single most important influence on housing styles and decor, and on attitudes about the home and family, in fact, were the critics of American home life who edited and wrote for the popular magazines. Although not themselves designers, Edward Bok of the *Ladies Home Journal* or Herbert S. Stone of *The House Beautiful* saw domestic architecture as a symbol of the larger society; their pages advocated simpler and more efficient houses while at the same time demanding changes in the social structure. So influential was *Godey's Lady's Book*, which published some 450 house plans between 1846 and 1892, that its publisher, Louis Antoine

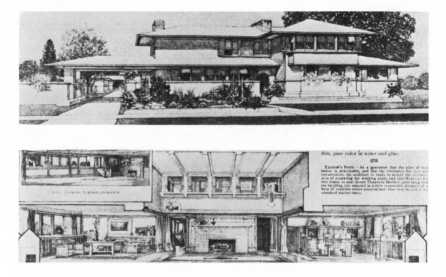

Frank Lloyd Wright's first model home for the *Ladies Home Journal*. TOP: exterior view. BOTTOM: interior view. (*Ladies Home Journal*, 1901)

Godey, declared in 1849: "In one place, . . . it has been suggested to call [it] Godeyville, so numerous have been the cottages put up there from our plans." By 1868 *Godey's* estimated that more than four thousand cottages and villas had been built from plans published in the magazine.[51] *Godey's* followed popular taste through Regency and Gothic, Italianate, Mansard, Queen Anne and "sincere" Eastlake. Its function was to popularize rather debased versions of advanced designs for the mass market, and once *Godey's* located the fashion, the magazine became increasingly an index to popular taste.

By the 1870s there was a clearly defined and widely circulating literature of pattern books, domestic guides and journals to provide builders and readers with up-to-date models for homes and popular domestic advice. The best known of these, *The American Builder and Journal of Art*, published under various titles between 1868 and 1895, carried articles on architectural theory, designs by trained architects of both sexes, models from pattern-book designers, practical advice on home sanitation by Catharine Beecher and manufacturers' specifications. Magazines like *The House Beautiful* featured articles on public health, tenement reform and a range of domestic issues—and articles supporting the women's suffrage movement and women's active involvement in every aspect of work and

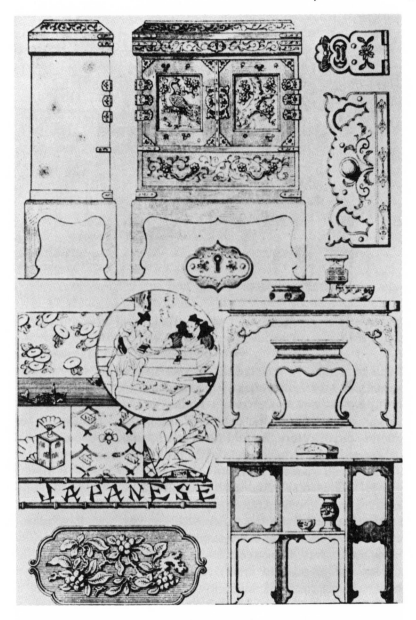

Fred T. Hodgson's interpretation of "Our Grammar of Ornament—Japanese."
(*National Builder*, 1905)

civic life—as well-as house plans designed to appeal, theoretically, at least, to all classes. Ellen Henrotin, a "lady manager" of the World's Columbian Exposition, president of the Chicago Woman's Club and then of the National Federation of Women's Clubs, wrote a regular column entitled "The Woman's Forum," in which she described connections between home and community, giving accounts of women in factories, the Consumer's League and city-planning associations.

As standardized housing became more accepted, the social implications of this architectural uniformity were of concern to reformers like Charlotte Perkins Gilman and Jane Addams, as well as to readers of magazines and pattern books, the former tying the need for common architectural standards to a balanced egalitarian society, the latter insisting, in such places as *American Homes and Gardens*, that "if the unusual is emphasized in a design, there must be a lessening of the artistic qualities." Seventy-five to ninety percent of the people, estimated Chicago's Radford Architectural Company in a 1905 pattern book, "wish to build . . . economical, standardized, simplified homes."[52] This shared aesthetic of the early twentieth-century house relied, especially in middle-class housing, on five principles: a complex technological system; the kitchen as a central focus; simplicity in outline and ornament, inside and out; reduced square footage as the number of rooms and partitions declined and the floor plan opened up; and finally, houses becoming more alike as the individuality of each dwelling became less emphasized. Builders, then, might promote individualized plans, but since they were based on a common cultural understanding of what should take place within the home, who should oversee it and who should mix together, the spatial organization was in fact prescribed. The patterning of rooms included distinct kinds of spaces —for presenting the ideal home to guests, for domestic work and for privacy. Zones for women and men, for adults and children, for family and guests called for particular furnishings, materials and shapes of rooms.[53]

The focus on the kitchen is a case in point: its sudden prominence points to a growing interest in scientific values and rational planning for every sphere of life. The kitchen became the center of the modern house, the focus of attention in most pattern books, domestic science textbooks and women's magazines, replacing the parlor as the favorite subject of housing guides and books of decorating advice. For example, *Carpentry and Building* reprinted from *The American Kitchen* a series on planning the model kitchen by the Chicago domestic scientist Nina C. Kinney. *Indoors and Out*, a fashionable journal of upper-class country life, described the "office" of the country estate where the housewife carried on her communications with the world outside, complete with a telephone, mailbox, filing cabinet for bills and a telescope for watching approaching visitors. Isabel McDougall, writing in *The House Beautiful*, described "An Ideal Kitchen" as "something on the lines of a Pullman-car kitchen, or a yacht's galley, or a laboratory . . . [with] the scientific cleanliness of a surgery."[54]

With chapters on boudoirs, drawing-rooms and libraries but no mention of the kitchen, Edith Wharton's *The Decoration of Houses* was clearly out of date a decade after its publication. The kitchen was, however, the focus of Charlotte Perkins Gilman's criticism of bourgeois domestic life. In *Women and Economics*, published the same year as Wharton's *Decoration of Houses*, Gilman prophesied a world where women would enjoy the economic independence of work outside the home for wages and the social freedom of family life in private kitchenless houses or apartments connected to central kitchens, dining rooms and day-care centers. In *The Home: Its Sphere and Influence* (1903), she condemned the existing home as an archaic holdover from preindustrial times and called for the complete mechanization and collectivization of all of its functions. Even Gilman, however, was looking for a way to *preserve* the home: although she accused men of abandoning to women "the chamber-work and scullery work . . . all that is basest and foulest,"[55] she did not suggest that women and men share domestic work; rather, she argued for paid women domestic workers—that is, one class of women to work for another class of women. Nor was she radical in her proposed organization of women's work: she did not design, for the world of women and men, a mode of voluntary cooperation (as she would later do in a fictional utopian world without men); rather, she espoused corporate forms of domestic organization as both efficient and profitable. In fact, in an article in *Harper's Bazar* of 1907 called "Why Cooperative Housekeeping Fails," she called the corporate structure "the true line of advance" and urged "making a legitimate human business of housework; having it done by experts instead of by amateurs; making it a particular social industry instead of a general feminine function, and leaving the private family in the private home where it belongs."[56]

These same themes were treated fictionally in Gilman's journal, *The Forerunner*. In *What Diantha Did*, which ran serially in that journal in 1909–10, Diantha establishes a restaurant, a cooked food delivery service and a cleaning service; when her business prospers, she hires a female architect to design twenty kitchenless houses and an apartment hotel. Endowed with the skills conservative domestic economists of the day insisted women should acquire, Diantha Bell is a successful entrepreneur whose employees are carefully supervised, well paid and protected from sexual harassment; although they have formed a "House Workers' Union," there are no conflicts between labor and management. Diantha's triumph, the "Hotel de las Casas," is a "pleasure palace" with swimming pool, tennis courts, rooms for billiards, cards, reading, lounging and dancing, a roof garden, flowers and winding shaded paths between the houses, and "great kitchens, clean as a hospital."[57]

Unlike most of her contemporaries, Gilman welcomed the increased residential densities of urban areas, which she believed would make possible and profitable socialized cooking, laundry and child care—though she was not the first to propose such collectivization. As Dolores Hayden has shown in *The Grand Domestic Revolution*, schemes for cooperative housekeeping were developed in the utopian communities that flourished in America particularly from 1840 to 1880: Shakers, Harmonists, Fourierists at Brook Farm, Oneida Perfectionists, Rappites, communitarians at Zoar, Amana and Modern Times—the group of "free lovers" on Long Island with which Stephen Pearl Andrews, Victoria Woodhull and Tennessee Claflin were associated, as was Marie Stevens Howland, who was to become an important domestic reformer. In Cambridge, Massachusetts, former Brook Farm sympathizers and Harvard intellectuals joined Melusina Fay Peirce (wife of the philosopher Charles Saunders Peirce) in organizing a producers' and consumers' cooperative in which participating women were to charge their husbands for domestic services. In 1868 and 1869 Peirce published several articles in the *Atlantic Monthly* in which she applied the principles of economic cooperation to housekeeping. Denouncing the private home, she suggested that women establish neighborhood centers equipped for large-scale cooking, baking, sewing and laundry. Although her own Cambridge Cooperative Housekeeping Society lasted less than two years (because of inadequate capital, poor management and male opposition), Peirce began a dialogue on domestic reform that engaged many women in the last decades of the nineteenth century.

Between 1874 and 1875 Marie Stevens Howland, working with a civil engineer and an architect, developed plans for an entire city of kitchenless houses and apartment hotels, with twenty-four-hour child-care facilities, central kitchens and laundries, all staffed by "skillful people"—paid servants living above the facilities. Like Gilman, Howland created a fictional

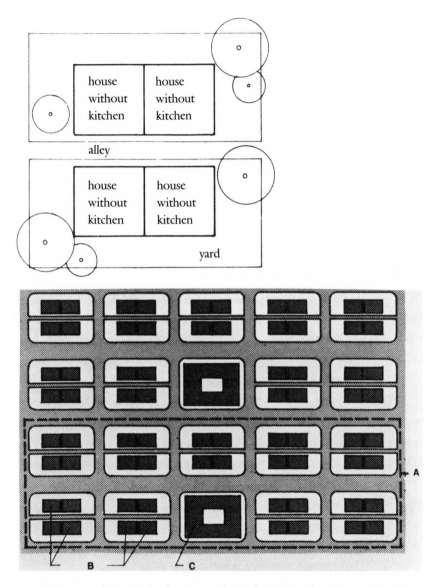

TOP: Diagram of four kitchenless houses by Beth Ganister, based on written descriptions by Melusina Fay Peirce. BOTTOM: Diagrammatic plan of (A) cooperative residential neighborhood, (B) thirty-six kitchenless houses and (C) one cooperative housekeeping center. Drawn by Paul Johnson from descriptions by Peirce in *The Atlantic Monthly*, March 1869. (Dolores Hayden, *The Grand Domestic Revolution*, 1981; courtesy, MIT Press)

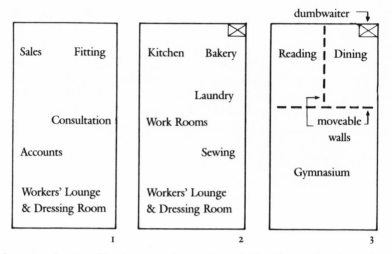

Diagrammatic plan of headquarters for a cooperative housing society drawn by Beth Ganister from written descriptions by Melusina Fay Peirce in *The Atlantic Monthly*, December 1868. (Dolores Hayden, *The Grand Domestic Revolution*, 1981; courtesy, MIT Press)

world in which all of this was possible: *The Familistère* of 1874 describes the establishment of an industrial community in New England with collective housekeeping and child care. Unlike Gilman, however, Howland was associated with the free-love movement; in fact, her novel calls "the loss of respectability as defined by hypocrites and prudes"[58] the first step toward the full development of woman. Gilman admired Marie Howland's research on child care, but she discouraged any association between Howland's life-style and her own interest in the professionalization of child-care and domestic services. Because social critics saw the apartment hotel as "no place for a lady" and conservative architects called it "the most dangerous enemy American domesticity had to encounter,"[59] Gilman promoted the apartment hotel as an environment for happy marriages.

Each of these reformers identified economic independence for women as the real basis for lasting equality between women and men; and each argued that the physical environment must change in order for women to enjoy economic independence. Lacking the tact, power and resources of a Bertha Palmer, Charlotte Perkins Gilman failed as her predecessors had done to bring together the interests of different constituencies into a program of concerted action. Peirce had been most concerned

Views of the Woman's Hotel, an apartment hotel for working women, showing office, parlor, bedrooms, bathrooms, dining room, laundry, boiler room and driven wells. (*Harper's Weekly*, April 13, 1878)

about middle-class housewives, Howland about sex reform, Gilman about employed women for whom homemaking was a second job. Housewives with the time to give to domestic reform had few managerial skills; employed women had more skills, but less time; and the sex reformers gave their best energies to other issues. And none of these reformers saw the problem from the point of view of the cooks, maids and laundresses employed by one out of ten families in 1900.[60]

Recognizing women professionals as her most important supporters, Gilman carefully defined a path for domestic reform that relied on "professional" housework, avoided claims for housewives' cooperatives where work was shared, and rejected living arrangements where sex might be shared as well as work, Hayden points out. And Gilman's ideals were attractive to some women in the Socialist party, some members of the National American Women's Suffrage Association and of the General Federation of Women's Clubs and some men, especially architects and urban planners. Professional women like Henrietta Rodman of the Feminist Alliance, Alice Constance Austin of the Llano Cooperative Colony and Ethel Puffer Howes of the Institute for the Coordination of Women's Interests tried to develop large-scale communities of kitchenless houses or apartments based on Gilman's ideas.

Some home economists and social settlement workers—becoming prominent in the 1890s with the establishment of the National Household Economic Association (which confirmed Gilman's "businesslike" methods) and the American Home Economics Association—encouraged the efforts of ordinary housewives to cooperate and improve their domestic situation. Most talented professional women, however, gave their attention to developing their skills in environmental analysis and institutional management in order to attain government jobs or university positions. For women like Ellen Richards of MIT or Jane Addams of Hull-House, a domestic revolution meant an extensive analysis of scientific child care, nutrition and sanitation. Moreover, the real purpose of a place like Hull-House was to introduce new city-dwelling immigrants to an environment of cultured taste and healthful order so that, with the proper models, immigrant women could reproduce middle-class homes.

By the 1930s alternatives to middle-class homes like Gilman's were no longer significant issues in women's magazines or at women's conferences. Indeed, after World War II, government support for the development of vast commuter suburbs increased restraints upon middle-class women spatially and socially, isolating them from each other and keeping them in a position of economic inequality without position in the paid labor force. To later generations of women and men, accustomed to the alienation of suburban living in monopoly capitalist society where private houses and consumer appliances account for an ever-increasing proportion of the gross national product, Charlotte Perkins Gilman would seem, were she known, a remote visionary feminist.[61]

IV

Most visionary of Gilman's works is *Herland*, a utopian novel that anticipates many of the concerns of contemporary feminists—that theorists of culture like Freud and Lévi-Strauss, for example, reduce psychological interaction or kinship networks to the paired heterosexual couple; that Marx in focusing on the economic issue of production deals with women only marginally, ignoring the equally important issue of reproduction; that the patriarchal mode of competition, upon which our socioeconomic system is based, is antithetical to the female experience, which freed from patriarchal assumptions would develop instead a mode based on cooperation. At the same time, however, *Herland* belongs to the utopian impulse in America which begins as early as the "citty upon a hill" of 1630, reaches its great momentum during the decades before the Civil War, has another resurgence toward the end of the century with a whole spate of utopian novels, the best known of which was Edward Bellamy's *Looking Backward* of 1888, and continues down to the present day with the communal experiments of the 1960s and 1970s and the recent feminist utopias of such writers as Marge Piercy, Joanna Russ and Ursula LeGuin. *Herland* is a very different sort of novel from *What Diantha Did*. In the earlier novel, Gilman invented the ultimate capitalism, where human interactions are reduced to buyer-seller relationships and domestic labor is still performed by women. *Herland*, on the other hand, posits a world of cooperation, a world in which the mother-child isolation of the private home has been transformed into a community of women, much like the world pictured by Mary Cassatt in her mural for the Woman's Building at White City.

The relationship to the works collected in the Woman's Building, in fact, provides a context for assessing *Herland*. That the Woman's Building contained a library of thousands of books by women, 2,400 from New York alone (later donated to the State Library of New York at Albany); that after the Fair was over, Thomas Wentworth Higginson (who had published in the *Atlantic Monthly* in 1884 an article entitled "Should Women Learn the Alphabet?") donated his "Galatea Collection" of one thousand books by women to the Boston Public Library; that another collection, the "Biblioteca Femina" (named after the first documented women's library in Italy, created in 1842), was established at Northwestern University in Evanston, Illinois, would have surprised Virginia Woolf, who bemoaned the fact that there were no books by women on the shelves of the British Museum. Among the books in the Woman's Building Library were the collected works of Harriet Beecher Stowe and the writings of Catharine Beecher, of Margaret Deland (*John Ward, Preacher*) and Helen Hunt Jackson (*Ramona*) and of best sellers Frances Hodgson Burnett (*Little Lord Fauntleroy*), Margaret Sidney (Harriet Lothrop, *Five Little Peppers*) and Kate Douglas Wiggin (*The Birds' Christmas Carol*).[62] Many of these books were based on home and family, some of them pragmatic solutions to problems, like Catharine Beecher's *Treatise on Domestic Economy* or Candace Wheeler's *The Art of Home Decorating*. Others were works of fiction, often set in a distant time or place, usually lessons in connubial bliss or in overcoming adversity. In imaginative writing, action (the pragmatic approach to problems) translates into plot, usually with a complicated apparatus of reconciliation; such romances by women as well as men topped the best-seller lists year after year at the end of the nineteenth century. In fact, successful popular fiction by women was written according to what might be called a "model fiction plan," whose rigid pattern, like that of the model house plan, provided a comforting sense of order in a time of social upheaval.

In 1900, for example, Mary Johnston's *To Have and To Hold*, for five months the best of best-sellers, bought by over a quarter of a million readers,[63] describes a young English heroine who flees to the American colonies to escape marriage with a nobleman aptly named Lord Carnal and finds true love with a heroic Virginian. Frances Hodgson Burnett's *The Shuttle* (1907) presents a similar plot, but with the American Girl as hero: a young American heiress is married to a wicked decadent English nobleman who abuses her and their crippled son and prevents her seeing or corresponding with her family. At long last, her younger sister arrives on the scene; brave, strong and heroic, she determines to save the by-now nearly demented heiress. Female boldness is not invulnerable to male carnality, however, and luckily for the American Girl, rape by her swinish brother-in-law is prevented just in time by the male hero—presumed to be dead—who appears brandishing his sword, vanquishes the villain, carries the brave young woman off on his horse (she has fainted from the

Award given to Connecticut Lady Managers, World's Columbian Exposition, Chicago, 1893. (Jeanne Weimann, *The Fair Women*, 1981; courtesy, Academy Chicago Publishers)

pain of a broken ankle), and soon the once-divided family is together again, with everyone on the way to restored health and happiness.

It is not true, then, that women did not write: ever since Hawthorne had complained about "that damn'd mob of scribbling women," their sales had been steadily climbing until Gene Stratton-Porter, for example, topped the list with over eight million copies of her books sold at the turn of the century.[64] These books by women were usually sentimental versions of home and family—written for children (like *Mrs. Wiggs of the Cabbage Patch*) but read by adults—or fables of courtship and reconciliation, no matter how strong the female hero. (Indeed, some of the strongest female heroes were created by men, Theodore Dreiser's Sister Carrie and David Graham Phillips's Susan Lenox, for example). That is to say, it is indeed difficult to find the kind of books Virginia Woolf was thinking of: books explicitly female in their vision, in their narrative structure, in their language, books whose writers withdraw from patriarchal culture into the indistinctly mapped and terribly difficult space of the self in order to generate new modes of being and of expression. Initial steps in this imaginative journey are often—not surprisingly—tales of madness and suicide, or tales that express great ambivalence in criticizing cultural patterns without being able to envision viable alternatives. The position of an Edith Wharton, whose *House of Mirth* was a great success when it was published in 1905, is not so very different at its starting point from that of Henry James's Olive Chancellor, in *The Bostonians*, except for Wharton's wonderfully bitter sense of irony, or from that of Henry Adams, caught between Virgin and Dynamo, residual and dominant cultures, with no emergent mode at the boundaries of the imagination. Mocking at the same time as she creates, in *The Decoration of Houses* and in most of her novels, the world of the drawing-room, Wharton expresses the deep ambivalence women writers felt about exploring and naming their own experience. The problem she sets up has exactly the danger of which modern psychologists, sociologists and anthropologists warn: when one discards the old patterns without being able to generate a new mode of being, one's environment fails to cohere in a meaningful way—which can be not a matter of complexion only, as in "The Valley of Childish Things," but of life and death.

Perhaps the most interesting treatment of this theme is Kate Chopin's *The Awakening*, which upon publication in 1899 caused its author's expulsion from the St. Louis literary club and was banned for its frankness from libraries across the country. Edna Pontellier in this novel discards old patterns—house, husband, children, lover—in her search for a mode of being that corresponds to the awakening of body and spirit she is experiencing. Unfortunately for Edna, in her fragile beginning stages of self-awareness, the only models available to her are Mademoiselle Reisz, a talented musician with a deformed body and an offensive personality, who dedicates herself totally to her art, and Adèle Ratignole, a "mother-woman" who is as fair and blooming a model of nurturance as the chosen women of *Herland*. Mademoiselle Reisz tells Edna, "The bird that would soar above the level plain of prejudice must have strong wings"; and Madame Ratignole implores her to "think of the children." Edna Pontellier is not a "mother-woman": she tells Adèle, "I would give my life for my children, but I wouldn't give myself"; neither, on the other hand, are her wings very strong.[65]

In her search for self, Edna neglects her social duties as Mr. Pontellier's wife, sends her children to their grandmother's farm, and moves out of her husband's house to her own "pigeon house." She paints, but not well enough to devote herself to art; her new set of friends seems shallow; the excitement of the races grows stale; her attentive lover bores her. Even Robert Lebrun, whom she thinks she loves, is not enough to build a world on because, she realizes, witnessing the birth of Adèle Ratignole's child, that loving him poses the eternal problem of "mother-woman." So she returns to the sea, to the place of her original awakening—but this time death seems to her the one available act of free choice. That act, however, partly impulsive, and one of great ambivalence, is described in words both of despair and exultation and pictured in two very different final images—a bird with a broken wing and the erotic Venus rising from the sea.

Like Chopin, Charlotte Perkins Gilman found the given pattern to be one of negation, of negative space. A story like "The Yellow Wallpaper" is based on her own experience when, after the birth of her child, she was confined by S. Weir Mitchell, the eminent physician (and popular novelist) who in the late nineteenth century treated women (Edith Wharton among them) for neurasthenia. His regimen included complete bed rest, with all reading and writing materials forbidden, and force-feeding (often through the rectum). Women would return to their families after the Dr. Mitchell treatment plump and quiet. In Gilman's story, a woman who has just given birth is confined to a nursery room by her doctor/husband and his sister, "a perfect and enthusiastic housekeeper" who "hopes for no better profession" and "thinks it is the writing which makes me sick!" The wallpaper in the room has a hideous pattern with bulbous staring eyes: "Up and down and sideways they crawl, and those absurd unblinking eyes are everywhere."[66] The wallpaper changes with the light: by moonlight it becomes bars, and gradually the writer sees a woman behind the bars, becomes that woman and creeps about the room afraid to go outside.

Confinement to a nursery room is very different from the *imagined* landscape of childhood. The sea to which Edna Pontellier returns at the end of *The Awakening*, for example, is like the bluegrass meadow where she would throw out her arms as if swimming when she walked, "beating the tall grass as one strikes out in the water." Like the sea, this childhood meadow was an escape—from the repressive atmosphere of Edna's Calvinist father's house—and such spaces, like the house of Léonce Pontellier, the room of the yellow wallpaper, the Valley of Childish Things, are spaces that enclose and entrap, not spaces that free the imagination. This is precisely what Erik H. Erikson failed to perceive when he drew his conclusions that female children reproduce in their play spatial representations of their anatomy. His contemporary Edith Cobb, on the other hand, concluded from an experiment similar to Erikson's that "what the child wanted to do most of all was to make a world in which to find a place to discover a self."[67] She found a relationship between the imaginative child and a landscape that had been important in what she calls the "middle-age" of childhood—from six to twelve—when the environment is experienced in some especially evocative way, and that there is a returning, among persons of genius, to this landscape of childhood in order to renew the power and impulse to create at its very source.

One would hope, then, that a feminist utopia would create something like the vast spaces of childhood freedom, where the imaginative person—freed from both the "exquisite discomfort" of the drawing-room and the middle-class comfort of the model house—can indulge in the reverie that leads to creativity. *Herland*, however, holds out the same false hopes as White City; as the American men who invade this land of women observe, "It's like an exposition. . . . It's too pretty to be true." Although the novel begins with a negation of the conventional fictional mode—there are no adventures, one of the men complains, because there is nothing to fight—it is, in a way, a feminist novel in reverse: it moves *from* an ideal world of female cooperation back to a world of marriage, of probable invasions from the outside world with its disease, pollution and stress, and even to the eclipse of a separate language based on a reverence for Motherhood and Nature. Herland women, in fact, choose to be exactly what Edna Pontellier refused to be: mother-women. Gilman assumes that the desire to be mothers is an innate part of the female condition and in *Herland* presents the same glorification of home and motherhood that she had advocated in her earlier *The Home: Its Work and Influence.*

Gilman's work bears some resemblance to that of contemporary feminist thinkers like Shulamith Firestone, who would have women control reproduction not by parthenogenesis as in *Herland*, but by modern technological means where children are born outside of the mother's body, thus eliminating the raison d'être for sexual oppression, and like Juliet Mitchell, who would make the socialization of children a major goal in a new feminist schema; but there are great similarities as well to the nineteenth-century ideology that claimed women as the morally superior sex. The rhetoric of *Herland*—not surprisingly, for Gilman was a descendant of the Beechers—is in fact puritanical: like the Puritans leaving the Old World for the New in order to purify, and return to, the existing church, Gilman's novel advocates an open-ended withdrawal from a polluted culture. Thus Herlanders take over reproduction, the socialization of children, work and the relationship to the natural world. They create a world of "beauty, order, perfect cleanness, and the pleasantest sense of home over it all," a world that gets rid of the "cultivated attitude of mind toward women" to discover the "older, deeper, more 'natural' feeling, the restful reverence which looks up to the Mother sex."[68] And the purpose of it all, as in Puritan ideology, is to return to and to purify the existing world.

It must finally be said, however, that something is missing from *Herland*, something of the sort William James found missing from Chautauqua. Visiting this famous summer retreat in upstate New York in 1896, James found a "sacred enclosure," where "sobriety and industry, intelligence and goodness, orderliness and ideality, prosperity and cheerfulness, pervade the air. . . . Beautifully laid out in the forest and drained and equipped with means for satisfying all the necessary lower and most of the superfluous higher wants," the town included a college, a chorus of seven hundred voices, athletic fields, schools, religious services, daily lectures, "no . . . diseases, no poverty, no drunkenness, no crime, no police," and "perpetually running soda-water fountains." In his essay "What Makes a Life Significant?," published in 1899, James describes how in leaving Chautauqua he catches a flashing glimpse through the window of a speeding train of "a workman doing something on the dizzy edge of a sky-scaling iron construction," and he feels a great "wave of sympathy with the common life of common men."[69] Clearly James is part of a culture that values some form of the heroism of manly labor so important to Louis Sullivan; yet he is worth attending to, as he points to a ubiquitous vision of a middle-class paradise, from White City to the model house to *Herland*, that at the turn of the century represents an official image of America perfected. Still, the appeal of *Herland* lies in its women who have grown up from that useless, confining innocence of the past, women who use, control, shape the new technology for very human ends. Gilman presents women who share a language that is experiential and not oppressive. She presents a harmony between mind and body and nature that is enviable. And above all, she asks the important questions about what is female and what is male that make it possible for us to envision alternatives to our present-day stressful, discordant, disastrously competitive world.

V

Martha Graham regularly based a set of exercises on the haptic experience of space: her students would be asked to hold, push, pull and touch pieces of space and places in space. This kind of training, she believed, mobilized the entire body "to touch and feel space, so that movement becomes not a vague indescribable set of reflex actions, but an articulately felt interaction with the positive stuff of space." Dancer and space animate each other as partners, so that not only is the dancer in relationship to the space outside the body, but also senses an essential relationship to the inside: "the 'center,' the inside, must be felt before the dancer can confidently move in space, the outside."[70]

The mathematician Henri Poincaré also worked with the idea that we take our own bodies as instruments of measurement in order to construct space—not geometrical space or a space of pure representation, but a space belonging to "instinctive geometry." Poincaré concludes that "every human being has to construct first this restricted space, . . . and then is capable of amplifying—by an act of imagination—the restricted space to the 'great space where he can lodge the universe.'"[71]

Poincaré was really distinguishing here between *place* and *space*; the security of the one (the sense of center) is a precondition of the experience of the other. Similarly, geographer Yi-Fu Tuan finds that "space" and "place" require each other for definition. "From the security and stability of place," he writes, "we are aware of the openness, freedom, and threat of space, and vice-versa. Furthermore, if we think of space as that which allows movement, then place is pause; each pause in movement makes it possible for location to be transformed into place."[72]

Anthropologist Edward Hall believes that each of us has a "spatial envelope"—an internalization of fixed space learned early in life, a mold into which a great deal of behavior is cast. Linking space and behavior, he sees one's orientation in space as ultimately tied to survival and sanity: to be disoriented in space is to be psychotic.[73] As a cultural anthropologist, Hall understands experience as that which is perceived through a set of culturally patterned sensory screens—which differ from culture to culture—and one's use of space (what he calls "proxemics") as a specialized elaboration of culture.

Hall does not suggest, as Virginia Woolf did, that man's use of space, or experience of space, is different from woman's, though clearly, her cultural patterning has been different. Sociologist Shirley Ardener, however, describes the way in which, because in any given society the life pattern of women differs markedly from that of men, ground maps and social maps for women and men do not match. She points out that space reflects social organization, and that once space has been bounded and shaped, it is no longer merely a neutral background: it exerts its own influence. The "theatre of action," she argues, to some extent determines the action. "The environment imposes certain restraints on our mobility, and, in turn, our perceptions of space are shaped by our capacity to move about." Like Hall, she concludes, *"Behaviour and space are mutually dependent."*[74]

As I noted at the beginning of this chapter, my concerns are with the relationship of space to the female *imagination*, a function not to be divorced from behavior. My question is this: if in America, where, as Tocqueville observed in 1835, "more than anywhere else in the world, care has been taken constantly to trace clearly distinct spheres of action for the two sexes, and both are required to keep in step, but along paths that are never the same," and if women have been conditioned not to move in space, as Erikson proved, but to stay fixed in their model houses, then what *is* the relationship, in America, of space to the female imagination?

The first condition, obviously, is freedom—freedom to move, as Tuan suggests, between shelter and venture. With this freedom, "in the solitude of a sheltered place the vastness of space beyond acquires a haunting presence."[75] Spaciousness, then, means being free; freedom implies space. It means having the power and enough room in which to act. It means having the ability to transcend the present condition, and that transcendence implies, quite simply, the power to move.

It is not only, then, as Virginia Woolf suggested, that women have had no spaces to themselves, not only that they have been forbidden spaces reserved for men. Trapped as she has been at home, a home that in America has been "not her retreat, but her battleground . . . her arena, her boundary, her sphere . . . [with] no other for her activities,"[76] woman has been *unable to move*. She has been denied, in our culture, the possibility of dialectical movement between private spaces and open spaces—open as in "free to be entered or used, unobstructed, unrestricted, accessible, available, exposed, extended, candid, undetermined, loose, disengaged, responsive, ready to hear or see as in open heart, open eyes, open hand, open mind, open house, open city, . . . all those [places] . . . open to . . . freely-chosen and spontaneous actions."[77] But let us not forget the room of one's own, for that is the other condition.

If the dancer must know her center before she can move in space, if journey means an absence from a starting point, if one's own body is the measure of the restricted space necessary to imagining "the great space" where one can lodge the universe, then this parable, I believe, points the way to the female discovery of felicitous space.

The religious mystic Jeanne Le Ber, a minor character in Willa Cather's *Shadows on the Rock*, is the subject of a legend in seventeenth-century Montreal. Choosing a life of silence and solitude, she builds a small three-room house for herself. The bottom room, which looks onto a garden, is where she receives her food and can attend mass without being seen; she sleeps in the middle room; the top room is her atelier where she makes and embroiders beautiful altar-cloths and vestments that go out from her stone chamber all over the province. She calls her room her earthly paradise: it is my center, she says, my element. There is nothing more delicious, and I prefer my cell to all the rest of the universe.

During the severe Canadian winter, the story of "the recluse" is told and re-told with loving exaggeration. This story is her incomparable gift, "some living beauty,—a blooming rose-tree, or a shapely fruit-tree in fruit," and in the long evenings, when someone would speak the name of Jeanne Le Ber, it gave out fragrance. People love miracles, Cather writes, not as proof or evidence, but because they are the actual flowering of desire. "From being a shapeless longing, it becomes a beautiful image; a dumb rapture becomes a melody that can be remembered and repeated; and the experience of a moment, which might have been a lost ecstasy, is made an actual possession and can be bequeathed to another."[78] This is Cather's own "incomparable gift": the ability to seize those moments of epiphany and transform them into miracles.

Willa Cather was writing before the recent time when women began to acknowledge what poet Susan Griffin calls "the roaring inside us." Her Jeanne Le Ber points the way with her "space full of curiosity about her, and the place which records her image. Space which she embroiders. Space which she covers in quilts. Space which she makes into lace. Space which she weaves. Where she builds the house of her culture. . . . Space where, in her circling motion, she found an opening."[79] This is the beginning.

BOOK II
Edith Wharton

Each room in a house has its individual uses, and whatever the uses of a room, they are seriously interfered with if it be not preserved as a small world by itself.

—Edith Wharton and Ogden Codman, Jr.,
The Decoration of Houses

CHAPTER 2

Argument by Design

An American Virgin would never dare command;
an American Venus would never dare exist.
—Henry Adams, *The Education of Henry Adams*

In 1893 the French poet Stéphane Mallarmé went to see an unusual performance by the American dancer Loïe Fuller, who was by that time beginning to patent costumes, mechanical stage devices and lighting techniques with which she created disembodied, abstract images. The audience would have been seated in a darkened hall. On a stage draped with black velvet curtains, standing on a false glass floor beneath which calcium or electric lights were positioned to illuminate and color her voluminous draperies, Loïe Fuller would begin to move to the music of Wagner, Debussy, Pierné, Berlioz, Scriabin, unfurling hundreds of yards of silk in a whirl of light and color to become fire, a butterfly, a lily. To Mallarmé she was "an enchantress . . . [who] creates her own environment, draws it out of herself and gathers it in again in a silence of quivering silk." He recognized in this "phantasmagoria" the "personification of his dream of the ideal theater—without scenery, without words, where space and time had no importance, where reality would not intrude between the idea and the audience."[1]

In the same year, in Loïe Fuller's own country, Woman as disembodied, abstract image welcomed visitors to the World's Columbian Exposition in Chicago. At the eastern end of White City stood Daniel Chester French's 65-foot-high statue of the Republic and at the western end Frederick MacMonnies's Columbia Fountain with its massive allegorical figures; Augustus St. Gaudens's commanding figure of Diana decorated the gilded dome of McKim, Mead and White's Agricultural Building;

Elihu Vedder, *Rome, or The Art Idea*, 1894. (Courtesy, The Brooklyn Museum, Gift of William T. Evans)

massive female allegorical statuary adorned Peabody and Stearns's Machinery Hall; and in the Woman's Building were to be seen Mary Fairchild MacMonnies's and Mary Cassatt's oversize murals of *Primitive Woman* and *Modern Woman*. Elsewhere, public buildings were adorned with murals like Edwin H. Blashfield's *Washington Laying Down His Command at the Feet of Columbia* at the Baltimore courthouse, in which the enthroned Columbia is surrounded by classical personifications of the Virtues carrying emblems of War, Peace, Abundance and Glory. Homes of the wealthy conflated women with mythological figures in such paintings as Thomas Dewing's representation of Maria Oakley (Mrs. Stanford White) as Hymen, or in the Greek caryatids Augustus St. Gaudens designed to support the mantelpiece in the house of Cornelius Vanderbilt II—not "goddesses but *women*," according to Kenyon Cox, their form, however, "leaving as it were, a diaphanous veil between it and our eyes and a mystery for the imagination to penetrate." Cox, St. Gaudens, Blashfield, along with Will Low and Walter Shirlaw, designed paper and metal currency that featured female allegorical figures of the Virtues, and in the pages of magazines and newspapers, the Gibson Girl—aloof, statuesque, and yet sensuous—embodied "the highest type of womanhood."[2]

The European counterpart of the symbolic Woman at the turn of the century was rather different. Gustav Klimt, for example, cast the Gibson Girl as a naked Judith or Salome, the masses of her hair set off by a

Designs for American currency. TOP: Silver certificate, series of 1896, educational note, designed by Will H. Low and engraved by Charles Schlect. (Courtesy, Division of Numismatics, National Museum of History and Technology, Smithsonian Institution) MIDDLE: Twenty-dollar gold piece, Liberty side, designed by Augustus Saint-Gaudens, 1907. (Courtesy, American Numismatic Society, New York) BOTTOM: Design for a one-hundred-dollar bill by Kenyon Cox, 1912. (Courtesy, The Cleveland Museum of Art, Gift of J. D. Cox)

flowering of gold-leaf geometrical ornament forming a background for and partially covering her body, making of her some elaborately powerful icon who holds in one hand the head of Holofernes or John the Baptist. Variants of this theme and style are to be found in Art Nouveau posters, decorative panels, illustrations, jewelry, costumes and theater sets. Woman is ornamental and mysterious, a combination of sensuality and purity often identified with flowers—but "that mixture of perfume and mustiness that flowers give off when the water in the vase hasn't been changed," Mario Praz commented: "In a word, the breath of decadence. A decadence that assumes the pose of springtime. They thought they understood Donatello and Botticelli, but their spokesmen were named Max Slevogt, Khnopff, Klimt, Bistolfi"—and, he might have added, Redon, Beardsley, Mucha.[3]

In the works of Alphons Mucha, one of the founders of the Art Nouveau movement and "virtually its official graphic artist," this image of woman becomes, especially in his posters depicting actress Sarah Bernhardt, "the personification of womanhood." His barefoot, flowering goddesses in their diaphanous gowns become part of decorative motifs of frames that cannot contain them: the image spills from its boundaries in sensual triumph. In illustrations with titles like *Profile of a Woman with Orchids in a Decorative Frame* and *Woman with Lilies*, the lines of the woman's body, her costume, her jewels, her hair become the shapes of petals and leaves and stems: the woman herself is a flower.[4]

The Paris Exposition of 1900, for which Mucha designed the gigantic Pavilion of Man, marked the apogee of Art Nouveau. And the living symbol of Art Nouveau was Loïe Fuller. In fact, so prominent was her influence in this vast assemblage of decorative arts, one observer noted, that the entrance to the Exposition should have been crowned not with "the 'Parisienne,' stiff as a dressmaker's dummy," but with "an effigy of Loïe Fuller swirling under the projectors." The dancer had her own theater, conceived in her own image, its sculptured plaster curtain facade meant to simulate "an immense veil of pleated plaster caught in mid-flight" and crowned by a life-sized dancing figure, its entrance flanked by dancing figures, and at night its white surface shimmering "in a rainbow of glistening splendor" provided by the play of multicolored lights.[5]

Although he was in Paris in 1900, Henry Adams seems to have missed Loïe Fuller entirely. In fact, he was frankly baffled by the art of the Paris Exposition. He had "looked at most of the accumulations of art in the storehouses called Art Museums," he wrote in the *Education*, "yet he

Alphons Mucha, *Sarah Bernhardt, "La Plume,"* 1896. (Courtesy, S.P.A.D.E.M., Paris/V.A.G.A., New York)

Theodore Rivière, Loïe Fuller in *The Lily Dance*, marble, ca. 1898. (Courtesy, The Fine Arts Museums of San Francisco, Gift of Mrs. Alma de Bretteville Spreckels to the Museum of Theater and Dance)

did not know how to look at the art exhibits of 1900. He had studied Karl Marx and his doctrines of history with profound attention, yet he could not apply them at Paris." It is at this point that Adams wanders off to the Gallery of Machines, here before the dynamo engine that he feels the new force of the twentieth century and senses "the break of continuity [that] amounted to [an] abysmal fracture." It is in front of the dynamo that he decides that "in any previous age, sex was strength." Woman was goddess "because of her force; she was the animated dynamo, . . . the greatest and most mysterious of all energies; all she needed was to be fecund." Venus and Virgin become one for Adams as he studies the dynamo, but sex as Force belongs to the past: "An American Virgin would never dare command; an American Venus would never dare exist." American artists use sex only for sentiment, he decides; American art, like American language and American education, is sexless. Still puzzled, he wanders off in search of his friend Augustus St. Gaudens, who as "a survival of the 1500's; he bore the stamp of the Renaissance, and should have carried an image of the Virgin round his neck, or stuck in his hat," can be expected, when they stand together before the Virgin of Amiens, to share with Adams a sense of her tremendous force. For St. Gaudens, however, the Virgin remains "a channel of taste"; like the artists of his day, he sees goddesses "only as reflected emotion, human expression, beauty, purity, taste," not as power.[6]

The distinction between force and taste, between physical and spiritual power which Adams believed a single entity before 1900, is a distinction of some significance insofar as the American "Renaissance" is concerned. The term "Renaissance" was one self-consciously used by American architects, painters, sculptors, decorators, landscape architects and writers of the turn of the century, particularly by the "guild" who designed palatial homes for the American robber barons in direct imitation of those of Italian and French merchant princes, who collaborated on the World's Columbian Exposition—"the greatest meeting of artists since the fifteenth century"—and who founded the American Academy in Rome. "We ourselves, because of our faith in science and the power of work, are instinctively in sympathy with the Renaissance," art connoisseur Bernard Berenson wrote; "the spirit which animates us was anticipated by the spirit of the Renaissance. . . . That spirit seems like the small rough model after which ours is being fashioned."[7]

The term "Renaissance" is indeed appropriate for a period in which, as Henry Adams suggested, the new force of technology rendered all of the structures that were embodiments of passion and inspiration in the past empty and meaningless forms through which people move in alienated isolation. Exactly the same paradigm shift occurred in the Italian High Renaissance: a momentous cultural change in this period is suggested by the interactions of human figures in the spaces of paintings and buildings. Studying floor plans, reproductions of furnished rooms, paintings and narratives, architectural historian Robin Evans finds in mid-seventeenth century, like Adams studying the later "Renaissance," two discernible separate realities which would form an unbridgeable gap and mark the beginnings of modern life. On the one hand there was a communal reality—in architecture "an extended concatenation of spaces to flatter the eye," and on the other "a careful containment and isolation of individual compartments in which to preserve the self from others."[8] In his examination of the floor plans of Raphael's Villa Madama, begun in 1518, with its multiple passageways through rooms and its extended gardens, Evans sees a pattern of movement similar to that of Raphael's late paintings, in which people are sensuously interrelated. The matrix of connected rooms was appropriate to a society that "feeds on carnality, that recognises the body as the person and in which gregariousness is habitual," Evans argues, just as in the nineteenth century a corridor plan was "appropriate to a society that finds carnality distasteful, that sees the body as a vessel of mind and spirit, and in which privacy is habitual."[9]

Evans sees in any house plan a picture of social relationships. In the Villa Madama, although most spaces around the central axis were symmetrically composed, there was no duplication: every room was different. The building seems to be an accumulation of enclosures—chambers, loggias, courts, gardens—the overall pattern of which was less definite than the component spaces.[10] Every room has more than one door; some have two, three or four, a feature that since the early nineteenth century has been considered a fault in domestic buildings of any size because, as Robert Kerr warned his readers in *The Gentleman's House* (1864), of "the wretched inconvenience caused by 'thoroughfare rooms' which made domesticity and retirement unobtainable."[11] In the Villa Madama, as in virtually all domestic architecture prior to 1650, there is no qualitative distinction between the way through the house and the inhabited spaces within it. Passages and staircases are used to connect one space to another, not as general distributors of movement—which means that "during the course of a day paths would intersect, and that every activity was liable to inter-

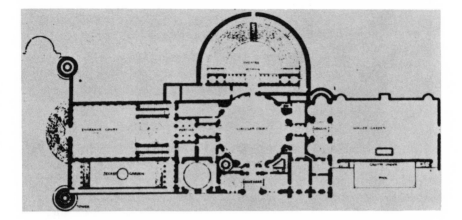

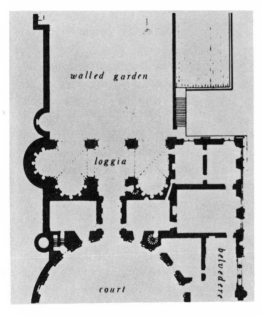

TOP: Raphael's Villa Madama, plan by Antonio da Sangallo (redrawn). BOTTOM: Villa Madama plan, detail. (Robin Evans, "Figures, Doors, and Passages," *Architectural Design* 48 [1978])

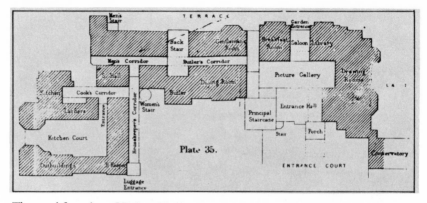

Thoroughfare plan of Robert Kerr's Bearwood, 1864. (*The Gentlemen's House,* 1864; reproduced in Robin Evans, "Figures, Doors, and Passages," *Architectural Design* 48 [1978])

cession." Company was the ordinary condition and solitude the exceptional state.

In the mid-seventeenth century, the house begins to have two domains, an inner sanctuary of inhabited, sometimes disconnected rooms and unoccupied circulation space. And this division of spaces into public and private suggests a different sense of self: for the first time the self was felt to be "not just at risk in the presence of others, but actually disfigured by them"—a notion, Evans suggests, that is at the root of our modern sense of intimacy as a form of violence, of relationships as forms of bondage, of finding liberty in the escape from the "tyranny" of society. Personal space has become "a territorial envelope in which we . . . shroud our bodies against the assaults of intimacy."[12]

Evans's study of Renaissance structures, together with Henry Adams's analysis of the American Renaissance, suggests that artifacts and narratives are rich complementary sources of evidence in periods of cultural change; and since those changes are similar in kind, we should be able to identify in the structures of the American Renaissance the tensions of the earlier period between public and private spaces.[13]

Adams had argued in the "Dynamo and Virgin" and "Vis Inertiae" chapters of the *Education* that women hold the key to history; the sexless American woman, as he saw her, diverted from her axis, sought a new field. It should be possible, then, to measure woman, in Adams's terms, against the field she no longer seems to fit. The structures that contain— or fail to contain—women are the houses in which they live, the material things of their lives, and the illustrations and stories that instruct them in ways of perceiving themselves and relating to others.

A true Renaissance woman, Edith Wharton provides an appropriate index to the period; for not only was her *Decoration of Houses* a handbook for interior designers of the period, but in that book and in her *Italian Villas and Their Gardens* she expressed great admiration for the original plans of Raphael's Villa Madama. Moreover, these books and her novels, rich in detailed descriptions of interiors, the floor plan of her own house in Massachusetts, the plans for the gardens and photographs of the interiors of her French houses, and the paintings and painters named in her novels together comprise a great lode of information about human enclosures and human interactions.

When in 1904 Henry James returned to America after a twenty years' absence for the visit he would re-present in *The American Scene*, the most "happily effective" part of that journey was six or seven weeks "of leisure on the way to legitimation, of the social idyll, of the workable, the expensively workable, American form of country life" with Edith Wharton at The Mount in Lenox, Massachusetts. He remembers the time "contentedly, [as] a single strong savour"; here he was able to enjoy both "concentration" and "conversation, . . . the play of social relation." The Mount was, for James, different from other American buildings that totally lack *penetralia*—by which he meant "some part . . . sufficiently *within* some other part, sufficiently withdrawn and consecrated, not to constitute a thoroughfare."[14]

The Mount James visited was composed of a series of different kinds of spaces: spaces for servants (the ground floor kitchen, scullery, laundry and servants' dining room; the first floor cook's, housekeeper's and butler's workrooms; the second floor maids' closets sewing and linen rooms; the third or attic floor with eight rooms opening off a connecting corridor); spaces for social relation (the first floor with a large hall dividing service rooms on the right from a long gallery running most of the length of the rest of the house connecting den, library, drawing-room and dining-room); spaces for privacy (the second floor with Edith Wharton's suite of rooms in the eastern corner, her husband's room and bath, and three guest rooms—including Henry James's facing the terrace—all separated from one another by a long corridor).[15] The house was situated on a large tract of gently rolling land in the Berkshire mountains. It was se-

The Mount, Lenox, Massachusetts, exterior. (Photograph by Warren Fowler, 1984; courtesy, Edith Wharton Restoration, Inc., Lenox, Massachusetts)

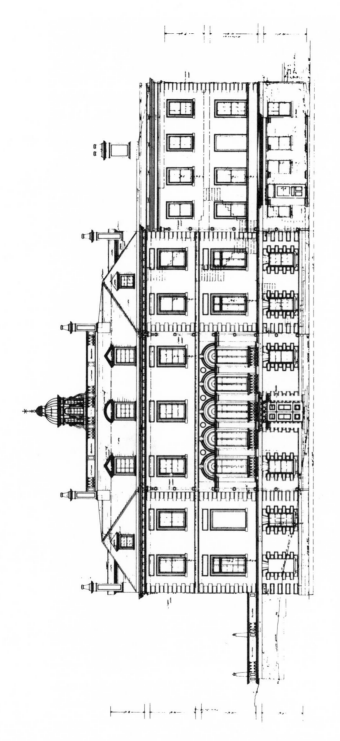

West elevation of The Mount, Hoppin and Koen, architects. (Courtesy, Avery Architectural and Fine Arts Library, Columbia University)

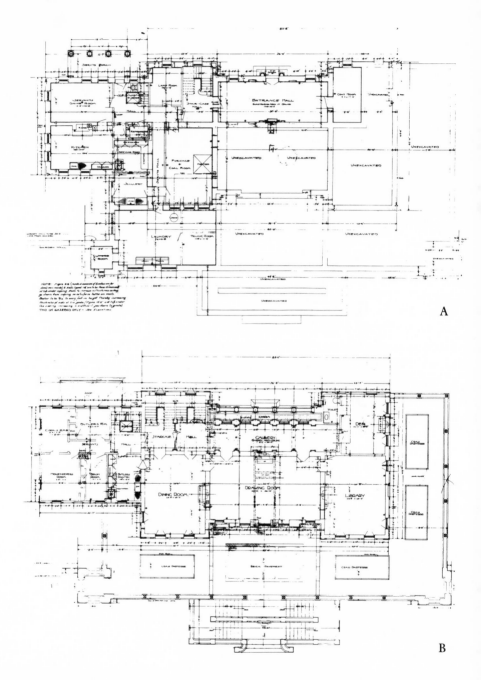

A

B

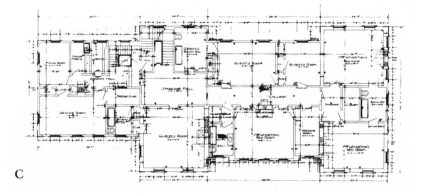

C

Plans of The Mount, Hoppin and Koen, architects. A: Basement plan. B: First-floor plan. C: Second-story plan. (Courtesy, Avery Architectural and Fine Arts Library, Columbia University)

cluded, and yet from the terrace at the rear, the vista extended all the way to Laurel Lake. From the terrace one could descend the broad stone steps to the left or to the right and wander in the elaborate gardens, intricately laid out as another series of enclosed spaces.

The idea of the whole was generally Wharton's, though she collaborated with Ogden Codman, Jr., whom she dismissed early in the planning stages, and Francis V. L. Hoppin, known mostly for his artistic rendiñ-ons of architects' plans (particularly in the office of McKim, Mead and White). Her conception is carefully articulated in *The Decoration of Houses*, in which *"house decoration"* is *"a branch of architecture,"*[16] and the house plan a clue to the kind of life lived in a house. Though Wharton notes in that book that "the styles especially suited to modern life . . . [are] those prevailing in Italy since 1500,"[17] her model was not the Italian Renaissance *palazzo*, but its successor, the English country house, specifically Belton House in Lincolnshire (attributed to Sir Christopher Wren), as the cupola at the top of The Mount signals. Distributors of movement—doorways, passageways, stairways—in Edith Wharton's house would insure that human interaction was controlled, not random.

Passing the gate house at the entrance to The Mount, the stables and greenhouses, the visitor journeys through a deliberately planned intermediate zone between "nature" and "civilization": the "sugar maple allée," the winding drive through the wooded terrain and around a granite outcropping, is a passage through a sequence of spaces leading to the

View of Laurel Lake from the terrace of The Mount. (Courtesy, Beinecke Rare
Book and Manuscript Library, Yale University)

house itself. Reaching the front door, with its "necessary ornament . . . of
locks, hinges and handles," one would confront "an effectual barrier"; for
the purpose of the door, as Wharton had noted in *The Decoration of
Houses*, was not only to admit, but to exclude. This house, this door
announces, is a retreat.

The front door opens at ground level; the visitor is admitted into a
kind of subterranean space, where the carved fountain and rippling plaster
walls suggestive of dripping water contribute to the sense of a grotto.
Ascending the stairs to the main part of the house, one would pass
through another large and confined enclosure—the hall, which stands "in
relation to the rooms of the house," Wharton had written, as "a public
square in relation to the houses around it," thus retaining "its original use
as a passageway"—into the long gallery. Drawn into predetermined patterns, one would move from passageway to passageway with a sense of
what Wharton called "spaciousness and repose."[18] One would have felt a
tension between public and private both reassuring and enticing: although the public rooms connect, and each has multiple doorways, there
is a clear sense of leaving one and entering another because their "room-
characters," as James would have called them, were so distinctive. The
passage through the gallery is a kind of journey, with intriguing choices to
be made.

Wharton deliberately avoided at The Mount the picturesque irregularity of the still-popular "Villa in the Italian Style"[19] designed by Alexander Jackson Davis and Andrew Jackson Downing in the 1850s, or of the "Hudson River Bracketed" in her own novel of that name, with the probable attendant picturesque irregularity of human intercourse to be found in country houses like the Trenors' or the Gormers' in *The House of Mirth*. Wharton believed in "harmony and proportion" in human relationships, in domestic arrangements and in artistic expression. "If proportion is the good breeding of architecture," she noted in *The Decoration of Houses*, "symmetry, or the answering of one part to another, may be defined as the sanity of decoration. The desire for symmetry, for balance, for rhythm in form as well as in sound, is one of the most inveterate of human instincts."[20] At The Mount the hall and dining room on the right match in size and shape the den and library on the left, surrounding with classical regularity the central drawing-room and gallery; yet the journey from the gallery through the house offers "penetralia" into a variety of spaces. This is accomplished partly by the way in which the doors are hung so that "they screen that part of the room in which the occupants usually sit," and also by placing the doorways not in the center, but near the ends of the long side of a room so that "the privacy of the greater part of the room is preserved." (Wharton then restored "equilibrium" by placing in a line with the door, at the other end of the same side-wall, a piece of furniture corresponding in height and width to the door.)[21] Moreover, from each doorway one's eye would have been carried beyond the room to the landscape, the relationship between the two having been carefully established—French windows opening to the floor, for example, deliberately chosen over a large expanse of plate glass to make the outside "*as seen from a room* . . . part of the wall-decoration."[22]

There are spaces for greeting guests, for dining, for taking a quiet cup of tea before the fire, for intimate conversation, for concentration. "Each room in a house has its individual uses," Wharton believed, and "whatever the uses of a room, they are seriously interfered with if it be not preserved as a small world by itself." Having wandered into the farthest corner of such a house, one would not expect to be interrupted—and in *The House of Mirth* Lily Bart *surprises* Lawrence Selden and Bertha Dorset in a Sunday morning tête-à-tête in the library of the Bellomont country house. Nor would one be likely to have access to Edith Wharton's private quarters, for the stairway to the upper levels of the house is deliberately set off from the public spaces of the first floor. Had the stairs, "the main

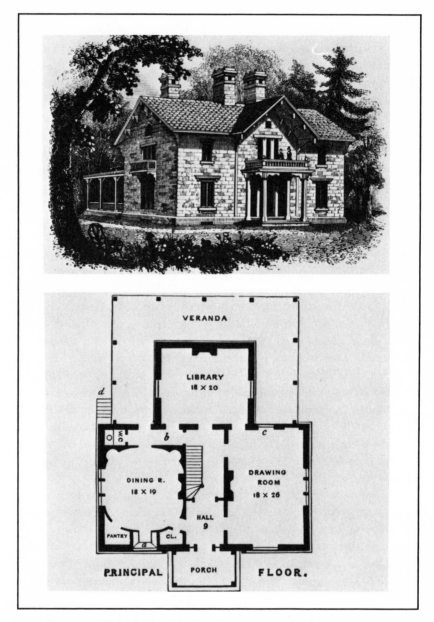

TOP: A cottage villa in the bracketed mode. BOTTOM: Plan for a "cottage villa." (Andrew Jackson Downing, *Cottage Residences, Rural Architecture and Landscape Gardening*, 1852 rev. ed.; courtesy, American Life Foundation, 1967)

The library at The Mount. (Courtesy, Beinecke Rare Book and Manuscript Library, Yale University)

artery of the house," been carried up through the hall, there would have been no security from intrusion by those "in no way concerned with the private life of the inmates."[23] Servants, apparently, even cleaned the big house invisibly. When in *The House of Mirth* Lily Bart encounters a char-woman scrubbing the steps in the hallway outside Lawrence Selden's flat, it is an annoyance to have to lift her skirts and squeeze past the woman with her buckets and brushes; but when the same encounter is repeated inside the house where Lily lives, it is a violation of personal privacy.

What emerges most clearly from this plan is a sense of *order*: the careful symmetry allows for no unexpected mingling of servants and mas-ters, no penetration of guests into private quarters, no romantic hermit-ages in the gardens, but rather a kind of social interaction that is carefully planned, controlled, deliberate. The plan says: patterns of movement here express certain kinds of long-standing social traditions; and at the same time this house is a projection of an idealized self, a retreat, a series of protective enclosures. Patterns of movement can be read from the plans of The Mount—and also patterns of stillness.

The Mount was not Edith Wharton's only house, but among her country houses and city houses—"Pencraig" in Newport, Rhode Island, and a pair of adjoining town houses on Park Avenue in New York; The Mount and a flat on the rue de Varenne in Paris; Ste. Claire near Hyères, France, and Pavillon Colombe at St. Brice-sous-Fôret near Paris—it was the one she called her first real home and the only one she would build. While The Mount was under construction, she published two volumes of tales, a novel, *The Valley of Decision*, a novella, *The Touchstone*, and *Italian Villas and Their Gardens*. In 1904, when Henry James came to visit at her newly completed home in Lenox, she was at work on *The House of Mirth*, learning, she would later say, how to construct a novel.[24]

Wharton must have been preoccupied that year with theories of construction, architectural and literary. She was at the beginning of her career and Henry James—with whom she had opportunities for countless conversations on their long walks and drives through the Berkshire countryside and in the quiet recesses of The Mount—was at the end of his. It was in 1904 that James published *The Golden Bowl*, a novel in which he abandoned "living creations," Wharton would later say, in pursuit of an impossible ideal: "As he became more and more preoccupied with the architecture of the novel he . . . subordinated all else to his ever-fresh complexities of design."[25] There is a kind of doubling in *The House of Mirth* reminiscent of the "co-ordinating consciousness" of *The Golden Bowl*, but in this case it is a doubling not of points of view, but of scenes. Indeed, the importance of the "illuminating incident" was the great thing Wharton learned from James, particularly in *The Golden Bowl*, where, for example,

> the deeply, the doubly betrayed Maggie, walking up and down in the summer evening on the terrace of Fawns, looks in at the window of the smoking-room, where her father, her husband and her step-mother (who is her husband's mistress) are playing bridge together, unconscious of her scrutiny. As she looks she knows that she has them at her mercy, and that they all (even her father) know it; and in the same instant the sight of them tells her that "to feel about them in any of the immediate, inevitable, assuaging ways, the ways usually open to innocence outraged and generosity betrayed, would have been to give them up, *and that giving them up was, marvelously, not to be thought of.*"[26]

The House of Mirth is in narrative structure about the downward path of the protagonist through a series of actual houses, but as the title from Ecclesiastes suggests,[27] it has also to do with symbolic houses, and as a "house of fiction"[28] it bears a great deal of resemblance to the plan of The Mount. It is a skewing of that plan, however—a bringing together of classical purity and sensuous decadence—that sets the novel in motion. The background of *The House of Mirth* is the American Renaissance, with all of its tensions; its key is Henry Adams's woman diverted from her axis, a devotee of taste rather than a source of power, the Art Nouveau decoration, Lily Bart.[29] The original title of the book—"A Moment's Ornament"—suggests Lily's role, which is not to say that ornament in her world is frivolous; indeed, she is part of a carefully elaborated plan: she is an "argument from design."[30]

The design of the whole can be most clearly seen by isolating its "illuminating moments": multiplied, they shimmer in a series of reflecting mirrors, or they stand as the foci of kaleidoscopic turns that refract their images as distorted patterns. At the center of *The House of Mirth* is Lily, alone and motionless, posed for a series of *tableaux vivants*, in the ballroom of the house of the nouveaux riches Wellington Brys, as Joshua Reynolds's *Mrs. Lloyd*. We know this is the center because it is here that Lawrence Selden, the most important of reflectors, says that he sees before him "the real Lily Bart" (135). *Mrs. Lloyd* (Joanna Leigh), painted in 1766 during Reynolds's classical phase, would seem to be a goddess come to earth, or a visitor from the Forest of Arden, so inappropriately is she dressed for the out-of-doors.[31] Her bare feet in thin sandals and the lines of her long, flowing robes accentuate rather than conceal the sensual lines of her body, and she is engaged, as she bends forward from the marble monument against which she leans, in the very human activity of carving her lover's name onto the bark of a tree. The setting, indeed, seems more English landscape park than forest, a re-creation of a Grecian valley; the marble monument, the inscription on the tree invite us to "read" the landscape as a series of lines, shapes and contours in a formal design. We have here a Woman, herself an artistic creation, in a Garden, which according to Reynolds was itself a form of Art.[32]

As the trees in the painting serve only to frame Mrs. Lloyd, so Lily Bart dominates her setting. As one of the Brys' guests observes of her impersonation, "there isn't a break in the lines anywhere," from the magnificently coiled masses of her abundant hair to the slightly upturned arch of her bare foot:

> Here there could be no mistaking the predominance of personality—the unanimous "Oh!" of the spectators was a tribute, not to the brush-work of Reynolds's "Mrs. Lloyd" but to the flesh and blood loveliness of Lily Bart. She had shown her artistic intelligence in selecting a type so like her own that she could embody the person represented without ceasing to be herself. It was as though she had stepped, not out of, but into, Reynolds's canvas, banishing the phantom of his dead beauty by the beams of her living grace. The impulse to show herself in a splendid setting—she had thought for a moment of representing Tiepolo's Cleopatra—had yielded to the truer instinct of trusting to her unassisted beauty, and she had purposely chosen a picture without distracting accessories of dress or surroundings. Her pale draperies, and the background of foliage against which she stood, served only to relieve the long dryad-like curves that swept upward from her poised foot to her lifted arm. The noble buoyancy of her attitude, its suggestion of soaring grace, revealed the touch of poetry in her beauty that Selden always felt in her presence, yet lost the sense of when he was not with her. Its expression was now so vivid that for the first time he seemed to see before him the real Lily Bart, divested of the trivialities of her little world, and catching for a moment a note of that eternal harmony of which her beauty was a part. [134–35]

Tableaux vivants to an unfurnished mind, with the most skillful lighting and the most delusive interposition of layers of gauze, remain "only a superior kind of wax works"; but to the responsive fancy they give "magic glimpses of the boundary world between fact and imagination." Selden is one who yields to "vision-making influences as completely as a child to the spell of a fairy-tale," a spell cast here by the theatrical setting for these tableaux—the recently built house of the Brys, which

> was almost as well-designed for festal display as one of those airy pleasure-halls which the Italian architects improvised to set off the hospitality of princes. The air of improvisation was in fact strikingly present; so recent, so rapidly-evoked was the whole *mise-en-scène* that one had to touch the marble columns to learn they were not of cardboard, to seat one's self in one of the damask-and-gold arm-chairs to be sure it was not painted against the wall.

All of this pleases Selden: all he asks of the very rich when he joins them is that they "live up to their calling as stage-managers," and he surveys both scene—an immense ballroom with a stage at one end behind a proscenium arch curtained with folds of old damask—and company—"a surface of rich tissues and jewelled shoulders in harmony with the festooned and gilded walls, and the flushed splendours of the Venetian ceiling"—with frank enjoyment. From the moment the curtains part on a group of nymphs dancing across a flower-strewn sward in the rhythmic postures of Botticelli's *Spring*, the pictures succeed each other for him with the rhythmic march of some splendid frieze "in which the fugitive curves of living flesh and the wandering light of young eyes have been subdued to plastic harmony without losing the charm of life" (131–33).

The various tableaux have been staged under the direction of the "distinguished" portrait painter Paul Morpeth, who bears a certain resemblance to John Singer Sargent and will appear again in *The Custom of the Country* as Claud Walsingham Popple. Each of the representations depends partly for effect on the rich and sumptuous setting of the painting chosen: a typical Goya, Titian's daughter, a characteristic Vandyck, Kauffmann nymphs garlanding the altar of love, a Veronese supper, a group of Watteau's lute-playing comedians lounging by a fountain. Lily's decision not to depend upon dress or setting—not, for example, to present Tiepolo's Cleopatra—makes her tableau stand out from the others. Yet Lily is indeed a work of art, no less than the symbolic Woman of the American Renaissance murals, the decorative woman of Art Nouveau or Loïe Fuller's "lily." She is "the real Lily Bart" in that the real Lily Bart is one who is always engaged in "making up," whether she is decorating herself and posturing for a particular audience or studying herself in the mirror. What is different in this tableau is the frank presentation of Lily's *body*, an acknowledgment of an erotic nature that is never mentioned in her society, though its currents run deep beneath the surface.

The same group will reenact this illuminating moment later on in Monte Carlo. Selden, alone there and unaware that his New York acquaintances are in the vicinity, stands on the Casino steps, surveying "the white square set in an exotic coquetry of architecture, the studied tropicality of the gardens, the groups loitering in the foreground against mauve mountains which suggested a sublime stage-setting." Feeling "the renewed zest of spectatorship," he watches the desultory groups in the square

> dissolve and re-form in other scenes . . . [while] the last moments of the performance seemed to gain an added brightness from the hovering threat of the curtain. The quality of the air, the exuberance of the flowers, the blue intensity of sea and sky, produced the effect of a closing *tableau*, . . . heightened by the way in which a . . . conspicuous group of people advanced to the middle front, and stood . . . with the air of chief performers. . . . Their appearance confirmed the impression that the show had been staged regard-

less of expense, and emphasized its resemblance to one of those "costume-plays" in which the protagonists walk through the passions without displacing a drapery. The ladies stood in unrelated attitudes calculated to isolate their effects, and the men hung about them as irrelevantly as stage heroes. [183–84]

The appearance of Lily Bart suggests to him a comparison with the earlier tableau: "Then . . . [her beauty] had a transparency through which the fluctuations of the spirit were sometimes tragically visible; now its impenetrable surface suggested a process of crystallization which had fused her whole being into one hard brilliant substance. . . . to Selden it seemed like that moment of pause and arrest when the warm fluidity of youth is chilled into its final shape" (191–92).

This pair of tableaux has reverberations in the framing scenes of the book, the one occurring in Selden's flat, to which the two friends retire for a cup of tea, and the other the closing tableau of the book, when Lily lies motionless on her boarding-house bed and Selden arrives, too late, to tell her that he has loved her all along. In the first we see Lily pausing before the mantelpiece, studying herself in the mirror while she adjusts her veil: "The attitude revealed the long slope of her slender sides, which gave a kind of wild-wood grace to her outline—as though she were a captured dryad subdued to the conventions of the drawing-room; and Selden reflected that it was the same streak of sylvan freedom in her nature that lent such savour to her artificiality" (13). And in the final scene, "though the blind was down, the irresistible sunlight poured a tempered golden flood into the room, and in its light Selden saw a narrow bed along the wall, and on the bed, with motionless hands and calm unrecognizing face, the semblance of Lily Bart. That it was her real self, every pulse in him ardently denied" (325).

These scenes, in turn, reflect other tableaux. Following the performance of artistic impersonations at the Brys', the actors during an interlude of music wander among the audience "diversifying its conventional appearance by the varied picturesqueness of their dress" (135). Lily, however, remains typically aloof from the crowd in order to prolong the effect she has produced; she has a second opportunity to show herself as the throng moves into the empty drawing-room where she stands, flowerlike, expanding in the light of approving glances. She gives her arm to Selden and they pass through a long suite of rooms to the conservatory, which has "the fragrant hush of a garden . . . [on] a midsummer night":

Hanging lights made emerald caverns in the depths of foliage, and whitened the spray of a fountain falling among lilies. The magic place was deserted: there was no sound but the plash of the water of the lily-pads. . . . Selden and Lily stood still, accepting the unreality of the scene as a part of their own dream-like sensations. . . . At length Lily withdrew her hand, and moved away a step, so that her white-robed slimness was outlined against the dusk of the branches. [137]

These echoes of *Mrs. Lloyd* repeat, in turn, another series of scenes set at Bellomont, the country estate of Lily's friends the Trenors. In the first of these, Lily stands leaning against the balustrade above the sunken garden, "a spot propitious to sentimental musings," at some distance from the animated group beneath her. She knows that Percy Gryce, a young millionaire she has made up her mind to "catch," is watching her, and her only response is "to sink into an attitude of more graceful abstraction" because, fully aware of the extent to which the volubility of others enhances her own repose, she deliberately exploits the contrast in order to throw her own charms into greater relief. Again, she seats herself on the terrace steps, leaning her head against the honeysuckles wreathing the balustrade, stepping into, as it were, an eighteenth-century landscape painting: "The fragrance of the late blossoms seemed an emanation of the tranquil scene, a landscape tutored to the last degree of rural elegance. In the foreground glowed the warm tints of the gardens. Beyond the lawn, with its pyramidal pale-gold maples and velvety firs, sloped pastures dotted with cattle; and through a long glade the river widened like a lake under the silver light" (46–49). Determining to put the finishing touches to Mr. Gryce's subjugation, she decides to ask him to accompany her to the country church, imagining his response to "the sight of her in a grey gown of devotional cut, with her famous lashes drooped above a prayer book"; but unfortunately for this design she is "like a water-plant in the flux of the tides." Characteristically, however, she impulsively thwarts her own careful plans: in this case she makes sure that Lawrence Selden sees her setting off at a gait hardly likely to get her to the church before the sermon, then stops to sink into a rustic seat at a charming spot (53, 61). Later, Lily and Selden set off on the ascending slopes, their path winding across a meadow with scattered trees, dipping into a lane plumed with asters and purpling sprays of bramble, and the light quiver of ash-leaves, through which "the country unrolled itself in pastoral distances." Like Mrs. Lloyd, Lily has "no real intimacy with nature," but she does recognize "the appropriate" and is keenly sensitive to scene as fitting back-

ground. So she stands, the lady in the landscape—this time the picturesque Hudson River valley, with "its calmness, its breadth, its long free
reaches," its foreground of "sugar-maples [that] wavered like pyres of
light," then "a massing of grey orchards, and here and there the lingering
green of an oak-grove. Two or three red farm-houses dozed under the
apple-trees, and the white wooden spire of a village church showed beyond the shoulder of the hill; while far below, in a haze of dust, the high-
road ran between the fields." Selden at this moment sees Lily as "a wonderful spectacle"; and it is always at such moments that he is most drawn
to her—in his detached way. When she weeps, for instance, he observes
that "even her weeping was an art" (63, 64, 66, 72). Desire, for him, is
ethereal: true human intercourse, he says, should take place in a "republic
of the spirit." Lily, always aware that she *is* a spectacle, understands fully
that what most draws Selden to her—the ornamental grace that most
enhances, for the connoisseur, this pastoral moment—might embody an
idea but is not in itself spiritual. "I can never even get my foot across the
threshold," she tells him. And in a wonderfully ironic underscoring of this
pastoral moment, American fashion, their idyll is disturbed by the intrusion of the machine into the garden:

> They stood silent . . . , smiling at each other like adventurous children who
> have climbed to a forbidden height from which they discover a new world.
> The actual world at their feet was veiling itself in dimness, and across the
> valley a clear moon rose in the denser blue. Suddenly they heard a remote
> sound, like the hum of a giant insect, and following the high-road, which
> wound whiter through the surrounding twilight, a black object rushed
> across their vision. [70–71, 73–74]

Toward the end of the book, by which time Lily will have descended
through a number of social layers, each symbolized by increasing disorder
in domestic spatial and human arrangements, this scene, inverted, will be
repeated. Lily takes a walk with Simon Rosedale, a glossy and overweight
little businessman of enormous wealth who has hopes of catapulting himself through marriage into the upper reaches of society. Rosedale's view of
Lily, though certainly less spiritual, is not so different from Selden's: to
him she is the woman who would "wear . . . [a crown] as if it grew on
her." He has proposed marriage to Lily and has been repulsed; but by the
time of their walk on "one of those still November days when the air is
haunted with the light of summer, and something in the lines of the landscape, and in the golden haze which bathed them, recalled . . . the Sep-
tember afternoon when she had climbed the slopes of Bellomont with

Selden," she has nearly reached bottom and is ready to accept Rosedale
(176, 253). He, however, now has a condition: Lily must "buy" her way
back into society by using, as blackmail, a packet of letters he knows she
has in her possession.

The mirrors shift again, and we have another pair of scenes. The first
is the opening chapter of the book: it is the one where Lily, leaving
Selden's flat, is blocked on the stairs by the charwoman with her scrub-
brushes and bucket. When Lily encounters the woman again on the stairs
in Mrs. Peniston's house, she has "the odd sensation of having already
found herself in the same situation but in different surroundings" (99).
This time, however, the woman examines Lily with "unflinching curiosity," a prelude to her reappearance at Lily's door with a packet of letters—
from Bertha Dorset, a married woman and one of the Bellomont set, to
Lawrence Selden. Lily buys the letters because she thinks Selden would
want her to. She does not read them, but she does not destroy them—yet.

This pair of scenes suggests still another series, for Lily has been
taking tea with Selden, which in the atmosphere of his flat with its warm
background of old bindings against which Lily's drooping profile is outlined, is a ritual of long-standing tradition. He kneels by the table to light
the lamp under the kettle; she measures out the tea into a little tea-pot of
green glaze: "As he watched her hand, polished as a bit of old ivory, with
its slender pink nails, and the sapphire bracelet slipping over her wrist, he
was struck with the irony of suggesting to her such a life as his cousin
Gertrude Farish [a woman who lives simply, economically and altruis-
tically] had chosen. She was so evidently the victim of the civilization
which had produced her, that the links of her bracelet seemed like manacles chaining her to her fate." Soon afterward, Lily takes tea with Percy
Gryce on the train to Bellomont. With the taste of Selden's caravan tea on
her lips, Lily has little inclination to drink the railway brew but because
she understands the importance of the ritual, she performs it perfectly, in
order to give the last touch to Mr. Gryce's enjoyment: "he watched her in
silent fascination while her hands flitted above the tray, looking miraculously fine and slender in contrast to the coarse china and lumpy bread. It
seemed wonderful to him that any one should perform with such careless
ease the difficult task of making tea in public in a lurching train" (7, 19).
Finally, late in the book Lily takes tea with Rosedale, this time with little
sense of ceremony, for she is ill with fatigue and worry, but with the same
effect as she has had on her male companions during the earlier version of
this scene:

As she leaned back before him, her lids drooping in utter lassitude, though the first warm draught already tinged her face with returning life, Rosedale was seized afresh by the poignant surprise of her beauty. The dark pencilling of fatigue under her eyes, the morbid blue-veined pallour of the temples, brought out the brightness of her hair and lips, as though all her ebbing vitality were centered there. Against the dull chocolate-coloured background of the restaurant, the purity of her head stood out as it had never done in the most brightly-lit ball room. [289–90]

The ritual quality of meals and conversations, celebrations and ceremonies measures precise degrees of meaning in the lives carried on in the structures Wharton so carefully builds. Gerty Farish, for example, who has to Lily's eye "a horrid little place, and no maid, and such queer things to eat," serves Selden a dinner with "wonderful effects," after which they move to the sitting-room, "where they fitted as snugly as bits in a puzzle," and sip coffee from her grandmother's egg-shell cups (7, 154–55). The importance of this ceremony is not in the setting, but rather in the preserving of a tradition handed down in old cups. This dinner, like the taking of tea in Selden's flat, contrasts sharply with dinner at Bellomont where Gus Trenor, "his heavy carnivorous head sunk between his shoulders, as he preyed on a jellied plover," sits at one end of the table, his wife "at the opposite end of the long bank of orchids, suggestive, with her glaring good-looks, of a jeweller's window lit by electricity. And between the two, what a long stretch of vacuity!" Lily deplores this scene because it is not "picturesque," for the same reason that in her childhood she had wished for six dozen fresh lilies-of-the-valley on the luncheon table each day. Yet for her Gerty's flat is not picturesque: it is in a cramped blind-alley of life at the top of dull and narrow stairs destined to be mounted by dull people. Inside, she virtually fills the flat; her very movements nearly overturn Gerty's fragile tea-table and Lily, steadying the cups as she sits, sighs incoherently, "I'd forgotten there was no room to dash about in—how beautifully one does have to behave in a small flat!" (55, 264–65).

How well Lily chooses, then, when she displays herself only, with no expressive background, as Reynolds's *Mrs. Lloyd*. For in this carefully constructed series of echoing scenes spreading out from the central tableau, Lily has no place, no room, no setting. She is "unsphered"; she is "rootless and ephemeral" (261, 319). Her fall—not a moral fall, but rather a downhill drifting—is through layers of social strata, none of which provides a foothold, a place to put down roots.

The House of Mirth is a superimposing of one structure upon another: a series of classically balanced spaces, settings for parallel scenes; a series of lines that would be parallel were it not for their increasingly crooked and wavering character toward the bottom. The latter are the houses of Trenor, Bry, Dorset, Gormer, Fisher, Rosedale, Hatch, against which a descending diagonal line can be traced indicating the fall of Lily Bart. The harmoniously balanced life represented in the houses and furnishings of *The Decoration of Houses* and articulated in the plan for The Mount, where public and private are carefully distinguished and movement carefully controlled, rests upon principles of tradition, balance, proportion. In *The House of Mirth*, as these principles are increasingly violated—as conflation of public and private multiplies, as disorder in spatial arrangements comes increasingly to reflect chaotic human intercourse, as these spatial arrangements cease to function as retreats but become instead *scenes*, as Henry James so appropriately named American spaces—there is a corresponding lack of moral center. It is as if Wharton took the classical house plan, with its harmony and proportion, and turned it, skewing it, then turned it a bit more for each of the stops along Lily's downhill path, so that the sense of fixedness becomes less sure and more off center as the novel progresses.

Regularity can be measured against the house of Mrs. Peniston, where Lily lives until her aunt dies and disinherits Lily in favor of a cousin whose behavior is more regular. Mrs. Peniston's house, in fact, offers a model of frozen precision: the rooms are arranged with "glacial neatness," and the little mirrors, affixed to the upper windows "so that from the depths of an impenetrable domesticity . . . [one] might see what was happening in the street," show Mrs. Peniston to be "a looker-on at life." The complacent ugliness of the black walnut, the slippery gloss of the vestibule tiles and the odor of sapolio and furniture polish make Lily feel "buried alive in the stifling limits of Mrs. Peniston's existence" (37, 100). Even her own large, comfortable and frivolously enlivened room seems, with the dead Mr. Peniston's monumental black walnut bedstead and wardrobe and the magenta flock wall-paper "hung with large steel engravings of an anecdotic character," as dreary as a prison. In the drawing-room, conversation with Mrs. Peniston is as limited and unvarying as the arrangement of its furnishings: of equal importance are the discussion of whether the old Van Osburgh Sèvres was used at the bride's table and Mrs. Peniston's checking the ormulu clock, surmounted by a helmeted Minerva enthroned between two malachite vases, for dust with her lace handkerchief.[33] In the upstairs sitting-room Mrs. Peniston receives confidences. She sits in a "black satin arm-chair tufted with yellow buttons, beside a bead-work table bearing a bronze box with a miniature of Beatrice Cenci in the lid," and the distaste Lily feels for these objects is that of a prisoner regarding the fittings of a court-room: "the pink-eyed smirk of the turbaned Beatrice" is associated in her mind with "the gradual fading of the smile from Mrs. Peniston's lips" (108–10, 169).

Lily finds release from the rigid straightness of Mrs. Peniston's house in the more relaxed and opulent atmosphere of the Trenors' Bellomont country house. Here Lily's "craving for the external finish of life" is gratified: card-players in a firelit room with trays of tall glasses and silver-collared decanters nearby, a hall "arcaded, with a gallery supported on columns of pale yellow marble," tall clumps of flowering plants in the angles of the walls, crimson carpets, and a great central lantern overhead shedding a brightness on the women's hair and jewels as they move. Her own room at Bellomont has "softly-shaded lights, her lace dressing-gown lying across the silken bedspread, her little embroidered slippers before the fire, a vase of carnations filling the air with perfume, and the last novels and magazines lying uncut on a table beside the reading-lamp." At the same time, Bellomont is a place of "large tumultuous disorder, . . . where no one seemed to have time to observe any one else, and private aims and personal interests were swept along unheeded in the rush of collective activities." The relaxation of standards at Bellomont is suggested by the garden, "a perspective of hedges and parterres leading by degrees of lessening formality to the free undulations of the park," and by the fact that the house itself is grafted onto another one. The original was an old manor-house, the only surviving portion of which is the library, a long spacious room, filled with tradition, from "its classically-cased doors, the Dutch tiles of the chimney, and the elaborate hobgrate with its shining brass urns," to the old family portraits and shelves of pleasantly shabby books (24–25, 229, 39, 59). A slightly discordant note is sounded in the way the Trenors use this room—not as a place to read, but rather as a smoking-room or a retreat for flirtation, and it is here, in fact, that Lily comes looking for Lawrence Selden for just that purpose, expecting him to be reading, but finding him, instead, in a tête-à-tête with Bertha Dorset.

The Trenors' town-house is on Fifth Avenue, just down from the Brys'—the setting for the *tableaux vivants*, a house with a wide, white facade and rich restraint of line suggesting "the clever corseting of a redundant figure"—and not far from Simon Rosedale's new house, built by a man who came from "a *milieu* where all the dishes are put on the table at once," its facade "a complete architectural meal" (159–60). While the Trenors' house is being renovated—not to be outdone by the Brys, they are adding on a 150-foot-long ball-room—Judy Trenor stays mostly at Bellomont, a fact her husband Gus uses to his advantage when he arranges to have Lily visit him in town on the pretext of a summons from Judy. Lily arrives to find the furniture "wrapped up in . . . slippery white stuff," and the discordant note of the cloud of cigar-smoke is a kind of warning—which Lily does not at first heed because "the sight of such appliances in a drawing-room" is not unusual in her set, where "smoking and drinking were unrestricted by considerations of time and place"—of Gus's "disorderly" intentions to make Lily "pay up" (160, 141).

Judy's learning that Lily has been borrowing money from her husband, Mrs. Peniston's learning of Lily's gambling, Bertha Dorset's jealousy over Lawrence Selden, and Selden's witnessing Lily's exit from the Trenor town-house all combine to make Lily suddenly homeless and friendless. Having frustrated her own chances to marry, without financial means of her own or skills with which to earn her living, she drifts, like a water-plant in flux, from one increasingly disreputable situation to another. The Gormer milieu, for example, represents "a social out-skirt which Lily had always fastidiously avoided," but once she is in it, it seems "only a flamboyant copy of her own world, a caricature approximating the real thing as the 'society play' approaches the manners of the drawing-room." The only difference between the Gormers and the Trenors, Van Osburghs and Dorsets was "in a hundred shades of aspect and manner, from the pattern of the men's waistcoats to the inflexion of the women's voices. Everything was pitched in a higher key, and there was more of each thing: more noise, more colour, more champagne, more familiarity" (234).

If the Gormers' milieu is vulgar, that of Mrs. Hatch is an "atmosphere of torrid splendour" where the people Lily meets are as strange as the surroundings: "wan beings as richly upholstered as the furniture, beings without definite pursuits or permanent relations, who drifted on a languid tide of curiosity from restaurant to concert-hall, from palm-garden to music-room, from 'art exhibit' to dress-maker's opening." The daily details of Mrs. Hatch's life are as disconcerting to Lily as the chaotic eclecticism of her hostess's rooms: Mrs. Hatch's habits are marked by such

"Oriental indolence and disorder" that she and her friends seem "to float together outside the bounds of time and space." With no definite hours and fixed obligations night and day flow "into one another in a blur of confused and retarded engagements, so that one had the impression of lunching at the tea-hour, while dinner was often merged in the noisy after-theatre supper which prolonged Mrs. Hatch's vigil till day-light." This lack of boundary, this incoherence of movement amounts to a complete inversion of the plan in which "all hung together in the solidarity of . . . traditional functions." At Mrs. Hatch's Lily has the "odd sense of being behind the social tapestry, on the side where the threads were knotted and the loose ends hung." The "vast gilded void of Mrs. Hatch's existence" makes clear to Lily the well-ordered lives of her former friends, with their inherited obligations and their share in "the working of the great civic machine" (274–76).

It is not only Mrs. Hatch and her surroundings that are lit up, for Lily, "in a blaze of electric light, impartially projected from various ornamental excrescences"; it is the frightening similarity to Lily herself. If Mrs. Hatch is described as rising from "a vast concavity of pink damask and gilding . . . like Venus from her shell"—the sexless American Venus who would fill Henry Adams with despair, this one's large-eyed prettiness having "the fixity of something . . . under glass"—Lily herself has been "brought up to be ornamental," "fashioned to adorn and delight." She is "like some rare flower grown for exhibition, a flower from which every bud has been nipped except the crowning blossom of her beauty" (273, 297, 301, 317). And if somewhere in the background of Mrs. Hatch's (like Sim Rosedale's) world there was a real past, "peopled by real human activities, . . . strong ambitions, persistent energies, diversified contacts with the wholesome roughness of life," Lily is on her way to discovering that world when she leaves Mrs. Hatch's. Hotel life—rooms with a cramped outlook down a sallow vista of brick walls and fire-escapes, lonely meals in a dark restaurant with unpleasant smells—is only an intermediate stop; Lily is headed for the working-class world of the boarding-house and factory, or to join forces with Rosedale as "superfine human merchandise." Within this given framework she must sink to the bottom unless she can, in Rosedale's "terms of businesslike give-and-take," agree to a "revision of boundary lines," using herself as a "transfer of property" (274, 247, 256, 259).

It is not simply seeing herself as a commodity in the latter alternative that disgusts her; throughout the book this realization has led her to repulse a series of suitors more eligible than Rosedale. Nor is it a sense of his power—the extension of Rosedale's business accomplishments into his private life—that bewilders her. It is rather that in the spelling out of the particulars, the *naming* of this transaction, Lily begins to see that such arrangements are without moral boundaries, that they rest upon distrust, that they are *base* appropriations of power (258–60). Her would-be-ac-complice assumes, as a matter of course, that she might try "to cheat him of his share of the spoils" because his is a Dynamo-structured world where rape and machine force become means to power. Lily's body for Rose-dale's money—a transaction dependent on Lily's renewing her own power through the base ploy of using Bertha Dorset's love letters to Lawrence Selden as blackmail, letters that Rosedale has put into her hands for just such a purpose—is a complete inversion of the "republic of the spirit."

For this tasteful Virgin raised to adorn and delight, these republics of spirit and of the business world are equally impossible alternatives. To suggest that Lily should at this point take charge of her own life, that she should adjust to the "blotched wall-paper and shabby paint," the parlor with its "discoloured . . . engravings of sentimental episodes" that disgusts even Rosedale, that she should work, is to ignore the fact that she has been raised as a hot-house flower, that her role models come from "an extensive perusal of fiction" and from symbolic representations of Woman in painting, statuary, magazine illustration and even on dollar bills, that she has been taught to accept "with philosophic calm the fact that such existences as hers were pedastalled on foundations of obscure humanity," that it is "in the natural order of things" to allow the orchid, "basking in its artificially created atmosphere . . . [to] round the delicate curves of its petals undisturbed by the ice on the panes." This hot-house flower, thrown into "the mud and sleet of a winter night," will wither and die; and this is what happens to Lily, taken from "that little illuminated circle in which life reached its finest efflorescence" into the "dreary limbo of dinginess [which] lay all around" (287, 298, 33, 150). The fault is not Lily's; as Wharton would comment, "a frivolous society can acquire dramatic significance only through what its frivolity destroys." *The House of Mirth*, then, is not only about "a society of irresponsible pleasure-seekers," but about the "tragic implication" of the power of such frivolity to debase people and ideals.[34] The hot-house flower and the working-class woman in the mud and sleet are equally products of this debased society.

Wharton renders Lily Bart vulnerable on two counts: she detaches her from any soil in which she might put down roots—she is as devoid of background as Reynolds's *Mrs. Lloyd* or as symbolic representations of American Woman—and she endows her with greater fastidiousness than "the average section of womanhood." The first deprives Lily of a sense of self and makes her like that "water-plant in flux";[35] the second prevents her from becoming either a member of "frivolous society" or of the working class, while it gives her an increasingly lucid consciousness.

The paradox is that Lily lacks what Wharton would later call "that great nutritive element" at the core of self.[36] Having grown up "without any one spot of earth being dearer to her than another," she has inherited rootlessness from her parents, who had been "blown hither and thither on every wind . . . , without any personal existence to shelter them from its shifting gusts"; and in her life there has been "no centre of early pieties, of grave endearing traditions, to which her heart could revert and from which it could draw strength for itself and tenderness for others." The past that lives in the blood, Wharton writes, "whether in the concrete image of the old house stored with visual memories, or in the conception of the house not built with hands, but made up of inherited passions and loyalties" is what gives power to individual existence, "attaching it by mysterious links of kinship" to human striving. Lily's homelessness, then, deprives her of something fundamentally human; finally she is even poorer than a working-class woman like Nettie Struther, who has been able to gather together the fragments of her broken life and build herself a *shelter*. Lily comes to see that both her drawing toward men as mates and her drawing away from them have been premonitions of the same thing: a vision of her life as a series of disintegrating influences, with "all the men and women she knew . . . like atoms whirling away from each other in some wild centrifugal dance." She comes at last to see her life as one of terrible silence and emptiness: "she felt as though the house, the street, the world were all empty, and she alone left sentient in a lifeless universe" (319, 321).[37]

It is because of this lack of shelter, which Lily senses that none of the men in the novel can provide for her, and which she cannot provide for herself out of her own experience, that houses for her are only settings, rooms only scenes in which to posture and pose. Thus we see her watching herself in a succession of mirrors—in Selden's flat, in her own room and in the drawing-room at Mrs. Peniston's, at Bellomont, in Gerty's flat—to count the lines marring her face, to practice expressions, to watch herself as if she were a picture in a frame. She seems "to watch her own figure retreating down vistas of neutral-tinted dulness" in Mrs. Peniston's house; she looks at herself as a philanthropist and sees her frame enlarged; she sees herself advancing toward intimacy and then dissimulating, using "her beauty to divert attention from an inconvenient topic" (101, 112, 114). The great lesson of her early life has been that "beauty is only the raw material of conquest, and that to convert it into success other arts are required"; and so we see her deliberately assume a "mask of a very definite purpose" at the train station (later in the book it will be a "tragic mask") and get into the train "with the instinctive feeling for effect which never forsook her" (34, 3, 215, 17). In the space of a few moments at Selden's flat, we see her gaze at him "with the troubled gravity of a child," pose against his collection of old bindings as a rare object in herself while she gathers material for her next scene, adjust her veil before his mirror in an attitude calculated to reveal the long slender slope and "wild-wood grace" of her body, and then mock herself with "the clothes are the background, the frame, . . . they don't make success, but they are a part of it" (9–13). At Bellomont we see her playing, for Percy Gryce, at looking languid—"full of a suffering sweetness; she carried a scent-bottle in her hand"—and for Gus Trenor, as a deliberate contrast to his own red massiveness, at looking fresh and slender. Similarly, in Sim Rosedale's opera box she affects "well-poised lines and happy tints" that lift her "to a height apart by that incommunicable grace which is the bodily counterpart of genius!" (67, 116).

Always conscious "of her own power to look and to be so exactly what the occasion required"—refusing, for example, to be a bridesmaid on the grounds that "she was [so] much taller than the other attendant virgins, her presence might mar the symmetry of the group," and because she sees herself as "the mystically veiled figure occupying the centre of attention"—she looks for scenes "in which every detail should have the finish of a jewel, and the whole form a harmonious setting to her own jewel-like rareness." Even other people are pieces of scenery (89, 87, 90, 121). The "buffeting of chances" that keeps her in an attitude of uneasy alertness, however, also teaches her to be an impromptu actress; she knows how to bear herself in difficult as well as in easy situations: "She had, to a shade, the exact manner between victory and defeat: every insinuation was shed without an effort by the bright indifference of her manner" (97–99). At Monte Carlo, for instance, when Bertha Dorset publicly dismisses Lily from the yacht on which she has been a guest,

Dorsets, Stepneys, Brys are all actors in and witnesses to "the miserable drama." The women avert their eyes and the men cower behind the women; but Lily looks her hostess straight in the eye, puts on a faint smile of disdain which lifts her "high above her antagonist's reach," gives Mrs. Dorset "the full measure of the distance between them," and only then turns to offer her own explanation and extend her hand to Selden, smiling, "Dear Mr. Selden, . . . you promised to see me to my cab" (227, 218–19).

That others treat Lily as an actress simply confirms her own inclinations: social roles, especially in this glaring exposé, are based upon expectations of reciprocal performance; that is part of the social ceremony that comes to be taken for "reality."[38] Selden sees her as a spectacle; Mrs. Fisher sees her as "an interesting study" and later as some "impenetrable surface suggest[ing] a process of crystallization which had fused her whole being into one hard brilliant substance" (189, 191–92). Indeed, Lily's social descent is marked by the "hard glaze of indifference [that] was fast forming over her delicacies and susceptibilities," each concession to expedience hardening the surface a little more. The artist Paul Morpeth, struck by Lily's "plastic possibilities," wants to paint her—"not the face: too self-controlled for expression; but the rest of her—gad, what a model she'd make!" (235, 237). Not everyone is taken in by Lily's skills as an actress, however. Both Gus Trenor and Sim Rosedale tell her not to "talk stage-rot," and Mrs. Peniston is unmoved by the "troubled loveliness" of Lily's face, put on to effect sympathy; she shrinks back apprehensively, feels her very furniture to be contaminated and decides to disinherit Lily (145, 257, 171, 127).

Lily's fastidiousness is more physical than moral: what she craves and feels entitled to is "a situation in which the noblest attitude should also be the easiest." She has no clearly formulated standard of judgment or behavior; indeed, most of her actions, from taking tea with Selden alone in his bachelor flat to taking too many drops of the chloral which ends her life, are impulsive. Her fastidiousness is, however, consistent in relation to her own body. She can set sail on the Dorset yacht because it is a comfortable temporary berth—despite the fact that she has been asked aboard to occupy George Dorset while Bertha has an affair with another man. She can live with the questionable Gormers because "the shade of a leafy verandah" is better than a broiling Sunday in town. She can join the disreputable Mrs. Hatch because of "the luxury of lying once more in a soft-pillowed bed, and looking across a spacious sunlit room at a breakfast-table set invitingly near the fire. . . . The sense of being once more lapped and folded in ease, as in some dense mild medium impenetrable to discomfort, effectually stilled the faintest note of criticism" (262, 273). She can put on clinging draperies that reveal every line of her body, but she is repulsed by men who want to touch her. She takes money easily from Gus Trenor, but his touch makes her feel "a momentary shiver of reluctance," "a thrill of vexation," a "shock to her . . . consciousness" (85, 91, 146). It is this personal fastidiousness that is at the root of her attraction to the rather meager Percy Gryce. It has been because Lily feels imprisoned in Mrs. Peniston's drawing-room and in the great gilded cage of Bellomont and fears that she may wind up in something like Gerty Farish's cramped flat that she angles for Gryce, deciding that were she to become for him what his Americana has been, "the one possession in which he took sufficient pride to spend money," she would "so . . . identify herself with her husband's vanity that to gratify her wishes would be to him the most exquisite form of self-indulgence" (54, 49). In the world in which Lily moves, space is money, and more space means less human contact. If her size is such that she fills the space in which she is placed, extending like the decorative woman of Art Nouveau beyond the frame, enough money would give "a soaring vastness" to her life. Her whole being dilates in an atmosphere of luxury: "it was the background she required, the only climate she could breathe in" (89, 26). And that such freedom has a price is also at the root of her impulsive neglect of Gryce.

Simon Rosedale, who has no drawing-room manner at all, makes the unspoken connection between money and sex explicit. He offers Lily freedom from thinking about money, but he appraises her as if she were a piece of bric-à-brac; he runs his small stock-taking eyes over her "as though he were a collector who had learned to distinguish minor differences of design and quality in some long-coveted object" (176, 14, 96, 300). Lily, for whom even contact with the charwoman gives a sense of contamination, knows the meaning of these exchanges: she can only consider such a solution of her difficulties because she does not "let her imagination range beyond the day of plighting." Her personal fastidiousness has a moral equivalent: "when she made a tour of inspection in her own mind there were certain closed doors she did not open" (248, 82).

Selden is attractive to her because he does not press upon her any sense of personal bondage in his "republic of the spirit." On the other hand, his not thinking about money is, for Lily, an impossible condition of citizenship in the republic, for "the only way not to think about money is to have a great deal of it"—words Rosedale uses in proposing to her a very different sort of existence. Selden is unattractive, then, because he does not have enough money: intercourse with him would be "an ideal state of existence, . . . the last touch of luxury; but in the world as it was, such a privilege was likely to cost more than it was worth." Selden can see that she is expensive—that "she must have cost a good deal to make, that a great many dull and ugly people must . . . have been sacrificed to produce her." He regards her with Epicurean fascination: one can almost see him walking round her as if she were some object in a glass case, wondering at her external finish—"as though a fine glaze of beauty and fastidiousness had been applied to vulgar clay"—but musing, "a coarse texture will not take a high finish; and was it not possible that the material was fine, but that circumstance had fashioned it into a futile shape?" (69, 88, 5).

  If Lily has been raised to adorn and delight—to regard her beauty, enhanced by learned arts, as her greatest asset—it has been with the explicit purpose of getting a husband: she will continue to cost a great deal. The dressing up of her body, the posing of it in suggestive ways, is a learned and alienating use of her body, preliminary to giving it up to another. Because social bonding is for Lily physical bondage, while at the same time it is impossible for her to be independent, all spaces available to her are prisonlike. She sees herself as chained by the very links of her bracelet, "like manacles," to her fate, or like Orestes pursued by the Furies; and Selden sees her as Andromeda, her limbs numb with bondage, waiting for Perseus (himself) to rescue her (17, 148, 159).[39] Selden's "republic of the spirit" seems to be the only free space; and in the open air with Selden Lily feels herself to be two persons, "one drawing deep breaths of freedom and exhilaration, the other gasping for air in a little black prisonhouse of fears." From then on this sense of doubleness—of the free person chained to another (64, 148)—will remain with her because, of course, there is no way for her to escape her body. The freedom Selden holds out to her is detached not only from social constraints and from money but from physical realities as well.[40]

  The final space in which Lily lives is a very small one—a room in a boarding-house. Its privacy is visual only; smells and sounds permeate the thin walls. From a rigidly ordered plan, her movement has been one of slippage to a milieu of complete disorder. The direction of Lily's movement has been irreversible from the moment she perceived herself to be, at Mrs. Hatch's, behind the social tapestry. From there it is only a short distance to the shop where Lily attempts to work in the back room among women who make Mrs. Trenor's hats and discuss the details of her life, and to the boarding-house where the "machinery" that makes one scene flow into another "without perceptible agency" is no longer carefully concealed. Another might have used this vision to construct a new life plan, but Lily, "for all her dissatisfied dreaming, had never really conceived the possibility of revolving about a different centre: it was easy enough to despise the world, but decidedly difficult to find any other habitable region." As she tells Selden in their last scene together, "I am a very useless person. I can hardly be said to have an independent existence. I was just a screw or a cog in the great machine I called life, and when I dropped out of it I found I was of no use anywhere else. What can one do when one finds that one only fits into one hole? One must get back to it or be thrown into the rubbish heap" (301, 261–62, 308).

At this moment Lily intends to "get back to it." She has in her dress, next to her body, one of the few signs of human passion in the novel—Bertha Dorset's love letters to Lawrence Selden. If she threatens to make public these very private pieces of sensuality, she can with a single stroke buy a place with Bertha Dorset's social and Sim Rosedale's financial protection. Forced to this alternative, she has come to bid Selden farewell, and to bid farewell, too, to the old Lily, recognizing that the action she is about to take—both the use of the letters and the merging of her life with Rosedale's—so revises the boundaries that she and Selden will never again be able to meet in the old way. But communication fails her: "it seem[s] incredible that any one should think it necessary to linger in the conventional outskirts of word-play and evasion"; she has passed beyond the pattern of "well-bred reciprocity, in which every demonstration must be scrupulously proportioned to the motion it elicits, and generosity of feeling is the only ostentation condemned" (306–7). In her "strange state of extra lucidity," the fastidiousness that has been both her undoing and the mark of her sense of self is too strong to allow her to violate herself in this way. As she leaves, she throws the letters into the fire, taking the first step toward putting her life into some final order.

She has a vision of what such order might be when she leaves Selden's flat. Weak and cold with fatigue and helplessness, she meets Nettie Struther, the working woman whom she once helped. Nettie takes Lily home to a "miraculously clean" and warm little kitchen and tells her how she has been able to pick herself up from poverty, illness and abandonment to begin again. Holding Nettie's baby, feeling for a moment "a sense of warmth and returning life," Lily glimpses for the first time a structure based on human contact. Returning to her tenement room, she puts her clothes in order, folding away last the Reynolds dress; she puts her papers in order, using the whole of her small legacy from Mrs. Peniston to pay her bills and the large debt to Gus Trenor; she faces clearly not only the external poverty of her life, but its "inner destitution" (313–16, 318). And then she lies down on her narrow bed, taking enough chloral to insure sleep. As she lies there, it seems to her as if Nettie Struther's baby is there with her. Her final sense is that of rounding her body to stroke and to protect the child, making of her own body a shelter to enfold her child-self. In this final, distinctly sensual embrace of self and another, Lily breaks through at last the separating and isolating structures of her life.

CHAPTER 3

Urban Pastoral

In whatever form a slowly-accumulated past lives in the blood—whether in the concrete image of the old house stored with visual memories, or in the conception of the house not built with hands, but made up of inherited passions and loyalties—it has the same power of broadening and deepening the individual existence, of attaching it by mysterious links of kinship to all the mighty sum of human striving.
—Edith Wharton, *The House of Mirth*

The House of Mirth ends with the death of a beautiful woman, the subject—best suited to "the lips . . . of a bereaved lover"—Poe had called "the most poetical topic in the world."[1] That the setting for Lily Bart's death is a stripped-down interior suggests, however, an important imaginative difference between Poe and Wharton. We have seen that for Wharton compositional structures—floor plans—are indications of human order and disorder, intimacy and separation; so their parts—individual rooms—are imaginative structures containing and expressing human meaning. Poe explored this notion in his essay, "The Philosophy of Furniture," suggesting the way in which a camera might linger among the objects of the room, hover briefly over the supine woman and focus on the grieving man at her side—although in this essay the figure on the sofa is male, and he is asleep, not dead, in a room that radiates tranquility. Wharton's camera focuses our attention on a dead woman in a bare room, destroyed by a culture that has taught her to experience herself only as a beautiful object to be appreciated—or bought—by men.

Structures that provide clues to imaginative difference are also the subject of Guy Davenport's essay, "The Geography of the Imagination." "The difference between the Parthenon and the World Trade Center, . . .

between Bach and John Philip Sousa, between Sophocles and Shake-speare, between a bicycle and a horse, though explicable by historical moment, necessity, and destiny, is before all a difference of imagination," Davenport writes.[2] He means a spatial—that is to say, a geographical imagination, one that functions diachronically as well as synchronically. Davenport is interested in the way in which persons of great imaginative reach travel across time and space, bringing together or re-creating sym-bols from different cultures. His first example is Poe's "Philosophy of Furniture" of 1840, the year in which Poe also published a collection of stories, *Tales of the Grotesque and Arabesque*. *Grotesque*, according to Dav-enport, comes from the writings of Sir Walter Scott and means something close to Gothic; it also refers to the fanciful decoration of Italian grottoes or caves with statues of ogres and giants from legend, which gives the word its sense of *freakish, monstrous, misshapen*. *Arabesque* means the intri-cate, nonrepresentational, infinitely graceful decorative style of Islam. Had Poe wished to designate the components of his imagination more accurately, Davenport suggests, he would have called his book *Tales of the Grotesque, Arabesque, and Classical*, for these are the three kinds of images to be found in Poe's tales and in the ideal room he sketched in "The Philosophy of Furniture": "landscapes of an imaginative cast—such as the fairy grottoes of Stanfield, or the lake of the Dismal Swamp of Chapman" (the grotesque), and "three or four female heads, of an ethereal beauty... in the manner of Sully" (in the classical mode) hang on "a glossy paper of silver-grey tint, spotted with small arabesque devices of a fainter hue."

Davenport goes on to find these three structures in the work of Oswald Spengler, a man who, sitting "night after night, from 1912 to 1917 ... in a long, almost empty room in a working-class district of Berlin, writing a book by candle light," could have been invented by Poe. Spen-gler's book, *The Decline of the West*, describes the rise, growth and decline of three cultures: the Apollonian, or Graeco-Roman; the Faustian, or Western-Northern European; and the Magian, or Asian and Islamic. By "culture" he meant a people's "formative energy" that lasts for thou-sands of years and matures into "a civilization"—its inevitable decline. His feeling for the effeteness of a finished culture was precisely that of Poe in "The Fall of the House of Usher" and "The Murders of the Rue Morgue," both stories about the "vulnerability of order and civilized achievement."[3]

Davenport seems not to have noticed that everything in the room in which Poe found such lightness, grace and clarity is red. "Repose" is achieved partly through harmony of color. The keynote of rich crimson silk draperies fringed with gold appears everywhere in profusion and determines the character of the room: crimson-tinted window panes, a thick crimson carpet, glossy wallpaper spotted with the prevalent crimson, two large sofas covered in crimson silk, some light and graceful hanging shelves with golden edges and crimson silk cords, a lamp with a crimson-tinted ground-glass shade throwing a "magical radiance" over all. The person on the sofa *sleeps*: he is oblivious to the ostentatious display of American wealth that surrounds him (in the first half of the essay), to the violence of its glare and the rage of its glitter. Like the innermost room in the castellated abbey where Prince Prospero, in "The Masque of the Red Death," has separated himself and his court from the rest of the world, this room glows red, the blood-red glow of the red windows in the darkened castle sanctum: "Blood was its Avatar and its seal—the redness and the horror of blood."[4]

This red fascinated Mario Praz, who understood Poe as "the first physiognomist of the interior" and took the title of Poe's essay for his own *La filosofia dell'arredamento*, which has been translated as *An Illustrated History of Furnishing*. Through the lens of his own particular perspective, Praz saw "those infinite perspectives" of nineteenth-century room arrangements as reflections of the male self, existing "to mirror man, . . . to mirror him in his ideal being." The interiors of these rooms whose representations in painting Praz studied were, however, like the room Poe described, little images of secret enclosure, retreats from contemporary realities. The red of the textiles in so many nineteenth-century interiors "almost speaks" to Praz, like the red flannel underclothes that ladies wore at the time, suggesting "an ardent, repressed, passionate nature." In the roundness of the bulbs and globes of the kerosene lamps he sees "the exaggerated curves of the female form imposed by the fashion magazines of the last thirty-five years of the 19th century, . . . a true if unconscious parody of sex, so deliberately ignored and repressed . . . by the conventions of the time."[5]

The distinction Praz made between exterior and interior is a cultural distinction between male and female. Those infinite perspectives that come down to us from Renaissance humanism "put man at the centre of his cosmology. Palaces, parliaments and battlefields were settings for the historical fight between man born into a divine order, and man achieving a new one."[6] To be born female, on the other hand, has been to be born into a world in which one's body has value and significance as an object for exchange between men. As Lily Bart knows, her choice is between giving herself or *acting* that she gives herself, a division of self that John Berger identifies as gender-specific:

> To be born a woman has been to be born, within an allotted and confined space, into the keeping of men. The social presence of women has developed as a result of their ingenuity in living under such tutelage within such a limited space. But this has been at the cost of a woman's self being split into two. A woman must continually watch herself. . . . Whilst she is walking across a room or whilst she is weeping at the death of her father, she can scarcely avoid envisaging herself walking or weeping. . . .
> One might simplify this by saying: *men act* and *women appear*. Men look at women. Women watch themselves being looked at. This determines not only most relations between men and women but also the relations of women to themselves. The surveyor of woman in herself is male: the surveyed female. Thus she turns herself into an object.[7]

One might argue, however, that the man who surveys himself surveys his female self: his object-self. Poe's sleeping man in "The Philosophy of Furniture" is in a sense his reclusive self, secluded from the chaos of the external world; the rooms are the man—like the woman in an early Wharton story called "The Fullness of Life" whose nature is like "a great house full of rooms: there is the hall, through which everyone passes in going in and out; the drawing-room, where one receives formal visits; the sitting-room, where the members of the family come and go as they list; but beyond that, far beyond, are other rooms, the handles of whose doors perhaps are never turned; no one knows the way to them, no one knows whither they lead; and in the innermost room, the holy of holies, the soul sits alone and waits for a footstep that never comes."[8] In "The Bolted Door," a story much influenced by Poe, Wharton would later describe a man who feels a "prisoner of consciousness":

> In the long night hours, when his brain seemed ablaze, he was visited by a sense of his fixed identity, of his irreducible, inexpugnable *selfness*, keener, more insidious, more unescapable, than any sensation he had ever known. He had not guessed that the mind was capable of such intricacies of self-realization, of penetrating so deep into its own dark windings. Often he woke from his brief snatches of sleep with the feeling that something material was clinging to him, was on his hands and face, and in his throat—and as his brain cleared he understood that it was the sense of his own personality that stuck to him like some thick viscous substance.[9]

Similarly, Prince Prospero in "The Masque of the Red Death," deciding that "the external world could take care of itself," shuts himself up in a set of rooms that are his physical embodiment. The extensive and magnificent structure of his deep seclusion, girded and bolted against either ingress or egress, is the design of his own "eccentric yet august taste" and the scene of a "voluptuous" masquerade. Whereas most palatial suites "form a long and straight vista" with sliding doors revealing a "view of the whole extent," the Prince's rooms are "so irregularly disposed" that they twist and turn in upon each other.[10]

Poe "resonated" in Edith Wharton's imagination, R. W. B. Lewis suggests, because of his fictional dramas of the trapped consciousness.[11] And certainly she shared with Poe as well—in *The House of Mirth*, for example—a concern for the vulnerability of order and civilized achievement. In *The Custom of the Country*, as we shall see, the voluptuous masquerade and irregular, slithering movements Poe described are signs of a poisonous nature that threatens the very structure of ordered civilization.

Just after completing *The House of Mirth* Wharton wrote to her Scribner's editor William Brownell, who had pleased her by appreciating the novel's "architecture," to ask when his projected essay on Poe would appear: "I should like to get in that Nicaean bark with you—and in time gently steer it toward the 'far-sprinkled systems' that Walt sails among. Those two, with Emerson, are the best we have—in fact, the all we have."[12] The reference to Whitman suggests another dimension to Wharton, one that created not only the man trapped behind "the bolted door," but also the image of a face that "suggested a hundred images of space, distance, mystery."[13] Poe, like the fin de siècle artists who so admired him,[14] had delineated in an eerie red glow the nightmarish world of the diseased imagination; Wharton, with certain affinities to Poe, particularly in her ghost stories, had as well an intensely social and energetic side, a Whitmanesque side.[15]

It is Whitman's rhythmic structures that interest both Ralph Marvell in *The Custom of the Country* and Edith Wharton in *A Backward Glance* (the title of which comes from Whitman), and at the time in her life when Wharton was reading Whitman, the passionate sweep of his rhythms must certainly have "resonated" for her imagination.[16] Wharton must also have admired the way Whitman was able to hold in perfect tension the value of the past and the energy of the present. He celebrates the technological as sublime; yet the poet who embraces the wonders of the modern world stands firmly rooted in the past in such a poem as *A Passage to India*:

Singing my days,
Singing the great achievements of the present,
Singing the strong light works of engineers,
Our modern wonders, (the antique ponderous Seven outvied,)
In the Old World the east the Suez canal,
The New by its mighty railroad spann'd,
The seas inlaid with eloquent gentle wires;
Yet first to sound, and ever sound, the cry with thee O soul,
The Past! the Past! the Past!17

As the great poet of the city—Wharton's city—Whitman meant something rather different from Wharton by the word *city*. Hardly one to embrace multitudes, Wharton's idea of city had to do with civilization, or *civilized*, that is, "the daily companionship of the same five or six friends, . . . [a] pleasure . . . based on continuity."18 Whitman was less exclusive: he included the "common prostitute," the corpse in "the city dead house," the "felons on trial in courts," the knife-grinder whose work makes "sparkles from the wheel" and "the city's ceaseless crowd."19 Wharton's city, the one she valued, was, to borrow the language of German sociologist Ferdinand Tönnies, a *Gemeinschaft*, while Whitman's, though he worked hard at spinning a community out of himself that would embrace his fellow citizens, was a *Gesellschaft*.20 So was the modern city novel, the city novel of Wharton's own time, a *Gesellschaft*: it took for its subject the *city*, a place defined by "the works of engineers" and one that displaced the very continuity Wharton valued.

Consider, for example, John Berryman's description of the city novel and of Theodore Dreiser as our "most impressive" chronicler of American urban life. Even such "flatulent" prose as this in *The Titan*: "To whom may the laurels as laureate of this Florence of the West yet fall? . . . This singing flame of a city, this all America, this poet in chaps and buckskin, this rude, raw Titan, this Burns of a city!" cannot lessen, for Berryman, the power with which Dreiser presents his "treacherous, brutal, corrupting, insolent, ego-sane" hero Frank Cowperwood. Comparing *The Titan* with "the very small number of successful novels . . . devoted to America's principal activity to date"—William Dean Howells's *The Rise of Silas Lapham, A Hazard of New Fortunes* and parts of *The Landlord at Lion's Head*; Sinclair Lewis's *Babbitt, Arrowsmith* and *Main Street*; and other Dreiser novels, *An American Tragedy* and *Sister Carrie*—Berryman finds that Howells and Lewis "won't do." The products of the American business world glow and shine for George F. Babbitt and his creator, as well as for Silas Lapham, who is "deeply moved" when he declares his paint "the best

. . . in God's universe." Dreiser's Cowperwood, on the other hand, is unmoved by things of the real world: gas companies and street railways are *means* to ends; "what Cowperwood aims at is *control*—control of the fastest-growing, most involved services of a great crude city, control of his bankers and associates, control of his enemies financial and political, . . . control of big physical establishments, control of certain women, . . . control of works of art. This is not a businessman, but a predator," comparable in his ruthless cunning and blunt male egotism to nobody.[21]

It is curious—or perhaps not so curious—that Berryman identified "city" only with "blunt male egotism." Although he might have been unaware of Charlotte Perkins Gilman's warning in *Women and Economics* of 1898 that the problem of women is at the very heart of our social structure, the key to mankind's deviance from true humanness,[22] surely he might have recalled similar pronouncements by Gilman's (and Dreiser's) contemporaries Henry James and Thorstein Veblen. Or he might have turned to Dreiser's *Sister Carrie* in which role playing and disguise are the hallmarks of the great city.

The Titan was published in 1913, the same year as Edith Wharton's *The Custom of the Country*, the book Sinclair Lewis said influenced him most in writing *Babbitt* (which he dedicated to Wharton). Wharton's city novel was preceded by another, *The Fruit of the Tree* (1907), in which the frivolous lives of the rich are shown to be supported by the inhuman conditions under which factory employees work and live. That Edith Wharton, known almost entirely for her depictions of Old New York society, should explore as background the details of working-class lives is not as surprising as it might seem. In turn-of-the-century periodicals like the *Atlantic Monthly*, one could find side by side such contrasting views of city life as Charles Mulford Robinson's description of Chicago's White City as "Aesthetic Progress" and Jacob Riis's depiction of "The Tenement House Blight."[23]

By 1910—the closest census to *The Custom of the Country* and *The Titan*—45.5 percent of some 92.5 million Americans were living in cities, as opposed to only 24.8 percent of nearly 40 million in 1870, a fivefold growth, from 9 million city residents in 1870, to 42 million in 1910.[24] The age of the Dynamo saw the Model T Ford and the flight of the Wright brothers' airplane, the formation of the Progressive party and the muckraking activities of Ida Tarbell and Lincoln Steffens, antitrust legislation, minimum wage laws and the organization of the IWW, a flood of immigrants to East Coast cities chronicled by photojournalist Jacob Riis in

How the Other Half Lives and *The Battle with the Slum*, and the Armory Show, which shocked former president Roosevelt with the painting of a naked lady going downstairs.

Roosevelt, who would run for president again on the Progressive ticket, was a friend of Wharton's. He gently rebuked her, she said, for portraying in her first novel, *The Valley of Decision*, the illicit liaison between the Duke of Pianura and his mistress.[25] Perhaps because the novel is set in the past—indeed, it is a wonderfully evocative description of the life of *settecento* Italy—the novel's theme of political reform seems to have escaped Roosevelt's notice. Other critics viewed *The Valley of Decision* as "unique and astonishing," and compared it to Stendahl's revolutionary novel, *The Charterhouse of Parma*. In fact the book was the kind of bridge between the past and present that Roosevelt himself was: the Duke who seeks to institute a new constitution that would curtail the power of the church is a man with "a certain piety for the past, and catholicity of taste" that makes him "preserve the rooms and gardens of Pianura unchanged, while adding new galleries, mss., coins."[26] Her novel was the kind of bridge between past and present that Edith Wharton was. Imagine her in 1903, the year after the publication of *The Valley of Decision*, taking her first long rides by motor car to gather material for *Italian Villas and Their Gardens*, a book that is a celebration of the Renaissance: "In a thin spring dress, a sailor hat balanced on my chignon, and a two-inch tulle veil over my nose, I climbed proudly to my perch, and off we tore across the Campagna, over humps and bumps, through ditches and across gutters, wind-swept, dust-enveloped, I clinging to my sailor hat. . . . We did the run [to Caprarola] in an hour, and I was able to see the villa and gardens fairly well before we tore back to Rome."[27]

Vance Weston, Wharton's alter ego in *Hudson River Bracketed*, also writes a successful first novel set in the past; and then he turns, as Wharton did (with a bit of friendly advice from Henry James), to a novel—he calls it *Loot*—about the city in which he lives. In *The House of Mirth*, *The Fruit of the Tree* and in her own "Loot,"[28] Wharton would demonstrate that she fully understood power and control. Her vision was different from Dreiser's: not only did she focus on her own upper class, seeing the nouveaux riches as the "Invaders," but the wide-angle lens through which Dreiser saw panoramic anonymity was very different from her focus on the "moment of illumination." The manners and customs of her Old New York are presented as tribal rituals, under siege by characters every bit as treacherous, brutal, corrupting, insolent and ego-sane as Dreiser's.

It is not "blunt male egotism" that is the destructive force in *The Custom of the Country*. A woman like Undine Spragg cannot control street railways and gasworks like Frank Cowperwood—there was no female counterpart in real life for the financier upon whom Cowperwood is based—or waterworks and mines like Elmer Moffatt, in Wharton's novel, who rises from ne'er-do-well in midwestern Apex City to Wall Street multimillionaire. Undine, however, can manipulate to her advantage the men to whom she attaches herself, and with a calculated coolness that matches her father's business transactions she sets out to sell what she has—her good looks—to the highest bidder. In its destructiveness and ruthlessness, this "blunt female ego" more than matches the blunt male ego of a Dreiser novel; and Wharton portrays here a type equally grotesque, the American Woman.

Like Lily Bart, Undine Spragg in *The Custom of the Country* suggests in her long sinuous lines and lively masses of reddish-tawny hair the Art Nouveau woman; but Undine is a more crude and more powerful version of Lily. Undine's power lies partly in her ability to perfect imitation into something of an art. We often see her rehearsing—"making up" before a mirror, practicing gestures, gliding, swaying, moving her lips in soundless talk and secret pantomime—and she learns quickly the way to dress, move, posture, gesture, adorn herself. Unlike Lily, Undine begins unsphered, and she voluntarily steps "out of her social frame" when it suits her to do so.[29] At the beginning of *The Custom of the Country* she lives, appropriately, in a New York hotel with her parents, nouveaux-riches "Invaders" from Apex City. Undine has been married, briefly and secretly in Apex, will marry Ralph Marvell, divorce him for Peter Van Degan (with whom she lives for two months), then aim higher for the French Count Raymond de Chelles, find his rural château and fixed family customs a prison, and divorce him for the by-now richest of them all, Elmer Moffatt, her ruddy, plump, unscrupulous, razor-sharp Apex beau, who manages to buy for their house the ancestral tapestries from the French château. Neither the tapestries nor the wreckage along the way mean much to Undine; because she is so unfixed herself, people and places are unreal except as cues and settings, obstacles or milestones.

Undine's behavior is not only selfishly destructive; it suggests as well an imagination warped and limited by the culture that has produced it. Undine chooses certain, available ways to power (over men) because in her society other means—those chosen by Elmer Moffatt or Frank Cowperwood, for example—*were* closed off to women. On the other hand, although Undine's activities are essentially meaningless, her crude middle-class attempt to model herself on the type of woman Lily Bart represents is, in her context, a creative outlet for her energies in a certain way. In other words, Wharton's position is essentially a *moral* one: her depiction of the city implies certain values, misunderstood, flaunted, superseded by the Undine Spraggs and Elmer Moffatts—a point to which I shall return. First I want to make clear that to argue that men write one kind of city novel and women another would be to make a simple equation between the physical body and experiential differences based on the kinds of assumptions that underlie Erik Erikson's experiments with children's play-world constructions. Phallocentric culture does impose on both sexes certain roles, definitions, self-perceptions. For example, when one has made the wrong identification with the symbols of the culture in which the meaning of sexual difference is invested, operations can be done on the exterior so that others will perceive the physical structure as reflecting the interior state. This mutilation of the body, this amputation of female sexual parts to insure that a woman cannot disrupt the social order is no worse, according to anthropologist Juliet Blair, than structuring woman's self-perception so that her identity is shaped according to meanings imposed by the phallocentric culture. "To experience oneself only in relation to men works like surgery on the mind, dividing the whole woman: virgin/whore, intellect/body, reproduction/decoration,"[30] she writes; it is to be condemned to consider oneself always in relation to how one is seen by others.[31]

The difference between Wharton's Lily Bart and Undine Spragg is just such a division, more clearly seen in the splitting of female characteristics into Bessy Westmore and Justine Brent in *The Fruit of the Tree*, and into May Welland and Ellen Olenska in *The Age of Innocence*. Wharton well understood the negative conditioning that would make an energetic and ambitious girl-child, like the one in "The Valley of Childish Things," leave the bridge building to the John Roeblings and the skyscrapers to the Louis Sullivans rather than risk total alienation. She was familiar with the way in which, excluded from the male sphere of making, inventing and shaping culture, woman is preoccupied with herself, with creating herself as an object, with considering her body in relation to costume and setting.

This, in fact, may be Wharton's real attraction to Whitman. The city is the setting par excellence, and to the extent that Whitman creates his own performance, he makes himself up and makes up his world. As Blair has shown, the actress in modern society, although she comes to see herself as "face and body, divided and assessed, and *herself* ignored,"[32] has the opportunity to find, create, invent herself with each new role. In an odd inversion, the "real" actress is able to demonstrate the existence of a "hidden interior life" and to create contexts in which human interaction may be inter-*personal*—that is, without the masks determined by social role-playing.[33]

In our culture, Blair points out, the skills required of actors are regarded as feminine: "it is unmanly to show grief, depression or even the delights of victory; and it is narcissistic to practise these expressions in front of a mirror."[34] It is woman's profession, on the other hand, to empathize, understand and identify with a whole range of female roles, from princess to prostitute. "Making up" becomes, then, for the skilled actress, *making up*—inventing, creating, taking control of her world. This is exactly what Undine Spragg does in *The Custom of the Country*.

Who is this woman, this American who lays siege to both Old New York and the Faubourg St. Germain, one of whose names suggests "some fabled creature whose home was in a beam of light," the other her down-home origins in Apex City? So often do we see her practicing illusions before the mirror and then playing them for an audience that we come to understand that "the quality of the reflecting surface" *is* Undine (21, 157). We see her rehearsing widening her eyes trustfully and making her smile limpid as a child's and then repeating this performance for her father when she wants money, or alternatively secretly sucking lemons, nibbling slate-pencils and drinking pints of bitter coffee to simulate a look of ill-health; we hear her listen by "trying to think far enough ahead to guess what [others] . . . expect her to say, and what tone it would be well to take," and understand that "it was instinctive with her to become, for the moment, the person she thought her interlocutors expected her to be" (246–47, 53, 386). She goes to art galleries to learn to fling herself into rapt attitudes before canvases, to the theater to practice for the audience during intermission what she sees on the stage; she learns from *Lili* Estradina, who has "several different personalities, . . . as if the one of the moment had been hanging up a long time in her wardrobe and been hurriedly taken down as probably good enough for the present occasion" (48, 60, 384). Undine's parts range from suffering the disarrangement of her draperies while composing with her son a pleasing picture of motherhood, to contrasting herself to the showy ostentation of the Nouveau Luxe by assuming an air of soft abstraction that emphasizes her "graces of reserve," to becoming "a new Desdemona," hanging on every word of Elmer Moffatt's "epic recital of plot and counterplot" in his "conflict with the new anthropophagi" (267–68, 278–79, 537). Moffatt, the Olympian hero of Wall Street (252, 254), is, in fact, the exact counterpart of Undine. Ralph Marvell, in trying to understand Moffatt's business dealings, makes explicit the relationship of business to acting; at the same time, he makes clear another connection, that between acting (making up) and writing (making up):

> In Paris, in his younger days, he had once attended a lesson in acting given at the Conservatoire by one of the great lights of the theatre, and had seen an apparently uncomplicated rôle of the classic repertory, familiar to him through repeated performances, taken to pieces before his eyes, dissolved into its component elements, and built up again with a minuteness of elucidation and a range of reference that made him feel as though he had been let into the secret of some age-long natural process. As he listened to Moffatt, the remembrance of that lesson came back to him. . . . as Moffatt talked he began to feel as blank and blundering as the class of dramatic students before whom the great actor had analyzed his part. The affair was in fact difficult and complex, and Moffatt saw at once just where the difficulties lay and how the personal idiosyncrasies of "the parties" affected them. Such insight fascinated Ralph, and he strayed off into wondering why it did not qualify every financier to be a novelist, and what intrinsic barrier divided the two arts. [261–62]

The Custom of the Country is about these two interconnected kinds of power, one financial, one sexual, both of which seek to invent, create, control the world. It is also about a city within a city, repository of a very different set of values. And it is about the power of imagination, of words.

In suggesting that Wharton created an "urban pastoral," I mean "pastoral" in a particular way.[35] Wharton's ironic attitude toward "the republic of the spirit" in *The House of Mirth* and her treatment of the "rural" in *Ethan Frome* as a place of desolation make clear that she neither attributed healing qualities to nature nor urged a withdrawal from society. Her milieu was necessarily urban, and even at The Mount, valued life was *civilized*. Wharton's criticism of Wall Street is based on something other than Undine's "air of a person unused to sylvan abandonments," her inability to adapt her beautiful back "to the irregularities of a tree-trunk," her assumption that she is entitled to "unite floral insouciance with Sheban elegance." It has more to do with the fact that Undine's mind is "as destitute of beauty and mystery as the prairie schoolhouse in which she had been educated," that her ideals are "as pathetic as the ornaments made of corks and cigar-bands" with which she once learned to adorn herself, as opposed to an imagination like Ralph Marvell's, "peopled with . . . varied images and associations, fed by so many currents from the long stream of human experience" (141, 149, 147).

One can dismiss Ralph Marvell as weak and out of touch with "reality," as his friend Charles Bowen does, arguing that "poor Ralph was a survival, and destined, as such, to go down in any conflict with the rising forces" (280). Ralph does imagine his creative self as inhabiting an inner world, where he comes and goes with a "joy of furtive possession," and which he protects by weaving about himself "a secret curtain." This inner world is his sea-cave, "a secret inaccessible place with glaucous lights, mysterious murmurs, and a single shaft of communication with the sky" (76). The image suggests Andrew Marvell's "The Garden," where "delicious solitude" is preferred both to "rude" society and to a luscious vegetable abandonment to sensuality;[36] yet the secret, inaccessible place reminds us of Poe as well. Ralph himself links his imaginative withdrawal to Whitman, the poet whose naked contact with the earth enables him to create a *language* that will be a means of contact with the human community; and this suggests a complexity to Ralph's (and Wharton's) vision and the need for a definition of "pastoral" that encompasses the reality of Ralph's situation.

In "What Is Pastoral?" Paul Alpers argues that the meaning of a pastoral *landscape* resides not in the landscape itself but in its character as "a privileged spot, a *locus amoenus*," and that the pastoral singer is not necessarily a representative shepherd or goatherd but a representative man. Virgil depicts in the *Eclogues*, for example, two *equally representative* shepherds—one is secure in the way of life he has known; the other has been dispossessed of his farm and is going into exile. Both are representative of human singing and a way of life. The poem does not, in any simple sense, express nostalgia: "rather, it contains an anatomy of nostalgia, which one feels all the more keenly because it reponds to a real situation and expresses feelings of concrete, ordinary loss." Virgil develops these two versions of pastoral, Alpers maintains, "in the *literary, social and political world* of Rome." Shakespeare, too, by pastoral meant not the "natural" world, but "what the French mean by *le monde*, society, the human community." *As You Like It* is a striking piece of evidence "that shepherds' lives, not landscape, are at the heart of pastoral." Shakespeare thus makes explicit what has always been clear about pastoral— "that it is a sophisticated form, that it is of the country but by and for the court or city."[37]

It is in this sense that I mean *The Custom of the Country* is an "urban pastoral": the "custom" of the country is, in fact, anticustom, antiritual; it threatens to destabilize and eclipse a world of civilized ritual which for Wharton was the meaning of "city." Partly the threat has to do with the strength of "the rising forces"; but partly the Old New York families who retire to their shelters, like the sleeping man Poe described in "The Philosophy of Furniture," make errors in judgment. Ralph Marvell, for example, overestimates himself and underestimates Undine, as Raymond de Chelles will do. Ralph imagines himself Perseus rescuing the lovely rockbound Andromeda, but as in the Jacobean play from which *The Custom of the Country* takes its name, women in this story are stronger than men. When Ralph, lured by the sea-creature Undine, makes the mistake of choosing her as the companion of his sea-cave, he wills his own vulnerability, his own dispossession: the Marvell/Dagonet world will not only be forced to recognize, but to sacrifice Ralph himself to a world that revolves about a central sun of gold (256, 193).

As their names suggest, Ralph *Marvell* and his grandfather *Urban* Dagonet are the keys to the city within the city. The principles that enclose them are those Wharton held dear: harmony, balance, proportion, a kind of order that corresponds to a standard of "honor or conduct, of education and manners . . . —the moral wealth of our country," the remaining "drops of an old vintage too rare to be savoured by a youthful palate."[38] The old houses in which they live *are* the people of the city. When Ralph Marvell looks at his grandfather's symmetrical old red house-front with its frugal marble ornament, he feels as if he might have been looking into a familiar human face. The people who live in this house, Ralph's grandfather and mother, are so closely identified with it that "they might have passed for its inner consciousness as it might have stood for their outward form." Their view of life is expressed in the very lines of their furniture.

Down the street are houses of a different sort, like Peter Van Degan's, with its Blois gargoyles on the roof, a muddle of misapplied ornament over a thin steel shell of utility: "The steel shell was built up in Wall Street, the social trimmings were hastily added in Fifth Avenue, and the union between them was . . . monstrous and factitious." Like the Dagonet house, the Van Degan house represents the people who live in it—a union monstrous and factitious between the bloated, froglike Peter

Van Degan and Ralph's delicate cousin Clare Dagonet. Inside the house are two drawing-rooms, his and hers. One is a "gilded and tapestried wilderness" where a fashionable portrait of Clare hangs opposite one, by a powerful artist,[39] of her husband, who regards her with the "satisfied air of proprietorship." The inner drawing-room, however, reflects another Clare: in luminous shadow stand old cabinets and consoles, pale flowers in vases of bronze and porcelain, and an old lacquer screen behind Clare's head "like a lustreless black pool with gold leaves floating on it; and another piece, a little table at her elbow, had the brown bloom and the pear-like curves of an old violin" (452–53, 318–20). The division of sexual lives and roles suggested here is the dominant tone of the book, and divorce, its main action, a symbol for a fundamental split in American culture between order and chaos. The division is not, however, drawn on the clearly sexual lines laid down by Henry Adams: if Clare preserves a small spot of harmony and order in the Van Degan world, Ralph Marvell is less successful against the onslaught of Undine Spragg.

Undine is "real" enough in that she represents forces typical of early twentieth-century America; and it is this power that attracts Ralph, Undine's other suitors—and Edith Wharton. What each of the suitors who gets caught in Undine's "meshes" fails to recognize, however, is that Undine is an *imitation*. She is most at home in a hotel sitting-room, a flowered, cushioned and lamp-shaded "delusive semblance of stability," or in the crowded dining-room of the Nouveau Luxe, where one finds "an endless perspective of plumed and jewelled heads, of shoulders bare or black-coated, encircling the close-packed tables," a scene always the same even when the individuals were not. Charles Bowen sees this Paris restaurant as the epitome of "the factitious," where the customers have "the incorrigible habit of imitating the imitation." The Nouveau Luxe represents what unbounded material power had devised for the delusion of its leisure: "a phantom 'society,' with all the rules, smirks, gestures of its model, but evoked out of promiscuity and incoherence while the other had been the product of continuity and choice" (281, 272-73).

The "other" is, for example, the dinner given by Ralph's sister, Laura Fairford. Undine has expected to view the company through a bower of orchids and to eat "pretty-coloured *entrées* in ruffled papers." Instead, Ralph brings her to a small house with no gilding; and she is served plain roasted meat in a dining room with no lavish diffusion of light and coffee in a book-lined room that reminds her, with its old-fashioned wood fire instead of a gas log or a polished grate with electric bulbs behind ruby glass, of the old circulating library at Apex. Undine is equally surprised by the conversation: instead of a series of solos, there seems to be a concert, with Laura "drawing in the others, giving each a turn, beating time for them with her smile, and somehow harmonizing and linking together what they said." This world is a puzzling blur of half-lights, half-tones, eliminations and abbreviations for Undine; she feels "a violent longing to brush away the cobwebs and assert herself as the dominant figure of the scene" (31-32, 34, 37).

Dominance, power, control: just how much does Undine possess? Bound by her sexual/cultural frame and by the limits of her own imagination, Undine believes like others of her time and place, that a change in space can effect a change in identity, and she does indeed exchange one space for another, each more opulent, more heavily gilded. Like the fisherman's wife in the fairy tale, however, to whom her watery name links her, she is never satisfied. If she begins with fashionable hotel life, realizing that "there was something still better beyond, then—more luxurious, more exciting, more worthy of her," she ends with one house in Paris, its ballroom resplendent with the Chelles ancestral tapestries, and another on Fifth Avenue in New York, an exact copy of the Pitti Palace in Florence. Yet on the horizon the same black cloud of dissatisfaction hovers because she still feels "that there were other things she might want if she knew about them." Unable to articulate to herself what it is that she longs for, she focuses on yet another role—something she can never get, something that neither beauty nor influence nor millions could ever buy for her because she is divorced: she can never be an Ambassador's wife, the one part, she says to herself, she was really made for (54, 586, 591, 594).

Part of the point, of course, is that all of Undine's choices are limited: like Henry James's Isabel Archer, who has every grace Undine lacks and money of her own, the only choice is to be someone's wife. Lacking Isabel's old-fashioned American self-reliance, however, Undine, both "fiercely independent" and "passionately imitative," learns never to trust her impulses, but to watch and dissimulate, to disguise and play roles. Although she wants "to surprise every one by her dash and originality, . . . she cannot help modelling herself on the last person she met." Charles Bowen, who serves as a kind of detached commentator on the action of the story, thinks that Undine is to be pitied. Her limitations are not her fault, he says, but that of the American "system." Whereas the center of a European marriage is place and family, the center of an American marriage is business, and the woman merely "a parenthesis," forced to make

fallacious little attempts to trick out the leavings tossed her by the preoccupied male—the money and the motors and the clothes—and pretend to
herself that *that* is what really constitutes life. Undine, he says, is simply a
"monstrously perfect result of the system: the completest proof of its
triumph" (19, 207–8). But is she to be pitied?

Bowen, in fact, underestimates Undine's power. Using his own image, if the American woman is "a parenthesis," she encloses or sets off the
man. Undine destroys Ralph and ruins the life of his family—mother,
grandfather, sister, cousin Clare, their son. Her disregard of ritual and of
ritual objects is not only thoughtless but destructive of patterns that give
meaning to life. On her honeymoon, for example, she destroys the identity of the heirloom jewels that Ralph has given her, including his grandmother's wedding ring, by having them more fashionably reset. She is too
busy celebrating the completion of her own portrait with a ride in Peter
Van Degan's fast car to remember her son's second birthday, celebrated in
her husband's family by gifts like Clare's old silver porridge bowl, used by
generations of Dagonets. As the Marquise de Chelles, she surreptitiously
calls in a connoisseur to price the ancestral tapestries at Saint Désert in
order to have more money for dresses and trips to Paris. Raymond de
Chelle's judgment is harsher than Bowen's. Like his kinsman Alexis de
Tocqueville, he blames America for Undine: "In the United States a man
builds a house in which to spend his old age, and he sells it before the roof
is on," Tocqueville had written; "he settles in a place, which he soon
afterwards leaves to carry his changeable longings elsewhere. . . ; he will
travel fifteen hundred miles . . . to shake off his happiness."[40] As one of
Undine's victims, Chelles, however, has no pity. "You lay hands on things
that are sacred to us!" he tells her, and you sense only money:

> You come among us from a country we don't know and can't imagine, a
> country you care for so little that before you've been a day in ours you've
> forgotten the very house you were born in—if it wasn't torn down before
> you knew it! You come among us speaking our language and not knowing
> what we mean; wanting the things we want, and not knowing why we want
> them; . . . ignoring or ridiculing all we care about—you come from hotels as
> big as towns, and from towns as flimsy as paper, where the streets haven't
> had time to be named, and the buildings are demolished before they're dry,
> and the people are as proud of changing as we are of holding to what we
> have—and we're fools enough to imagine that because you copy our ways
> and pick up our slang you understand anything about the things that make
> life decent and honourable for us! [545][41]

Undine, in "assert[ing] herself as the dominant figure of the scene," reduces everyone around her—especially the men—to supporting roles. She copies what she needs, or she takes what she wants, and when she no longer has a use for someone, she discards him or her. In just this way does the Count in the Fletcher and Massinger *Custom of the Country* assert his right to enjoy—or to ransom, that is, sell—the first night with the bride of any of his subjects: it is the custom of the country to use women's bodies for his pleasure. Undine, however, does not even get pleasure from her various sexual encounters. Personal entanglement means "bother." The jewels and clothes, the admiring glances, the feverish activity of balls and dinners and theatrical performances, her name in the newspapers, are all gratifying; but "the pleasures for which her sex took such risks had never attracted her." She uses her body in a way that is "as clear, as logical, as free from the distorting mists of sentimentality, as any of her father's financial enterprises" (224, 353-54, 364). Ralph is surprised to learn that Undine regards intimacy "as a pretext for escaping . . . into a total absence of expression," and she herself "always vaguely wondered why people made 'such a fuss,' were so violently for or against such demonstrations." She is able to achieve a kind of coolness in her sexual transactions that "Mr. Spragg might have felt at the tensest hour of the Pure Water move" because her physical reactions are "never very acute. . . . A cool spirit within her seemed to watch over and regulate her sensations, and leave her capable of measuring the intensity of those she provoked." This coolness allows her to sever human relationships as easily: Abner Spragg's informing on his old friend James J. Rolliver, Undine's divorcing Ralph or Chelles have exactly the same meaning. As long as a husband is "distinctly ornamental," it amuses her to have someone like the Count "in her train, . . . driving about with him to dinners and dances, waiting for him on flower-decked landings, or pushing at his side through blazing theatre-lobbies"; this answers "to her inmost ideal of domestic intimacy" (151, 294, 507). Chelles is right that Undine does not understand his language. Hers is one neither of words nor of human contact—gesture, glance, touch, embrace—but the language of buying and selling. A name is either valuable or "debased currency"; and her own—"we called her after a hair-waver father put on the market the week she was born," Mrs. Spragg tells Ralph—links her to the currency of the "Invaders." Only Elmer Moffatt intuitively understands her language—the "wants" for which her "acquired vocabulary had no terms"—and she his: "Every Wall Street term had its equivalent in the language of Fifth Avenue, and while he talked of

building up railways she was building up palaces." Only Moffatt deals
with her on her own terms; he drives as ruthless a sexual bargain as she,
and under his cool eye she becomes "no more compelling than a woman
of wax in a show case" (361, 80, 536–37, 574).

Undine is quite literally unable to speak. At the Fairfords' dinner she
can only answer, "I couldn't really say," or "Is that so?" to remarks addressed to her. Since she can remember nothing about "pictures" or plays
and never reads, "banter" only gives her a dizzy sense of being, or not
being, in the "stronghold of fashion"; and those who regard conversation
a necessary part of ritual finally stop inviting her to small dinners because
she has nothing to say, because she does not understand (36–38, 541, 527).
What she does not understand is some mysterious *code*—"antecedents, . . .
rules, . . . conventions," a "structure of . . . rights and sanctions," "a definite and complicated code of family prejudices and traditions," a system
where money is not used for immediate individual gratification, but is
"the substance binding together whole groups of interests," those of the
future as well as those of the present (161–62, 469, 481, 495). Thus she sees
the Boucher tapestries only as "mirrors reflecting her own image." Because
she does not understand it, this code to Undine—and to Abner Spragg
and Elmer Moffatt as well—lacks the "morality" of her own American
code. If Abner Spragg's business principles are "elastic," his "code of domestic conduct" is rigid. Elmer's is the same: committed to "the Wall
Street code" of "swift adjustments," he can recommend that Undine trade
her son to the Marvells for the money to have her marriage annulled so
that she can marry into the Catholic French aristocracy (529, 248, 261). He
can later recommend a quick (American) divorce from Raymond de
Chelles when the more advantageous role becomes that of Railroad
Queen of Fifth Avenue. That Moffatt regards the results of these "adjustments"—Ralph's suicide, the outrageous scandals for both old families—
as business casualties is not to say that his code has no "morality" of its
own. Wharton makes clear that the frightening thing about the American
business code's becoming *the* American language is its rhetoric of purity.
Moffatt's ultimatum to Undine—"If you want to come back you've got to
come . . . [as my wife], not slink through the back way when there's no
one watching, but walk in by the front door, with your head up, and your
Main Street look" (572)—coupled with his reducing her to a wax woman
in a showcase reveals a puritanical attitude that fears the rich, sensuous
and deeply gratifying contact of human action, "the dissonance and unexpected conflicts of a society's history."[42] A half century later sociologist

Richard Sennett would call this "the myth of a purified community" and relate it both to a "purified" identity and to the planning of American cities. The Wall Street code, and especially its product Undine Spragg in *The Custom of the Country*, exemplify what Sennett calls a defensive pattern which fixes *in advance* a self-image that filters out threats of social experience, that measures events in terms of how well they correspond to a preexistent pattern and does not permit any unexpected experience a reality of its own. Such an attitude—the "making [of] oneself a fixed object rather than an open person liable to be touched by a social situation"—in denying the possibility of change, denies the very idea of history.[43]

To identify in Undine Spragg and in the world of business with which she is associated a particular kind of *order* when I have been stressing all along her disorderly and destructive abandon is to identify a pattern of contradictions Wharton sets up in this novel: order/disorder, representation/imitation, pastoral/urban, tradition/self-determination. These contradictions between the social and the natural self, held by Wharton in creative tension, express her very real needs to protect and to cut loose from the constraints of a complex society. To say that Undine lacks this tension, that her behavior is determined externally by social forces unrelated to inward impulses is to say that she is selfish, that she devalues the human world and sees value only in the world of things. Her lack of connection with the human community is made manifest by her inability to speak, and her power is greatest when she deprives an other of the power of language.

Speech—words—are quite literally at the core of the community Wharton would build. Undine's language disability separates her from other human beings as clearly as Laura Fairford's skill in fostering communication—herself the shepherdess, her house the *locus amoenus*—creates community. Raymond de Chelles loses the ancestral tapestries to Undine; yet through language, he asserts himself in the face of her power. In the speech in which he tells Undine that she does not understand language, and therefore the things that make life decent and honorable, he asserts his own ability to see clearly, and to speak clearly, over her inability to see anything at all beyond herself; thus he undermines the reality of her power. Ralph Marvell, on the other hand, in his inability to confront Undine's power, makes his own powerlessness into a kind of virtue. Ralph's is the kind of innocence in the face of power that Rollo May calls "pseudoinnocence," or blindness, as opposed to "authentic innocence," or that which leads to spirituality.[44] Unable to speak in the face of Undine's perfidiousness, Ralph makes no claims against her divorce action and thus loses his son; by his blindness and inarticulateness, he is as much the agent of his own destruction as is, for example, Melville's Billy Budd. Communication, May suggests, recovers the original "we-ness" of the human being: "authentic communication depends on authentic language." Communication implies the presence of "social interest"; it leads to community—that is, to understanding, intimacy and mutual valuing. Like Wharton, May defines community as "a group in which free conversation can take place." It is the place where "I can accept my own loneliness, distinguishing between that part of it which can be overcome and that part of it which is inescapable"[45]—and, Wharton would add, can be turned to creative use.

The "custom of the country," then, is to subvert community by destroying the kinds of structures that encourage and preserve communication. Such custom divides a society between those who, Poe-like, inhabit the solitary spaces of an imagination—widely ranging though it may be—alienated from the world of "glare" and "glitter," and men who, as Carlyle put it, have "grown mechanical in head and heart,"[46] whose women use their own bodies as commodities. In the sense that the pastoral is a song, Wharton sings of our loss, in order to keep alive a very real and important human tradition.

CHAPTER 4

Purity and Power

Society does not exist in a neutral, uncharged vacuum. It is subject to external pressures; that which is not with it, part of it and subject to its laws, is potentially against it. . . . Ideas about separating, purifying, demarcating and punishing transgressions have as their main function to impose system on an inherently untidy experience. It is only by exaggerating the difference between within and without, above and below, male and female, with and against, that a semblance of order is created.
—Mary Douglas, *Purity and Danger*

Material things are a kind of language: the structures of everyday life are expressions of ritual and relationship, of patterns of movement and mediation, of meditation and enclosure. Floors, walls, doors, windows and their materials, coverings and their placement, cookware and tableware, furnishings and decoration, textiles and clothing all speak of an existence in time and space, alone and with others. These things tell us that here a life was lived in a particular way.

Material things are a language of place. Fashion, for example, the phenomenon that eliminates one style and imposes another, is a Western notion, a Western language. For centuries, furnishings and clothing in Chinese, Japanese and Indian cultures remained unchanged except for times of political upheavals that affected the whole social order. And it is not by coincidence, cultural historian Fernand Braudel argues, that political and economic control was seized by those "fickle enough to care about changing the colours, materials and shapes of costume, as well as the social order and the map of the world—societies, that is, which were ready to break with their traditions."[1]

Material things are a language of class. The poor have few possessions and often live crowded together in ways that are hardly ideal projections of self. If all the world were poor, Braudel points out, the question of fashion would not arise: "Everything would stay fixed. No wealth, no freedom of movement, no possible change."[2]

Material things are a language of gender. They speak of a world in which women are private property to be contained, more or less, in non-public areas belonging to men. Yet they suggest another—unspoken—language as well, one that derives from memory, secret and collective, one that suggests ritual and gesture, movement and stillness, one in which woman figures not as object but as subject.[3]

In the little "hieroglyphic world" of Old New York that Edith Wharton explores in *The Age of Innocence*, spoken language often fails as a means of communication; the common language in this world is that of sign and gesture. At the end of the novel young Dallas Archer says to his father, "You [and Mother] never did ask each other anything, did you? And you never told each other anything. You just sat and watched each other, and guessed at what was going on underneath. A deaf-and-dumb asylum, in fact. Well, I back your generation for knowing more about each other's private thoughts than we ever have time to find out about our own."[4]

It would be possible, in fact, to know a great deal about the characters in *The Age of Innocence* if they did not speak at all. Their settings—the spaces in which they move—reveal what we will learn from action and dialogue, much as the orchestral setting for an aria can prefigure a singer's destiny or the action about to be unfolded. We understand, for example, the two women who embody the choices Newland Archer must make about his life from the fact that May Welland will furnish her house exactly like her mother Augusta's, with purple satin and yellow tuftings in the drawing room, "sham buhl tables and gilt vitrines full of modern Saxe," while Ellen Olenska's house has "something intimate, 'foreign,' subtly suggestive of old romantic scenes and sentiments . . . in the way the chairs and tables were grouped, . . . in the vague pervading perfume that was . . . like the scent of some far-off bazaar, a smell made up of Turkish coffee and ambergris and dried roses" (71–72). We learn about old Catherine Mingott, the family matriarch, from the way in which "with characteristic independence she had made her reception rooms upstairs and established herself (in flagrant violation of all the New York proprieties) on the ground floor of her house; so that, as you sat in her sitting-room window with her, you caught (through a door that was always open, and a looped-back yellow damask portière) the unexpected vista of a bedroom with a huge low bed upholstered like a sofa, and a toilet-table with frivolous lace flounces and a gilt-framed mirror." And we know Newland Archer from the fact that he is determined to furnish his own room, his library, according to his own taste—with a dark embossed paper, "'sincere' Eastlake furniture, and the plain new bookcases without glass doors" (28–29, 205, 73).

Edith Wharton believed that manners and customs, styles and tastes filter down from above: "no matter under what form of government," she wrote in *The Decoration of Houses*, changes "usually originate with the wealthy or aristocratic minority, and are thence transmitted to other classes. Thus the *bourgeois* of one generation lives more like the aristocrat of a previous generation than like his own predecessors. This rule naturally holds good of house-planning," she continued, justifying her reliance upon examples for her book from illustrations of villas, palaces and large country estates, "and it is for this reason that the origin of modern house-planning should be sought rather in the prince's mezzanin than in the small middle-class dwelling."[5] This somewhat controversial notion that Wharton states as "fact" seems to be borne out in the fiction of Wharton's contemporaries. An immigrant woman like Anzia Yezierska, for example, writing about the Jews of Hester Street in New York, describes the kind of squalor and poverty that Jacob Riis captured in photographs in *How the Other Half Lives*, *The Battle with the Slum*, *The Children of the Poor* and other works. Families in Yezierska's stories live crowded together in one room, struggling to keep clean and to create with little a sense of ritual in the daily meal, the shared glass of tea. In a story like "The Lost Beautifulness," written the same year as Wharton's *The Age of Innocence*, Hannah Hayyeh, an immigrant woman who works as a maid, has longed "ever since she first began to wash the fine silks and linens for Mrs. Preston . . . to have a white-painted kitchen exactly like that in the old Stuyvesant Square mansion."[6] In "A Window Full of Sky," Yezierska uses the same image for the imagination freed from the confines of cramped daily life that Wharton would use in an early story like "Mrs. Manstey's View," in *Ethan Frome* when the trapped man focuses "on a square of moon-suffused sky" crossed by a crooked tree branch visible through his window, and in *Hudson River Bracketed* when the same sunlit scene gives Vance Weston the vision of his new novel.[7] In *The Bread Givers* (1925), Yezierska's protagonist, Sara Smolinsky, begins life in a Hester Street room—one of two, the family's crowded with junk, the father's study packed with books. Space here is not only divided traditionally between male and female (a Jewish tradition, but one we see in *The Age of Innocence* as well, where Newland Archer has a whole upper floor to himself, while his mother and sister "squeezed themselves into narrower quarters below"); it is also determined according to class. Being forced to give up the second room is to the scholar-father in *The Bread Givers* the last indignity, but his wife tells him, "Only millionaires can be alone in America."[8] The father's need becomes the daughter's determination: when Sara breaks away from Hester Street, what she wants most is that room of her own. The "fat *yenteh*" who shows her a little coffin of a room where three girls sleep in a bed and "there's yet a place for a fourth," hears Sara's request for her own room with a fierce look and the declaration, "This is a decent house. I'm a respectable woman"; and Sara realizes for the first time in her life "what a luxury it was for a poor girl to want to be alone in a room." This room becomes the symbol of her progress, from the filthy cellar closet with "a separate door to myself—a door to shut out all the noises of the world" to the vow to tear herself out of the dirt and have only "clean emptiness" to, finally, a plain room, "beautiful and empty."[9] She claims this right, unheard-of in the old country, as if she were as rich as Newland Archer, who asserts his right to furnish his room in his own way and feels invaded when his wife visits him there; it is her right as an American.

The optimistic tone of Yezierska's stories is a result of her immigrants' fierce determination to carve out for themselves a piece of what they perceive as the great material abundance of America, and in this they are not unlike Wharton's Sim Rosedale in *The House of Mirth* or Elmer Moffatt in *The Custom of the Country*. By 1913, however, as Wharton makes clear in *The Custom of the Country*, "progress" had come to mean the ruthless destruction of rituals and traditions—quite literally in World War I the rape of the powerless by the powerful. And for a woman as bounded by rituals and traditions as she was, moving at this time from the Faubourg St. Germain where she had lived for over twenty years could only have added to her sense of displacement. She must have felt a need "to restore both continuity and rootedness to her existence"[10] as she turned back to the "age of innocence," to re-member those moments, those frozen rituals in her past which, if stifling, gave to life stability and order, creating a hero whose chief assertion of individuality was his preference for "sincere" Eastlake furniture.

Charles Locke Eastlake's *Hints on Household Taste* of 1868 (first published in America in 1872 and reprinted seven times before 1890)[11]
was one of the most popular pattern books of the late nineteenth century.
Unlike earlier pattern books for the master carpenter, Eastlake's and those
that followed were meant to improve the taste of the middle-class home-
owner. In *Hints on Household Taste* Eastlake argues that "real art" is simple
in form; it has no "tricks" in frivolous ornament or design—veneering one
wood on top of another, for example—to make an object look like something other than what it is. In other words, as Wharton indicates, it is
"sincere." "Real art" is also *moral*: reasoning from the man to his dwelling,
"his artificial body," Eastlake argues that "form is silent speech, and as we
know that a man is uneducated if he speak ungrammatically, or unrefined
if he use vulgar language, so when he voluntarily surrounds himself with
ugly shapes we know that he is ignorant, or that his taste is bad." Using
the "essential principles of beauty, such as harmony, balance of parts,
symmetry," Eastlake separates "the good from the bad, . . . the fit from the
unfit."[12] In light of Wharton's own stress on harmony, balance, symmetry
in *The Decoration of Houses*, it is difficult at first to understand why in her
book "nothing even remotely savors of Eastlake or the *Lady's Book*."[13] Alan
Gowans's astute introduction to Eastlake's *History of the Gothic Revival*
(1872) helps us to understand how Eastlake took for granted a fundamentally new concept of what architecture is all about, one that has shaped the
way we continue to think about art and architecture.

Like Newland Archer in *The Age of Innocence* (and like Edith Wharton), Eastlake read Ruskin, and he took the well-known critic to task not
for being a "dictator of taste," but because as a critic of painting Ruskin
had not understood the principles of "good architecture"—that is, he had
not recognized the importance of the honest use of materials and direct
expression of structure in the thirteenth century. But this is a fundamentally new concept of architecture, one that ignores the fact "that architecture everywhere was always traditionally motivated by the social function
it serves," Gowans argues, and on those grounds, *all* historic architecture
is bad. "The whole idea of architecture projecting an image of social or
religious or political conviction, as it had for thousands of years past—the
basic principle inherent in Egyptian pyramids and Greek temples, in Versailles, Hagia Sophia, in the Colosseum and Angkor Vat—has simply
vanished from Eastlake's consciousness," Gowans writes, and "in its place
has come the idea of architecture as a Work of Art, to be appreciated by

persons of Cultivated Taste who understand its Principles—principles derived from the art itself, independent of social context."[14] This fundamentally new way of thinking about the arts, which begins in the 1860s and by
the 1890s is assumed, is based on the notion that "taste" is central to the
creation of architecture, rather than on an understanding that all styles are
trivial unless they relate to and derive from a total complex of social
values.[15]

   This is Henry Adams's distinction, in "The Dynamo and the Virgin," between force and taste. In Edith Wharton's *The Decoration of
Houses*, the distinction is between *taste* and *principles*, the latter underlying a particular way of life Wharton believed essential not only to manners
and customs but to the fundamental order and harmony that give life
meaning. Modern decoration with its superficial graces is an equivalent of
modern civilization, that "varnished barbarism," Wharton had written:
"Only a return to architectural principles can raise the decoration of
houses to the level of the past." She had only scorn for the eclectic house
whose rooms represented a variety of styles and for the modern room with
its lack of balance and its confusion between the essential and the inessen-
tial. She took Eastlake to task for focusing on furniture and ornament to
the exclusion of doors, windows or fireplaces because she believed that
decoration is only valid when it is a branch of architecture—that is, when
it is organic.[16] Wharton's linking of Newland Archer's preferences in
tasteful decoration to "sincere" Eastlake is, then, a devastating criticism:
he is a man of "taste" rather than a man of principle—or at least, he is a
man whose principles are determined externally, according to taste.

   Once understand the importance of Taste in "the age of innocence"
and we see it as the key to a whole system of values; the word fairly leaps
out from almost every page. It is Archer's highly developed taste that
makes him feel "distinctly. . . superior" to other "chosen specimens of old
New York gentility" in matters intellectual and artistic; yet he does not
separate himself from "the habit of masculine solidarity" because "it
would be troublesome—and also rather bad form—to strike out for himself" (8). We understand without being told that Archer "was at heart a
dilettante, and that thinking over a pleasure to come often gave him a
subtler satisfaction than its realization" when we see him lingering in his
Gothic library (in his mother's house) rather than getting to the Opera on
time because in New York "it was 'not the thing' to arrive early at the
Opera; and what was or was not 'the thing' played a part as important . . .
as the inscrutable totem terrors that had ruled the destinies of his forefa-

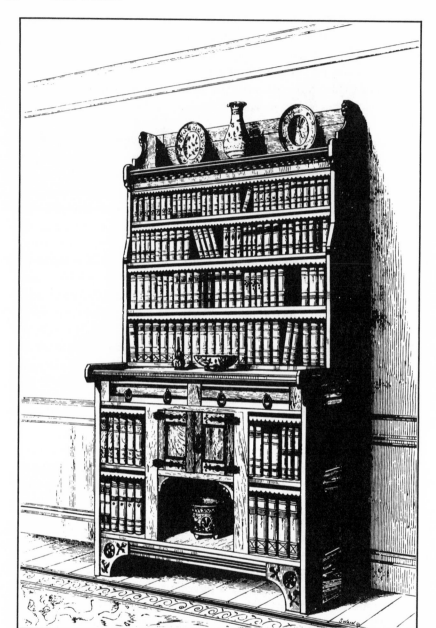

Library bookcase. (Charles Eastlake, *Hints on Household Taste*, 1868; courtesy, Dover Publications)

Mantelpiece shelves. (Charles Eastlake, *Hints on Household Taste*, 1868; courtesy, Dover Publications)

thers thousands of years ago." His use of "two silver-backed brushes with his monogram in blue enamel to part his hair" and his never appearing in society "without a flower (preferably a gardenia) in his buttonhole" are part of the same "unalterable and unquestioned law" of his world that decrees "that the German text of French operas sung by Swedish artists should be translated into Italian for the clearer understanding of English-speaking audiences": all of these things seem "natural" to Newland Archer. What is "unnatural" is something that is "an offense against 'Taste,' that far-off divinity of whom 'Form' was the mere visible representative and viceregent": a young woman seated in the box of his betrothed who is wearing an unusual dress, one with no tucker, which shocks and troubles Archer in the way it slopes away from her thin shoulders, exposing his fiancée to an influence "careless of the dictates of Taste" (4–5, 9, 15). The young woman in the simple navy-blue dress is Ellen Olenska, and she shocks Archer's mother and sister as well, two single women who live in an unclouded harmony of tastes, cultivating ferns in Wardian cases, making macramé lace and wool embroidery on linen, collecting American Revolutionary glazed ware, subscribing to "Good Words," and reading Ouida's poems. Newland's sister Janey disparages Madame Olenska's "dark blue velvet, perfectly plain and flat—like a nightgown," and wonders why she does not change her name from the ugly Ellen to Elaine. And Mrs. Archer says simply, "dear May is my ideal"—May, who at the Opera sits slightly withdrawn, dressed all in white, her modest tulle tucker fastened with a single gardenia, touching with her white-gloved fingertips one of the immense bouquets of lilies-of-the-valley Archer sends her daily (34, 40, 153, 5–6). We have seen May before: her indestructible youthfulness seems not hard or dull, but "primitive and pure," as if she represented "a type rather than a person; as if she might have been chosen to pose for a Civic Virtue or a Greek goddess" (188–89).

Newland's taste for May, then, is as culturally predictable as his manner of dress, his Gothic library, his sense that it is "deeply distasteful . . . to do anything melodramatic and conspicuous, anything . . . the club box condemned as bad form," or his taste in art and literature. He has been "saturated with Ruskin" and has a taste for John Addington Symonds, Vernon Lee's "Euphorion," the essays of P. G. Hamerton and Walter Pater's *The Renaissance*. His talking easily of Botticelli and speaking of Fra Angelico with a faint condescension does not mark him, in Wharton's eyes, as a sophisticate: as any reader of *False Dawn* knows, taste for the old masters was soon to be superseded by an interest in Italian primitives. Newland's aesthetic taste is more sophisticated than that of his mother or sister: they prefer novels "about peasant life, because of the descriptions of scenery and the pleasanter sentiments, though in general they liked novels about people in society, whose motives and habits were more comprehensible, spoke severely of Dickens, who 'had never drawn a gentleman,' and considered Thackeray less at home in the great world than Bulwer" (321–22, 71, 341). But his taste is less sophisticated than Ellen Olenska's: the books scattered about her drawing-room (where they should be "out of place")—Paul Bourget, Huysmans, the Goncourt brothers—the pictures on her walls, and the house itself on an unfashionable street have the "curious" effect of reversing his values and bewildering him (71, 74, 104). Ellen can say, "It seems stupid to have discovered America only to make it into a copy of another country.... Do you suppose Christopher Columbus would have taken all that trouble just to go to the Opera with the Selfridge Merrys?"[17] But Newland is, as his journalist-friend Ned Winsett tells him, "like the pictures on the walls of a deserted house: 'The Portrait of a Gentleman,'" one of the "last remnants of the old European tradition that your forebears brought with them. But you're in a pitiful little minority: you've got no center, no competition, no audience.... You'll never amount to anything, any of you, till you roll up your sleeves and get right down into the muck." As if a gentleman could abandon his own country, Newland responds to himself: "One could no more do that than one could roll up one's sleeves and go down into the muck. A gentleman simply stayed at home and abstained. But you couldn't make a man like Winsett see that; and that was why the New York of literary clubs and exotic restaurants, though a first shake made it seem more of a kaleidoscope, turned out, in the end, to be a smaller box, with a more monotonous pattern, than the assembled atoms of Fifth Avenue" (240, 126).

Edith Wharton had in 1920 a very specific reason for wanting to examine the "smaller box." In naming her protagonist Newland Archer, she seems to promise the reader a hero something like Henry James's Christopher Newman and a novel something like *The Portrait of a Lady*, which James intended, at least, to center in the young woman's consciousness. Wharton's protagonist is much more like James's Lambert Strether in *The Ambassadors*, however, who at exactly Archer's age at the end of *The Age of Innocence*, finds himself in love with a woman whose passionate and foreign nature is at odds with the world whose ambassador he is.[18] Strether's famous advice—"live all you can"—is the choice Newland Archer does not make; his choice is for keeping separate two worlds, one the "monotonous pattern," the other a secret world of the imagination, the sort of choice Wharton, in *A Backward Glance*, said she herself had made.

Edith Wharton was also fifty-seven, Newland Archer's age, when she wrote *The Age of Innocence*, and this novel is a kind of fictional "backward glance," a visitation, like that in Henry James's "The Jolly Corner," made to wake "all the old baffled forsworn possibilities . . . into such measure of ghostly life as they might still enjoy." The fifty-six-year-old protagonist of James's story, a sort of fictional treatment of *The American Scene* written at the end of his life, is a returned American who, after an absence of thirty-three years, wanders by night through the house of his youth in search of his lost self; "with habit and repetition he gained to an extraordinary degree the power to penetrate the dusk of distances, . . . to resolve back into their innocence the treacheries of uncertain light, the evil-looking forms taken in the gloom by mere shadows." Like Newland Archer in *The Age of Innocence*, Spencer Brydon in "The Jolly Corner" finds that "all things come back to the question of what he personally might have been, how he might have led his life and 'turned out,' if he had not so, at the outset, given it up." James's protagonist goes back to this question deliberately, to open the inner door of his locked consciousness, to wander in an immense space, the scale of which is "inordinate," the rooms of which "gloomed . . . like mouths of caverns; only the high skylight that formed the crown of the deep well created for him a medium in which he could advance, but which might have been, for queerness of colour, some watery under-world."[19] The reader will recognize echoes here of Ralph Marvell's sea-cave in *The Custom of the Country*, of Newland Archer's secret world in *The Age of Innocence*, of Edith Wharton's "secret garden" in *A Backward Glance*. Unlike Marvell and Archer, however, James's Spencer Brydon chooses to confront his "alter ego," this "sentinel guarding a treasure"; he is willing, by projecting "the magic lantern of childhood" on his other self, the self he might have been, to be "thrust . . . out of his frame." The doppelgänger Brydon finally tracks down is a man with a mutilated hand and ravaged face, a grotesque horror, a presence whose identity fits his own at no point; and at the moment of achieving this "duplication of consciousness," Brydon *loses* consciousness.[20]

Wharton's Newland Archer is willing to run no such risk in *The Age of Innocence*. When at the end of the novel he stands, a free man at last, beneath the windows in Paris of the woman he has in tormented secrecy loved for twenty-nine years and says to himself, "It's more real to me here than if I went up," he chooses to keep separate his two lives. To the end he insists on the "reality" of his inner world—it is "the fear lest the shadow of reality should lose its edge" that sends him back to his hotel alone—but its "realness" can be maintained only by keeping it imaginery, by protecting it if not from loss, at least from change in the world of the physical and concrete. Wharton, however, in writing the novel, *is* bridging two worlds: Ellen Olenska in the apartment on the rue de Varenne, Wharton's own street in Paris, and Newland Archer, gazing up at the windows from the street below, resemble two sides of Edith Wharton. *Resemble*—to be similar to, to simulate—describes the relationship between Wharton and her male protagonist in *The Age of Innocence* in the same way that Lily Bart and Undine Spragg (both of whom bear nicknames of the young Edith Wharton, Lily and "Puss") are semblances of Wharton, often exaggerated or distorted, and that May Welland is another, perhaps a portrait of what Wharton feared she might have become had she not escaped.

The need to turn back to the past in 1920 was occasioned by real things in Wharton's life. She had lived in France all through the First World War, for one thing, and had spent most of her time in war-relief activities. Turning back to fiction after the War, she found that she had to distance herself from the horrors she had witnessed, from the deliberate rape and destruction of a country she loved. Ruins of places like Gerbéviller, "simultaneously vomited up from the depths and hurled down from the skies, as though she had perished in some monstrous clash of earthquake and tornado," filled her with cold despair. This was no accident of nature "but a piously planned and methodically executed human deed":

> From the opposite heights the poor little garden-girt town was shelled like a steel fortress; then, when the Germans entered, a fire was built in every house, and at the nicely-timed right moment one of the explosive tabloids which the fearless Teuton carries about for his land-*Lusitanias* was tossed on each hearth. . . . One old woman, hearing her son's death-cry, rashly looked out of her door. A bullet instantly laid her low among her phloxes and lilies; and there, in her little garden, her dead body was dishonoured.[21]

At the same time, these years brought the death of her friends Henry James, Howard Sturgis, Egerton Winthrop and others—sorrows "not single spies but in battalions," Wharton wrote in *A Backward Glance*. "My spirit was heavy with these losses. . . . I had to get away from the present altogether . . . [and] I found a momentary escape in going back to my childish memories of a long-vanished America, and wrote 'The Age of Innocence.'"[22]

These two works, *A Backward Glance* and *The Age of Innocence*, spring from the same impulse, and both begin with the purpose of fixing an image of security, the autobiography with a child dressed for and engaged in the ritual of taking a walk on Fifth Avenue with her father, and the novel with a family of Old New Yorkers dressed for and engaged in the ritual of attending the Opera at the old Academy of Music building. Wharton's intention is similar in the two works: she journeys into her own past, a past that she had rejected, in order to recapture a time of lost stability and to achieve a reconciliation with that past.

The Age of Innocence is not, of course, autobiography, but a novel; and in the context of the novel, the reconciliation with the past is an ambivalent one. We know that Newland Archer lives one life committed to his family, profession and community, and another that seems equally real, a "kind of sanctuary" for his secret thoughts and longings that becomes "the scene of his real life, of his only rational activities" (262). Yet at the end of the novel the reader is left to wonder what Archer has received from family and community to compensate him for the loss of a companionate and passionate relationship with Ellen Olenska—particularly the reader of other Wharton novels in which it is not at all clear that the American family *was* nurturing. In the novels that precede *The Age of Innocence*, the presentation of the family as destructive and oppressive might be explained in terms of the defensiveness—about her career and her divorce—Wharton's own family aroused in her. Thus can Lily Bart's suicide as the only alternative to marriage in *The House of Mirth* (1905), the entrapment of a man and two women in a living tomb of frozen silence in *Ethan Frome* (1911), the incestuous attraction and distrust in *The Reef* (1912) and in *Summer* (1917) be accounted for as well as the divorce between the sexes in American life in *The Custom of the Country* (1913). The novels that follow *The Age of Innocence*, however, present even more devastating depictions of the family: a "hideous and degrading" competition between two women for one daughter in *The Old Maid* (1924), a competition between a mother and daughter for the same man in *The Mother's Recompense* (1925), the meaninglessness and outrage of all family intercourse in *Twilight Sleep* (1927), incestuous attraction again and the destruction of children by irresponsible parents in *The Children* (1928). And while she was writing *The Age of Innocence* (in 1919), Wharton began the "unpublishable fragment" for the uncompleted ghost story "Beatrice Palmato," which together with the plan for the tale, describes a family relationship marked by incest, madness and death.

Given all of this, it is difficult to see *The Age of Innocence* as a novel of reconciliation;[23] rather, Newland Archer achieves a kind of balance between two lives, and he prefers his way of tacking back and forth to a full commitment to one life or the other. Archer might see "good in the old ways" and "good in the new ways," but Wharton was well aware of repression of the self in the old ways and fragmentation of the self in the new. The attraction of the old here, despite the formidable allure of the sensuous "disorder" of Ellen Olenska, is as the necessary counterbalance to war and death that Wharton needed as she worked on this novel. Newland Archer, in fact, is exactly as important as a *center* in this novel as his room full of "sincere" Eastlake furniture is important in May's house: *The Age of Innocence* is not really "about" Newland Archer at all; it is about the little "hieroglyphic world" in which he lived—a world not of men, but of women.

If we think of *The Age of Innocence* in this way, we see its resemblance to a work like Virginia Woolf's *Mrs. Dalloway*, written just five years later. Responding similarly to the cataclysmic events of the first quarter of the twentieth century, Woolf sets up two structures in *Mrs. Dalloway*—one of war and one of roses, represented by Septimus Warren Smith, a shell-shocked soldier returned from the war, and by Clarissa Dalloway, a rich man's wife. The novel builds simultaneously toward Smith's suicide and Mrs. Dalloway's party. Woolf was examining here two different modes for social organization, Lee Edwards suggests: "solitude, fragmentation, abstraction, rigidity, and death on the one side, or communion, harmony, spontaneity, and life on the other. Wars and parties, shell shock and roses, authority and individuality, death and life, 'manly' and 'feminine' are counters. . . . The politics of *Mrs. Dalloway* are such that life is possible only when roses, parties, and joy triumph over war, authority, and death. Clarissa's celebrations—ephemeral and compromised though they may be—are a paradigm of sanity, a medium through which energy can flow in a world which is otherwise cruel, judgmental, and frozen."[24]

These masculine and feminine structures of war and roses were horribly clear to the Edith Wharton who wrote *Fighting France* in 1915. War meant a deliberate destruction of all that gave life meaning: "The photographs on the walls, the twigs of withered box above the crucifixes, the old wedding-dresses in brass-clamped trunks, the bundles of letters laboriously written and as painfully deciphered, all the thousand and one bits of the past that give meaning and continuity to the present—of all that accumulated warmth nothing was left but a brick-heap and some twisted stove-pipes!" And even worse was the violation of Ypres, bombarded to death, but with the outer walls of the houses still standing so that it presented the distant semblance of a living city, while near by it seemed a disemboweled corpse:

> Every window-pane is smashed, nearly every building unroofed, and some house-fronts are sliced clean off, with the different stories exposed, as if for the stage-setting of a farce. In these exposed interiors the poor little household gods shiver and blink like owls surprised in a hollow tree. A hundred signs of intimate and humble tastes, of humdrum pursuits, of family association, cling to the unmasked walls. . . . It was all so still and familiar that it seemed as if the people for whom these things had a meaning might at any moment come back and take up their daily business.[25]

Wharton found that in hundreds of such houses of open towns the hand of time had been stopped. She found a convent where the orderly arrest of life "symbolized the senseless paralysis of a whole nation's activities. Here were a houseful of women and children, yesterday engaged in a useful task and now aimlessly astray over the earth." But she also found women beginning to build again the structures that support life—nuns, for example, at work in the fields, one of whom, turning up a hob-nailed sole, told her: "All the women are working in the fields—we must take the place of the men." And, Wharton wrote, "I seemed to see my pink peonies flowering in the very prints of her sturdy boots!"[26] She would carry these flowers back half a century to *The Age of Innocence*, which was for her an oasis, a compromised oasis, a frozen world of ritual that offered sanity in its very repetition: she held before her scenes in "suitable" rooms in old New York houses and pictures from summers at Newport where athletic rituals were carried out on the hemmed turf of the small bright lawns.

The repetition of rituals, anthropologists point out, is particularly characteristic of female structures. Woman's body, for one thing, assigns to her a repetitive role in the reproduction of the life cycle, while the male transcends the life cycle "artificially," through the medium of technology and symbols, asserting and declaring this transcendence, or "culture," superior to "nature."[27] Lacking in value or status to the extent that they are confined to domestic activities, cut off from the social world of men and from each other, women gain power and a sense of value in one of two ways: they can transcend domestic limits either by entering the men's world or by creating their own society. In a separate society, purity rituals become particularly important—elaborate norms for "strict dress and demeanor, modesty, cleanliness, and prudishness"—because these are devices for contrasting their world with the men's world and of establishing grounds for order and status. The convent is the most extreme example of such a world: it is a pure and moral society of women, a world wholly their own in which "the very symbolic and social conceptions that appear to set women apart and to circumscribe their activities may be used by women as a basis for female solidarity and worth."[28]

Wharton knew a great deal about cultural anthropology. She read Darwin, Huxley, Spencer "and various popular exponents of the great evolutionary movement," and she made skillful use of works like *The Golden Bough* in analyzing her own former world in tribal terms and in dramatizing its rituals.[29] The important rituals in *The Age of Innocence*— the family landau rolling "from one tribal doorstep to another," the "religious solemnity" of exclusive dinners—are female rituals (69, 62). Lawrence Lefferts and his kind who carry on clandestine affairs, Julius Beaufort who comes to a dishonorable financial smash-up, count only as the sort of disorder that threatens the community and against which the rituals of the women, acting in concert, offer protection. The men might remain behind for brandy and cigars, but they must always return to the drawing-room world of the women. The world of *The Age of Innocence* bears a certain resemblance to Dion Boucicault's popular melodrama *The Shaughraun*—which Newland Archer goes to see repeatedly—where the action is dominated by Tom-Sawyerish highjinks to save a political prisoner who has already been pardoned by Queen Victoria.[30]

The audience who attends *The Shaughraun*, like the audience who attends the Opera, regards what happens onstage as a performance meant to be entertaining—but the far more important performance takes place offstage. That Gounod's *Faust* both opens *The Age of Innocence* and is repeated toward the end of the novel with "the same large blonde victim . . . succumbing to the same small brown seducer" gives the opera, however, a significance beyond entertainment or setting (320). We know from *The Fruit of the Tree* that the importance of the Faust story for Wharton was not only in the aspiration toward the moment of ecstasy, but in the resignation with which one must accept what inevitably follows. Characters in her novels come to an understanding like that of Faust who says "This is the moment!" only at "the end when he'd nothing left of all he began by thinking worth while." As in *Faust*, the moment one wants to hold fast to is not, "in most lives, the moment of keenest personal happiness, but the other kind—the kind that would have seemed grey and colourless at first: the moment when the meaning of life began to come out from the mists—when one could look at last over the marsh one had drained."[31] Moreover, the second part of Goethe's *Faust* begins with Faust's invocation to "The Mothers"—those dangerous powers of darkness fundamental to creativity. As Wharton's young writer-hero in *Hudson River Bracketed* learns, the distinction between real and "surface" art is a difference between knowing, like Faust, "the mysterious Mothers, moving in subterranean depths among the primal forms of life," and being "Motherless."[32]

In *The Age of Innocence*, soprano Christine Nilsson, literally the first person to whom the reader is introduced, must have suggested such a primal force. "What a pity she is not the heroine of the tale, and I didn't make her!," Henry James wrote after seeing her perform: she must have seemed to him even more vital, more energetic, larger and bolder than someone like his own actress Miriam Rooth in *The Tragic Muse*.[33] The powerful Nilsson would have been familiar to Wharton's readers, who must have felt the sharpness of her contrast between a woman who has chosen to play a part with deliberation and genius—and who will have the opportunity to play other parts—and the frozen rituals enacted by the audience.

The offstage performance takes place in the Mingott box, from which "the Matriarch of the line" is conspicuously absent. Mrs. Manson Mingott may once have ruled Old New York with her "strength of will and hardness of heart, and a kind of haughty effrontery," but by 1870 "Catherine the Great" is like "a doomed city": an "immense accretion of flesh" has changed her from an active woman into "something as vast and august as a natural phenomenon." So fat that she is immobile, with "moral courage" she still suggests the disorder of the "inaccessible wilderness near the Central Park," startling and fascinating her visitors with her ground-floor arrangement of sitting-room giving onto an unexpected vista of bedroom, recalling "scenes in French fiction, and architectural incentives to immorality such as the simple American had never dreamed of." It is, however, only "a stage-setting of adultery," Archer reflects when he goes with May, a Mingott granddaughter, to receive their betrothal blessing, in which old Catherine leads a blameless life (13, 14, 28, 29).

The two Mingott granddaughters in the Opera box suggest a redefinition of community since Granny Mingott's time: the boundaries have shifted to exclude the passionate and bohemian Ellen; they enclose the pure and Diana-like May. It is Newland's valuing of the world contained within that box, his wish to protect and preserve it, and his quick sense of something that offends against "Taste" that takes him to the Mingott box to persuade May to announce their engagement early, adding the strength of his family to that of hers to affirm their respectability—or reinforce their boundaries—in the face of what he perceives as disorder.

One way to read this novel is to see May Welland and Ellen Olenska as the traditional light and dark ladies of this script, as two modes of dealing with "reality"—those represented by the girls in "The Valley of Childish Things," one of whom stays at home to play with her beads while the other goes out into the world to learn about building bridges. Newland perceives May as "a light under ice"; she embodies "the steadying sense of an inescapable duty" (193, 207). Where he imagined her as a comrade, he will learn that "such a picture presupposed, on her part, the experience, the versatility, the freedom of judgment, which she had been carefully trained not to possess"; he will come to fear that her "niceness" carried to the supreme degree is only "a dull association of material and social interests held together by ignorance on the one side and hypocrisy on the other." May is the other side of the coin from Undine Spragg in *The Custom of the Country*: "that terrifying product of the social system he belonged to and believed in, the young girl who knew nothing and expected everything." As May Archer she will keep her Diana-like innocence "that seals the mind against imagination and the heart against experience" (44–45, 43, 146).

In contrast to the safe and ordinary way of May, Ellen suggests "tragic and moving possibilities outside the daily run of experience." Her eclectic education has been "expensive but incoherent," including such outlandish activities as "drawing from the model" and playing in quintets with professional musicians. Unlike May, who is stiffly bedecked and elaborately bejeweled for each social occasion—wearing her wedding dress to the Opera, for example—Ellen chooses clothes like the unadorned dark velvet she wears to the Opera and a fur-trimmed lounging robe at home which seem exotic in their simplicity: they express Ellen's moods and emphasize her body. Recognizing the possibilities of individual freedom and experience, instinct and variety, cultural and sexual richness in Ellen, Newland sends her not lilies-of-the-valley but yellow roses that are "too rich, too strong, in their fiery beauty" (115, 60, 80).

Katherine Cornell as Ellen Oleska in the dramatized version of Edith Wharton's *The Age of Innocence*. (Courtesy, Beinecke Rare Book and Manuscript Library, Yale University)

The "too rich" reveals which way Newland will choose, but to read the novel in this way is to fail to see that he is not really part of either world; it is to discount his limitations and the limits of his perception. With Ellen, Newland is unable to transcend his "stock phrases" and "hackneyed vocabulary"; and she does not speak his language: with no common language, they cannot understand each other (112, 309, 133, 171).[34] But neither do Newland and May speak the same language: they communicate "without a word," "in an atmosphere of faint implications and pale delicacies" which binds him to an "inarticulate lifetime." May is the center of an "elaborate system of mystification," the power of which, because Newland does not fully understand it, makes him feel impotent. He begins to suspect that May's innocence is an artificial product—"untrained human nature was not frank and innocent; it was full of the twists and defenses of an instinctive guile"—and to feel "oppressed by this creation of factitious purity, so cunningly manufactured by a conspiracy of mothers and aunts and grandmothers and long-dead ancestresses" (17, 356, 45, 46).

Newland Archer is trapped both by his own limitations and by forces he does not understand, by meaningless words or by wordless meanings. Expressing seemingly radical sentiments about human freedom—"women ought to be free—as free as we are"—he understands that his words are meaningless, that "'nice' women, however wronged, would never claim the kind of freedom he meant, and generous-minded men like himself were therefore—in the heat of argument—the more chivalrously ready to concede it to them. Such verbal generosities were in fact only a humbugging disguise of the inexorable conventions that tied things together and bound people down to the old pattern." What he does not realize, however, is that the "freedom" of the chivalrous men is just as much of a humbugging disguise as their verbal generosity. Like the women, he is "versed in the arts of the enslaved" (42, 44, 305).

To read *The Age of Innocence* as a failed love story, then, is to believe that "the play's the thing," that the script offers Newland Archer a choice between May Welland and Ellen Olenska, a Faust-like opportunity to transform his reality. He is in fact fated to remain in the old pattern precisely because there is in May's "innocent" world a sophisticated shrewdness which, without asking questions, instinctively protects that world, relentlessly patrolling its boundaries against the forces of disorder. The power of this world is such that even the professional lives of the men count for little: Newland, a lawyer, can be called home from work to give his attention to domestic problems, and even the nature of his work, when it relates to family matters, can be dictated—as when The Family makes clear to him what sort of legal decision he is expected to make about Ellen Olenska's divorce.

Because Newland's social conditioning makes him more comfortable in May's world than in Ellen's, he flees with "instinctive recoil" from Ellen, the very vocabulary of the freedom she suggests seeming "to belong to fiction and the stage," and from "an atmosphere so thick with drama." He flees to May, for her script is safer; it calls for a woman to be static, fixed against a scenic backdrop with "that faculty of unawareness" that makes her seem transparent, her blood a preserving fluid (109, 116, 188–89). He is able to respond to her "Diana-like aloofness" with a "glow of proprietorship," as at that first Opera scene, when he walks with her in the park, at the Newport archery match; he communicates with her in "the code in which they had both been trained," and in choosing her, he chooses safety and enclosure—a world that "lay like a sunlit valley at their feet" (7, 210, 81, 206, 266, 25).

This hieroglyphic world of Old New York is a kind of "heaven"—a place for the "blessed," where other women seem not to feel the needs that Ellen Olenska expresses; it is a place where no one cries, peopled by "children playing in a graveyard," or children "lighting a bunch of straw in a wayside cavern, and revealing old silent images in their painted tomb" (133, 113, 78, 207, 214). It is the world of the luxurious Welland house and of "the density of the Welland atmosphere, so charged with minute observances and exactions" that it becomes for Newland a narcotic: "the heavy carpets, the watchful servants, the perpetually reminding tick of disciplined clocks, the perpetually renewed stack of cards and invitations on the hall table, the whole chain of tyrannical trifles binding one hour to the next, and each member of the household to all the others" makes any other less systematized and less affluent existence seem unreal and precarious. The life Newland is expected to lead as May's husband seems equally unreal and irrelevant. When he flees from Ellen, in whose house time literally has stopped, to May, his "here was truth, here was reality," upon seeing her standing Diana-like in the garden of St. Augustine, is exactly as perceptive as Lawrence Selden's "here was the real Lily Bart" when she poses in the tableau in *The House of Mirth* (217, 70, 141). It seems, in fact, that it is impossible for Newland to tell what the "real thing" is at all. May's is the world where "the real thing was never said or done," but Ellen's is the world "of fiction and the stage." The only place where "real" things happen to him is in the theater of his imagination where he plays opposite Ellen Olenska:

> [There was] a kind of sanctuary in which she throned among his secret thoughts and longings. Little by little it became the scene of his real life, of his only rational activities; thither he brought the books he read, the ideas and feelings which nourished him, his judgments and his visions. Outside it, in the scene of his actual life, he moved with a growing sense of unreality and insufficiency, blundering against familiar prejudices and traditional points of view as an absent-minded man goes on bumping into the furniture of his own room. Absent—that was what he was: so absent from everything most densely real and near to those about him that it sometimes startled him to find they still imagined he was there. [262]

The great irony of Newland Archer's self-preoccupation is that both of his roles—as May's husband, as Ellen's lover—are minor roles. The scenes in which he figures to himself with such importance are poignant because, like some of our own experiences, they are so set apart from or so much at the mercy of the more powerful forces of the drama. Archer quite literally reenacts melodrama, for example, by repeating twice a scene from *The Shaughraun*—the one where the hero steals up behind the woman he loves and lifts one of the velvet ribbons of her dress to his lips without her having noticed him. In the first of these two scenes, Newland stands by the shore of Granny Mingott's Newport house, watching Ellen who faces away from him. She seems transfixed, and he says to himself, "If she doesn't turn before that sail crosses the Lime Rock light I'll go back." She does not turn; he walks back up the hill. In the later scene, an older Newland waits beneath Ellen's windows in Paris. When the lights come on and a servant closes the shutters, "as if it had been the signal he waited for, Newland Archer got up slowly and walked back alone to his hotel" (216, 361). Both times—as in the play—Ellen knows he is there; in neither case does she acknowledge his presence, just as in the climactic moment of the story, she will decide not to consummate their affair.

The scene at the new Metropolitan Art Museum highlights the difference between Newland and Ellen that has been suggested throughout the novel. They meet after a long separation, when Ellen, who has moved to Washington, returns because Granny Mingott has had a stroke—which literally signals the demise of the old order. Newland wants Ellen—he feels "burnt up in a great flame" when he sees her—but he does not want "an ordinary hole-and-corner love affair." Ellen, however, forces him to look not at visions but at realities. "Is it your idea," she asks him, "that I should live with you as your mistress—since I can't be your wife?" He has no words for what he wants; he flounders, "I want—I want somehow to get away with you into a world where words like that—categories like that—won't exist. Where we shall be simply two human beings who love each other, who are the whole of life to each other; and nothing else on earth will matter." Ellen laughs at him, asking, "Oh, my dear,—where is that country? Have you ever been there?" She makes a practical suggestion: she will come to him once and then return to Europe alone. Newland believes that it might be possible to trap her, but he also believes that he loves her: "If I were to let her come," he muses, "I should have to let her go again." He seizes the moment, however. Her face is "flooded with a deep inner radiance," his heart "beat[s] with awe"—but they look at each other "almost like enemies" (288–90, 312–13).

Ellen does not come to Newland. A meeting between Ellen and May has interfered with this plan; she sends his key back and does not see him again until she departs for good. According to May, she and Ellen have had "a really good talk"; they have understood each other. May has in fact lied to Ellen about her pregnancy; acting with the knowledge and approval of the family, Granny Mingott has promised to guarantee Ellen's financial independence, and Ellen has found female bonding to be more compelling than individual heterosexual passion. The bargain to which Ellen has agreed is sealed in the ritual dinner, "a conspiracy of rehabilitation and obliteration," May's triumph (315, 339).

Because of the way we are used to reading novels, the romance of Newland and Ellen at first obscures the force of the countersubject: the inexorableness of the offensive launched by the women in *The Age of Innocence*. Ellen Olenska suggests disorder, but it is not for this alone that she will finally be expelled. Her aunt, Medora Manson, a "gaunt and mincing lady . . . in a wild dishevelment of stripes and fringes and floating scarves" suggests disorder, too, especially in her association with Dr. Agathon Carver, itinerant leader of a free-love community (184). Both Ellen Olenska and Medora Manson are marginal people: they exist close to the borders of the community and as such are necessary in defining its boundaries.[35] But where Medora's kind of disorder is frivolous and ineffectual (like Agathon Carver's "Valley of Love"), Ellen Olenska's disorder is dangerous because it threatens to displace the existing pattern with some powerful other pattern. She is what anthropologist Mary Douglas would call a "polluting person," who is always in the wrong. She has "simply crossed some line which should not have been crossed and this displacement unleashes danger for someone."[36] It is not just that Ellen has been married (to a notorious European count), or that she is rumored to have had affairs, but that unlike Medora Manson, she represents the European kind of threat to the "official innocence" of May's world that Madame de Vionnet, in Henry James's *The Ambassadors*, represents to the world of Woollett, Massachusetts; she threatens to pollute the little sphere of order and purity with a sexual and cultural richness that would destroy it.

Spatially, ritually, and thus physically and psychologically, so complete is the women's control over their world that they can command without speaking. May, trimming the lamp in Newland's "sincere" Eastlake library, can depend upon his understanding the unspoken communication in which her "You must go and see Ellen" is embedded. In the code in which they have both been trained, her straight look and cloudless smile make these words mean:

> "Of course you understand that I know all that people have been saying about Ellen, and heartily sympathize with my family in their effort to get her to return to her husband. I also know that, for some reason you have not chosen to tell me, you have advised her against this course, which all the older men of the family, as well as our grandmother, agree in approving; and that it is owing to your encouragement that Ellen defies us all, and exposes herself to the kind of criticism of which Mr. Sillerton Jackson probably gave you, this evening, the hint that has made you so irritable. . . . Hints have indeed not been wanting; but since you appear unwilling to take them from others, I offer you this one myself, in the only form in which well-bred people of our kind can communicate unpleasant things to each other: by letting you understand that I know you mean to see Ellen when you are in Washington, and are perhaps going there expressly for that purpose; and that, since you are sure to see her, I wish you to do so with my full and explicit approval—and to take the opportunity of letting her know what the course of conduct you have encouraged her in is likely to lead to." [266]

May has, of course, become expert in the use of this kind of power because she has no other real power—power in the world of men, political power—outside the little closed society. We know from *French Ways and Their Meaning*, *A Backward Glance* and *The Custom of the Country* that Wharton valued not a separate world of women, but a world in which men and women intermingled, a world of conversation and stimulation, of continuity and tradition.[37] We know from *The House of Mirth* that the elevation of woman to deity on the one hand and her diminution to child on the other produced the same result: permanent residence in "the valley of childish things." And yet the community of women in *The Age of Innocence* has a greater importance than a similar one in Henry James's *The Bostonians*.[38] Both writers present a female society in decline, but Wharton's is the decline of the matriarchal vigor and daring of Granny Mingott into a Bachofean kind of matriarchal deity—the Victorian "perfect woman" of "unblemished beauty . . . chastity and high-mindedness."[39] As a woman's real power declines, Wharton suggests, so the protection of a world separate and increasingly characterized by purity and order assumes importance. The world of cultural and sexual richness that Ellen Olenska embodies is impossible in America precisely because Ellen's is a heterosexual world, a shared world, a world "rich and deep" in that it is "based on the recognised interaction of influences between men and women."[40] Yet if Ellen comes "home" to escape from the "horrors" of the European world (represented by her decadent and unscrupulous husband), it must be because though she can communicate, she has no real power to order the world, not even to the extent that May has power. Ellen—the intruder who cannot be tolerated in the closed community— sees qualities worth preserving in May's world. May herself is brave and strong and generous: she can offer, during her engagement, to set Newland free to love another woman; dying she tells her son that she has understood Newland's sacrifice of the thing he most desired.

May's triumphal dinner, then, the "tribal rally around a kinswoman about to be eliminated from the tribe," is an expressive reaffirmation of female bonding. It is a statement of where the boundaries of the community are and of an intention to delineate and protect those boundaries as a means of preserving the community. It is the culmination of a pattern of behavior and belief that can be traced through the novel—from the time when the women first decide to offer Ellen protection, to their concern that she live in an appropriate neighborhood, their attempts to dissuade her from initiating a divorce suit, and finally to their efforts to get her to return to her husband, whatever his qualities, because in attracting one of their husbands, she threatens the community itself. From each of these family judgments, once May has held up the straw to the wind to see which way his loyalties lie, Newland has been excluded—just as at the final ceremonial dinner, "a band of dumb conspirators" eating canvasbacks, taking life in the Old New York way "without effusion of blood," he is not even there: he floats "somewhere between chandelier and ceiling," the music he hears in the two syllables of Ellen's name flickering against the social reality of May (334–35). He does not understand how all of this has come about: the menu and the guest list and the flowers have been chosen by May, her mother and her mother-in-law in the same way as Ellen has gone in her grandmother's carriage to visit the shunned and humiliated cousin Regina Beaufort while the men refuse to have anything to do with her husband, and in the same way as May and Ellen have had their talk which has led to the agreement that Ellen return to Europe. Newland still thinks, when he looks at Ellen's long pale fingers, that he will follow her, but remembering his "a gentleman simply stayed at home and abstained," one knows that he will not, that the most important things in his life will take place in his "sincere" Eastlake library: May's breaking to him the news of her first pregnancy, the christening of their first child, discussions of the children's futures, the scene of his being persuaded by the governor of New York to take up politics. Since his love for Ellen has depended all along on his keeping her "just there, safe but secluded," that is exactly the way she must remain for him—so dreamlike that he will not even be able to imagine what her life is like; he will come to think of her "abstractly, serenely, as one might think of some imaginary beloved in a book or a picture: . . . the composite vision of all that he had missed" (173, 246, 347).

The nature of Ellen's life must remain for Newland conjectural, for by his own choice, in the domestic and social sphere, at least, his own limited vision has been reduced by the orderliness May's boundaries have imposed. By the end of the novel, when he has accepted these boundaries and has even been able to carve out for himself a certain amount of influence in the public sphere, it is too late for Newland Archer to redefine himself, although May is dead, their daughter makes no attempt to maintain the twenty-inch waist, and their son is soon to be married to a Beaufort bastard. If he has missed something—Ellen Olenska, whom he has envisioned living in some quiet and obscure corner of Paris, but now imagines from the location of her apartment in the Faubourg St. Germain enjoying a life (like Wharton's) intensely rich, filled with good conversation and social activity—Newland Archer does well not to enter this world. Had he done so, no doubt Ellen Olenska would have received him graciously, but he would not have felt at home; he would have found the rich atmosphere "too dense and yet too stimulating for his lungs," an "incessant stir of ideas, curiosities, images and associations" (358–59). In Newland Archer's pause, Wharton poses, on the threshold of the modern world, a disturbing question about the creation of order and the exercise of power: in the split between public and private spheres of order and influence, who is to say which is artificial—that is, sub-ordinate—and which is "real"?

CHAPTER 5

"Making Up"—and Making Up

The Room of the Dressing

She falls into this labyrinth. Into the room of the dressing where the walls are covered with mirrors. Where mirrors are like eyes of men, and the women reflect the judgments of mirrors. Where the women stand next to each other, continue dressing next to each other, speak next to each other as if men were still with them. As if men could overhear their words. The room of the dressing where women sometimes speak in code. The room where each makes her own translation. The room where the women keep to themselves and she teaches her daughter to put on make-up. The room of the half real. . . .

And she says she is suffocating. And she says the horizon is a lie. And the air is filled with stories about her. And she says space denies her. The room in which the women are lost. The labyrinth from which they do not escape. Which keeps them going around in circles. The room in which the women lose their way and are no longer anywhere. . . .

The Room of the Undressing

Craters of the moon. *She lets herself fall. She falls into the room of her wants. . . . Where her voice has endlessly demanded her to go. This room which reveals her. . . . The room of the revelation of all she thought horrible, and of her endlessly demanding body. Of all she shrank from in herself. This room filled with herself. She fell into this room. This room of outcasts.* Where we uncover our bodies. Where we meet our outcast selves. . . . *This room filled with darkness. . . . The room which she said she needed. The room without which she was sure she would perish. The*

*first room in which she experienced space. This place where she could fi-
nally breathe. The place where she breathed out the stories she had not
believed. . . . Where she began to believe the horizon. This room of her
wants. Of her desiring. . . . This place which allows her to exist.*

—Susan Griffin, *Woman and
Nature: The Roaring Inside Her*[1]

The text of Wharton's published autobiography, *A Backward Glance*,
is illustrated with photographs of her own choosing, presumably intended
as commentary. They present to us an image that reinforces the "feminine
me" of the word pictures: a woman dressed in laces, bows, furs and gloves,
a graceful descendant of portrayed Stevenses, Rhinelanders and Joneses, a
figure "placed" in Newport, Lenox, Paris and Hyères. Collectively, these
images fix Wharton in *this* world, as she intended they should, for as she
insists, this "feminine *me*" was as equally real as the "other *me*." The
autobiography is a demonstration that Wharton could—and did—exist in
two worlds, as carefully separated as her division of public and private
rooms in *The Decoration of Houses*.

The writer of the carefully modulated passages of *A Backward Glance*
betrays no "roaring": Wharton's description of finding her own space is
filled with self-conscious monitoring of her own behavior—a self-consciousness that both obscures and suggests something *behind* the picture,
something that is not there, that takes place in another setting, that is not
quite "suitable," to borrow the keyword of Wharton's *The Decoration of
Houses*. "The world is not to be reinvented," the introduction to that
book states clearly:

> *Suitability* as used in this book is rooted in the traditions of the Graeco-
> Roman world. . . . tradition lays down the ground rules, and they are an
> expression of what life is all about. One of civilization's tasks is to find
> rituals which give human existence significance. The rites of daily life are
> ritualized by *suitable* rooms, *le decor de la vie*. They must be classical rooms
> because classical architecture is the only architecture that expresses human
> dignity and greatness. The classical house is a prefiguration of a society
> which affirms a hierarchy of values. These are the ground rules. All of this is,
> of course, quite opposed to the contemporary odyssey of the self-centered
> self.

"Self," here, has negative connotations; and yet it is the self that creates. In
The Decoration of Houses, this conflict is resolved by a clear distinction
between public and private. No rooms could be more "dressed" than

Edith Wharton, about 1884. (Edith Wharton, *A Backward Glance*, 1934)

those Wharton describes in this book; yet privacy is "one of the first requisites of civilized life." A comfort not to be exchanged for "vast openings and extended 'vistas,'" privacy is attained by keeping the doors between the rooms of a house—each a small, specific world in itself—shut.[2]

Edith Wharton, about 1934. (Edith Wharton, *A Backward Glance*, 1934)

Wharton published *A Backward Glance* in 1934, but three years later, in the year of her death, she began again to tell her story because she realized, she said, that her view of her own case was that of a sentimentalist, and that the intervening years had given her a new sense of "the everaccumulating thickness of the obstructions" that now lay between her and the last half of the nineteenth century: "Everything that used to form the mode of our daily life has been torn up, trampled on, destroyed; & hundreds of little incidents, habits, traditions, which, when I began my 'Backward Glance' seemed too utterly insignificant to set down, have since taken on . . . historical importance. . . . It is such bits of vanished life that I should like to gather up now. . . ."[3]

In this final version of her autobiography, details from the fictional stories Wharton had made up throughout her long life become intermingled with the story of her life: the several layerings of her life story— "Memories," "Life and I," *A Backward Glance*, "A Further Glance"—are like the performances of a good repertory company, which Wharton says in "A Further Glance" she much preferred to the newer "star" system. In fact, she writes, though theater-going was one of the great emotions of her life, "standing up like summits catching the light when all else was in shadow," she distrusted "the bodily representation of characters who already live so visibly in my imagination that anyone else's conception of them interferes with that intense inward vision . . . for, five minutes after I have watched the actors in a new play, I have formed an inner picture of what they ought to look like and speak like; and as I once said in my rash youth . . . , 'I always want to get up on the stage & show them how they ought to act.'" Theater, for Wharton, was "largely a matter of listening to voices"[4]—like writing stories, where characters spoke to her, "with their own voices"; as soon as the dialogue began, she became "merely a recording instrument."[5]

To re-imagine her life, then, becomes to write a story, and to write requires first the falling in to "that intense inward vision." The setting for this story comes, as usual, from everyday life: a line of "little 'brown-stone' houses . . . marched up Fifth Avenue . . . in an almost unbroken procession from Washington Square to the Central Park . . . like [an] aging ladies' boarding-school taking its daily exercise." The set is in fact re-created with great precision, from the number of steps leading to the front doors of the brown-stone facades, their monotony broken here and there by a brick front, and further toward Central Park, in the wilderness first occupied by the haughty Mrs. Mason Jones (the Mrs. Manson Mingott of *The Age of Innocence*), by yellowish-green lime-stone (of the sort occupied by Newland and May Archer in that novel); to the width of the facades, the furnishing of hall-ways, drawing-rooms and libraries (the ladies collecting old fans and old lace, the gentlemen bound volumes of old books and paintings—sometimes originals, more often copies—of old masters); to the kinds of carriages one would be likely to pass in a ride down Fifth Avenue, from the C-spring barouche of Mrs. Astor to the "shabby little covered cart drawn by a broken-down horse and labelled in large letters *Universal Exterminator*." On one such ride that took place in Wharton's seventeenth year, there suddenly appeared a remarkably dashing little brougham, painted canary yellow, in the depths of which one caught a glimpse of a lady "whom I faintly remember to have been dark-haired, well dressed & enchantingly pale, with a hat whose brim, lined with cherry-colour, shed a lovely glow on her cheeks. It was an apparition surpassing in elegance & mystery any that Fifth Avenue had ever seen; but when I cried: 'Oh, Mamma, look—what a smart carriage! Do you know the lady?' I was hurriedly drawn back into the depths of our own brougham, with the stern order not to stare at strange people, and whenever the yellow brougham passed to turn my head away and look out the other window." This incident contains the core of Wharton's story of her youth and of the development of her creative self: the repressiveness of social mores presided over by her colorlessly correct mother was to force the young Edith Jones to turn inward, to imagine for herself the lively performance supplied by these clues. Being an obedient daughter, she says, "I always, thereafter *did* look out the other window when the yellow brougham passed; but that one & only glimpse of forbidden loveliness furnished my imagination with images of enchantment. . . . And in the empoverished [*sic*] emotional atmosphere of my youth such a glimpse of forbidden fascination was like the distant image of palm-trees in the desert."[6]

Looking back on my childhood, Wharton would write, "I have often sighed to think . . . how pitiful a provision was made for the life of the imagination behind those uniform brown-stone façades, & then have concluded that, . . . the creative mind thrives on a reduced diet." The average well-to-do New Yorker was "starved for a sight of the high gods. Beauty, passion & danger were automatically excluded from . . . life . . . & the moral atmosphere resulted in a prolonged immaturity of mind." One can see this, she says, by penetrating the vestibules of the brown-stone houses, decorated according to Owen Jones's "Grammar of Ornament," into the carefully guarded interiors. Following her down the narrow hall we are admitted to a long, deep drawing-room rather like Mrs. Peniston's in *The House of Mirth*:

> The tall narrow windows were hung with three layers of curtains . . . through which no one from the street could possibly penetrate, & over them lace embroidered tulle curtains richly beruffled, & draped back under the velvet or damask curtains which were drawn in the evenings. This window garniture always seemed to me to correspond, symbolically, with the super[im]posed layers of under-garments worn by the ladies of the period—& even, alas, by the little girls. They were in fact almost purely a symbol, for in many windows even the inner "sash-curtains" were looped back with wide satin ribbons, in order to allow the secluded dwellers within a narrow

glimpse of the street; but no self-respecting mistress of a house (a brown-stone house) could dispense with this symbolic window-lingerie, & I remember that one of the many things I did which shocked & pained my mother-in-law not the least was the elimination, in our house in the country, of all the lace & dotted muslin draperies which should have intervened between ourselves & the robins on the lawn.[7]

What is the meaning of this seventy-five-year-old woman's "shocking" gesture of removing for us the symbolic lingerie that protects the monotony behind the brown-stone fronts? Why does she wish to tantalize her readers with the forbidden image of palm trees in the desert? What kind of memorial is it that she wishes to create for herself as she insists, yet again, upon her own historical importance?

The title of Wharton's published autobiography is suggestive, for Whitman, like the lady in the yellow carriage, was off-limits for the little girl who grew up behind the brown-stone facade. His poetry circulated "among the very advanced intellectuals, was kept under lock & key, & brought out, like tobacco, only in the absence of 'the ladies,' to whom the name of Walt Whitman was still unknown."[8] Moreover, the borrowing of Whitman's title is a clue that Wharton's *A Backward Glance* is a kind of deathbed preface to her works—or, like Whitman's, to her *work*. In "A Backward Glance O'er Travel'd Roads" Whitman asserts that the poem is the man and the man is the poem, that *Leaves of Grass* is the creation of a Persona (the voice of America in the Nineteenth Century, full of Good Cheer, Content, Hope, of courageous and lofty manhood, chanting "the great pride of man in himself"), and that *Leaves of Grass* is "the outcropping of my own emotional and other personal nature—an attempt, from first and last, to put *a Person*, a human being (myself . . .) freely, fully and truly on record. . . . No one will get at my verses who insists upon viewing them as a literary performance, . . . or as aiming mainly toward art or aestheticism."[9] All of his work, according to Whitman, is autobiography. All of the work—like Wharton's—is fabulation. Though the *intention* of fiction and of autobiography are different, the finished autobiography aims to present the final, perfected, fixed Persona.

Whitman's keyword is "performance," an appropriate term for autobiography, which is an act of self-dramatization, a formal mode of maintaining the reality of reality. "The autobiographer discloses the truth and at the same time fixes it by making it, paradoxically, more real, truer,"

Barrett Mandel says of Whitman. "The autobiographer assembles words *now* in order to demonstrate that a life was lived, that it had a particular meaning, and that it was capable of making an impact on others. The results are, in Whitman's phrase, 'full of life now.'"[10]

"Performance" is a keyword for Wharton as well. Characters in Wharton's novels continually perform for one another; their performances "highlight the common official values of the[ir] society"; they act in ways accepted (even expected) by other performers. Performances, as Erving Goffman argues, can be (and are) repeated; they take place in particular settings: "furniture, décor, physical layout, and other background items which supply the scenery and stage props for the spate of human action played out before, within or upon it." In fact, the performance can only begin in the appropriate place and must terminate upon leaving it.[11] If we look, then, at the opening passage of *A Backward Glance*, we see that the stage is set for a familiar performance: the little girl and her father are taking a walk, but nothing *moves*. Old New York, the last "drops of an old vintage too rare to be savoured by a youthful palate," is fixed, like the desperately uniform brown-stones, in time and space—as is the veiled and muffled little girl who holds the hand of her big, strong father.[12] She is fixed, too, and hidden, by her costume. Once she is "dressed," as Simone de Beauvoir has written, even the least sophisticated of women "does not present *herself* to observation: she is, like the picture or statue, or the actor on the stage, an agent through whom is suggested someone not there—that is, the character she represents, but is not. It is this identification with something unreal, fixed, perfect as the hero of a novel, as a portrait or a bust, that gratifies her; she strives to identify herself with this figure and thus to seem to herself to be stabilized, justified in her splendor."[13]

In her seventy-second year, the writer who would come to think of herself "as an old woman laying a handful of rue on the grave of an age which had finished in storm and destruction"[14] began the autobiography she would publish: "There's no such thing as old age; there is only sorrow." Then she began again with a picture of "the little girl who eventually became me."[15] Times are juxtaposed here: the time recalled—by writer and reader, the time of the writer writing, the time of the reader reading.[16] Something in the writer's life triggers a picture, which in turn triggers a picture for the reader. In "the space in which the re-creation of the illusion occurs," somewhere between the text itself and one's imagination, the reader intuits what it was like to *be* this person, thus bringing to the reading yet another "time." As I read Wharton's autobiography, in other words, the content of my own memory pictures and the complex feelings that underlie them provide yet another context for the narrative. It is the *context* disclosed through writing, Barrett Mandel argues—and, I would add, through reading—that is the stuff of autobiography.[17] Reading Wharton's autobiography triggers for me a picture; the deeper relevance or context of that picture has to do with needing comfort and protection at certain times in one's life, and this in turn colors my reading of an elderly woman's writing:

> It was on a bright day of midwinter, in New York. The little girl who eventually became me, but as yet was neither me nor anybody else in particular, but merely a soft anonymous morsel of humanity—this little girl, who bore my name, was going for a walk with her father. The episode is literally the first thing I can remember about her, and therefore I date the birth of her identity from that day.
>
> She had been put into her warmest coat, and into a new and very pretty bonnet, which she had surveyed in the glass with considerable satisfaction. . . . As the air was very cold a gossamer veil of the finest Shetland wool was drawn . . . over the wearer's round red cheeks like the white paper filagree over a Valentine; and her hands were encased in white woollen mittens.
>
> One of them lay in the large safe hollow of her father's bare hand; her tall handsome father, who was so warm-blooded that in the coldest weather he always went out without gloves, and whose head . . . was so far aloft that when she walked beside him she was too near to see his face. It was always an event in the little girl's life to take a walk with her father, and more particularly so today, because she had on her new winter bonnet, which was so beautiful (and so becoming) that for the first time she woke to the importance of dress, and of herself as a subject for adornment—so that I may date from that hour the birth of the conscious and feminine *me* in the little girl's vague soul.[18]

The "truth" of this picture is not its *content*. The writer quite literally sees someone else, "she," not "I": a soft anonymous morsel of humanity, a subject for adornment, veiled like a Valentine, with a vague soul. It is Wharton the writer, not this little girl, who as the walk proceeds down Fifth Avenue, sees in the double line of low brown-stone houses "a desperate uniformity of style" and in the water reservoir "a truncated Egyptian pyramid," who notices that the gentle landaus, broughams and victorias moving at decent intervals have "decorum." The "feminine *me*" that this little girl presents is Wharton as she might have become: Wharton the writer creates herself here as her own fictional heroine. Like her Jamesian counterpart, Wharton, the returned American, stalks the ghost of her-self—as she might have been—in the mansion of her childhood.[19] The sense of otherness about the picture is deliberate; the gossamer veil veils not only the little girl, but the little girl's double, the other *me*, one who makes up stories. Wharton had described in an earlier version of her autobiography the two lessons of childhood: to learn and to look pretty. The implication is that it is the pretty little girl's double, the other *me*, who grew up to write stories; yet what is "making up," as Wharton called the double's imagining, but embellishment? There is a puzzling harmoni-ous opposition to Wharton's "I always saw the visible world as a series of pictures, more or less harmoniously composed; and the wish *to make the picture prettier* was, as nearly as I can define it, the form my feminine instinct of pleasing took."[20]

Both the sad, lonely, elderly woman and the writer ascribe a great deal of importance in this opening scene to the little girl holding her father's hand. It is as if the self being justified is indelibly marked by what Beauvoir called *féminitude*—"a culturally determined status of difference and oppression." The act of recollection must begin here, with this mo-ment of at-one-ment, because with the introduction of the double, Whar-ton's purpose becomes, as Nancy Miller suggests in another context, to "justify an unorthodox life by writing about it . . . —to *reinscribe* the original violation, to reviolate the masculine turf."[21] Thus Wharton, in beginning this work of self-justification, must back up all the way to the creation of an image she believed would please her father, a static, passive, female *child*, made even prettier in this picture than in the original—at least so I, as reader, reexperiencing my own sense of "otherness," the old dichotomy of my self and the image I was expected to present, interpret.

Like other autobiographies—none of which is an objective and dis-interested pursuit—*A Backward Glance* is a search "for a hidden treasure, for a last delivering word, redeeming in the final appeal a destiny that doubted its own value."[22] Like other autobiographies by women, there is a hidden agenda, one that for Wharton is painful and ambiguous: though a woman may fly in the face of traditional expectations (as Wharton did in choosing career and divorce), she is no less a human being of merit; though she may seem the outlaw, the real fault lies with society and its laws. This last point is so important that it is at the core of all of her fictions—the "fictional fiction" and the "fictions of autobiography," as Germaine Brée calls the illuminating "matrix of fabulation."[23]

The Wharton-as-child of this autobiography, at the moment of her walk perceiving herself for the first time as a subject for ornament, plays the same role as a Lily Bart, embellished and fixed before the mirror of the decorated drawing-room that gives back her reflection, Lily who is most "real," as the other characters say to themselves, when costumed and motionless, she portrays a *tableau vivant*. Thus the *context* behind the content of the picture at the beginning of *A Backward Glance* is this: the child who is "a subject for ornament" and the woman who is "A Moment's Ornament" (as *The House of Mirth* was first titled) are one and the same; the text, in either case, is literally the female body—encased, veiled, embellished, but also static and secure. The elderly woman presenting this picture says all of these things: I was oppressed, I was loved, I was beautiful.

The little girl "who eventually became me" is a fairy tale creation: her bonnet is magic, her father is godlike and the now-extinct New York through which they walk is "good"—a safe, guarded, monotonous world in which, according to the epigraph from Goethe, *it is impossible to write poetry*. But the lesson of all fairy tales is that reality can be transformed.[24] In this "good" world—this world of safety, protection and comfort—a little girl learns that she has been made as a subject for adornment, and that her world is a "valley of childish things" which it is necessary to leave for another in which poetry *can* be written. On the other hand, this "good" world *was* good for Wharton: it was the repository of values unknown in the world of "telephones, motors, electric light, central heating, . . . X-rays, cinemas, radium, aeroplanes and wireless telegraphy," which Wharton equated with her country's moral impoverishment.[25] The elderly woman, looking back on her life, confesses to the attraction of two lives which seemed always to be in conflict: the one ornamental and social, lived in this "good" world, the other imaginative and contemplative, in which the writer was consumed by a passion to "make up" stories. Her autobiography is her opportunity for reconciliation, and the little girl with whom the book begins is a gesture of atonement made by Wharton the storyteller, who remains in control, attempting here to perfect her destiny and to join her lives in a completed whole.

The room of the undressing, the private space, was necessary for the existence of the "other *me*," the little girl who "makes up," the one who had imagined tales, Wharton recalled, "since my first conscious moments; I cannot remember the time when I did not want to 'make up' stories." *This* little girl had only to hold a densely printed book—Washington Irving's *The Alhambra* was best—and turning the pages as she walked, she would be "swept off full sail on the sea of dreams." In the telling of this tale, the adult writer both presents and protects this little girl:

> The fact that I could not read added to the completeness of the illusion, for from those mysterious blank pages I could evoke whatever my fancy chose. Parents and nurses, peeping at me through the cracks of doors (I always had to be alone to "make up"), noticed that I often held the book upside down, but that I never failed to turn the pages, and that I turned them at about the right pace for a person reading aloud as passionately and precipitately as was my habit.
>
> There was something almost ritualistic in the performance. The call came regularly and imperiously; and though, when it caught me at inconvenient moments, I would struggle against it conscientiously—for I was beginning to be a very conscientious little girl—the struggle was always a losing one. I had to obey the furious Muse; and there are deplorable tales of my abandoning the "nice" playmates who had been invited to "spend the day", and rushing to my mother with the desperate cry: "Mama, you must go and entertain that little girl for me. *I've got to make up.*" . . . I did not want them to intrude on my privacy, and there was not one I would not have renounced forever rather than have my "making up" interfered with. What I really preferred was to be alone with Washington Irving and my dream.[26]

This "other *me*," the little girl who makes up stories, makes up, in fact, the little girl who stands pretty and passive with her hand in her father's. And making up both little girls, of course, was Wharton the writer. As the words "ritualistic" and "performance" suggest, this *other* little girl also acts out an oft-repeated scene. She is a self-conscious actress performing for parents and nurses peeping at her through the cracks of doors, and because she has been praised, or has heard herself praised, she repeats the performance that is guaranteed to win smiling approval from the supervising adults. In fact, the regular and "imperious" call seems almost a reflex action (like "nature's call") in response to an uncomfortable situation—the "nice" playmates. There was a sure way to find relief from discomfort, but the privacy, not to be intruded upon by the playmates, had to include parents and nurses peeping through the cracks of doors—this was the stage set—in order for the ritual to be successful. It is difficult to tell whether the self-consciousness is the little girl's or the writer's, remembering the little girl. The little girl must have known that she was watched while she was engaged in making up, and she probably understood that the ritual in which she participated was a means of securing approval; but the layering of that ritual with another struggle, one against an expected pattern of behavior, is the work of the mature writer, the elderly woman, and she presents it now, to us, her readers, for approval.

The little girl's choice of *The Alhambra* is "real" enough. The outline for the autobiography—a numbered list of "clues"—includes (before "Learning to read") "Washington Irving in dark blue paper cover (Galignani edition?). Preferred a dense heavy page with very black characters."[27] Yet the selection of *this* book refers us to the adult Edith Wharton, the one who wrote *The Decoration of Houses, Italian Villas and Their Gardens, Italian Backgrounds,* and who set her novels with a wealth of architectural detail. For interspersed with the tales in *The Alhambra* are architectural descriptions of Moorish Spain, and Irving's purpose—"to revive the traces of grace and beauty fast fading from its walls; to record the regal and chivalrous traditions . . . and the whimsical and superstitious legends of the motley race now burrowing among its ruins"[28]—suggests Wharton's chronicles of the manners and customs of her Old New York.

The mature writer who makes up stories does not merely "revive the traces of grace and beauty" in her record of Old New York, however; like the little girl who "makes up," she needs to re-invent the past, to take control. This, as the mature writer tells it, is the way the little girl begins: in the outline of the autobiography is a reference to "My first attempt to write. . . . A story in which Mrs. Smith calls on Mrs. Brown, who says: 'If I had known you were coming I should have tidied up the drawing-room.' Rebuke from my mother: 'Drawing-rooms are *always* tidy.' Discouraged, I abandon literary career." Later in the outline, in the "making up" section (where "making up a story" has been changed to "making up"), we read: "'Mamma, will you go and amuse the little girl? I have to make up,' etc."[29] In other words, *The Alhambra,* the private room into which others could peep, signaling both a need to retreat and a need to be watched, and the manner of self-presentation—adornment, gesture, tone of voice—are all necessary conditions for fantasizing. And being watched is necessary to the creation of *illusion*: once all the cues are in place, "from those mysterious blank pages I could evoke whatever my fancy chose." The first little girl's being muffled and veiled, adorned and adorning, was discomfiting to the writer who left that static image behind; yet being fixed, as both little girls are, offers a certain amount of comfort. Silence is necessary to "making up," but complete solitude could be frightening.

The upside-down *Alhambra* appears again in the chapter called "The Secret Garden," which Wharton says she hesitates to begin on the grounds of wishing to repudiate the assumption that one's own work is of lasting interest to others. The hesitation is real enough, but the reason for it is not the one Wharton gives. Not only does the very writing of an autobiography either assume or set out to demonstrate that one's work and life are of lasting interest to others; but the real grounds for ambivalence must be, in Wharton's schema, the revelation here of the private, the imagining and writing self. What Wharton proposes now to lay bare is the connection between the world of the imagination and the dark, hidden world suggested by the strangely sexual title of this chapter describing her creative process. Finally, we are about to be admitted to the "room of the undressing," to be privy to the *real* Edith Wharton, the one offstage.

Though Wharton was a remarkable gardener, there is little of nature, rank or cultivated, in the "Secret Garden" chapter. Rather, we are invited to descend into the realm of the unconscious, with its haunting overtones of the supernatural, beginning with Wharton's likening herself to the weavers of the Gobelins tapestries who, working on the underside, find close contemplation of the finished work to have the quality of nightmare.[30] Here is the famous passage about her storytelling:

> I can only say that the process, though it takes place in some secret region on the sheer edge of consciousness, is always illuminated by the full light of my critical attention. What happens there is as real and as tangible as my encounters with my friends and neighbours, often more so, though on an entirely different plane. It produces in me a great emotional excitement, quite unrelated to the joy or sorrow caused by real happenings, but as intense, and with as great an appearance of reality; and my two lives, divided between these equally real yet totally unrelated worlds, have gone on thus, side by side, equally absorbing, but wholly isolated from each other, ever since in my infancy I "read stories" aloud to myself out of Washington Irving's "Alhambra," which I generally held upside down.[31]

Two things are important about this passage. One is how explicit an example it is of Wharton's process in the autobiography: she offers us the word "secret" and takes us to the "sheer edge of consciousness," promising to reveal what lies beyond, or underneath, tantalizing the aroused and curious reader. Then she leads us away, defining this secret region by its opposite, the "real" world of friends and neighbors, which goes on, side by side, with the other, finally diverting our attention once again with the picture of the precocious little girl. The other thing any reader of Wharton must notice is how closely this passage resembles her fictional descriptions of characters with secret places, how the "matrix of fabulation"—the core of the imaginative process—is the same in autobiography and in fiction. Wharton here is but another of her fictional heroes—her male self, perhaps: Ralph Marvell in *The Custom of the Country*, with his "secret, inaccessible, mysterious" sea-cave, the metaphor for his inner world protected by a "secret curtain," where he came and went with the "joy of furtive possession";[32] Newland Archer in *The Age of Innocence*, with a kind of sanctuary within himself, "the scene of his real life, of . . . the ideas and feelings which nourished him, his judgments and his visions";[33] Vance Weston in *Hudson River Bracketed*, with his "secret doors" opening on to the deepest part of him, where he became "a child let loose in an unknown garden," and created the world of "his inner stage [where] one by one his characters came on, first faintly outlined, then more clearly, at last in full illumination" in "that one small luminous space."[34] All of these characters manifest the same ambivalence toward these secret creative spaces that Wharton conveys in the autobiography; they try to dwell in both worlds, the world of public and domestic life and the world of the secret garden. In the autobiography the reader is presented always with two worlds, two identities; the "secret garden" exists, but our entrance to it is blocked by the re-invoking of the precocious, prepubescent child.

In the first, unpublished version of the autobiography, the reader comes closer to the underside of the tapestry, yet even here nightmare becomes enchantment, and sensuous rapture is transmuted into myth: "Nothing compared to the sensuous rapture produced by the sound and sight of . . . words. . . . They were visible, almost tangible presences. . . . Like the Erlkönig's daughters, they sang to me so bewitchingly that they almost lured me from the wholesome noonday air of childhood into some strange supernatural region where the normal pleasures of my age seemed as insipid as the fruits of the earth to Persephone after she had eaten of the pomegranate seed."[35] The linking of something unwholesome in the strange supernatural region of darkness where words were heard and seen and felt—and made up—with creativity is deliberate, for the very dedication of the published autobiography, *A Backward Glance*, will be "to the Friends who every year on All Souls' Night come and sit with me by the fire."

"All Souls'," which refers to the night when the dead can walk, is also the title of Wharton's last published story. The subject of this story is silence and solitude, and its protagonist is the mistress of a large country house who lives alone, like Wharton in her old age, dependent on her servants. On All Souls' Eve, she takes a bad fall on her doorstep just as she meets a strange, witch-like old woman, and during the terrible night that ensues, she endures total and painful isolation in her mysteriously deserted house, meeting with only a continuously falling blanket of snow, numbing cold and unbroken silence. The narrator of the story, like the narrator of *Ethan Frome*, imagines what it *must have been like* to experience such total and terrifying solitude, something that must have been very much on Wharton's mind at the end of her life. The characters who people the pages of *A Backward Glance* are all, save herself, dead people, and she is very literally calling them back for a visit, for a last performance, where she, as scriptwriter and director, is in complete control.

The more closely one reads the autobiography, the more convinced one becomes that there is *something that is not there*, "something" that eludes the reader. Wharton suggests in this chapter that the process of creativity *is*, for her, a ghost story: the apprehension of a ghost takes place "in the warm darkness of the prenatal fluid far below our conscious reason," and the cardinal rule of the ghost story was that "the teller . . . should be well frightened in the telling"—frightened partly by the unearthly visitations, but also by the strange and disturbing sexual innuendoes of violent, possessive, homoerotic or incestuous passion that vibrate through these tales. Her ghost stories are told by narrators who *imagine what it must have been like* to be watched in the night by a pair of horrible red eyes, for example, in "The Eyes," to experience ghostly visitations in "The Triumph of Night," to be unable to distinguish the dead from the living in "Miss Mary Pask," to be lured to the underworld in "Pomegranate Seed." Wharton means for us to understand that the narrator's and reader's trance-like state of receptivity—her ghosts need only "silence and continuity"[36]—is exactly the same as the writer's: "What I mean to try for is the observation of that strange moment when the vaguely adumbrated characters whose adventures one is preparing to record are suddenly *there*, themselves, in the flesh, in possession of one, and in command of one's voice and hand. It is there that the central mystery lies, and perhaps it is as impossible to fix in words as that other mystery of what happens in the brain at the precise moment when one falls over the edge of consciousness into sleep."[37] A character's suddenly being *there*, in possession of her—an experience of "great emotional excitement" but also a terrifying one (it was the *furious* Muse, the little girl had said)—this was also the way the writing began. This was, for Wharton, the "spectral element" in her creative life:

> Several times, in this way, a name to which I can attach no known association of ideas has forced itself upon me in a furtive shadowy way, not succeeding in making its bearer visible, yet hanging about obstinately for years in the background of my thoughts. . . . I want to try to capture . . . an impression of the elusive moment when these people who haunt my brain actually begin to speak within me with their own voices. The situating of my tale, and its descriptive and narrative portions, I am conscious of conducting, . . . but as soon as the dialogue begins, I become merely a recording instrument, and my hand never hesitates because my mind has not to choose, but only to set down what these stupid or intelligent, lethargic or passionate, people say to each other in a language, and with arguments, that appear to be all their own. . . . these people of mine, whose ultimate destiny I know so well, walk to it by ways unrevealed to me beforehand. Not only their speech, but what I might call their subsidiary action, seems to be their very own.[38]

Watching Wharton watch herself as the automatic recording device takes over, we are kept from penetrating any further into the "garden." Its "secret" becomes a tease, a coyness, a mask, a performance conducted by Wharton—who is conscious not only of conducting but of our watching her conduct. Like the little girl who needed to be watched by peeping grownups while "making up," Wharton here needs a means of reconnecting herself to the society from which she estranges herself and in which she feels estranged. The language of mysterious tongues which she says she hears and records is, of course, a *social* construct, one that comes from and enables her to return to society. As she "records" language, however, to the extent that she shapes it, she makes it up. In losing control, paradoxically, she creates another world where she is in control.

Writing begins as an antisocial act—a withdrawal from ritualized order and control into the private spaces of the "secret garden"—and implies the possibility of social reconnection on one's own terms. "Making up"—this struggle, this urge toward release, toward annihilation, this dismembering and re-membering is an other ritual, one connected in some disturbing way with the world of the supernatural. Writing, for Wharton, seems like being haunted.

In "Life and I," Wharton had described her chronic fear of "some dark undefinable menace, forever dogging my steps, lurking, & threatening," which seemed most formidable and pressing when she returned from her daily walk. It was while she waited on the step for the door to be opened—exactly at the transition point between freedom and enclosed-ness—that she could feel it "behind me, upon me & . . . was seized by a choking agony of terror."³⁹ Exactly this kind of agony is experienced by the little girl who pauses on the threshold of her father's library, averting her eyes from the scene of her first "secret ecstasy": "Whenever I try to recall my childhood it is in my father's library that it comes to life. I am squatting again on the thick Turkey rug, pulling open one after another the glass doors of the low bookcases, and dragging out book after book in a secret ecstasy of communion. . . . perhaps it was not only the 'misunder-stood' element . . . that kept me from talking of my discoveries. There was in me a secret retreat where I wished no one to intrude."⁴⁰ What is "misunderstood?" What is "secret?" It is her *discoveries*—what she "makes up." In one world she "makes up" for her father; in the other world, she "makes up" stories. To "make up" is to "make the picture prettier," to embellish—herself, her art. If she were to be intruded upon while "making up," in "secret ecstasy," she would be "misunderstood"; yet not to be intruded upon is to be left alone, outside. That paradox is the agonizing point between her two worlds.

To give oneself up to fantasy—and what else is making up?—is to surrender to *dis*order. The disorderly fantasies of the "secret garden" are private and secret—taboo, like sexual passion in Wharton's (perceived) Old New York. Wharton's biographers have noticed this connection; ac-cepting her clues as "fact," they often link two passages from the autobiog-raphy: the one where Wharton's mother, Lucretia Rhinelander Jones, discourages the budding writer's first comedy of manners with the words "drawing-rooms are always tidy," and the one describing the same Lucre-tia's refusal to give her daughter, on the eve of her marriage, any concrete information about sexual intercourse.⁴¹ Given the repressive atmosphere of Edith Wharton's world, it makes sense that her one passionate love affair was carried on in secret, and written down—not in the published autobiography but in "secret diaries." And given her social context, it is not so strange that she should consider her written-down description of sexual passion at its most disorderly *secret*, and label it "unpublishable." That this fragment from the secret garden needed to be written suggests a need to *know*, at what was for Wharton the most fundamental level, the passion central to her story: to write, to order, was first to surrender to *dis*order.

"Beatrice Palmato," as Wharton called this "unpublishable fragment," and a plot *for a ghost story*, part of a projected volume entitled "Powers of Darkness," are found together among Wharton's papers. "Beatrice Palmato," a graphically erotic description of a father and daughter engaging in oral intercourse in the (probably untidy) drawing-room, is not mentioned in the plot summary; the latter refers only to *"some hidden power* controlling her, . . . some strange initiation, some profound moral perversion." Although this "unpublishable fragment" is unique among Wharton's manuscripts, Cynthia Griffin Wolff points out a specific connection to the autobiography: the construing of Mr. Palmato's phallus as his "third hand" recalls the large, bare, warm hand of the little girl's father in *A Backward Glance*.[42] The point is not a suggestion of an illicit relationship between Wharton and her father, but rather Wharton's fascination with the idea of incest (implicit or explicit in *Summer, The Reef, Twilight Sleep* and *The Children*) as an attack on the very foundations of the social order. This attraction to disorder—"secret" in *A Backward Glance* and "unpublishable" (i.e., punishable) for the fragment—makes one wish for a fuller depiction of such passionate characters as Ellen Olenska, who commits her indiscretions "offstage." *The Age of Innocence*, however, written in the same year as "Beatrice Palmato" and also concerned with order and disorder, was so publicly acceptable that it won the Pulitzer Prize in 1920. In the published novel, though Newland Archer and Ellen Olenska flirt with the violation of social taboos, their love affair is never consummated because they are consumed with guilt;[43] in "Beatrice Palmato," the affair—not only consummated but part of an old pattern—is punished by madness and death. Since it is Wharton who created "Beatrice Palmato," she, finally, is the one in violation of societal taboos, the one who imagines both the "swooning sweetness" and the "terror [and] humiliation."[44] That the Wharton pictured in *A Backward Glance* imagined and wrote down "Beatrice Palmato" illustrates how well she could also shroud her creative process and jam the messages of its importance with counter signals.

It was in her "secret garden" that Wharton gave herself up to "reverie," that most important precondition of creativity. When philosopher Gaston Bachelard suggests that "by dreaming on childhood, we return to the lair of reveries, . . . which have opened up the world to us[, that] it is reverie which makes us the first inhabitant of the world of solitude," he means that the return, in a tranquil reverie, to "the slope of childhood solitudes" is a happy reexperiencing of freedom achieved by an imaginative return to the landscape of childhood.[45] For Wharton, however, indulgence in reverie was both necessary and painful, and indulging in reverie left one open to two risks: one was the sense that no one would understand; the other was the risk of disappearance.

Wharton offers two parables at the beginning of her chapter on "coming out" in society, two tales told by a young man whom she met at a yachting party and was never to see again—stories that seem unrelated to anything else in the chapter, or in the book, for that matter. One is a Hawthornesque tale about a young physician who dabbled in a strange experiment. He ordered his little orphan-boy assistant to watch over and stir without stopping a certain chemical mixture that was to serve for a very delicate experiment. Returning at the appointed time, the doctor finds the mixture successfully blent, but beside it, the boy dead of the poisonous fumes. The physician cannot understand why the fumes should have been poisonous, so he performs an autopsy to find out, and discovers that the boy's heart has been transformed into a mysterious jewel. He brings it to his mistress, who agrees that it is beautiful but tells her lover, "I wear no ornaments but earrings. If you want me to wear this jewel, you must get me another one just like it."

The other story is about a young man who spends a weekend at a big country house where he has never been before. He is seated at dinner next to one of the most captivating young women he has ever met, but at the end of their delightful conversation, the young lady reveals that she is a ghost—and suddenly the seat that she has occupied is empty. After dinner the hostess apologizes for putting him next to an empty chair: "We expected my dear friend Mrs. ——; but just as you arrived we had a telegram announcing her sudden death—and there was not even time to take away her seat." Without comment, then, Wharton goes on to "the regular afternoon diversion at Newport," and one wonders at the abruptness of the transition from one world to another.[46]

The fumes of creativity, as we have seen, can be poisonous, and bringing her jewels from one world to the other could be a dispiriting experience. Wharton saw her own literary success, a puzzling and embarrassing phenomenon to her old friends and family, as creating a kind of constraint that increased with the years: "None of my relations ever spoke to me of my books, either to praise or blame—they simply ignored them; and among the immense tribe of my New York cousins, though it included many with whom I was on terms of affectionate intimacy, the subject was avoided as though it were a kind of family disgrace, which might be condoned but could not be forgotten."[47]

The risk of living in the spectral world, on the other hand, carried with it the sense of the döppelganger, as Georges Gusdorf understood in his classic essay on autobiography:

> If exterior space—the space of the world—is a light, clear space where everyone's behavior, movements, and motives are quite plain on first sight, interior space is shadowy in its very essence. The subject who seizes on himself for object inverts the natural direction of attention; it appears that in acting thus he violates certain secret taboos of human nature. . . . [How] complex and agonizing [is] . . . the encounter of a man with his image. . . . The image is another "myself," a double of my being but more fragile and vulnerable, invested with a sacred character that makes it at once fascinating and frightening.

The apparition of a double is, in most folklore and myth, a death sign, Gusdorf points out.[48] One thinks of Poe's story, "The Man of the Crowd," where the narrator follows an unknown man who wanders all night in the London crowd until he loses himself altogether, becoming the other;[49] or of Hawthorne's "Wakefield," who in leaving his place for solitude risks disappearing altogether.

Edith Wharton, then, in *A Backward Glance*, fixes her image to prevent it from disappearing. Unlike her friend Henry Adams, who "never got to the point of playing the game at all; he *lost himself* in the study of it,"[50] Wharton attempts to reconcile her two lives by tacking back and forth between the private space and the public place, lingering in the ghostly reverie of the one, participating in the "ceremony" of the other.[51]

Ceremony, for Wharton, had to do with establishing a coterie of friends and a series of places of her own. As the photographs illustrating her text demonstrate, Wharton first fixes herself in the past, and then quite literally "makes it new" in the tradition of American autobiography.[52] If the American drawing-room (of New York and Newport) was a place of "exquisite discomfort," as she made clear in *The Decoration of Houses*, then The Mount, her flat on the rue de Varenne in Paris, Pavillon Colombe in St. Brice-sous-Forêt, and Sainte-Claire in Hyères were places of comfort and contentment. If at first Wharton suffered from the indifference of her family and friends—and from her own difference—recognition as a writer transformed her life: "I had made my own friends," she would write, finding that "intimacy and continuity were the first requisites of social enjoyment." From The Mount to the houses in France, small parties of congenial friends succeeded one another as her guests; her idea of "society" was "the daily companionship of the same five or six friends," a pleasure based on "continuity." These were political, literary and artistic figures—"my books were . . . [my] introduction"—Theodore Roosevelt and Henry Cabot Lodge, Paul and Minnie Bourget, Howard Sturgis, Gaillard Lapsley, Percy Lubbock, John Hugh-Smith, Robert Norton, Bernard and Mary Berenson, Royall and Elisina Tyler, and especially Walter Berry and Henry James.[53]

The presence of Henry James—"one of the great intelligences" of Wharton's life—pervades *A Backward Glance*; it surrounds the "Secret Garden" chapter, and so strongly is he felt in the book that he seems to offer Wharton the cornerstone for her own house of fiction: it is as if she stands "in a square and spacious house," with a number of possible windows, a portrait of a lady. "Place the centre of the subject in the young woman's own consciousness," James had said to himself in writing his *Portrait of a Lady*, and his Isabel Archer begins as a young woman "affront[ing her] . . . destiny."[54] The lesson of the *Portrait*, however, is what Isabel must learn from Madame Merle: "Every human being has his shell, . . . the whole envelope of circumstances. . . . One's self, one's furniture, one's garments, the books one reads, the company one keeps—these things are all expressive."[55]

This might be Edith Wharton's text—at least the one she presents in *A Backward Glance*, where the odyssey of the self must lead back into the world. Wharton made of her recorded life a work of art; as such, it is a work of pattern-making, of inclusion and omission, of selection and arrangement, a work in which the "'I' . . . half discovers, half creates itself."[56] The artist who made it was one who described "moderation, fitness, relevance" as qualities that insure permanence in art. "There is a sense in which works of art may be said to endure by virtue of that which is left out of them, and it is this 'tact of omission' that characterizes the master-hand," Wharton had written in *The Decoration of Houses*. "There is no absolute perfection, there is no communicable ideal; but much that is empiric, much that is confused and extravagant, will give way before the application of principles . . . regulated by the laws of harmony and proportion."[57] What is "left out" of *A Backward Glance* is considerable: adolescence, marriage, divorce, love affair, pain, isolation, self-doubt—all that which disturbs the image of two lives poised in perfect balance. Clearly Edith Wharton presents herself here as having surmounted and transcended the obstacles to creativity, and in so doing, as having reconciled the disturbing opposites of her life and achieved a life of harmony and proportion.

Like Henry James, Edith Wharton created her own great good place, but with the loss of one after another of her "inner circle" of friends, she was left alone, like the ghostly "Miss Mary Pask," who says to herself, "you couldn't be lonelier if you were dead." Unlike the heroine of Wharton's last story, "All Souls'," who determines never to return to the house which has been the scene of her ghostly visitations, Edith Wharton at the end of her own life sits warming her hands at the fire fed by "the dry wood of more old memories," feeling life "the saddest thing there is, next to death," and yet finding "those magical moments" which make the world "a daily miracle."[58] These words seem to call out for comfort, but how can one comfort a persona? If I have been witness only to a public performance, then I can have no conception of the private except my own construction, made from what is given and what is left out, and from my own experiences that I bring to the reading of *A Backward Glance*. Wharton's choice—a positive one—is to seize "those magical moments" and conduct now for us, her readers, one last performance: choosing actors, set, language, she can call us back to witness the presentation of a final, perfected version of her life.

Or so it would seem. Three years later, feeling like a lone survivor of another world as her death approached, separated from "the era of the New Deal" by "mountains of wreckage," "new Babels or new havoc," she would begin again with greater urgency. The purpose now becomes not only to justify, but to reconstruct the "habits, habitudes" of a vanished life. This last piece, never completed, was to be her monument to her age, one in which, monotonous as it was, the imagination could flourish. She speaks to us almost as one of her own ghostly characters, from beyond the grave; her voice comes to us as from one already embarked on that last voyage: "It is such bits of vanished life that I should like to gather up now, & make into a little memorial like the boxes adorned with exotic shells that sailors used to fabricate in the long leisure between their voyages. That the shells will be very small, & the box when made a mere joke of a thing, (unless one puts one's ear to the shells—& how many will?) is what I should like to forestall my critics [from saying] by mentioning that I have already foreseen."[59] It is as if she is saying, I have already lived through the passing of my age; I foresee now my own death, but lest I be eclipsed, here is my memorial, fashioned as a monument to the historical importance of the age I represented. And so you do not forget, I will re-present it to you one more time. And she does, setting the stage, setting in motion once again the processing of Old New Yorkers, prominent among them the little girl with the vivid imagination who will re-create them (not always to their liking) and in so doing immortalize them—and herself.

CHAPTER 6

The Figure in the Landscape: "Winter" and "Summer"

This wielding of the unreal trowel.
—*Walter Scott's Diary* (December 26, 1825)

House and garden must be studied in relation to each other, Wharton insisted as early as 1904, and both must be considered as part of the enclosing landscape. The great architects of the Italian Renaissance, she wrote in *Italian Villas and Their Gardens*, successfully fused art and nature by adapting the architectural lines of the garden to the house it adjoined, to the requirements of the inmates of the house and to the surrounding landscape. As in *The Decoration of Houses*, it was the "harmony of design" that impressed her most about the Italian garden: "by *thinking away* the flowers, the sunlight, the rich tinting of time," the "accessories of the fundamental plan," one becomes aware that "the inherent beauty of the garden lies in the grouping of its parts—in the converging lines of its long ilex-walks, the alternation of sunny open spaces with cool woodland shade, the proportion between terrace and bowling-green, or between the height of a wall and the width of a path, . . . the distribution of shade and sunlight, of straight lines of masonry and rippled lines of foliage, . . . [of] the relation of . . . [the] whole composition to the scene about it." It is the *principles* of these great gardens that one should extract for application at home, Wharton maintained. The old Italian garden was not meant to be translated, but to be lived in. Pieces of it cannot be transplanted; however, it is possible to create "*a garden as well adapted to its surroundings as were the models which inspired it*" by adhering to the principles of the Italian garden: "grounds . . . as carefully and conveniently planned as the house,

Parterres on Terrace, Villa Belrespiro (Pamphily-Doria), Rome. (Edith Wharton, *Italian Villas and Their Gardens*, 1904; courtesy, Da Capo Press)

with broad paths (in which two or more could go abreast) leading from one division to another, . . . clipped into shape to effect a transition between the straight lines of masonry and the untrimmed growth of the woodland to which they led, . . . each step away from architecture . . . [being] a nearer approach to nature."[1]

Neither "natural" nor timeless, in fact, the plans for the gardens Wharton admired represent the same kind of restructuring of exterior space that we have already seen in interiors: in layout, size, relationship to surroundings and emphasis on the *visual* experience, the ornamental or pleasure garden represented a model of a spacious, rational and human world—"order given visible form."[2] This princely garden, as Bacon called it, regardless of its location, belonged to the city. Designed as a *spectacle* of spatial harmony and order, with its emphasis on symmetry, correct proportion and a pleasing relationship among the parts, it was "a space created by urban tastes and intellect," J. B. Jackson argues, which flourished whenever and wherever cities were powerful and rich. Where previously the garden had sought isolation from its surroundings, in the seventeenth century the villa, as Wharton noted, became the prominent element in the layout and determined the garden's location, so that terraces and avenues served visually to prolong the formal interior and also to dominate the landscape by great avenues and vistas in the same way as the axis came to symbolize the classical city. Any spatial organization as self-conscious and calculated as the seventeenth-century pleasure garden inevitably raises the question of what group it is intended for, Jackson suggests. It was the scene of "mock tournaments, masquerades, banquets, the dramatization of myths and legends, farcical imitations of pleasant life, . . . masques, . . . a background for some dramatic performance, some ballet or *tableau vi-vant*"—of Lily Bart's posing as the lady in the garden. Indeed, as Wharton's word *scene* suggests, the pleasure garden was "essentially an artificial environment designed to give form and place and visibility to the actions of a particular group of people, . . . [establishing] a new relationship between theater and actors, and eventually between the city and its inhabitants."[3]

What this classical garden replaced was a space given over to delight in the physical and symbolic—trees and vegetables, hundreds of varieties of herbs with strong odors like lavender, marjoram, thyme and sage. "The pure flower-garden, the garden of absolute pleasure, the garden altogether divided from utility, is a very late fancy of the human mind," Geoffrey Grigson writes. "In our own language a garden is first an enclosure, a garth, a yard (as we still say in vine*yard*) in which plants were grown—plants to eat, plants to dose oneself with, plants magically useful, even as well plants to delight by their inflorescence."[4] Taste and smell were reliable guides to the uses of plants, but each plant had as well external characteristics—its sign, its signature—corresponding to its inner qualities. Herbs thus provided the garden with fragrance and with a familiar set of symbols that were part of its design.[5] Indifferent to "the view," the sixteenth-century gardens were protected from contact with the wider, undisciplined landscape by a wall or a hedge of trees. Few complemented the spatial organization of the house; usually they were "divided into distinct, independent rectangles, each of which contained a different composition of fruit trees, flowers, herbs, vegetables or symbolical devices. The visitor was confronted with a series of surprises, of separate divisions lacking any overall unity or even a central axis." Such a garden, Jackson argues, requires of us that we learn how to read and interpret its design and contents, that we be "initiates and believers, not mere spectators."[6] By their incomprehensibility—to outsiders—these become *secret* gardens, little hieroglyphic worlds.[7]

The belief in the symbolic and healing properties of herbs was kept alive after the mid-seventeenth century among peasants, foresters, hermits and village healers; particularly in the New World the belief survived that health is to be had by living close to untrammeled nature. For the most part, however, from the mid-seventeenth century on, plants became scientifically classified and catalogs for gardens appeared contemporaneously with pattern books for houses, "as if plants were acquiring a two-dimensional visibility before being experienced as living forms." A flood of such books appeared describing and picturing plants as *ornaments*, offering designs for parterres—elaborate tapestry-like flowerbeds—and advice for arranging compositions of flowers, rotating them according to time of flowering, planting and caring for them. It is this concern for the visual that led to the conception of the garden as an art of views and perspectives, of broad avenues extending from castle terrace to the remotest horizon, to the design of the landscape as the theater of human interaction. What was new, Michel Foucault notes in *The Order of Things*, was not the curiosity about particular plants, but "the space in which it was possible to see them and from which it was possible to describe them." The classical garden represented "not the desire for knowledge, but a new way of connecting things both to the eye and to discourse. Serving as inspiration for the City Beautiful movement in America, this scenic environment with its emphasis on axial composition and bilateral symmetry was indeed a new way of making history."[8]

The classical conception of house, garden and landscape as expression of a particular way of ordering the structures of daily life represents a moment in time of great importance to Edith Wharton, a moment bounded on one side by unstructured, sensuous and symbolic human interactions and on the other by the chaos, fragmentation and isolation that characterize the modern period. From her attempts to impose upon the rocky and stubborn soil of New England a classical house and garden to her reestablishment of continuity and order after the War, we can trace her conscious attempt always to arrest the chaos around her by conquering, dominating, planting, cultivating space, the ground, the earth—herself not the lady in the landscape, but the gardener, the landscape architect.

Just after the War, in the spring of 1918, Wharton motored out to a suburb north of Paris with her friend Elisina Tyler to take a look at what

Pavillon Colombe, St. Brice-sous-Forêt, France. (Photographs by the author)

would become her summer and autumn home, Pavillon Colombe at St. Brice-sous-Forêt. The route was through pleasant market-gardens and acres of pear and apple orchards, Wharton would recall in *A Backward Glance*: "The orchards were just bursting into bloom, and we seemed to pass through a rosy snow-storm to reach what was soon to be my own door." Despite the dirt and squalor of the house, she fell in love with it. "At last I was to have a garden again—and a big old kitchen-garden as well, planted with ancient pear and apple trees, espaliered and in cordon, and an old pool full of fat old gold-fish; and silence and rest under big trees! . . . The little house [!] has never failed me since. As soon as I was settled in it peace and order came back into my life." The language here is an exact echo of the earlier description of Wharton's "two lives": "At last I had leisure for the two pursuits which never palled, writing and gardening; and through all the years I have gone on gardening and writing. From the day when (to the scandal of the village!) I chopped down a giant araucaria on the lawn, until this moment, I have never ceased to worry and pet and dress up and smooth down my two or three acres; and when winter comes, and rain and mud possess the Seine Valley for six months, I fly south to another garden, as stony and soilless as my northern territory is moist and deep with loam."[9] The other garden was that of Ste. Claire in Hyères, the ancient château on the French Riviera which Wharton leased in 1919 and later purchased, and where she would spend the rest of her winters and springs.

The choice of "Secret Garden" for the title of the chapter in Wharton's autobiography devoted to describing her process of writing, and of the passage from Scott for the epigraph, suggest that for Wharton gardening was yet another way of "making up."[10] Gardening and writing were ways to divide her life, like inside and outside, private and public, creative and social, home and away, winter and summer. But however she divided her lives which, she said, "went on side by side," the parts were reciprocal: winter and summer residences—New York and Newport, Paris and The Mount, Hyères and St. Brice-sous-Forêt; travel and homecoming; "making up" and making up. In the writing itself—the nightmarish ghost stories that probe the secret spaces of the unconscious and the novels of manners—there is pairing as well. In mid-October, we learn in *The House of Mirth* and *The Age of Innocence*, Fifth Avenue opens its shutters, unrolls its carpets, and hangs up its triple layer of window-curtains to announce the beginning of the winter season. In summer, New Yorkers roll up the carpets, cover the furniture and head for the country house or Newport, where the small bright lawns—turf carefully hemmed with flower borders and divided by winding paths of neatly raked gravel—become outdoor drawing-rooms. Bound by these carefully articulated spaces, Wharton's imaginative characters—Ralph Marvell, Newland Archer, Vance Weston—withdraw to secret rooms or caves, analogues of Wharton's own "secret garden" in *A Backward Glance*, where the language of gardening—"I have never ceased to worry and pet and dress up and smooth down my two or three acres," and of writing—"I shall try to depict the growth and

Château Ste. Claire, Hyères, France. (Photograph by the author)

unfolding of the plants in my secret garden, from the seed to the shrub-top—for I have no intention of magnifying my vegetation into trees!"[11]—reminds us of the reciprocity between making up, or adorning oneself, and "making up" stories. The extraordinary thing is that Wharton suggests here a mind-body fusion that she negates in the rigidly controlled structures of her houses, gardens and novels of manners. "*Secret* garden," with its connotations of incomprehensible symbols, of hieroglyphics, implies secret, blooming passion of a forbidden or illicit sort, flowers of creativity like those poisonous specimens Hawthorne cultivated in Rappaccini's garden, or like Baudelaire's *Fleurs du Mal*.

There are detailed plans for the gardens that are not secret,[12] from which we can see that Wharton conceived of these spaces, as one would expect, as a series of outdoor rooms, planned with that attention to classical harmony and balance called for in *The Decoration of Houses* and *Italian Villas and Their Gardens*. And in Wharton's correspondence we find the same meticulous attention given to the planning and "dressing up" of gardens that characterized the choosing of interior furnishings for her houses, the same careful eye for visual detail. Indeed, her correspondence

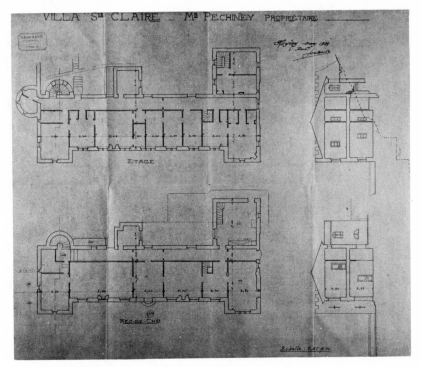

Plans for Edith Wharton's garden at Hyères by Leon David, landscape architect, 1909 (redrawn). (Courtesy, Beinecke Rare Book and Manuscript Library, Yale University)

from 1903 on reveals an increasingly thorough knowledge of things that grow in gardens, especially flowers: she studied catalogs, made lists, gave advice, sent off for and described rare specimens and even wrote articles on gardening for *Better Homes and Gardens*. From her letters, one might deduce that Wharton attended more to the deliberate choosing and placing of flowers than to choosing and shaping words and images in her fiction. Her gardens were to be perfect fusions of art and nature: wild nature in the garden is trained, pruned and structured.[13]

Like her houses, Wharton's gardens seemed to her to be extensions of her physical and spiritual self. She suffered, she wrote to her friend Sara Norton just after settling in at The Mount, from a several weeks' drought in western Massachusetts that made her garden "parched and brown, flowers & vegetables stunted, & still no promise of rain! You may fancy how our poor place looks, still in the rough, with all its bald patches

The Red Garden, viewed from the terrace at The Mount, ca. 1905. (Courtesy, Beinecke Rare Book and Manuscript Library, Yale University)

emphasized."[14] When her gardens bloomed, she, too, was in a state of well-being, like the hermit in "The Hermit and the Wild Woman" (1908) who expected to find his garden dried up after a two weeks' absence, but found instead a miracle—his plants all "fresh and glistening."[15] When her gardens suffered, as in the snowstorm of 1929 at Hyères, she wrote in her diary of the "torture" she was feeling for her "dead garden" in much the same language as she had used to describe the death of her beloved Walter Berry. To Gaillard Lapsley she wrote, "Oh, Gaillard, that my old fibres should have been so closely interwoven with all these roots and tendrils"—contracting herself that winter a severe chill and virus that nearly caused her own death.[16]

Gardening in Massachusetts seems to have been an unrewarding challenge, something like Ellen Olenska's attempts to wrest a life of richness and color from the emotionally stunted life in Old New York, or like Wharton's own descriptions of row after row of chocolate-colored brownstones and of being forced to look the other way when the one lively variation in her early life—the lady in the canary-colored carriage—crossed her path. "It used to be said that good Americans went to Paris when they died," she wrote in an article called "Gardening in France," but the saying should be qualified by adding that garden-loving Americans go to the suburbs of Paris. At any rate, she continued,

> to one who has fought for years with the ruthless gales of the Rhode Island sea-coast, and the late frosts and burning suns of the Massachusetts mountains, who has watched the mowing-down in a night of painfully nursed "colour-effects", and returned in the spring to the blackened corpses of carefully sheltered hemlock hedges and box-borders, who has learned from cruel experience the uselessness of trying to "protect" ivy, or to persuade even the tough ampelopsis to grow on sunny walls; to a gardener who has battled with such climates for twenty years, for the sake of a few brief weeks of feverish radiance, there is a foretaste of heaven in the long leisurely progression of the French summer.
>
> The mere fact that box, ivy, jasmine and climbing hybrid tea roses belong to the fundamental make-up of the least favored garden; that roses begin to bloom in June and go on till December; that nearly everything is "remontant" and has plenty of time to flower twice over; this blessed sense of the leisureliness and dependableness of the seasons in France, of the way the picture stays in its frame instead of dissolving like a fidgetty [*sic*] *tableau-vivant*, creates a sense of serenity in the mind inured to transiency and failure.[17]

It took two years of hard work, Wharton said, to smooth "the New England gardening wrinkles . . . from my brow and [restore] my confidence in the essential reasonableness of Nature." Her first task, at St. Brice, was to restore the main lines of the old garden, set the fountain playing, reestablish boundaries between the kinds of gardens—separating trees, kitchen garden, rock garden, park, terrace with its box-edged squares of turf—while uniting the whole into a little *hortus inclusus*.[18]

This is, of course, exactly the sort of enclosed space Wharton planned at The Mount: the classical house set firmly on the promontory of a rocky New England hillside, its landscape tamed into a series of formal outdoor rooms, the ground plan spreading out from the house plan to make of the whole a demonstration of ordering principles, a controlled space for gracious living. The question we might now ask—which Edith Wharton herself might have asked—is how appropriate was that house to that place; how well did Wharton's "summer drawing room"[19] suit the landscape of Lenox, Massachusetts? Henry James visited The Mount in summer. Gathering material for *The American Scene*, he tended to see all of America as a series of "scenes" and "spectacles," from the *villeggiatura* to the "landscape, which kept one in presence as of a world created, a stage set." His own role, once the "very *donnée*" of the piece was given to him—"the great adventure of a society reaching out into the apparent void for the amenities, the consummations, after having so earnestly gathered in so many of the preparations and necessities"—was to record "*that* drama," thickening the plot "from stage to stage." He must have envisioned a scene of high comedy for Edith Wharton, his "angel of devastation," for he described The Mount to Howard Sturgis as "a delicate French chateau mirrored in a Massachusetts pond (repeat not this formula,) and a monument to the almost too impeccable taste of its so accomplished mistress."[20]

In winter, when the unrelenting snow blanketed the landscape, obliterating all boundaries and forcing New Englanders back into lives behind the shuttered house-fronts of their isolated farmhouses, Wharton was in France, transferring her daily rituals—"making up" and making up—to the Faubourg St. Germain. It *amused* her to write there a tale of New England winter, she wrote to her friend Bernard Berenson, "to do that décor in the rue de Varenne."[21] The tale—called in the French translation *Hiver*—is one of numbness, deprivation, starvation, isolation unparalleled in her work; yet she would remember "the book to the making of which I brought the greatest joy and the fullest ease" as *Ethan Frome*.[22] *Summer*, Wharton's other New England tale, "known to its author and her familiars as the Hot Ethan," was also written "at a high pitch of creative joy."[23]

Ethan Frome was written when Wharton's marriage was in its final stages of dissolution and plans were under way to sell The Mount; *Summer* was written, she said, "while the rest of my being was steeped in the tragic realities of the war."[24] Like the planting of The Mount in the stern and stubborn New England soil, completing *Ethan Frome* and *Summer* seems to have given her the confident sense that she could—unlike her heroine Lily Bart, for example—structure and order experience.[25] At moments of intense chaos, in the most difficult situations, just at the time when the world around her seemed to be crumbling, Wharton seems to have felt new strength and power—in an odd way almost as if she were one of the characters in Henry James's *The Sacred Fount*, where a relationship, not unlike her own with Teddy Wharton, is established between the draining away of youth and power in one character and the concomitant increase in physical strength and mental acuity in another. From conditions of unremitting coldness and sickness and silence, from senseless suffering and ruin, Wharton could create moments of warmth and passion, and from the bare outlines of harsh givens make up stories that are the means of reestablishing communication and human interaction.

These two tales, *Ethan Frome* and *Summer*, are different from Wharton's other novels—and more like her ghost stories—in that their centers are "situation" rather than "character and manners," the two kinds of novels Wharton distinguishes in *The Writing of Fiction*. "Plot" in the novel of character and manners is "an arbitrarily imposed and rather spaciously built framework, inside of which the people concerned had room to develop their idiosyncrasies," as opposed to the novel in which "the situation, instead of being imposed from the outside, is the kernel of the tale and its only reason for being." Wharton's *Ethan Frome* and *Summer* are less like "Scott, Thackeray, Dickens [and] George Eliot" than like Hawthorne's *The Scarlet Letter*, the only great novel in English that Wharton would cite as a novel of situation.[26] Unlike her predecessors Mary E. Wilkins Freeman and Sarah Orne Jewett, who saw "the derelict mountain villages of New England . . . through . . . rose-coloured spectacles," Wharton was sure that her New England tales would displease those "who had for years sought the reflection of local life in the rose-and-lavender pages of their favourite authoresses."[27]

There were those who claimed that Wharton—"the brilliant outsider, a New York summer visitor for a mere six years"—did not know New England;[28] but Wharton insisted that after spending "ten years in the hill-region where the scene is laid, . . . I had come to know well the aspect, dialect, and mental and moral attitude of the hill-people." The colony of drunken mountain outlaws described in *Summer*, she said, was given to her in every detail by the rector of the Lenox church: "the lonely peak I have called 'the Mountain' was in reality Bear Mountain, an isolated summit not more than twelve miles from our own home. The rector had been fetched there by one of the mountain outlaws to read the Burial Service over a woman of evil reputation; and when he arrived every one in the house of mourning was drunk, and the service was performed as I have related it. . . . my friend . . . drove off alone with the outlaw—coming back with his eyes full of horror and his heart of anguish and pity."[29]

The relating of this incident does indeed link Wharton to Hawthorne and separate her from Jewett and Wilkins Freeman. Although Wharton begins by relating how she had the tale *of a past incident* from the rector "in the fashionable parish of Lenox," she has by the end of this description made the tale her own: she sees and feels, and she makes the reader see and feel, the rector's horror, anguish and pity. This is precisely what Hawthorne does in *The Scarlet Letter* when in "The Custom House" preface the narrator describes finding the fantastically embroidered scarlet letter A wrapped in a roll of foolscap on which is recorded the history of one Hester Prynne: when he places the letter A on his own breast, the tale becomes his own, a tactic Wharton would adopt for *Ethan Frome*. Wilderness for Hawthorne is wildness and outlawry, passion and horror. Similarly, Wharton's snowbound villages of western Massachusetts are "grim places, morally and physically: [where] insanity, incest and slow mental and moral starvation were hidden away behind the paintless wooden house-fronts of the long village street, or in the isolated farm-houses on the neighbouring hills; and Emily Brontë would have found as savage tragedies in our remoter valleys as on her Yorkshire moors."[30] In *Summer*, "the Mountain" is one sort of release from the starved lives behind the wooden house-fronts, but in its wildness—and in the resemblance of its name to "The Mountain" in Oliver Wendell Holmes's *Elsie Venner*, to the "Delectable Mountain" in Melville's *Pierre* and Hawthorne's "Ethan Brand," and to The Mount, Edith Wharton's summer home at Lenox—it has overtones of Wharton's "secret garden" as well.

There is neither passion nor horror in the stories of Sarah Orne Jewett and Mary E. Wilkins Freeman, but instead communities of women —women not young and beautiful, but mostly middle-aged and elderly, usually spinsters or widows, usually poor and "without prospects"—in which primary relationships are to other women. There are the two elderly sisters in Freeman's "A Mistaken Charity," one blind, the other nearly deaf, who care for each other, or the two sisters who share one best dress in "A Gala Dress." There is the amazing defiance of Sara Penn, in "The Revolt of Mother," who moves her family into the new barn her husband has built for the animals when he will not build a decent house for his family, or of Hetty Fifield in "A Church Mouse," who becomes the first woman sexton. In Jewett we have the loyalty of poor-house women to one another in "The Flight of Betsey Lane" and the centrality in their lives of conversation among elderly women in *The Country of the Pointed Firs*.

Jewett and Freeman write of a relationship to the land that is very different from either the classical harmony and balance of Wharton's estate or the wildness and horror of the Mountain. The two sisters in Freeman's "A Mistaken Charity" prefer their simple garden fare of greens and pumpkins and berries to the tidy comfort and proper nourishment of the old people's home. The young girl in "A White Heron" senses a kinship with the bird that is more important than men and money. "Poor Joanna," in *The Country of the Pointed Firs*, goes off to live by herself on an island, secure in the knowledge that the land will be good to her. Mrs. Todd, the central character in *The Country of the Pointed Firs*, cultivates a garden that predates the separation of the earth into spheres rational and wild: hers is a medieval herb garden, rife with pungent smells; she understands the secret lore of plants and uses them for healing. In fact, almost the first thing we learn about Mrs. Todd is that she "trod upon thyme," meaning both that she annihilates the division of time into pre- and post-classical, pre- and postmodern, and that she releases the odors of her garden with her body. She is at one with the earth, neither dominating it nor alienated from it.

In Hawthorne's "Ethan Brand," an old Jew appears in a mountain village with a diorama. Looking into the show-box, Ethan Brand, the returned lime-burner, is startled by the "heavy matter" he sees. But what he sees, according to the next viewer, is "nothing."[31] In Hawthorne's heavily symbolic landscapes, Ethan Brand has no place. "Oh, Mother Earth," he cries, just before taking his own life, "who art no more my Mother, . . . Oh, mankind, whose brotherhood I have cast off. . . !" Among the lonely characters of Nathaniel Hawthorne, none, perhaps, so haunts and lingers in the reader's consciousness as Ethan Brand. "The bleak and terrible loneliness in which this man had enveloped himself," as well as that of Hawthorne's Zenobia, the "tragedy-queen" of *The Blithedale Romance*, must have lingered in Edith Wharton's consciousness as she meditated on her own New England tale.[32] Both Ethan Brand and Zenobia are suicides. Wharton's Ethan Frome is a failed suicide, but as one of the village residents tells the narrator of Wharton's tale, "I don't see's there's much difference between the Fromes up at the farm and the Fromes down in the graveyard; 'cept that down there they're all quiet, and the women have got to hold their tongues."[33] Hawthorne's characters suffer the dilemma of head and heart—where Ethan Brand became a fiend "from the moment that his moral nature had ceased to keep the pace of improvement with his intellect," Zenobia, envisioning and speaking for a radical restructuring of society in which the relationships between the sexes would fundamentally be altered, suffers an unbearable wound to her heart. In separating himself from "the brotherhood of mankind," Ethan Brand will be reduced, finally, to a marble heart (a residue of which appears in the fragmentary tale told in Wharton's autobiography); "as the bright and gorgeous flower, and rich, delicious fruit of his life's labor—he had produced the Unpardonable Sin!" In defying Destiny by daring to swerve "out of the beaten track," Zenobia, as the exotic flower in her hair indicates, demonstrates a similar "pride and pomp, which had a luxuriant growth in . . . [her] character."[34] Wharton was less interested in the sinfulness than in the loneliness of such separation from humankind, on the one hand, and the masks or veils necessary to social role-playing—the name "Zenobia" was a mask in which Hawthorne's heroine appeared before the public—on the other. Coverdale, the narrator in *The Blithedale Romance*, who as his name suggests veils his own heart, seeks to learn what lies behind the masks; but like Ethan Brand, Coverdale would pry into the hearts of his fellow human beings and truly sympathize with none.

One need not linger too long on the actual correspondence between Hawthorne's and Wharton's characters. As Henry James said about the resemblance of Hawthorne's Zenobia to Margaret Fuller, there are facts of correspondence—Fuller's pride, passion, eloquence, her connection with the Transcendental community—and of "divergence from the plain and strenuous invalid" in "the beautiful and sumptuous Zenobia": it is an idle inquiry "to compare the image at all strictly with the model."[35] In other words, an author takes what she or he needs from a germ of life—or literature—and draws for the rest upon the imagination. Wharton's "germ" for Zenobia seems to have been this "plain and strenuous invalid," one, Hawthorne noted in his journal, whose "strong, heavy, unpliable, and in many respects defective and evil nature" was adorned "with a mosaic of admirable qualities."[36]

We know Zenobia, of course, through the narrator Coverdale, who would turn the whole affair—Zenobia's tragedy—into a ballad, just as we know Hester Prynne through the imagination of the narrator who finds her talisman and the bare record of her case in the attic of the Custom House. And this is the way we know Ethan Frome. In fact, we are told, there are several versions of "the Starkfield chronicle," the "deeper meaning" of which is in the gaps—the parts left to the imagination. And we as readers are invited to make up our own versions.

A female reader, for example, might make up a version different from the narrator's. He imagines Ethan as a victim of a shrewish, hypochondriac wife seven years his senior. But what was Frome's cousin like when she first came to the farm to help nurse Ethan's dying mother? For Ethan who, the narrator imagines, had lived with a deepening silence year by year and felt, once his mother had fallen ill, the loneliness of the house to be even more oppressive than that of the fields, Zenobia's volubility must have been "music in his ears" after the mortal silence of his long imprisonment:

> His mother had been a talker in her day, but after her "trouble" the sound of her voice was seldom heard, though she had not lost the power of speech. Sometimes, in the long winter evenings, when in desperation her son asked her why she didn't "say something," she would lift her finger and answer: "Because I'm listening"; and on stormy nights, when the loud wind was about the house, she would complain, if he spoke to her: "They're talking so out there that I can't hear you."

Then, she, too, fell silent, the narrator imagines. "Perhaps it was the inevitable effect of life on the farm, or perhaps, as she sometimes said, it was because Ethan 'never listened.' The charge was not wholly unfounded" (69, 72).

Whether, given her name, Zenobia has some tragedy of her own behind her, some suppressed passion buried before she married Ethan, clearly this marriage is as confining for her as for him. What must it be like to be Zenobia, a woman imprisoned on an isolated farm with only the taciturn and inarticulate Ethan for company? No wonder she is turning "queer." Men in such situations at least have contact with farm hands, other farmers, folks gathered at the post office, the stage driver; but Zenobia, when the chill and snow seals her off from all human interaction, must be driven inward in a way conducive to madness. As she feels herself shriveling up, growing more unattractive, another cousin arrives: colorful, cheerful, active, bright Mattie Silver. Her husband begins to shave daily and in many little ways to reveal that he is attracted to the younger and prettier newcomer. Then there is the "smash-up": no one knows just why Ethan and Mattie were sledding when he was supposed to be taking her to the train and picking up the new hired girl, but at any rate, there are the two injured people to care for now, and Mattie, the intruder, will be permanently paralyzed, Zenobia's burden.

This is not, of course, the story Edith Wharton's narrator makes up, but we as readers are given some license to imagine "other versions," and indeed, when *Ethan Frome* was dramatized by Owen and Donald Davis in 1936, quite a new Zenobia emerged. Leon Edel wrote to Wharton, after seeing *Ethan Frome* performed, that while the play was "beautifully mounted, winter scenes crisp and white against deep blue-night back-grounds, and interiors scrupulously conveying the atmosphere of the New England farmhouse," the principal characters "have been arbitrarily altered. Mattie Silver has turned into a giddy young girl, fluttery and insipid. Contrasted with her, Zeena emerges mature, dignified, and even sympathetic to an audience alienated by Mattie's excessive exuberance. Ethan is weak, indecisive, robbed of much of his stature and nobility." The play was, he felt, "yours and yet not yours."[37]

The given, the "situation" for any version of the tale begins with the landscape. Ethan, Zenobia, Mattie all succumb to the exigencies of the snow-bound village, where in the isolated farm-houses "insanity, incest and slow mental and moral starvation were hidden away." Like the land, Wharton said in her introduction to the tale, her characters were a series of "granite outcroppings"; the story *"contains its own form and dimensions."*[38] "It was not until I wrote 'Ethan Frome' that I suddenly felt the artisan's full control of his implements," Wharton would recall some twenty-three years after she wrote the tale. "When 'Ethan Frome' first appeared I was severely criticized by the reviewers for what was considered the clumsy structure of the tale. I had pondered long on this structure, had felt its peculiar difficulties, and possible awkwardnesses"—a set of simple and inarticulate characters, a more sophisticated "looker-on" who interprets them. "I am still sure that its structure is not its weak point."[39] If the situation—here the bleakness and privation of the New England land-scape—"seizes the characters in its steely grip," she would point out in *The Writing of Fiction*, "the central characters tend to be the least real." They are standard-bearers of the author's convictions "or the expressions of his secret inclinations. They are *his* in the sense of tending to do and say what he would do, or imagines he would do, in given circumstances, . . . mere projections of his own personality."[40]

In just this way are the lonely and inarticulate people buried alive in the snow-bound landscape bound up with the narrator of *Ethan Frome*, the more sophisticated looker-on, who is *free* to interpret and imagine. This newfound freedom, this ability to make of situations *stories*, must account for the joy and power Edith Wharton herself felt in creating *Ethan Frome*. Underneath the snow that buries the little village of Stark-field, the structure of her tale reveals, lie clues of Edith Wharton's secret garden.

As in *The Blithedale Romance* and *The Scarlet Letter*, then, as well as in ghost stories like Henry James's *The Turn of the Screw* and Edith

Wharton's "The Eyes," *Ethan Frome* is two stories, one about the narrator and one that the narrator makes up. To take first the tale made up by the narrator, the one the reader remembers: Ethan Frome, in order to support his ailing, nagging wife and her semiparalyzed cousin who lives with them, is tied to a mill and a farm from which he barely ekes out a living. He and the cousin had years before been much drawn to each other, we learn, and Zenobia, perceiving the growing attraction between Ethan and Mattie, determined to send Mattie away. In the narrator's version, Ethan dreams of fleeing with Mattie, but his financial and imaginative poverty makes freedom impossible. As he drives Mattie to the station, the pleasant thought occurs to him that they might have a farewell sled ride together. Then, at Mattie's urging, they take one more ride, this time aiming for the giant elm at the foot of the steep slope, intending, since they cannot live together, to die together. The plan miscarries: with a horrible irony, the lamed and scarred Ethan is, for the rest of his life, imprisoned with *two* dependent ailing women.

Edith Wharton wrote this part of the story several years before she completed the novella *Ethan Frome*.[41] Wishing to improve her French after moving to Paris, she wrote later in *A Backward Glance*, she engaged a young French tutor for conversations two or three times a week. The tutor, "too amiable ever to correct my spoken mistakes, . . . finally hit on the expedient of asking me to prepare an 'exercise' before each visit. The easiest thing for me was to write a story; and thus the French version of 'Ethan Frome' was begun, and carried on for a few weeks. Then the lessons were given up, and the copy-book containing my 'exercise' vanished forever. But a few years later, during one of our summer sojourns at the Mount, a distant glimpse of Bear Mountain brought Ethan back to my memory, and the following winter in Paris I wrote the tale as it now stands."[42] Several things happened in between. Wharton had a good deal of writing behind her by the time she began to revise her tale, for one thing: four novels, two novellas, four books of nonfiction, four collections of stories and two books of verse. She had met and fallen in love with Morton Fullerton, for another. By 1911 the affair was over, but this newly experienced passion would give an increased range and depth to her fiction, and her characters, from this point on, would have alternatives to entrapment, even if they did not use them or made bad use of them. Finally, Wharton had begun to read Joseph Conrad, whose narrator and his double in "The Secret Sharer" and "Heart of Darkness" would leave their mark on *Ethan Frome*.[43]

There are significant differences in the two versions of the story. In the first one, there is no narrator, no tragic accident, no "backward glance" or "making up," for the action all takes place in the space of a few days—and thus no lamed Ethan, no paralyzed Mattie; there is little detail given about the Frome house and the land seems, with its hard bright glitter, equally inaccessible and alienating, but less ominously threatening. In the earlier version, Ethan and Mattie have neither the one evening nor the sled ride together. When his wife (named Anna in the earlier version) goes away, Hart (the earlier Ethan) is afraid to be alone with Mattie: he loiters about the town instead of going home, finally warming himself up with a stiff drink. In the final scene Mattie and Hart bid each other a tearful farewell at the train station, she suicidally depressed, but forbidding Hart to do anything that would humiliate Anna or bring infamy upon herself.

In the later construction of *Ethan Frome*, a character with options is superimposed upon a character without options; this narrator comments on and interprets the story of his counterpart as Wharton did in making up the story, literally telling the tale as she wrote it: "I wrote the tale as it now stands, reading my morning's work aloud each evening to Walter Berry. . . . We talked the tale over page by page, so that its accuracy of 'atmosphere' is doubly assured."[44] Wharton's narrator, too, like the narrator of *The Scarlet Letter* in "The Custom House," is concerned with the accuracy of the atmosphere; it is in this way that the dreamworld—the place Hawthorne called "moonlight in a familiar room"—becomes real to the imagination. When the situation is real, the narrator can say: what if *I* were like Ethan Frome? I might have been like Ethan Frome. But the difference between us is that he is inarticulate, while I, in telling this story, free myself from such a trap.

That the narrator *is* Ethan Frome's counterpart is clear from the details about Ethan in the inner story which the narrator cannot have *known* in any objective sense. All that can be verified by direct observation or corroborated by reports of others—as opposed to what is "made up"—is the following: Ethan Frome at fifty-two looks like an old man; he walks with a limp, the result of a "smash-up" twenty-four years ago that has left his right side so shortened and warped that every step costs him a great effort and his forehead badly scarred with a deep red gash. He drives in every day from his farm to the post office, where the narrator sees him, and where Frome receives no communications from the outside world except the *Bettsbridge Eagle* and letters or packages addressed to his wife from patent-medicine manufacturers. The narrator learns from Harmon Gow, the stage driver, that Ethan Frome has always had to care for those around him—first his father, then his mother, then his wife—and that Ethan's "been in Starkfield too many winters. . . . Most of the smart ones get away," words that will linger in the narrator's mind. From Mrs. Hale, with whom he lodges, the narrator learns only that Mattie, before the accident, had a sweet nature and that the accident itself is, for Mrs. Hale, too terrible to talk about. Mattie Silver was Ruth Varnum's friend, before her marriage to Ned Hale, and it was to Lawyer Varnum's house that Mattie was brought after the smash-up. "If she'd ha' died, Ethan might ha' lived," she tells the narrator. From these hints, from the provocation of Mrs. Hale's silence, from his impressions of winter in Starkfield, when the village "lay under a sheet of snow perpetually renewed from the pale skies, . . . [a] mute melancholy landscape, an incarnation of . . . frozen woe, . . . a depth of moral isolation too remote for casual access," and from daily contact with Ethan Frome, the narrator pieces together his story (11, 7, 9, 14).

The narrator is an engineer, "sent up by my employers on a job connected with the big power-house at Corbury Junction, and a long-drawn carpenters' strike had so delayed the work that I found myself anchored at Starkfield—the nearest habitable spot—for the best part of the winter." He hires Ethan Frome to drive him daily to the train, and through this regular contact he learns enough to piece together his description of Frome. That Frome is a "ruin of a man" with "something bleak and unapproachable in his face" is due not only to the smash-up, the narrator decides, but to crushed hopes and a defeated sense of self. For example, when the narrator mentions his job in Florida the previous winter, Frome says that he, too, had once been "down there," and when the narrator leaves in Frome's sleigh a book that deals with new research in biochemistry, Frome begins to read it, telling the narrator that such things "used to" interest him. In the narrator's story, Frome "had always wanted to be an engineer, and to live in towns, where there were lectures and big libraries and 'fellows doing things'"; he had studied engineering at Worcester and had gone down to Florida on an engineering job before he was called back to the farm by his father's illness. Since then, "the inexorable facts [had] closed in on him like prison-wardens handcuffing a convict. There was no way out—none" (8, 3–4, 15–16, 71, 134).

One day there is a snowstorm so thick and constant that the narrator's train is blocked and Ethan Frome drives him all the way to Corbury

Junction. On the road, they pass the Frome farm, the "exanimate" saw-mill, the cluster of sheds "sagging under their white load," the orchard of "starved" trees, and a field or two, "their boundaries lost under drifts; and above the fields, huddled against the white immensities of land and sky, one of those lonely New England farm-houses that make the landscape lonelier." The narrator sees a house "unusually forlorn and stunted" be-cause it lacks what is known in New England as the "L"—that long, deep-roofed adjunct usually built at right angles to the main house and connect-ing it, by way of store-rooms and tool-house, with the wood-shed and cow barn. "Whether because of its symbolic sense," the narrator reflects, "the image it presents of a life linked with the soil, and enclosing in itself the chief sources of warmth and nourishment, or whether merely because of the consolatory thought that it enables the dwellers in that harsh cli-mate to get to their morning's work without facing the weather, it is certain that the 'L' rather than the house itself seems to be the centre, the actual hearth-stone of the New England farm." With Frome beside him, he hears the wistfulness in his companion's words and sees "in the dimin-ished dwelling the image of his own [Frome's] shrunken body" (19–21).

The house now faces an unused road. It once looked out upon an artery of connection to the world, but since the trains began running, "nobody ever comes by here to speak of," and Frome's mother, he sug-gests (like Mrs. Manstey in an earlier story), dies when she is cut off from the outside world. The sense of just how cut off becomes clear that eve-ning, when the continuing snow becomes part of the "thickening dark-ness, . . . the winter night itself descending on us layer by layer," and even the small ray of Frome's lantern is lost in this "smothering medium." Floundering through the deep drifts in the darkness, the two men at last reach Frome's place and decide to go no further for the night. Lifting his lantern inside the door, Frome reveals "a low unlit passage, at the back of which a ladder-like staircase rose into obscurity"; to the right "a line of light marked the door of the room which had sent its ray across the night," and from behind the door came the sound of a woman's voice "droning querulously." It is at this moment when the interior of Frome's house is revealed to him, the narrator says, that he "found the clue to Ethan Frome, and began to put together this vision of his story" (22, 23, 24–25).

So clearly is the house presented through the movements and ges-tures of its inhabitants that we can visualize its plan and understand the patterns of movement of the people who live there. The original house

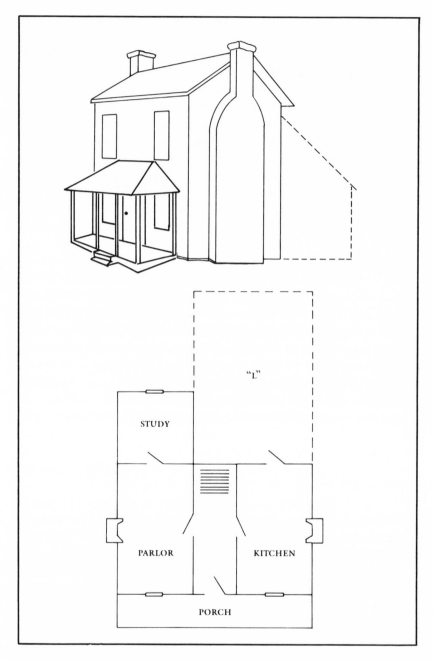

Author's conception of Ethan Frome's house, facade and plan.

plan was an image of classical harmony and balance. A typical New England hall-and-parlor house, it has a central front door that opens onto a passageway dividing the kitchen on the right from the parlor on the left. The stairs lead from the entryway to two bedrooms, one on the right and one on the left. The central floor plan promotes order in that Ethan can leave his muddy boots and raincoat in the passageway before entering the kitchen. Unlike visitors to an earlier version of a New England house who would have been ushered directly into the "hall"—the multipurpose kitchen, sleeping room, and visiting place—guests at this house must wait in the passageway to be ushered either into the kitchen or into the parlor.[45] Moreover, the front porch announces a tie to "the most considerable mansion in the village," the Hales', with its classical portico, small-paned windows through which can be seen the steeple of the Congregational church, and " 'best parlour,' with its black horse-hair and mahogany weakly illuminated by a gurgling Carcel lamp" (9–10).

The plan of the Fromes' house has, in fact, been subverted. In New England fashion, a small room, like a minister's study, has been added behind the parlor, and the now nonexistent "L" further contributed to the irregular outline of the house. The removal of the "L," however, means that the kitchen door at the back of the house is directly accessible from the outside, and it is Ethan's habit to go around to the back and enter the house in this way. His farm-hands also enter directly into the kitchen through this back door. Moreover, the kitchen is the only room in the house that is really inhabited. The Fromes are too poor to keep another fire going in the parlor, and the small room at the back, Ethan's room, is rarely used. It was to the parlor that Mattie was carried to begin her invalidism after the smash-up. The narrator must have slept in the small room behind the parlor.

The kitchen ought to be—as it is in the stories of Sarah Orne Jewett—a center of warmth, conversation, hospitality. The Frome kitchen is very cold when Ethan and the narrator enter, and not only because someone has allowed the fire to go out. It is a poor-looking place, even for that part of the country: one chair—Zenobia's—looks like a soiled relic of luxury bought at a country auction, and the rest of the furniture is of the roughest kind, "coarse," "broken," "unpainted," "meagre," like the food— the unappetizing "remains of a cold mince-pie in a battered pie-dish" (174–75). Ethan is trapped, the narrator imagines, in this house which seems an image of his own shrunken body, but which is really Zenobia's domain: he moves from her bedroom, where he lies beside her without moving, staring at the ceiling, to her kitchen, where he eats her meager portions and listens not to conversation but to querulous droning. In the narrator's version of the story there is a cat, which when Zenobia is not present sleeps in her rocking chair, but even the cat is not an image of warmth. Wharton did not like cats. ("The cat: a snake in fur," she wrote in her diary in 1924.)[46] Bound together in a proximity that does not warm, everyone in this tragic little circle is starved, cold, inarticulate and enslaved by poverty, their bodies, one another, by their inability to imagine for themselves, as the narrator can, other possibilities. Neither is redemption offered by the surrounding land: if Ethan does not go through the farm-yard—"bare's a milkpan when the cat's been round"—to get to his house, then he must go through the graveyard, passing the headstone that reads:

> SACRED TO THE MEMORY OF
> ETHAN FROME AND ENDURANCE HIS WIFE,
> WHO DWELLED TOGETHER IN PEACE
> FOR FIFTY YEARS.

And in winter, the heavy, unceasing snows threaten to obliterate not only the boundaries and identifying marks of the land, but to extinguish human life itself. The narrator's story begins, "The village lay under two feet of snow" (13, 80, 26).

At the moment that the narrator stands in the passageway of Ethan Frome's house, he begins to imagine the story of the life that goes on in the room with the light; he imagines himself as Ethan, trapped in that house, on that land. So Ethan in the beginning of the story stands in the frosty darkness outside the window of the church where animated young people are dancing. He looks in at a room that seems "to be seething in a mist of heat"; there are platters heaped with food, there is music, and the people inside are engaged in communication and contact—talking, laughing, touching, moving together to the music. Ethan walks Mattie home from the dance—they talk about the stars, about the big elm at the foot of the hill where Ned Hale and Ruth Varnum were almost killed in a sledding accident, about Mattie's plans—and when they reach the back of the house, Ethan stands looking in, this time at his wife:

> Against the dark background of the kitchen she stood up tall and angular, one hand drawing a quilted counterpane to her flat breast, while the other held a lamp. The light, on a level with her chin, drew out of the darkness her puckered throat and the projecting wrist of the hand that clutched the quilt, and deepened fantastically the hollows and prominences of her high-boned

face under its ring of crimping-pins. To Ethan, still in the rosy haze of his hour with Mattie, the sight came with the intense precision of the last dream before waking. He felt as if he had never before known what his wife looked like. [52–53]

The scene is repeated precisely when Zenobia goes to town to consult a new doctor and Ethan comes home to Mattie:

> . . . he caught a sound on the stairs and saw a line of light about the door-frame, as he had seen it the night before. So strange was the precision with which the incidents of the previous evening were repeating themselves that he half expected, when he heard the key turn, to see his wife before him on the threshold; but the door opened, and Mattie faced him.
>
> She stood just as Zeena had stood, a lifted lamp in her hand, against the black background of the kitchen. She held the light at the same level, and it drew out with the same distinctness her slim young throat and the brown wrist no bigger than a child's. Then, striking upward, it threw a lustrous fleck on her lips, edged her eyes with velvet shade, and laid a milky white-ness above the black curve of her brows. [81–82][47]

The repetition prepares us for the way, at the end of the story, Mattie will have become like Zenobia, a whining, dependent invalid, and suggests that all possibilities of escape for Ethan are delusory. His intercourse with Mattie, we learn throughout the story, is "made up of . . . inarticulate flashes" not really different from his intercourse with his wife. When he spends the night alone in his cold study, trying to imagine how he might escape with Mattie, the scene out the window that would give Vance Weston, in *Hudson River Bracketed*, the vision of his next novel—a "bit of crooked apple-bough against a little square of sky"—is for Ethan only "beauty of the night . . . poured out to mock his wretchedness" (135).[48]

In so small a space as the Fromes', patterns of human behavior become very complex. The only place for Ethan to shave, for example, is in the bedroom where Zenobia lies watching him, and it is from this unusual daily ritual that she knows he is attracted to Mattie. If you have only two dresses, one for good and one for everyday, if you have only one special dish among the common ones, then the putting on of that best dress as Zenobia does when she goes to town, the setting of the table with that special dish as Mattie does when she and Ethan have supper alone, are actions that acquire a great, even an ominous significance. If there is no garden, only barren farmland and a relationship to the land that is everything—including death—and "nothing," then keeping geraniums and hyacinths alive in winter, as Zenobia does, bids us look at her again, invites us to piece out yet another story from the gaps in this one. If there are only two chairs by the hearth to sit on and only one room to sit in, if you sit in the chair that is by custom someone else's, it is a more audacious statement than it would be in a house full of rooms and chairs. If you are "by nature grave and inarticulate," and in the dark vastness of the out-of-doors you are moved by such locutions as Mattie's description of the starry sky—"It looks just as if it was painted!"—believing, as Ethan does, that "the art of definition could go no farther, and that words had at last been found to utter his secret soul," then the lamplit room "with all its ancient implications of conformity and order," the only order you know, bids you out of habit to hold your tongue and not touch that which you have no right to touch (68, 34, 93). The "order" is, however, of that eerie sort peculiar to dreams, like the fragments of the broken pickle dish laid edge to edge on the shelf, an ominous portent of Mattie's own smash-up.

Ethan Frome affects us as readers so powerfully precisely because of this quality of nightmare.[49] Reading it again and again, knowing that the querulous droning voice we hear at the end of the narrator's introduction is that of the bright and vivacious Mattie Silver at the beginning of the story does not lessen the horror of the dream as we experience it one more time. *Ethan Frome* takes the structures of everyday life, the structures Edith Wharton knew—the carefully balanced house plan, a particular relationship between house and land mediated by some connecting extension of the house, the repeated rituals of daily living—and reduces them to their barest essence, takes from them all warmth and nourishment and possibility of human intercourse. Outside is the obliterating vastness of unbounded space; inside are the clearly marked boundaries of imprisonment.

Ethan Frome dreams, in the narrator's version, of being able to speak: during his hiatus with Mattie he feels constraint vanish, he sees her face change with each turn of their talk "like a wheat-field under a summer breeze," and becoming intoxicated with the sound of his own clumsy words, he longs to try new ways of using this "magic." Words, he senses, can overcome his imprisonment, can turn winter into summer, barrenness into a garden. The narrator, too, dreams the story of Ethan Frome. It does not come to him all at once as he stands in the dark passageway of the Frome house. The house affects him powerfully, as does the land in which he finds himself marooned for the winter. But like Wharton, who had the bones of the story several years before she was able to turn it into a successful work of fiction, the narrator must mull over the pieces, sort out the clues and dream the story for several years before he is able finally to set it down (91, 3). In the telling, he makes the tale his own; he has control—like Wharton, who experiences the relief of the dreamer awakened, the joy of learning to connect her two worlds.

In 1917, the year *Summer* was written, "I had my only real holiday," Wharton recalled, referring to a three-weeks' motor-tour of Morocco: "the brief enchantment of this journey through a country still completely untouched by foreign travel . . . was like a burst of sunlight between storm-clouds." The Moroccan trip, re-created in a volume called *In Morocco* in 1920, would also color *Summer*, "a short novel . . . as remote as possible in setting and subject from the scenes about me; and the work made my other tasks seem lighter. The tale was written at a high pitch of creative joy, but amid a thousand interruptions, and while the rest of my being was steeped in the tragic realities of the war; yet I do not remember ever visualizing with more intensity the inner scene, or the creatures peopling it."[50]

If we meditate on the sexual implications of the Great War, we must certainly decide that "it is one of those classic cases of dissonance between official, male-centered history and unofficial female history," Sandra Gilbert suggests; the events of this war had a very different meaning for men and women because the events themselves were different. As one young man at the front wrote to his fiancée about his radical alienation from the "normal" world she seemed to inhabit without him, "I feel a barbarian, a wild man of the woods [and] you seem to me rather like a character in a book or someone one has dreamt of and never seen." The phrase "a wild man of the woods" describes the way in which young men entering the polluted trenches of the War understood themselves to have been exiled from the very culture they had been deputized to defend, Gilbert argues.[51] They became increasingly alienated from their prewar selves, increasingly immured in the muck and blood of No Man's Land, while women, on the other hand, "seemed to become . . . ever more powerful. As nurses, as mistresses, as munitions workers, bus drivers, or soldiers in the 'land army,' even as wives and mothers, these formerly subservient creatures began to loom malevolently larger." As Nina Macdonald's verse put it, "Girls are doing things / They've never done before. . . . All the world is topsy-turvy / Since the War began."[52]

Edith Wharton observed that "many women with whom I was in contact during the war had obviously found their vocation in nursing the wounded"—like Zenobia Frome, who takes strength from others' sickness. "The call on their co-operation had developed unexpected aptitudes which, in some cases, turned them forever from a life of discontented idling, and made them into happy people."[53] She herself gave most of her energy during this time to war relief activities: she started a workroom for Parisian seamstresses, paying and feeding them to make garments and linens for hospitals and refugees; she opened three refugee hostels, one with a restaurant, free clinic and dispensary; following the German devastation of Belgium she opened five Children of Flanders houses, to which nuns and old people were also admitted, and where the older girls were taught lace-making so that they could become self-sufficient.[54]

Reversals in this "topsy-turvy" world fostered the formation of a metaphorical country like the queendom Charlotte Perkins Gilman called *Herland*, and the exhilaration of that state is dramatically rendered in wartime stories by women, Gilbert argues. These artists covertly or overtly celebrated a release of female desires; they "recorded drastic (re)visions of society that were . . . inspired by the revolutionary state in which they were living."[55] Wharton's literary response to the War was not, like Gilman's *Herland*, however, to envision alternative worlds without men, although as we have seen in *The Age of Innocence*, she believed the bonding of women in an earlier age to be the foundation of order and stability. In *Summer*, as in the fragmentary "Beatrice Palmato," she explored a "topsy-turvy" world in which harmony and balance, love and ritual have become eclipsed by chaos and destruction. It was not the War that created Wharton's interest in disorder, though certainly her response to disorder was heightened by the War. Antisocial impulses recur in her work from "The Valley of Childish Things" (1895) to *A Backward Glance* (1937), most explicitly in such pieces as "What the Hermits Saw" in *Italian Backgrounds* (1905), "The Hermit and the Wild Woman" (1908) and "Ogrin the Hermit" (1909). That she had a (hidden and suppressed) side to her of the "wild woman of the woods" is clear from her explorations of the underworld in the ghost stories written throughout her long career, in poems like "Pomegranate Seed," in stories like "Pomegranate Seed" and "The Lamp of Psyche." Like "Beatrice Palmato,"[56] *Summer* is an inversion of the Demeter-Persephone myth,[57] inverted, perhaps, because in 1917 there seemed to be no escape from the nightmare of a war that shattered all structures of civilization. Lawyer Royall's trip up the Mountain to rescue the baby daughter of a drunken convict and rear her like a Christian was, from his description, like a journey to the underworld; the baby's half-human, dying mother had been glad enough, he says, to let her go. Like similarly proper men in Henry James's *Watch and Ward* and *The Awkward Age*, however, Mr. Royall's feelings toward his adoptive daughter have been more Hadean than fatherly; he has been determined to have her, from the night he attempts to force his way into her room to the autumn day when he makes his second trip up the Mountain, rescuing a dazed and broken-hearted Charity by marrying her. As in "Beatrice Palmato," the "topsy-turvy" world not only unleashes the incestuous desires of old men for young girls; it makes possible the frank exploration of "wildness" in women—a flowering of desire that may indeed be related to a new sense of self at this time.

In this "Hot Ethan," everything in the once-frozen New England village is blooming. Charity Royall, the wild woman in this novel, experiences nature in a Whitman-like way—directly and sensuously. Like Jewett's Mrs. Todd, Charity takes pleasure in the smell and feel and sound of wild herbs and flowers—"the roughness of the dry mountain grass under her palms, the smell of the thyme into which she crushed her face, the fingering of the wind in her hair and through her cotton blouse, and the creak of the larches as they swayed to it"—though she lacks Mrs. Todd's "civility." Charity likes best to lie alone on a hilltop, just for the mere pleasure of feeling the wind and of rubbing her cheeks in the grass to feel its warm currents run through her. There among "the push of myriads of sweet-fern fronds in the cracks of the stony slope below the wood, and the crowding shoots of meadowsweet and yellow flags in the pasture beyond," a great "bubbling of sap and slipping of sheaths and bursting of calyxes was carried to her on mingled currents of fragrance. Every leaf and bud and blade seemed to contribute its exhalation to the pervading sweetness in which the pungency of pine-sap prevailed over the spice of thyme and the subtle perfume of fern, and all were merged in a moist earth-smell that was like the breath of some huge sun-warmed animal."[58]

Where in *Ethan Frome* the narrator experiences the relief of the dreamer awakened, *Summer* (created, Wharton said, as an interlude between storm clouds) is structured as a bit of dreamlike evanescence between the harsher reality of two nightmares. One is the Mountain, an alluring wilderness that seems to promise freedom from the "harsh code of the village," where over a hundred people live without any of the structures of civilization—school, church, sheriff—in poverty, filth, squalor and sickness, where randomly begotten children run wild, their slovenly parents living as no animal would, spending most of their time in drunken bouts or drunken stupors. The other is the town of Nettleton, which seems to offer a similar abandon on the Fourth of July, when "the whole night broke into flower. From every point of the horizon, gold and silver arches sprang up and crossed each other, sky-orchards broke into blossom, shed their flaming petals and hung their branches with golden fruit; and all the while the air was filled with a soft supernatural hum, as though great birds were building their nests in those invisible tree-tops" (238, 147). But this magic is as transitory as fireworks; what remains is the ominous sign of the abortionist and a nightmare of glitter, of sickening sweetness, of an incomprehensible oppression of things about to start into crazy motion, a Poe-like world of

> strawberry-cake, cocoanut drops, trays of glistening molasses candy, boxes of caramels and chewing-gum, baskets of sodden strawberries, and dangling branches of bananas[,] . . . banked-up oranges and apples, spotted pears and dusty raspberries; and the air reeked with the smell of fruit and stale coffee, beer and sarsaparilla and fried potatoes. . . . the pink throats of gramophones opened their giant convolutions in a soundless chorus; . . . bicycles shining in neat ranks seemed to await the signal of an invisible starter; . . . tiers of fancy-goods in leatherette and paste and celluloid dangled their insidious graces; and . . . wax ladies in daring dresses chatted elegantly, or, with gestures intimate yet blameless, pointed to their pink corsets and transparent hosiery. . . . everything she saw seemed to glitter . . . everything seemed to pass before her in a chaos of palms and minarets, charging cavalry regiments, roaring lions, comic policemen and scowling murderers; and the crowd around her, the hundreds of hot sallow candy-munching faces . . . became part of the spectacle, and danced on the screen with the rest. [133–34, 139]

Against the lure of the Mountain and the lure of the town stands the village of North Dormer, a sort of middle ground between these two threatening spheres of chaos. The houses with their scrubbed floors and dressers full of china, their smells of yeast, coffee and soap, like the rigid village code, seem to be signs of domestic and moral order. Yet this order is as deceptive as the allure of Mountain and town: as Wharton pointed out with reference to *Ethan Frome*, New England village houses are grim, morally and physically, places of insanity, incest and slow mental and moral starvation. Mr. Royall, for example, represents order not only in his profession as a lawyer, but also in the "cold neatness" of himself and of his house. In his patriotic speech for North Dormer Home Week, we see him as the moral leader of the village. Come home for good, he urges his audience: "North Dormer is a poor little place, almost lost in a mighty landscape: perhaps, by this time, it might have been a bigger place, and more in scale with the landscape, if those who had to come back had come with that feeling in their minds—that they wanted to come back for *good*." Underneath, however, Lawyer Royall represents disorder. He has failed as a lawyer in Nettleton, and his days at home are meaningless, without occupation and, for this articulate man, without conversation. Beneath the guise of order—the wish to protect Charity from the chaos of the Mountain, to offer her a home—lurks his nightmarishly incestuous desire for her young body. We remember him, despite his considerate protectiveness at the end of the novel, confronting her on the Fourth of July in Nettleton—drunk, in the company of disreputable women, his tie undone and dangling down his rumpled shirt-front: "His face, a livid brown, with red blotches of anger and lips sunken in like an old man's, was a lamentable ruin in the searching glare. . . . He stood staring . . . and trying to master the senile quiver of his lips; then he drew himself up with the tremulous majesty of drunkenness" (85, 24, 194, 151; emphasis original).

Exactly halfway up the Mountain there *is* a middle place, one that seems to promise harmony, fulfillment, possibility:

> The little old house—its wooden walls sun-bleached to a ghostly gray— stood in an orchard above the road. The garden palings had fallen, but the broken gate dangled between its posts, and the path to the house was marked by rose-bushes run wild and hanging their small pale blossoms above the crowding grasses. Slender pilasters and an intricate fan-light framed the opening where the door had hung; and the door itself lay rotting in the grass, with an old apple-tree fallen across it.
>
> Inside, also, wind and weather had blanched everything to the same wan silvery tint; the house was as dry and pure as the interior of a long-empty shell. But it must have been exceptionally well built, for the little rooms had kept something of their human aspect: the wooden mantels with their neat classic ornaments were in place, and the corners of one ceiling retained a light film of plaster tracery. [166]

This is the love-house, the meeting place of Charity, the Mountain girl, and Lucius Harney, the young architect from the city who is exploring New England villages for old houses of architectural interest. Harney is engaged to a city woman but is drawn to Charity's youth and freshness, almost hypnotized by her wildness. Their passionate summer love affair carried on in this little house partway up the Mountain, an old tumbledown place of once classical purity in a garden now running wild, like the house itself, is as vulnerable as Charity's body and as transitory as her youth: summer, evanescent as a dream, must be followed by the chill of autumn.

Charity, the transplanted Mountain flower. Schooled in the woods and fields surrounding North Dormer, unable to read the books in the village library where she works—books that fascinate and delight Lucius Harney, like the Starkfield people in *Ethan Frome*, Charity is inarticulate; yet she has an intuitive wisdom that the more articulate people in her life lack.[59] Out of her own "lonesomeness," for example, she understands that of Mr. Royall: "He and she, face to face in that sad house, had sounded the depths of isolation; and though she felt no particular affection for him, and not the slightest gratitude, she pitied him because she was conscious that he was superior to the people about him, and that she was the only being between him and solitude." For this reason, she does not go away to school; but she also has the wisdom beyond her young years to tell him, after he has tried to force his way into her room, that she must have another woman in the house with her. It is with this intuitive wisdom that she understands the difference between herself and Harney; she is lured by his words[60]—at first the most wonderful part of his endearments—but she distrusts them, too, in a deep and undefinable way, so that marrying him does not even occur to her:

> If ever she looked ahead she felt instinctively that the gulf between them was too deep, and that the bridge their passion had flung across it was as insubstantial as a rainbow. But she seldom looked ahead; each day was so rich that it absorbed her. . . . Now her first feeling was that everything would be different, and that she herself would be a different being to Harney. Instead of remaining separate and absolute, she would be compared with other people, and unknown things would be expected of her. She was too proud to be afraid, but the freedom of her spirit drooped.

Charity's inarticulateness separates her from Lucius Harney's world, the world outside North Dormer, in exactly the same way as her learned fastidiousness separates her from the Mountain. When he leaves her and she tries to write to him, "all the words that had been waiting had vanished." She feels her own pitiful inadequacy and senses with despair that "in her inability to express herself she must give him an impression of coldness and reluctance; but she could not help it." Her very attempt to enter this world of words deprives her, she feels, of "all spontaneity of feeling," making her "passively await . . . a fate she could not avert" (25, 180, 212–13, 233, 214).

Charity's inability to enter this world of words—Wharton's salva-
tion—makes her unable to control her fate in a world that excludes her on
both sides. The Mountain is where Charity, pregnant and abandoned,
hears the funeral service read over her mother, dead before her daughter
could get back to her; the town is where the words are read that tie
Charity to Mr. Royall, after his second trip up the Mountain to claim her,
in marriage. She seems hardly to understand the words in either case:
what she hears in the one is a comforting sound, "soothing the horror,
subduing the tumult, mastering her as they mastered the drink-dazed
creatures at her back"; and in the other a "memory of Mr. Miles [the
minister], standing the night before in the desolate house of the Mountain, and reading out of the same book words that had the same dread
sound of finality" (253, 278).[61] An alien in this world of words, Charity is
trapped with Mr. Royall, in North Dormer, in silence.

Wharton posits in her novel of summer landscape impossible alternatives. The issues of social order and the wildness of individual abandon
that she explored in *The Custom of the Country*, *The Age of Innocence*,
"Beatrice Palmato," the ghost stories and *A Backward Glance* are those
Hawthorne had explored in *The Scarlet Letter*, where the forest wilderness
brings out madness in the leaders of civilization, and in "The Maypole of
Merrymount," where the freedom of revelers amounts to an abandonment
of order to sexual pleasure, an order, albeit oppressive, without which
there would *be* no society. Understanding Wharton's need to order experience, what alternatives are there for Charity once she has eaten of the
pomegranate seed but the chaos of city and Mountain or the grimness of
the little town lost in the mighty landscape? If summer unleashes wild
desire, for Wharton there was the relentless wielding of the unreal trowel,
the reestablishing of boundaries, chopping down, if necessary, the giant
tree that disturbed the harmonious symmetry of the garden, the ceaseless
worrying and petting and dressing up and smoothing down of her *hortus
inclusus*, and when winter came, the flying south to "another garden, as
stony and soilless as my northern territory is moist and deep with loam."

BOOK III
Willa Cather

*How wonderful it would be if we could throw all the furniture out of the
window; and along with it, all the meaningless reiterations concerning
physical sensations, all the tiresome old patterns, and leave the room as
bare as the stage of a Greek theatre, or as that house into which the glory
of Pentacost descended; leave the scene bare for the play of emotions, great
and little—. . . . The elder Dumas enunciated a great principle when he
said that to make a drama, a man needed one passion, and four walls.*
—Willa Cather, "The Novel Démeublé"

CHAPTER 7

Another Way of Telling

You were listening. You were in the story. You were in the words of the story-teller. You were no longer your single self; you were, thanks to the story, everyone it concerned.

—John Berger, *Another Way of Telling*

The discovery of a tower in her garden marks the beginning of the education of Maggie Verver in Henry James's *The Golden Bowl*. Maggie is no Rapunzel, trapped in her tower and waiting for some knight of deliverance; she is more like Sleeping Beauty, and the outlandish pagoda in her blooming garden a sign of her own awakened sexuality and power. This situation—a newly discovered desire for her husband—which had been occupying "the very centre of the garden of her life" had

> reared itself there like some strange tall tower of ivory, or perhaps rather some wonderful beautiful but outlandish pagoda, a structure plated with hard bright porcelain, coloured and figured and adorned at the overhanging eaves with silver bells that tinkled ever so charmingly when stirred by chance airs. She had walked round and round it—that was what she felt; she had carried on her existence in the space left her for circulation, a space that sometimes seemed ample and sometimes narrow: looking up all the while at the fair structure that spread itself so amply and rose so high, but never quite making out as yet where she might have entered had she wished. She had n't wished till now . . . though her raised eyes seemed to distinguish places that must serve from within, and especially far aloft, as apertures and outlooks, no door appeared to give access from her convenient garden level. The great decorated surface had remained consistently impenetrable and inscrutable.[1]

The "outlandishness" of the image—the exotically ornamented artifice—suggests the outlandishness of the situation: Maggie's husband,

Prince Amerigo, is the lover of her father's wife, Maggie's friend Charlotte Stant; Maggie, who despite her marriage has been unable to separate herself from the King/Daddy, completes the foursome with Adam Verver, her stepmother's husband.

Discovery of the tower, which has heretofore limited the space left Maggie for circulation—she had walked round and round it—now offers her an opportunity to take control of her own life if she can find a way to enter it, for "no door appeared to give access to her own convenient garden level." This new power must be studied, she senses, in order not to destroy what she most wants to preserve: to act out "innocence outraged and generosity betrayed" would be the wrong way; that would be to give them up—Charlotte and the Prince—a strategy "marvellously, not to be thought of." Rather, she must find a basis, not merely momentary, upon which the Prince can meet her.[2]

This image of an American princess confronting a strange tall tower of ivory is a starting point for a study of Willa Cather's imaginative structures because it is an image that recurs, vastly changed to be sure, in her fiction early and late. Cather would depart, of course, from James's baroque prose; and her own "unfurnished room" would bear little resemblance to the "coloured and figured and adorned" structure of *The Golden Bowl*. She would, however, retain James's use of the invention itself, making use of that process—*invention*—in a very specific way.

Born in Virginia, raised from her ninth year on the Nebraska prairie land, educated in classics at the University of Nebraska in Lincoln, trained as a journalist (arts critic for Nebraska and Pittsburgh newspapers, editor for *McClure's* magazine), Willa Cather came to power as a writer when "Henry James and Mrs. Wharton were our most interesting novelists, and most of the younger writers followed their manner, without having their qualifications." The drawing-room was considered "the proper setting for a novel," she would later say about her own first novel, the sort of book she thought people expected her to write, "and the only characters worth reading about were smart people or clever people."[3] Twenty years after the publication of *Alexander's Bridge*, she would describe this first novel as "a studio picture"—shallow, conventional, superficial, *invented*. Soon after the book was published, Cather went for six months to Arizona and New Mexico, and, she recalled, "the longer I stayed in a country I really did care about, and among people who were a part of the country, the more unnecessary and superficial a book like *Alexander's Bridge* seemed to me. I did no writing down there, but I recovered from the conventional editorial point of view." The next book—her "novel of the soil"—was "a story about some Scandinavians and Bohemians who had been neighbours of ours when I lived on a ranch in Nebraska, when I was eight or nine years old." Writing *O Pioneers!* (the title comes from Whitman) was a different process altogether: "Here there was no arranging or 'inventing'; everything was spontaneous and took its own place, right or wrong. This was like taking a ride through a familiar country on a horse that knew the way, on a fine morning when you felt like riding. The other was like riding in a park, with someone not altogether congenial, to whom you had to be talking all the time."[4]

The "invented" studio piece was one obstacle Cather faced just after the turn of the century as she stood, poised like Henry Adams, between two kingdoms of force, neither of which allowed her the space she needed. The other obstacle was the naturalism of Dreiser and Norris, inspired by Zola, that was, she believed, "really nothing more than lively pieces of reporting, ... [stories that] are interesting and pertinent today, but lose their point by tomorrow."[5] The horns of her dilemma, then, are the invented artifice on the one hand—the world of the arranged drawing-room as opposed to the spontaneous ride in the open air, and on the other mere photographic detail *without* selection, arrangement, invention. "Art . . . should simplify," she wrote in her own "Art of Fiction." "That, indeed, is very nearly the whole of the higher artistic process; finding what conventions of form and what detail one can do without and yet preserve the spirit of the whole—so that all one has suppressed and cut away is there to the reader's consciousness as much as if it were in type on the page."[6]

What is this credo if not "invention"? Though Cather would reject "invention" in the sense of "devising, contriving, or making up; contrivance, fabrication"—her idea of the novels of James and Wharton and of her own first novel—"invention" as "the action of coming upon or finding; . . . finding out; discovery"[7] is quite another matter, one related to the musical invention (and musical analogies in her work are frequent). In this sense, "invention" is a technique Cather would "discover" rather early in her career and perfect as her own.

A musical invention is the art of spinning something complex out of something simple (a motive) that is given, as the original term for the baroque invention, *Fortspinnung*, suggests. An invention can be spun upon a ground—a repeated bass pattern with melodies written above it; it can take the form of a puzzle, such as Bach's puzzle canons following the *Goldberg Variations*, where the annotations leave to the ingenuity of the reader (or performer) the way in which later voices imitate earlier voices, whether they are to be inverted, reversed, begun at a different pitch. In this case, the rules for the invention are hidden, but suggested by the nature of the theme and by whatever clues are given, their complexity spun out, as Thomas Dowland had stated in 1609, according to "an imaginarie rule, drawing that part of the Song which is not set downe out of that part which is set downe. Or it is a Rule, which doth wittily discover the secret of a Song."[8]

As a "ground" from which the inner harmony of a musical invention proceeds, the golden bowl in James's last completed novel offers a starting point for understanding Cather's use of invention. This golden bowl—the other source of Maggie Verver's knowledge—is actually a crystal bowl, thickly gilded and with a fatal flaw, of the sort invisible to wealthy and naive Americans searching for perfection, very like the Prince himself whom Adam Verver chose for his daughter as "a pure and perfect crystal."[9] The flawed crystal bowl is, in turn, Maggie's gift to her father. It is the very same bowl that the Prince had earlier refused, on the eve of his marriage to Maggie, as a gift from his former lover Charlotte Stant. In a futile and belated attempt to suppress the evidence this object suggests, the meddlesome Fanny Assingham, who has arranged these irregular marriages, smashes the bowl. Maggie, to begin the process of restoring order, picks up the shining pieces, but finds that she can only carry two fragments at once, for the bowl has split neatly along its crack into two nearly equal parts, detaching itself from the solid foot. Attempting to fit the pieces together, she can only hold them with her own hands or lay the almost equal parts of the vessel carefully beside their pedestal and leave them thus before her husband's eyes.

Later, in that scene Edith Wharton had called "the illuminating incident" of *The Golden Bowl*,[10] Adam Verver, Prince Amerigo, Charlotte Stant—"magnificently handsome and supremely distinguished"—play bridge with Fanny Assingham while Maggie on the terrace watches them through the tall windows as she circles the beautiful room, much as she had earlier circled the tower in her garden. Maggie understands "the sharp-edged fact of the relation of the whole group, individually and collectively, to herself—herself . . . more present to the attention of each than the next card to be played." They might have been, Maggie thinks, "figures rehearsing some play of which she herself was the author." They might have represented any mystery they would; the point being predominantly that the key to the mystery, the key that could wind and unwind it without a snap of the spring, was there in her pocket—or rather, no doubt, clasped at this crisis in her hand and pressed, as she walked back and forth, to her breast. She walked to the end and far out of the light; she returned and saw the others still where she had left them; she passed round the house and looked into the drawing-room, lighted also, but empty now, and seeming to speak the more in its own voice of all the possibilities she controlled. Spacious and splendid, like a stage again awaiting a drama, it was a scene she might people, by the press of her spring, either with serenities and dignities and decencies, or with terrors and shames and ruins, things as ugly as those formless fragments of her golden bowl she was trying so hard to pick up.[11]

Holding in her hands the fragment of the flawed and broken golden bowl, Maggie suggests the weaving and the breaking of spells; rituals and rites of passage; tolerance and clarity of vision, acceptance and reconciliation, growth and the restoration of order characteristic of fairy tale and myth. The golden bowl itself is the kind of object that interested James as the means of casting "a literary spell," of reducing one's reader to "a state of hallucination," of "springing . . . [into] fruit from his seed"—in other words, an invention.[12]

Believing in the "plastic possibility" of his text, James agreed to collaborate on photographs for the New York Edition of his collected works with Alvin Langdon Coburn—not as illustrations of the novels and tales but rather as "a separate and independent subject of publication, carrying its text in its spirit." Nothing could have amused the author more, James says in the Preface to *The Golden Bowl*, than "the opportunity of a hunt for a series of reproducible subjects—. . . mere optical symbols or echoes, expressions of no particular thing in the text, but only of the type or idea of this or that thing." James and Coburn agreed that the photographs would speak for themselves, neither commenting on the text nor commented upon—"the idea, that is, of the aspect of things or the combination of objects that might, by a latent virtue in it, speak for its connexion with something in the book, and yet at the same time speak enough for its odd or interesting self." The shop in which the golden bowl might have been found, then, which figures as the frontispiece for this novel, "was but a shop of the mind, of the author's projected world, in which objects are primarily related to each other, and therefore not 'taken from' a particular establishment anywhere, only an image distilled and intensified, as it were, from a drop of the essence."[13]

This insistence of James upon the author's "projected world" at once separates Cather from and links her to the Jamesian novel. Discussing with her friend Willa Cather the passage from *Notes on Novelists* in which James says that the originator has one law and the reporter, however philosophic, another, "so that the two laws can with no sort of harmony and congruity make one household," Elizabeth Shepley Sergeant recalls that Cather suddenly leaned over, "and this is something I remembered clearly when *My Ántonia* came into my hands, . . . set an old Sicilian apothecary jar of mine, filled with orange-brown flowers of scented stock, in the middle of a bare, round, antique table" and said:

> "I want my new heroine to be like this—like a rare object in the middle of a table, which one may examine from all sides."
> She moved the lamp so that light streamed brightly down on my Taormina jar, with its glazed orange and blue design.
> "I want her to stand out—like this—because she *is* the story."[14]

Sergeant suggests in this passage that Cather made the transition, as she had not done in her last book, *The Song of the Lark*, from *reporter* to *originator* in *My Ántonia*. Sergeant's next sentence, however—"Someone you knew in your childhood, I ventured," which Cather confirms with a nod—suggests that Cather *begins* always with the reportorial; the actual living person, object, landscape provides the motive from which the invention is spun out.

The choosing of the photographs for his New York Edition was for James, on the other hand, less a meditation upon actual objects than an act of re-vision, just as the New York Edition in itself is a re-consideration of his works—a re-reading, a re-perusal, a re-representation, the old matter there to be re-accepted, re-tasted, exquisitely re-assimilated and re-enjoyed; the re-writing was the act of seeing—or *inventing* again upon the given matter of his projected world. James was uncomfortable with the world of the actual: I have noted the way in which he made landscape into a stage set in *The American Scene*, imagining trees and rocks as furniture in a drawing-room. Yet it was the reportorial urge that took him back to America in the year in which he published *The Golden Bowl*. *The American Scene* was, he said, a "re-appropriation" of his native land. Once there, however, confronted with the force that would provide the ground for Willa Cather's first novels, he found himself, for perhaps the first time in his long career, floundering for words to describe what he experienced with all of his senses.

Approaching his subject by "circumnavigation," as was his wont,

James found the American scene which he had come to study so over-flowing with suggestion that he asked himself whether his pair of scales—so used to weighing features of the *human* scene—might not be powerless to handle so much heavier an expression of character than he had antici-pated. But even in the chaos of confusion and change, sights and sounds and smells evoke memory: "out of the slightly dim depths of which, at the turn of staircases and from the walls of communicating rooms, portraits and relics and records, faintly, quaintly aesthetic . . . and all so archaically and pathetically . . . laid traps, of a pleasantly primitive order, for memory, for sentiment, for relenting irony; gross little devices, on the part of the circumscribed past, which appealed with scarce more emphasis than so many tail-pieces of closed chapters."[15] That is to say, James tries at first to respond to the "chaos of confusion and change" by treating the things he sees as projections of his inner world in his usual way: through the study of interiors as sets (staircases, walls, rooms); through the study of objects as images (portraits, relics, records) and as keys to unlock memory and sentiment—as subjects for irony. The "fury of sound," however, leaves James staggering. And the powerlessness he feels in confronting the "dauntless power" of the American city is exactly Henry Adams's sense of confusion and despair in confronting the force of the Dynamo. "The aspect the power wears . . . is indescribable," James wrote:

> it is the power of the most extravagant of cities, rejoicing . . . in its might, its fortune, its unsurpassable conditions, and imparting to every object and element, to the motion and expression of every floating, hurrying, panting thing, to the throb of ferries and tugs, to the plash of waves and the play of winds and the glint of lights and the shrill of whistles and the quality and authority of breeze-born cries—all, practically, a diffused, wasted clamour of *detonations*. . . . The universal *applied* passion struck me as shining unprece-dentedly out of the composition; in the bigness and bravery and insolence, especially, of everything that rushed and shrieked; in the air as of a great intricate frenzied dance, half merry, half desperate, or at least half defiant, performed on the huge watery floor. This appearance of the bold lacing-together, across the waters, of the scattered members of the monstrous organism—lacing as by the ceaseless play of an enormous system of steam-shuttles or electric bobbins (I scarce know what to call them), commensu-rate in form with their infinite work—does perhaps more than anything else to give the pitch of the vision of energy. One has the sense that the monster grows and grows, flinging abroad its loose limbs even as some unmannered young giant at his "larks," and that the binding stitches must for ever fly further and faster and draw harder; the future complexity of the web, all under the sky and over the sea, becoming thus that of some colossal set of clock-works, some steel-souled machine-room of brandished arms and ham-

mering fists and opening and closing jaws. . . . In the light of this apprehension indeed the breezy brightness of the Bay puts on the semblance of the vast white page that awaits beyond any other perhaps the black overscoring of science.[16]

The "monstrous organism" that rises out of the composition and so assaults James's sensibilities is John Augustus Roebling's Brooklyn Bridge: an ingenious network of wire cables, anchored on shore and passing over towers made of Maine granite, from which a roadway is suspended; a system of transportation linking the city (Manhattan) to the country (Brooklyn); a news item of interest to reporters of the 1880s; a subject for *invention* in the paintings of Joseph Stella, the poetry of Hart Crane, the photographs of Walker Evans in the first decades of the twentieth century. James might have seen in this "composition" the construct that gave outward form to his own great theme: the bridging of two distinct realities, the simple irreducible unity beneath the merciless shrieking clamor. Confronted with the tremendous force of this artifact, however, he is rendered not exactly inarticulate, but insensible: he can neither report nor originate. "I scarce know what to call" the enormously complex structure, he says, perceiving, as in Adams's alien kingdom of force, only "the black overscoring of science."

"Workmen, work, and tools, words and things . . . are all emblems," Emerson wrote in "The Poet," maintaining that most of us are so "infatuated with the economical uses of things, we do not know that they are thoughts," whereas the poet, "by an ulterior intellectual perception, gives them a power which makes their old use forgotten, and puts eyes and a tongue into every dumb and inanimate object."[17] The understanding of the made object as both thing and thought—a process at which both Henry James and Edith Wharton were expert so long as the context for understanding the "thing" was an intricately appointed social milieu—was Willa Cather's starting point. Cather imagines the artifact in the way anthropologist Robert Plant Armstrong suggests, as "an affecting presence, the perpetual, mythic enactment of a culture's essential structure."[18]

The bridge, in *Alexander's Bridge*, is a "thing." The report of the collapse of the long cantilever bridge under construction over the St. Lawrence River in Quebec appeared in the *New York Times* on August 30, 1907. Half of it, according to the *Times* article, "crumpled up and dropped into the water." The men at work on the span when the "grinding sound from the bridge at midstream" was heard rushed shoreward, but the distance was too great: "the fallen section of the bridge dragged others after it, the snapping girders and cables booming like a crash of artillery," trapping men who were hurt in the wreckage near the shore and killing more than eighty, among them the chief engineer, who had gone out on the bridge just before it collapsed.[19] The entire construction of the Quebec bridge had been hampered by faulty estimates and insufficient funds, later accounts reported, and the warning of imminent danger reached the engineer too late. All of these physical, concrete details become part of *Alexander's Bridge*, but the bridge in the novel is a "thought" as well as a "thing," or as Alan Trachtenberg says of Roebling's Brooklyn Bridge, not only a fact but a symbol—a construct with specific and powerful connotations in the collective American imagination.[20]

To begin with, the *presence* of Alexander's bridge is its great force: the most important piece of bridge-building going on in the world, the Moorlock bridge is a test, "a spectacular undertaking by reason of its very size," the longest cantilever in existence. Alexander himself is a veritable "Nestor *de pontibus*" (the wise man of bridges); he has, for example, been called to Japan at the emperor's request to institute reforms throughout the islands, not only in the practice of bridge-building but in drainage and road-making,[21] thus like the engineers who had built the Pacific Railroad, the Atlantic Cable and the Suez Canal in Whitman's "Passage to India," fulfilling the great mission of history:

> Lo, soul, seest thou not God's purpose from the first?
> The earth to be spann'd, connected by network . . .
> The lands to be welded together.[22]

For Whitman "India" was a form of consciousness, an idea of union: "Nature and Man shall be disjoin'd and diffused no more." But what Whitman failed to perceive was the basic conflict between two ways of life implicit in the massive transformation he proposed and men like Bartley Alexander carried out. The extension of such a vision of history had been spelled out by Thomas Ewbank, commissioner of patents, in his report to Congress in 1849. Man's work will not be finished, he said, until "the planet is wholly changed from its natural wilderness . . . into a fit theatre for cultivated intelligences." A steamer, according to Ewbank, was a mightier epic than the *Iliad*, and "a lever, hammer, pulley, wedge, and screw, are actual representations of great natural truth." Engineers and inventors held "the future destinies of the planet in their hands."[23]

Alexander's bridge, then, is a presence in its power to connect, to transport, to transform; his wife sees it as "the thing we all live upon, . . . the thing that takes us forward, . . . the bridge . . . into the future." But this bridge is not strong enough: because Alexander is "cramped in every way by a niggardly commission," he is forced to use lighter structural material than necessary and will produce a bridge with a fatal flaw (17, 37). It is the very flaw suggested in Whitman's "Passage to India," the flaw identified by Henry Adams and Henry James as an "abysmal fracture" between two kinds of force and suggested by the various cultural critics who described America, between the time of the Brooklyn Bridge and *Alexander's Bridge*, as divided between East and West, city and country, highbrow and lowbrow, activity and culture, nature and culture, feminine and masculine. *Alexander's Bridge* suggests that there is a disabling chasm inherent in the attempt to bridge by force past and present. The flaw is implicit in the bridge builder's very name: Alexander recalls the great conqueror (the tamer of rivers); but he also recalls Paris/Alexander in the *Iliad* who deserts his wife Oenone for Helen of Troy, an action that leads ultimately to the collapse of the Trojan empire.[24] Alexander's old teacher, Professor Wilson, who functions in *Alexander's Bridge* as a seer, has perceived this flaw from the beginning. "I always used to feel that there was a weak spot where some day strain would tell," he says to Alexander. "Even after you began to climb, I stood down in the crowd and watched you with—well, not with confidence. The more dazzling the front you presented, the higher your façade rose, the more I expected to see a big crack zigzagging from top to bottom, . . . then a crash and clouds of dust" (12).

Professor Wilson's prophecy refers only in a symbolic way to the flaw that will incurably disable the whole great span; he speaks, rather, of the disabling conflict inherent in Alexander's own nature. "No past, no future for Bartley; just the fiery moment," is the way his wife describes him: "The only moment that ever was or will be in the world!" (124, 8). She speaks of the tremendous force in him that has attracted her—this man of heroic proportions is as "hard and powerful as a catapult," full of "vigor and vehemence," with "the machinery . . . always pounding away" in his "powerfully equipped" nature—but suggests at the same time its limitation (9, 10, 13, 17). The force that exists only in the fiery moment cannot, like the physical, concrete structure, be a bridge between past and present; there is a self-consuming quality in its dynamic energy.

Where writers of one sort divide force from imagination (Hawthorne in "The Artist of the Beautiful," Wharton in *The Custom of the*

Country), others, like Cather, insist that force *is* energy and passion, that it is the essential quality of the artistic nature. Thus Alexander seems to have one of those marriages that American writers in their fiction seek, a bridge between passion and order, making possible freedom without chaos; and yet this union poses for Alexander an irresolvable conflict between instinctual and social needs. When Professor Wilson says to Alexander that he perceives a change in the engineer, one that makes him safe, he is seated comfortably in Alexander's study, a large room that looks out upon the Charles River to the Cambridge Embankment beyond. To Wilson the room is not what one might expect of an engineer's study, but rather a place where one feels at once "the harmony of beautiful things that have lived long together without obtrusions of ugliness or change. It was none of Alexander's doing, of course; those warm consonances of color had been blending and mellowing before he was born." Yet Alexander does not seem out of place there; rather, "it all seemed to glow like the inevitable background for his vigor and vehemence." The change is Winifred. It is her gracious concern for the details of domestic living that creates "a great sense of ease and harmony and comfort"; her rooms breathe "the peace of a rich and amply guarded quiet" (9–10, 5). The price for this order is the demands made on Alexander's time by boards of civic enterprise and committees of public welfare, the obligations imposed by his wife's fortune and position. Because he is expected to be interested in a great many "worthy endeavors" on her account as well as on his own, his life has become "a network of great and little details." The price of power, Alexander finds, is a kind of restraint. "Suddenly you discover that you've only been getting yourself tied up," he tells Wilson. "A million details drink you dry. Your life keeps going for things you don't want, and all the while you are being built alive into a social structure you don't care a rap about. I sometimes wonder what sort of chap I'd have been if I hadn't been this sort; I want to go and live out his potentialities, too" (37–38, 12–13). Conversely, the price of freedom from social restraints is that paid by all tragic heroes. In the great scene of disaster at the end of the novel, Alexander, with a letter of farewell to his wife in his pocket, trying to keep his head in a frenzy of falling and clutching men, imagines that his wife keeps him afloat by telling him that he can hold out a little longer. Surfacing from the depths of the river, he remembers that "there was something he wanted to tell his wife, but he could not think clearly for the roaring in his ears. Suddenly he remembered what it was. He caught his breath, and then she let him go" (125–27).

The divided self that Alexander is and tries to bridge in this novel is posed in the rather conventional terms of the hero torn between two women, one standing for freedom and the romance of youth, the other, as we have seen, for peace and order and domestic harmony—though Winifred is no "pale maiden": she is, among other things, a musical performer of "really professional" standards, one who plays with great brilliance and feeling, and whom Professor Wilson believes to be unique in her ability to support both a personal and an intellectual passion, one who is beautiful, composed, self-sufficient, and at the same time "strangely alert and vibrating" (14, 15).

Like Edith Wharton's Newland Archer, Alexander meets his lover in the mummy room of the Museum, which leads him to ponder "the lastingness of some things, or . . . the awful brevity of others." Like Archer, Alexander plays the game of walking away from the object of his desire "without turning round." He reflects, in his middle age, that "remembering Hilda as she used to be, was doubtless more satisfactory than seeing her as she must be now" (33, 35, 36). He can see himself, if he lives with her, losing what he values most, "dragging out a restless existence on the Continent—Cannes, Hyères, Algiers, Cairo—among smartly dressed, disabled men of every nationality; forever going on journeys that led nowhere; hurrying to catch trains that he might just as well miss; getting up . . . to begin a day that had no purpose and no meaning; dining late to shorten the night, sleeping late to shorten the day."[25] He finds that although the only happiness real to him comes in moments of "wild lightheartedness," he is "not a man who can live two lives. . . . Each life spoils the other" (133–34, 39, 82). As a matter of fact, *Alexander's Bridge* foreshadows the later *Age of Innocence*, though one image—where Alexander writes to Hilda that loving her makes him feel as if a second nature, one that threatens to absorb him altogether, has been grafted onto his, like "the little boy [who] drank of the prettiest brook in the forest and . . . became a stag" (102)—might have been suggested by Wharton's volume of poetry, *Artemis to Actaeon*, published in 1909.[26]

In *The Age of Innocence* Newland Archer cultivates, like Wharton herself, coexistence in two "equally real" worlds. Cather's treatment of the divided self, however, is different from Wharton's,[27] not only in the contrasting characterizations of the dilettantish Archer and the forceful Alexander, but in the way the problem of freedom—an issue for Cather herself—is posed. The writer is a young woman who grew up on the western prairies as "Willie" Cather (or "Wm. Cather, Jr.," as she signed herself),[28] a different person from the young woman who worked in the city and visited frequently the salon at 148 Charles Street in Boston.[29] And her hero Alexander's desire for the Irish actress Hilda Burgoyne—he thinks of her as a slim young boy—is, as he well recognizes, a longing for the freedom of his own vanished youth. She is attractive to him for the same reasons that Hilda Wangel in Ibsen's *The Master Builder* is attractive to a much older man: she embodies everything the engineer, in his middle age, lacks—youth, freedom, a pagan disregard for civilities. Ibsen's Hilda Wangel, a boyish young woman in hiking clothes, comes to the master builder's house to claim a promise made ten years earlier: he had built a tower on the old church in the village where she lived, had climbed to the very top to hang a wreath upon the weather vane, and that evening had kissed her—a child of twelve—and promised to build for her, when she was grown, her own castle with a tower. In the meanwhile, the master builder's success has been built upon a foundation with a crack: the burning down of his wife's property—the fire may have started from a crack in the chimney that Solness knew was there—has both claimed the lives of his children and made possible the housing development upon which his reputation rests. When Hilda comes into his life, his own new house is under construction. It must have a tower for her, she insists, and he must climb it—mortally afraid of heights though he now is—to hang the ceremonial wreath. "My castle must stand up—very high up—and free on every side," she tells him, "so I can see far—far out." It will have "a terribly high tower. And at the highest pinnacle of the tower there'll be a balcony. And out on that balcony I'll stand."

"Hilda—you're like some wild bird of the woods," Solness tells her. "You're like a dawning day. When I look at you—then it's as if I looked into the sunrise. . . . You, Hilda, are youth."

"Youth that you're so afraid of?" she asks him.

He nods, answering, "And that, deep within me, I'm so much hungering for."[30]

Cather's Hilda is an actress, a profession, Alexander imagines, that gives her freedom from ordinary social restraints: her constant slipping in and out of roles gives her a flexibility that his own constrained life, confined to one role, lacks; her seeming youth—or the remembrance of their common youth—gives back to him his own youth. Her performance as a ragged donkey-girl,[31] however, is professional, while his own performance is "foolish": night after night when he sets out to see her, he has a shadowy companion—"not little Hilda Burgoyne, . . . but some one vastly dearer to him than she had ever been—his own young self, the youth who had waited for him. . . ., had known him and come down and linked an arm in his." Not a man much given to reflection—his "dreams always took the form of definite ideas, reaching into the future"—he shares with Cather's later, most reflective of protagonists, Professor St. Peter, "a seductive excitement in renewing old experiences in imagination." This youth whom he cultivates, Alexander (like Ibsen's master builder) will learn, "was the most dangerous of companions" (40–41).

Alexander also embodies the nineteenth-century Romantic dream of freedom from social restraint, which in the early twentieth century becomes an ironic/nightmarish quest for the lost freedom of youth. Alexander at his desk in Boston, remembering himself as a little boy who would "leap from his bed each morning into the full consciousness of himself . . . , [of] Life itself," recalls the Louis Sullivan of the *Autobiography*; his reflection that "there was only one thing that had an absolute value for each individual, and it was just that original impulse, that internal heat, that feeling of one's self in one's own breast" recalls the Thoreau of *Walden*. There is something of both the Mark Twain of *Roughing It* and of Henry James's Christopher Newman in Alexander's sense of his "continuous identity" with "the boy he had been in the rough days of the old West, . . . the youth who had worked his way across the ocean on a cattleship and gone to study in Paris without a dollar in his pocket." And there is a foreshadowing of F. Scott Fitzgerald's Gatsby in Alexander's walk back to his London hotel from one of his solitary searches for Hilda and for his young self, "the red and green lights . . . blinking along the docks on the farther shore, and the soft white stars . . . shining in the wide sky above the river" (40–41).

The life Alexander leads—hardworking, controlled, serene—has "everything but energy"; the new force that overmasters him is a sullen and powerful disregard for everything but change (115). Alexander, struggling with his dual self, suggests the distinction Cather had drawn in a pair of journalistic pieces between James and Whitman, the two literary masters who at this point in her search for her own literary voice exerted some anxiety of influence. "Whitman communicates personal joy, but without order," she had written, while "James has the order of Mozart, but with him you must be content with quiet delight, and live without rapture."[32]

James's Maggie Verver, attempting to hold in her hands the three fragments of the flawed and broken golden bowl, uses what she has—her self, her own body—to bring together the disparate parts of experience and so restore order. She uses all of her self-restraint and all of her intelligence to achieve this reconciliation. The place where Henry James arrived at the end of his long career is the place where Willa Cather begins; but her perfectly balanced novel leads from the discovery of a crack to the destruction of the hero, poised, flawed and ultimately powerless, above a river—the Charles, the Thames, the Moorlock—the sound of whose rushing water "more than anything else, meant death; the wearing away of things under the impact of physical forces which men could direct but never circumvent or diminish" (117–18).

When Maggie Verver looks in upon the foursome in the drawing-room at Fawns, meditating upon a plan, the room seems to her "spacious and splendid, like a stage awaiting a drama, . . . a scene she might people, by the press of her spring." For Cather the theater becomes not the setting for social rituals that we see here and have examined in Wharton's fiction, but a metaphor for the new kingdom of force. Its footlights are a boundary line: one side is "the dead world of fact; but right beyond that line of lights are the tropics, the kingdom of the unattainable, where the grand passions die not and the great forces still work," she had written in a review of 1895.[33] Stepping across the boundary line in *Alexander's Bridge* to join forces with actress Hilda Burgoyne is for Alexander "the disaster that his old professor had forseen for him: the crack in the wall, the crash, the cloud of dust" (114).

For Cather, the building of the bridge is a necessary attempt, and its destruction is also necessary. Out of the rubble some things are saved, things that can be traced in Cather's progress as a storyteller. One is the interest in the divided self, a subject central to Cather's fiction, often presented in her early works as a conflict between woman and artist, and developed with an interest, finally, not so much in reconciliation as in creating a new context in which the force, passion and energy of the creative self can be preserved.[34] Another is the discovery that passion—the passion that tears Alexander apart as he writes to Hilda, "I used to think these four walls could stand against anything. . . . I am never at peace. I feel always on the edge of danger and change" (100–101)—is itself the core of all great art, and that art built upon passion requires not the most complex, but the most simple of structures. Her quoting of Dumas *père* in reviews between 1898 and 1901—that the great artist needs but four walls and one passion—becomes Thea's discovery in Cather's *Künstlerroman*, *The Song of the Lark*, and the core of her artistic philosophy in "The Novel Démeublé."[35] Finally, there is the use of the artifact itself.

The bridge in *Alexander's Bridge* is, as Alan Trachtenberg suggests of the bridge in Hart Crane's poem of that name, a "real factual bridge within the symbolic structure of imagined bridging, of crossing from one state of consciousness to another." Trachtenberg's contrast of Joseph Stella's paintings of the bridge that were to accompany the published text of Crane's poem with Walker Evans's photographs that were used instead suggests a means of understanding the difference between Cather's use of artifact in this early novel and the "affecting presence" that an artifact, carried successfully "from the brain to the hand," would be in her later works.[36] Stella had written in 1929 that "the verse of Walt Whitman— soaring above as a white aeroplane of Help—was leading the sails of my Art through the blue vastity of Phantasy, while the fluid telegraph wires, trembling around, as if expecting to propogate [*sic*] a new musical message, like aerial guides—leading to Immensity, were keeping me awake with an insatiable thirst for new adventures."[37] The flamboyance of the prose is present in the paintings, which prompted Stella's contemporary John Marin to make the kind of judgment that Cather had made of her *Alexander's Bridge*—that they were a kind of studio piece, having no more relation to the actual bridge "than if he had put up some street cables and things in his studio—painting a rather beautiful thing and called it the 'Bridge.'" Marin misses "the *experience* of the bridge in space" that he had tried to convey in his own *The Red Sun, Brooklyn Bridge* (1922). Stella's images elicit from the viewer "less a crossing into a new awareness than a recognizing of a familiar object transfigured into an image of heroic energies." Walker Evans's photographs, on the other hand, are supremely simple and austere: "They represent the bridge as stone and steel, as precise textures, and they site it just as precisely. . . . They are not merely recognitions of the bridge, but constructive visions, unexpected organizations of objects in space: not simply representations of Brooklyn Bridge, but also of the act of seeing, of the photographic discovery that form follows point of view. . . . Here the bridge is seen freshly, not merely looked at; it emerges, as it does in the poem, as the vision of a specific eye, as *someone's* palpable experience."[38]

Cather's bridge, appropriately enough in this first novel that was to link her to and suggest departures from the Wharton-James tradition, is both: a real, factual bridge within the symbolic structure of imagined bridging. Her hero Alexander, confronting and overmastered by the force of the new technology, builds a real structure, as different as possible from the tower in Maggie Verver's garden or from the monstrous organism of chaos that left Henry James reeling with despair, but one also different from the piece of pottery Thea Kronborg holds in her hands in *The Song of the Lark*, the pieced quilt the women make in *O Pioneers!*, Ántonia's fruit cave, or the attic sewing room in *The Professor's House*. Alexander's bridge is a familiar object transfigured into an image of heroic energies; but Alexandra, Thea and Ántonia in the next three novels are themselves earthbound and familiar centers of energy, while Professor St. Peter, the tower in his garden an image of the withdrawn and solitary individual, prefigures the reclusive mystic in *Shadows on the Rock*. The imagined bridging—the crossing from one state of consciousness to another, the act of discovery, takes place in this first novel when Alexander looks from the window of the train speeding him on his way to Moorlock on his final journey. The train passes through a gray country, the sky overhead is flushed "with a wide flood of clear color, . . . a rose-colored light over the gray rocks and hills and meadows," and under the approach of a weather-stained wooden bridge, Alexander sees

> a group of boys . . . sitting around a little fire. The smell of the wood smoke blew in at the window. Except for an old farmer, jogging along the highroad in his box-wagon, there was not another living creature to be seen. Alexander looked back wistfully at the boys, camped on the edge of a little marsh, crouching under their shelter and looking gravely at their fire. They took his mind back a long way, to a campfire on a sandbar in a Western river, and he wished he could go back and sit down with them. He could remember exactly how the world had looked then. [116]

Rereading *Alexander's Bridge* after Cather's death, her friend and companion Edith Lewis said that she found in the novel places of intensity and power, as if the author's true voice, "submerged before in conventional speech, had broken through, and were speaking in irrepressible accents of passion and authority." Lewis refers especially to this passage describing the boys around the campfire. "I recalled Vinteuil's 'little phrase' in Proust's great work," she said, "appearing and reappearing throughout the musician's compositions, until it becomes at last 'the masterpiece triumphant and complete.'" Lewis finds the "little phrase" in Cather's early story "The Enchanted Bluff," as a chapter in *My Ántonia*, "and at last . . . given its full and magnified expression in *Death Comes for the Archbishop*."[39]

Joseph Stella, *The Bridge*, 1922. (Courtesy, The Newark Museum)

Walker Evans, *Brooklyn Bridge*, 1930. (Courtesy, Arnold Crane Collection)

It is not Alexander who hears the "little phrase," but Edith Lewis—and the reader of Cather's stories in the context of her later work. Lewis makes a great deal from this fragment of a scene of some boys around a campfire; yet she is on the mark. As the "little phrase" becomes more insistent in Cather's work, as the inventions are spun out from this motive, Cather experiments with form to find the right expression for what she comes to understand as her own material. Sited precisely, the stories Willa Cather's characters tell—in front of the fire, in the kitchen, while baking, while quilting, under a tree, in the sickroom, on a journey—will come to be as precisely textured as the bridge, emerging as the vision of a specific eye, as *someone's* palpable experience.

The scene that Edith Lewis likens to Vinteuil's "little phrase" is like a fragment of a story: the group gathered around the campfire provides a context for storytelling. It is a piece of memory—for Willa Cather, as well as for Alexander, who "could remember exactly how the world had looked then." It invites the reader to listen to a tale beginning "once upon a time . . . ," a tale of faraway places, brought home by a traveler, or a tale of the past, best known by natives of a place.[40] The scene occurs in a specific time and place—that is, it is particular, fixed in history; at the same time it is universal, timeless, like memory: it defies history and the passing of time. Like a photograph, it preserves the particularity of the event recorded and at the same time elicits in the viewer or hearer a recognition of some past experience.[41]

The "little phrase" to which Lewis refers first occurs to Swann—in *Du côté de chez Swann*, published the year after *Alexander's Bridge*—as a revelation: "at a certain moment, without being able to distinguish any clear outline, or to give a name to what was pleasing him, suddenly enraptured, he had tried to grasp the phrase or harmony—he did not know which—that had just been played and that had opened and expanded his soul, as the fragrance of certain roses, wafted upon the moist air of evening, has the power of dilating one's nostrils." He finds it "entirely original, and irreducible to any other kind, . . . vanishing in an instant, . . . *sine materia*." The notes themselves vanish before the sensations awakened by the haunting phrase have developed sufficiently to escape submersion in succeeding or even simultaneous notes. In this ceaseless overlapping, "the *motifs* which from time to time emerge, barely discernible, to plunge again and disappear and drown, recognised only by the particular kind of pleasure which they instil, impossible to describe, to recollect, to name, ineffable" are pieces of memory, "facsimiles of those fugitive phrases, [that] enable us to compare and to contrast them with those that follow." Swann's memory has furnished him with

> an immediate transcript, sketchy and . . . provisional, which he had been able to glance at while the piece continued, so that, when the same impression suddenly returned, it was no longer impossible to grasp. He could picture to himself its extent, its symmetrical arrangement, its notation, its expressive value; he had before him something that was no longer pure music, but rather design, architecture, thought, and which allowed the actual music to be recalled. . . . It had at once suggested to him a world of inexpressible delights, of whose existence, before hearing it, he had never dreamed, into which he felt that nothing else could initiate him; and he had been filled with love for it, as with a new and strange desire.

Later, the little phrase eludes Swann. Although he can recall the exquisite and inexpressible pleasure of the moment when he first heard it, and can see in his mind's eye the forms it had traced, he is incapable of reproducing it, of humming it. Then one night, he hears it again, senses its approach "stealing forth . . . like a curtain of sound to veil the mystery of its incubation, . . . secret, murmuring, detached, the airy and perfumed phrase that he had loved." He learns its *name* (it comes from the *andante* of Vinteuil's sonata for piano and violin), and in naming the little phrase, he can have it to himself; he can "study its language and acquire its secret."[42]

The little phrase comes to Swann through the immediacy of hearing; that is why naming it is important to his being able to find it again and again, to learn it, to reproduce it for himself. The language of the little phrase is like the language of a story: it both speaks to his secret soul and ties him to the world, as indeed the little phrase *becomes* the story of *Swann's Way*, and Proust, who spins out the invention upon the little phrase, the storyteller.

I am suggesting that the process for Willa Cather was similar, that like Proust, like the storyteller, Cather discovered the importance of the little phrase, of memory and invention, as a key to imaginative structures, that upon hearing the little phrase, she journeys backward from the Jamesian novel, where "the chanter of the ballad . . . can never be responsible *enough*"[43] to the more primitive storytelling. A novel can be written about an Undine Spragg or a Bartley Alexander confronting the forces of the new technology with cunning or with energy, but a story is inclined to borrow from the miraculous; in fact, the art of storytelling depends to some extent on keeping a story free from explanation as one reproduces it.[44] The more the storyteller foregoes psychological explanation—the more it is simplified—the greater is the story's claim to a place in the memory of the listener; the more completely it is integrated into one's own experience, the greater is one's inclination to repeat it to someone else.[45]

The person listening to a story, unlike the solitary reader of a novel, participates in an experience that could be continued indefinitely.[46] There is even this sense of continuity and companionship in reading a story because in every true story there is a kinship with the oldest stories, with myth and fairy tale; there is memory, creating a chain of tradition that passes on a happening from generation to generation, epic remembrance that spins a web that all stories, one tying on to the next, together form in the end; and there is counsel, which teaches us "to meet the forces of the mythical world with cunning and with high spirits." Counsel depends upon the ability to be able to reach back in memory to a whole lifetime of experience—the teller's and what the teller adds from hearsay, from the experience of others.[47]

In these reflections by Paul Valéry upon the "almost mystical depth" of the silk embroideries of a woman artist, one comes close to the meaning of the story: "Light and shade form very particular systems, present very individual questions which depend upon no knowledge and are derived from no practice, but get their existence and value exclusively from a certain accord of the soul, the eye, and the hand." For the storyteller as well as the artisan, the relationship to one's material is that of a craftsperson whose task it is to fashion the raw material of experience in a solid, useful and unique way.[48]

Cather's stories are of course written down. Yet it is exactly toward this sense of the story of craft, as made object shaped by the coordination of soul, eye and hand, that she worked. There is just the hint of this conception in the early *Alexander's Bridge*, a novel carefully crafted from materials that were not her own, as she said in "My First Novels [There Were Two]," but from "situations and accents that were then generally thought to be necessary."[49] Cather had in fact described her art as "craft" as early as 1896. "It is an awful and fearsome thing, that short voyage from the brain to the hand," she wrote in a review for the *Nebraska State Journal*. "Art is not thought or emotion, but expression, expression, always expression. To keep an idea living, intact, tinged with all its original feeling, its original mood, preserving in it all the ecstasy which attended its birth, to keep it so all the way from the brain to the hand and transfer it on paper a living thing with color, odor, sound, life all in it, that is what art means, that is the greatest of all the gifts of the gods. And that is the voyage perilous, and between those two ports more has been lost than all the yawning caverns of the sea have ever swallowed."[50]

Vinteuil's "little phrase" is a series of notes in time—that is, they follow one another in a linear fashion, like history; but for Swann the sound of the little phrase stops time because, in the moment isolated, the inherently meaningless becomes filled with meaning. Since James Joyce, we have come to call these moments of revelation "epiphanies"— isolated instants in which the essential nature of something, "its soul, its whatness, leaps to us from the vestment of its appearance,"[51] recorded "with such intense precision that they . . . funnel thought through the specific into the general, concentrating tiny fleeting perceptions into large, timeless concepts."[52] Appearances, that is, take on meaning only as they are recognized. In fact, John Berger argues in *Another Way of Telling*, "appearances are so complex that only the search which is inherent in the act of looking can draw a reading out of their underlying coherence." The reading, or revelation, depends upon the search and upon the searcher with a memory of other appearances, other moments; revelation consists in *"the relation between the human capacity to perceive and the coherence of appearances."* Appearances, like oracles, depend on the quest or need of the one who listens or looks: "The one who looks is essential to the meaning found, *and yet can be surpassed by it.* And this surpassing is what is hoped for."[53]

Willa Cather's Alexander, looking from the window of his train at the group of boys around the fire, sees a scene that is past in an instant and yet triggers something in his memory. Like a photograph, what Alexander sees is an appearance both simple and complex: its simplicity is the way in which it is quoted directly, not translated; its complexity is the way in which both Alexander and the reader bring to this appearance a chain of memories. Alexander's bridge, on the other hand, while a real enough artifact, an affecting presence, is a thing translated for the reader, interpreted, imbued with symbolic meaning—the very difference between Joseph Stella's paintings and Walker Evans's photographs of Brooklyn Bridge: the one translates appearances while the other quotes directly. Cather discovers in this first novel, then, that appearances in themselves constitute a kind of language. As John Berger argues about photographs, appearances cohere—they make patterns in the context of other, recalled appearances; they suggest other appearances: appearances both distinguish and join events in that the recognition of an appearance requires the memory of other appearances.

A photograph is simpler than most memories in that its range is more limited; but thinking about the way in which both the photograph and the remembered depend upon and equally oppose the passing of time helps us to understand the relationship of memory to moments of revelation in Cather's stories. "Both the photograph and the remembered depend upon and equally oppose the passing of time," Berger writes. "Both preserve moments, and propose their own form of simultaneity, in which all their images can coexist. Both stimulate, and are stimulated by, the inter-connectedness of events. Both seek instants of revelation, for it is only such instants which give full reason to their own capacity to withstand the flow of time."[54]

Cather in her mature works will have traveled a great distance from what is only suggested in *Alexander's Bridge*. She will have abandoned translation for quotation—translation of the sort James used in *The Golden Bowl*, translation that we might now see as characteristic of the imaginative structures of Edith Wharton: secret revelations of her garden layered with interpretation, moments of epiphany controlled, if not repressed, in presentation to the reader.

In Cather's stories, tension—as in a series of photographs—will lie not so much in the mystery of the destination, the "waiting-for-the-end," but in "the mystery of the spaces between its steps towards that destination." Her stories will become *discontinuous*—separate moments, with increasingly greater spaces between them—and yet will achieve a new continuity through a tacit agreement about what is not said, about what connects the discontinuities, fused between teller and listener, neither of whom is at the center of the story, but at its periphery. At the center of the story are those whom the story is about. It is between their actions and attributes and reactions that the unstated connections are being made: "the story invests with authority its characters, its listener's past experience and its teller's words," as Berger writes; "the discontinuities of the story and the tacit agreement underlying them fuse teller, listener and protagonists into an amalgam ... which ... [is] the story's *reflecting subject.*" In other words, in uniting teller, tale and listener, the story—which creates culture by discovering and reinforcing tales to be told not only twice, but continuously—is a *process.*[55] This is Cather's great discovery in *Alexander's Bridge*: in the essence of that childhood experience lie the power and appeal, the authority of her story.

CHAPTER 8

Novel of the Soil

Painting is an essentially concrete *art and can only consist of the representation of* real and existing *things. It is a completely physical language, the words of which consist of all visible objects. . . . Imagination in art consists in knowing how to find the most complete expression of an existing thing.*

> —Gustave Courbet, *Courrier du dimanche,*
> December 25, 1861[1]

The appeal of childhood recalled is its simplicity. Safety, happiness, freedom inhere in time remembered as less complex, in spaces of vastness, unconfining, yet protective; places recalled seem havens that foster creativity. Childhood is valuable precisely because it is lost, recoverable only through memory. Thus the importance of the story, the photograph, the taste, smell or touch of an object that re-creates the sense of childhood freedom; so we value our storytellers who have the power to enclose us in that world again. While we listen, we invent a world, spinning out from what we hear more—or less—than what is given. We listen for words that soothe. We take counsel from our storytellers who give us back a time and place we thought lost.

If we hear these stories as pastoral, we should remember that although there are fortunate people whose childhoods are "lived in bubbles of light and warmth," as Yi-Fu Tuan observes in *Landscapes of Fear,* "for the generality of humankind this is unlikely to be true. The pure happiness of the young is a creed of the Romantic era, and we who are its inheritors show a natural tendency to suppress the sorrow and recall the joy as we rummage through the storehouse of memory."[2] This tendency must account for the way we continue to read—or misread—Willa Cather, as did a *Time* magazine reviewer of *A Lost Lady* (reissued in 1973 in celebration of the centennial of Cather's birth) who judged that novel "typical of the kind of prairie pastoral Cather did best."[3]

"Prairie pastoral!" Ellen Moers retorted. "*A Lost Lady* is an Electra story, raw and barbarous. Marian Forrester is a queen and a whore as well. She has betrayed the king—that traveler and conqueror of the West, the old, impotent railroad man Captain Forrester." Moers bids us consider the narrator's "pastoral" vision with ironic detachment: Niel Herbert, who poses as a disillusioned innocent, is in fact as inflamed as he is revolted by Marian Forrester's adulteries, and "as impotent in revenge as he is in lust." Mrs. Forrester is indeed the symbol of her age, Moers argues—an age when "civilized standards and aristocratic honor . . . slip . . . irrevocably into the past." She is also a great teacher—of Niel and of the reader—for she offers an education in the underpinnings of that vanishing age, bringing

> courage and beauty to her husband; romance and elegance to the magnates who stop at the Forrester house; civilization and style to the crude boys of the town; envy and drama to the women. And to Niel she brings the whole meaning of his life—too much meaning. For Niel is forced to see how it is done, this womanly mythmaking without which there would be no civilization, no "taming of the West." He sees the veils and the jewels, the rouge and the dyed hair, the brandy tippling, the teasing of little boys and old men; most of all, he sees with mingled yearning and rage the woman's fully sexual nature—"life on any terms."[4]

More is at stake here than the demystifying of childhood reveries in Cather's fiction. Moers's reading of *A Lost Lady* suggests a re-consideration of our cultural fantasies about the land and about the women and men who leave their marks upon the land, spinning their own—very different—fantasies as they move westward.

Contemporary perceptions of the American landscape as "pastoral" are rooted in a projection of male fantasies upon the land, Annette Kolodny has shown. In America—where in our descriptions of landscape from the seventeenth century on, we have taken the conventions of self-conscious (European) "literary" language for the vocabulary of everyday life—there has been a male need to experience the land as maternal because of the threatening, alien and potentially emasculating terror of the unknown: making "the new continent Woman was already to civilize it a bit, casting the stamp of human relations upon what was otherwise unknown and untamed."[5] In this American pastoral narrative, the movement back into the realm of the Mother, and then an attempted movement out of that containment in order to experience the self as independent, assertive and sexually active, is associated with violence and guilt. Yet our "most American" writers continued to embrace the myth of the eternal return, made possible by the discovery of a land unblemished and fertile upon which is projected "a residue of infantile experience in which all needs—physical, erotic, spiritual, and emotional—[can be] . . . met by an entity imaged as quintessentially female."[6] Or so critics would have us believe.

By "most American," literary and cultural critics seldom mean statistically most representative, most typical, most read, most sold, Nina Baym argues; rather, they resort to value-laden rhetoric to establish a particular version of culture, a version that embraces "their membership in the dominant middle-class white Anglo-Saxon group, and their modest alienation from it." That is, they define the boundaries of "Americanness" as containing the "contradictions" that they perceive to be the "very essence of the culture"—in other words, a "consensus criticism of the consensus" that plainly excludes many groups. And in pushing their particular version of "Americanness" to an extreme, "critics have 'deconstructed' [American fiction] by creating a tool with no particular American reference. In pursuit of the uniquely American, they have arrived at a place where Americanness has vanished into the depths of what is alleged to be the universal male psyche."[7]

In the "melodrama of beset manhood," as Baym calls the myth of "the pure American self divorced from specific social circumstances," the "deeply romantic" promise that "in this new land, untrammeled by history and social accident, a person will be able to achieve complete self-definition," woman is the entrapper and impediment. In female versions of the myth—Thea Kronborg in Cather's *The Song of the Lark*, Dorinda Oakley in Ellen Glasgow's *Barren Ground*, Anna Leath in Wharton's *The Reef*— women who, beset by the reigning male oligarchy, elect celibacy are said by our critics "to be untrue to the imperatives of their gender, which require marriage, childbearing, domesticity." Such novels are read as stories of female frustration; they are not perceived as commenting on, or containing, the essence of our culture, so we do not find them in the canon.[8]

The drama of the white male engaged in a struggle to assert his "active drive for individuation . . . against the current driving him toward maternal union"[9] is the concern not only of those whom critics call "our most respected writers"—Cooper, Thoreau, Melville, Faulkner, Frost and Hemingway,[10] and not only of literary critics, but of historians who perceive the schemas of men as characteristic of humankind.

The central fact of American imaginative writing for Richard Slotkin, for example, is the myth of the hero whose adventures of initiation and conversion enable him to achieve communion with powers that rule the universe. In the wilderness, something in his subconscious stirs up his hunting instincts: he tracks the wilderness beings, learns their secrets, and when he has established this connection with his prey, he uses his acquired skills against his teachers to kill or assert his dominance over them. In killing, Slotkin says, the hero is confirmed in his new and higher character and comes into full possession of the powers of the wilderness: "Through the ordeal and discipline of the hunt and its culmination in violence, the hero has achieved a regeneration of the spirit akin to the Puritan conversion experience."[11]

Or—he has achieved a "regeneration" similar to that Leo Marx finds in the pastoral narrative. In its simplest, archetypal form, Marx writes in *The Machine in the Garden*, the myth of America "affirms that Europeans experience a regeneration in the New World. They become new, better, happier men—they are reborn." This regenerative power is located in the natural terrain: "access to undefiled, bountiful, sublime Nature is what accounts for the virtue and special good fortune of Americans. It enables them to design a community in the image of a garden, an ideal fusion of nature with art. The landscape thus becomes the symbolic repository of value of all kinds—economic, political, aesthetic, religious."[12] That both Marx and Slotkin, in their different versions of the American landscape, exclude women is patently obvious; the only reason to say so is that such assertions are taken as "truth" in describing the content of imaginative statements—myth, history, literature—about American culture.

This conception of the American pastoral narrative as a "deeply romantic" promise held out by the beckoning, compliant, supportive "deeply feminine" landscape, the unsettled wilderness that in America offers to the male individual "the medium on which he may inscribe, unhindered, his own destiny and his own nature"[13]—just how useful an approach is it to Willa Cather's "novels of the soil"? What if we ask instead: What are women's narratives like? Do women see themselves as the "entrappers and impediments" in our "most American" experience? Do they see themselves as trapped by the language of the dominant culture—"infected" language, as Emily Dickinson called it? Do they write different plots, invent new language? And how do women perceive Nature? Is it "deeply feminine"? What sorts of fantasies do they spin about the land?[14] Or, on the other hand, as opposed to the "deeply romantic" promise of the pastoral narrative, what is a "real" response to landscape? Leo Marx's affirmation that "we can remain human, which is to say, fully integrated beings, only when we follow some such course, back and forth, between our social and natural (animal) selves"[15] is less than satisfactory so long as these terms are given gender value and exclude women from full participation in the human, or imaginative experience. References to a prescriptive patriarchal tradition that identifies "a myth of America which had nothing to do with the classical fictionalist's task of chronicling probable people in recognizable social situations"[16] has little to do with Willa Cather's perceptions of the land and her descriptions of the people who are of the land.

Standing in front of Jules Breton's *The Shepherd's Star*, I am thinking of Willa Cather. This painting depicts a woman standing barefoot on the earth, resting a moment, with both hands raised above her head, perhaps to steady the big pack of harvest gleanings that she carries on her shoulders. She is strong. Standing tall and solitary against the landscape, she seems larger than life, heroic; yet there is nothing particularly remarkable in her strength. She is portrayed without sentiment. She is exactly like the woman in the foreground of an earlier Breton painting, *The Recall of the Gleaners,* in which each of the sturdy peasant women, some bending, some standing with bare feet planted firmly on the ground, seems, as she moves forward with her burden, part of the earth. I think of Cather still as I meditate upon Breton's landscapes at Courièrres; François Bonvin's studies of women at work ironing, scouring, sweeping; the monumental sculpted forms of Jean François Millet's harvesters, shepherds, water carriers; the sensuous prairie landscapes of Rosa Bonheur. The exhibit is called "The Realist Tradition." Though these French painters hardly constitute a "school," the catalog cautions, they are "a rich mother lode" of nearly forgotten depictions of gleaners and plowmen, ragpickers and common laborers.[17] That Willa Cather is in my mind is pure intuition: I experience a moment of epiphany. I do not yet know that Cather loved these paintings and that she saw in the Barbizon landscapes her own Nebraska prairie land.

Jules Breton, *The Shepherd's Star*, 1887. (Courtesy, The Toledo Museum of Art)

A lonely young girl from Moonstone, Colorado—a little prairie town much like Cather's Red Cloud, Nebraska—has come to Chicago to study. Thea Kronborg, in Cather's *The Song of the Lark*, takes refuge in the Art Institute, where one picture—

> oh, that was the thing she ran upstairs so fast to see! That was her picture. She imagined that nobody cared for it but herself, and that it waited for her. That was a picture indeed. She liked even the name of it, "The Song of the Lark." The flat country, the early morning light, the wet fields, the look in the girl's heavy face—well, they were all hers, anyhow, whatever was there. She told herself that that picture was "right." Just what she meant by this, it would take a clever person to explain. But to her the word covered the almost boundless satisfaction she felt when she looked at the picture.[18]

Reviewing an exhibit at the Chicago Art Institute in 1901 for the *Lincoln Courier*, Cather herself had been especially taken with this painting of "the ugly little peasant girl standing barefooted among the wheat fields in the early morning," teaching the merchants and farm boys who come from Nebraska and Kansas "to hear the lark sing for themselves."[19] Cather first saw the works of the French Realists at the University of Nebraska in 1895, and her assessment at that time was as nonpolitical as Thea's. In a review for the *Nebraska State Journal* she compared the genre paintings of a Nebraska artist to Millet's peasant laborers. "Some people have tried to make political economy out of Millet's picture," she wrote, "but there is none there. There is only the poor pathos of labor and poverty. Millet painted for the sake of the people who suffered, never vexing himself about the cause of it. . . . The earth and air about Millet's laborers . . . would fascinate a mechanic and repel a poet."[20]

The next year Cather made a pilgrimage to Barbizon, with her friend Isabelle McClung, to see these landscapes for herself. Letters written home to the *Journal* describe this encounter as a "great imaginative experience"[21] and tell us that Cather found a striking resemblance in the Barbizon landscape to the countryside around her own Red Cloud and childhood homestead. "The wheat fields beyond the town were quite as level as those of the Nebraska divides," she wrote:

> The long, even stretch of yellow stubble, broken here and there by a pile of Lombard poplars, recalled not a little the country about Campbell and Bladen, and is certainly more familiar than anything I have seen on this side the Atlantic. To complete the resemblance, there stood a reaper of a well known American make, very like the one on which I have acted as super-

François Bonvin, *Woman Ironing*, 1858. (Courtesy, John G. Johnson
Collection, Philadelphia)

Jean-François Millet, *Harvesters Resting (Ruth and Boaz)*, 1853. (Courtesy, The Museum of Fine Arts, Boston)

Rosa Bonheur, *Plowing Scene*, 1854. (Courtesy, The Walters Art Gallery, Baltimore)

cargo many a time. There was a comfortable little place where a child might sit happily enough between its father's feet, and perhaps, if I had waited long enough, I might have seen a little French girl sitting in that happy, sheltered place, the delights of which I have known so well.[22]

Barbizon, then, is the first of the magical landscapes; the importance of the American Southwest—her first visit in 1912 is recounted in *The Song of the Lark*—would come later. It was the landscapes of the French Realists that first took Cather back to her own soil and to the strong pioneer women who seem to come straight out of Millet and Breton. Indeed, just after finishing *O Pioneers!* she likened her own process of composition to that of Millet, who taught her, she said, the process of simplification. "Art ought to simplify—that seems to me to be the whole process," she told an interviewer for the *Philadelphia Record* in 1913. "Millet did hundreds of sketches of peasants sowing grain, some of them very complicated, but when he came to paint 'The Sower,' the composition is so simple that it seems inevitable. It was probably the hundred sketches that went before that made the picture what it finally became—a process of simplifying all the time—of sacrificing many things that were in themselves interesting and pleasing, and all the time getting closer to the one thing—It."[23]

This is what young Thea, standing in front of Breton's *Song of the Lark*, means by her intuitive sense of the "rightness" of the picture. For the mature opera singer, the "rightness" is there in a characterization in exactly the same way as Cather the writer works to express in language the most complete representation of an existing thing. "You realized that she was beginning that long story, adequately, with the end in view," Gustav Mahler (who appears in *The Song of the Lark*) observes of Thea Kronborg's singing. "Every phrase she sang was basic. She simply *was* the idea of the Rhine music." "It's the idea, the basic idea, pulsing behind every bar she sings," another of her admirers says. "She simplifies a character down to the . . . idea it's built on, and makes everything conform to that. . . . Instead of inventing a lot of business and expedients to suggest character, she knows the thing at the root, and lets the musical pattern take care of her" (396, 422). As Thea's accompanist describes the process:

"When she begins with a part she's hard to work with: so slow you'd think she was stupid if you did n't know her. . . . All at once, she [will have] got her line—it usually comes suddenly, after stretches of not getting anywhere at all—and after that it kept changing and clearing. As she worked her voice into it, it got more and more of that 'gold' quality that makes her *Fricka* so

Jules Breton, *The Song of the Lark*, ca. 1860. (Courtesy, The Art Institute of Chicago)

different. . . . She was working on . . . [*Elizabeth*] years ago when her mother was ill. I could see her anxiety and grief getting more and more into the part. The last act is heart-breaking . . . might be any lonely woman getting ready to die. It's full of the thing every plain creature finds out for himself, but that never gets written down. It's unconscious memory, maybe; inherited memory, like folk-music." [448–49]

In *The Song of the Lark*, Thea Kronborg's "idea" in her art, the thing that makes it "right," is the imaginative representation of the real and existing things—both close and far away—in the unconscious memory. "Idea" in art, for singer and writer, is prompted, for example, by the childhood memory of prayer meetings in a small western town; it depends upon the re-imagining of one old woman with "sunken eyes that seemed full of wisdom, . . . black thread gloves, much too long in the fingers and so meekly folded one over the other. Her face was brown, and worn away as rocks are worn by water. There are many ways of describing that color of age, but in reality it is not like parchment, or like any of the things it is said to be like. That brownness and that texture of skin are found only in the faces of old human creatures, who have worked hard and who have always been poor." And this memory is joined to another, that of going to bed at night with a paper-bound copy of *Anna Karenina*, bought at the local drugstore because "the first sentence interested her very much, and because she saw, as she glanced over the pages, the magical names of two Russian cities." As she reads, Thea forgets "the hymns, the sick girl, the resigned black figures": it is "the night of the ball in Moscow." Both kinds of memory are equally real: "those old faces [which] . . . come back to her, long after they were hidden away under the earth, . . . full of meaning, . . . mysteriously marked by Destiny, . . . [and] the people who danced the mazurka under the elegant Korsunsky" (128, 130). And both are understood not as *idea* only—if the picture, the characterization, the language is "right"; these memories are re-created with the *passion* that Thea Kronborg's teacher says "is every artist's secret" (447).

Earlier I referred to Guy Davenport's notion that the key to the great works of the imagination is in the vastness of the vision: writers like Edgar Allan Poe, James Joyce, Samuel Beckett, for example, range geographically beyond the boundaries of their national identities to draw in their works from cultures that they know imaginatively. On the other hand, Henry Glassie's brilliant analysis of Samuel Beckett's work as a product of specifically Irish culture rests upon the point that in *Waiting for Godot* Vladimir and Estragon are just two Irish friends "passing the time."[24] For Cather, the simplification, the understanding of the most complete expression of a concrete, physical object, person, landscape— what she calls the "idea" that makes art "right"—comes from a richness of experience—both world and parish, as Sarah Orne Jewett suggested,[25] from a context both diachronic and synchronic.

For the French Realists, the immediate cultural context was the 1848

Revolution: "contemporary life" for these artists was "a serious and consistent confrontation of the life of the poor and humble, [and] the depiction of work and its concrete setting"—not as allegory but as a major subject for art.[26] Jules Breton described the strong influence of that revolution in terms of both idea and passion. "There was a great upsurge of new efforts," he wrote. "We studied . . . the new social stratum and the natural setting which surrounded it. We studied the streets and the fields more deeply; we associated ourselves with the passions and the feelings of the humble, and art was to do them the honor formerly reserved exclusively for the mighty."[27]

Breton's peasant women, Millet's working folk are specific nineteenth-century laborers performing in a particular place a routine task. And if they seem to prefigure the strong immigrant women of Cather's prairie novels, it is because there is also about them a suggestion of timelessness, of universality. The almost religious validity and moral beauty in these depictions of laborers has to do, to use Davenport's geographical language, with the variety of affinities in Millet's work, ranging from classically composed and sculpted forms, to the primitive strength of Egyptian figures, to arrangements of figures reminiscent of biblical themes, to the groupings of Dürer and Brueghel. The imaginative vastness in these paintings is not merely mythological or derivative; when Cather visited Barbizon some fifty years after Millet painted his peasants working the land, she *saw* this scene:

> The fields already cut were full of stackers; men in their long blue blouses that hang about their knees like skirts, and women bare-headed and brown faced and broad of shoulders. They all wore wooden shoes, their skirts were high above the ankle, and few of them wore stockings. After the rakers and stackers came the gleaners—usually women who looked old and battered, who were bent and slow and not good for much else. Such brave old faces as most of these field working women have, such blithe songs they hum and such good-humored remarks they bawl at a girl who sees too much of one particular reaper. There is something worth thinking about in these brown, merry old women, who have brought up fourteen children and can outstrip their own sons and grandsons in the harvest field, lay down their rake and write a traveler directions as to how he can reach the next town in a hand as neat as a bookkeeper's. As the sun dropped lower the merriment ceased; the women were tired and grew to look more and more as Millet painted them, warped and bowed and heavy. The horses strained in their harness, the ring dove began to call mournfully from the pine wood in the west and I found there was a touch of latent homesickness in the wide, empty, yellow fields and the reaper with the cozy seat which some little brown-skinned Barbizon

girl would have tomorrow. Storm clouds were piling themselves up about the gorgeous sunset, and we tramped silently back to Barbizon, through the little winding street where tired women sat on the wooden door steps, singing tired children to sleep.[28]

This description, sent home to the *Nebraska State Journal* in 1902, would appear again in Cather's novel, *One of Ours*, where a Nebraska farm boy is stationed during the War in a village like this one, with a sad and elderly Frenchwoman who shares with these strong peasant women such special marks of dignity as their handwriting, neat as a bookkeeper's, in which they write directions.

This same dignity characterizes women like Grandmother Burden in *My Ántonia* and Old Mrs. Harris in *Obscure Destinies*. In the latter story, "idea" and "passion" combine to re-evoke in language the memory of Cather's grandmother. In this story of women—a bright bookish young girl who is about to break away from the stifling small prairie town; her attractive mother, a former southern belle, resentfully trapped by her childbearing body; the exotic and intellectual neighbor, Mrs. Rosen—the focus is the old woman who rises before the rest of the family is awake to make breakfast, keeps her own few possessions neatly behind a curtain in her room that is also the family gathering place, reads to the children, takes care of the animals, and finds the money for her granddaughter's college fees. Deeply tied to her social and human context, Old Mrs. Harris is a woman whose every gesture is an expression of love and quiet dignity. The daughter and granddaughter, the Jewish neighbor, Mandy, the "bound girl" brought from the South, who in rubbing the old woman's swollen feet in a little tub of warm water at the end of the day performs "one of the oldest rites of compassion"[29]—all of them find Old Mrs. Harris "impressive" and recognize her lot as somehow their own.

Immigrant women like Cather's Swedish Alexandra Bergson and Bohemian Ántonia Shimerda, women who plough and reap, sweep, carry water, feed the animals and bake bread, are exactly as "real"—and as mythic and primal—as Millet's *Woman Returning from the Well*, of which the painter wrote:

I tried to make it impossible for one to take her either for a water-carrier or for a servant, but rather to show: that she had just drawn water for home use, water to make soup for her husband and children; that she was carrying a weight neither heavier nor lighter than the full baskets; that through the kind of grimace which is, so-to-speak, imposed by the weight pulling on her arms and the narrowing of her eyes caused by the light, one might surmise

Jean-François Millet, *The Water Carrier (Woman Returning from the Well)*, 1855–62. (Courtesy, IBM Corporation, New York)

an expression of rustic goodness. I avoided, as usual, with a kind of horror, any suggestion of sentimentality. On the contrary, I wanted to show her going about a daily task, the habit of a life time, along with other household tasks, in simplicity and good humor, without considering it a burden. I wanted to convey an idea of the coolness of the well and to show by its ancient appearance that many women had come there before her to draw water.[30]

The response of the critics to Millet's work—that he had done a new version of pastoral but a poetic and naive one nonetheless—has been like the response of critics to Cather's work: it is easier to invoke tradition, as T. J. Clark argues of Millet, more reassuring, particularly when a work might question one's basic assumptions, use a different language, speak to somebody else.[31]

"Realism," however, is a slippery term, with boundaries not at all clear, as the broad compass of the exhibit, "The Realist Tradition," demonstrates. Any work of art is, of course, *imagined*—in fact, a "Realist" like Flaubert could write that the imagined work is the *most* real—but the important thing for both the "Realist" painters and for Willa Cather was that things represented preserve "the ordinary indifference of their being."[32] This was the great achievement of the Realist movement in painting, Charles Rosen and Henri Zerner argue in their review of this exhibit: the acceptance of trivial, banal material and the refusal to ennoble it, idealize it or even make it picturesque. In literature as well as painting, they point out, this means an ascetic liberation from rhetoric—rhetorical figures of speech, conceived pictorially, idealizing formulas for pathos, the whole repertory of poses and gestures, an absence of moral comment and an unwillingness to characterize the most sordid and repulsive events as atypical, exceptional. Flaubert's intention "to write the *mediocre* beautifully, and at the same time to have it retain its aspect, its shape, its very words"[33] comes close, I believe, to Cather's intention. An admirer of Flaubert's "peculiar integrity of language and vision,"[34] in her novels Cather represents particular events as real not because they are special events, and not because they are beautiful, for to make them beautiful would be to make them special: beauty inheres not in the event, but in the story, imagined and set down in language.

In *O Pioneers!*, Cather's first "novel of the soil," Alexander becomes Alexandra, and the reality upon which the novel is built is no manmade object set upon, penetrating, spanning the land: the affecting presence of fact and artifact is the land itself. The great fact is the land. That is where we begin:

> Although it was only four o'clock, the winter day was fading. The road led southwest, toward the streak of pale, watery light that glimmered in the leaden sky. The light fell upon the two sad young faces that were turned

mutely toward it: upon the eyes of the girl, who seemed to be looking with such anguished perplexity into the future; upon the sombre eyes of the boy, who seemed already to be looking into the past. The little town behind them had vanished as if it had never been, had fallen behind the swell of the prairie, and the stern frozen country received them into its bosom. The homesteads were few and far apart; here and there a windmill gaunt against the sky, a sod house crouching in a hollow. But the great fact was the land itself, which seemed to overwhelm the little beginnings of human society that struggled in its sombre wastes. It was from facing this vast hardness that the boy's mouth had become so bitter; because he felt that men were too weak to make any mark here, that the land wanted to be let alone, to preserve its own fierce strength, its peculiar, savage kind of beauty, its uninterrupted mournfulness.[35]

The girl looks at the land and sees the future (the boy's mouth is bitter from the struggle and his eyes look to the past). The woman Alexandra, with hard work and imagination creates a "wide, map-like prospect of field and hedge and pasture" that surprises her friend Carl. "I would never have believed it could be done," he tells her. "I'm disappointed in my own eyes, in my imagination" (108).

How do we read this map of the land, this land that men have measured and spanned, divided and mastered, mythologized and idealized? Critics—even feminist critics who invert inherited structures—can lead us away from rather than toward Cather's meaning. Nina Baym, thinking perhaps of the vast hardness and fierce strength of this passage, suggests that Cather in *O Pioneers!* "adjust[s] the heroic myth to her own psyche by making nature out to be male."[36] Ellen Moers, on the other hand, suggests, like some critics of Georgia O'Keeffe's paintings, that Cather's Divide is an emblem of the female body—like Emily Brontë's moors, George Eliot's Red Deeps, Isak Dinesen's Black Valley. One of the most erotic landscapes in literature, Moers argues, is the one Thea Kronborg discovers in *The Song of the Lark*, the very same that Cather discovered in 1912 and which would have so decided an effect on her imagination in the writing of *O Pioneers!*. "Panther Canyon was like a thousand others," the passage begins,

> —one of those abrupt fissures with which the earth in the Southwest is riddled. . . . it was accessible only at its head. The canyon walls, for the first two hundred feet below the surface, were perpendicular cliffs, striped with even-running strata of rock. From there on to the bottom the sides were less abrupt, were shelving, and lightly fringed with *piñons* and dwarf cedars. The effect was that of a gentler canyon within a wilder one. The dead city lay at

the point where the perpendicular outer wall ceased and the V-shaped inner gorge began. There a stratum of rock, softer than those above, had been hollowed out by the action of time until it was like a deep groove.

But the greatest Cather landscapes are those evoked by the land she knew best, the Nebraska prairies: "The same sense of earthbound ecstasy fills them all, of physical dissolution on a limitless, undulating, high-lying plain under a limitless sky; of a solitary, primordial land antecedent to, perhaps hostile to human life."[37] Here is young Jim Burden's first impression, having like Willa Cather traveled from the lush Virginia mountain valleys, of the barren open land of frontier Nebraska in *My Ántonia*:

> There seemed to be nothing to see; no fences, no creeks or trees, no hills or fields. If there was a road, I could not make it out in the faint starlight. There was nothing but land: not a country at all, but the material out of which countries are made. . . . I had the feeling that the world was left behind, that we had got over the edge of it, and were outside man's jurisdiction. I had never before looked up at the sky when there was not a familiar mountain ridge against it. But this was the complete dome of heaven, all there was of it. . . . Between that earth and that sky I felt erased, blotted out.[38]

Citing the same passage, Elizabeth Hampsten argues that Cather has "invested topography with the idea, and then adjusted character to it." Though art and life may imitate each other, she writes, they are not the same, no more than Jim Burden's version of Ántonia is her own. Ántonia Shimerda's experience of her environment, had she written her own story, might have been more like that of one of the working-class women writing home, Hampsten says, reporting at too close a range to be found on a map, her language, concrete, uneuphemistic, unmysterious, with little generalization and no irony.[39]

If we refer to the diary entries, journals and letters of women traveling west and settling, like Ántonia Shimerda and Alexandra Bergson, on farms with their families, we find, as scholars who have recently studied and published these documents have shown, that the journey for women was an "anti-mythic" one. Women mythologized neither the landscape nor the trip itself. They traveled through an unknown landscape, neither virginal nor maternal, noting in their diaries not natural formations but numbers of graves; their journeys meant death and separation, illness, hardship, every kind of privation. Against the pain of separation and dislocation, noted continually, women filled their letters to each other with the kind of domestic detail meant to reinforce their bonds of friend-

Prairie, Webster County, Nebraska. (© Lucia Woods 1973)

ship. Neither hardy adventurers nor sunbonneted weepers, these vigorous, brave women, for whom the journey came at an unnatural place in their life cycles and was a violation of life's natural rhythms during their childbearing years, found in the journey west the challenge of maintaining domestic order against the disordered life of the frontier.[40]

One way of bringing order out of disorder was through the careful crafting of objects for daily use and enjoyment, works of art to be shared and handed down: quilts and coverlets, songs and stories. As Dolores Hayden and Peter Marris have shown, many patchwork quilts *are* women's maps of their journeys, views of their neighborhoods or architectural plans of places they knew. Quiltmakers of all classes and races "developed an elaborate design language based on forms derived from the natural and built environments. They used that common language to comment on women's experiences." Like storytellers, quiltmakers move from typical— or "real"—landscapes to metaphorical ones. Powerful evocations of time and place, quilts are both formal, in their search for design and pattern making, and personal, in their nature as gift, souvenir, portable embrace.[41]

The importance to women of mapping, or locating their experience in a precise and detailed way, is described in Cather's *One of Ours*. When news of the German invasion of Luxembourg reaches the Nebraska prairie where the Wheelers live, Claude's concern is for history and civilization— the passion of destruction that has seized a people he has known to be splendid, the waste of centers of learning and of human lives. His father thinks only of business—how much his wheat crop will bring in a war economy. Mrs. Wheeler, however, goes to the attic to find a map, just as "that night, on many prairie homesteads, the women, American and foreign-born, were hunting for a map,"[42] and this will be her first response to each battle of the War—to place it on her map.

The women whose quilts we now view on museum walls as "abstract art" and whose private papers we are now able to read bear a strong resemblance to Alexandra's mother in *O Pioneers!*: she is a woman who refuses to live in a sod house, goes twenty miles for fish, and if she were cast upon a desert island, "would thank God for her deliverance, make a garden, and find something to preserve." For Mrs. Bergson,

> Preserving was almost a mania. . . . Stout as she was, she roamed the scrubby banks of Norway Creek looking for fox grapes and goose plums, like a wild creature in search of prey. She made a yellow jam of the insipid ground-cherries that grew on the prairie, flavoring it with lemon peel; and she made a sticky dark conserve of garden tomatoes. She had experimented even with the rank buffalo-pea, and she could not see a fine bronze cluster of them without shaking her head and murmuring, "What a pity!" When there was nothing more to preserve, she began to pickle. The amount of sugar she used in these processes was sometimes a serious drain upon the family resources. . . . She had never quite forgiven John Bergson for bringing her to the end of the earth; but, now that she was there, she wanted to be let alone to reconstruct her old life in so far as that was possible. She could still take some comfort in the world if she had bacon in the cave, glass jars on the shelves, and sheets in the press. [29–30]

These resourceful women who accompany their men to the end of the earth bear a strong resemblance to quick-footed and energetic Grandmother Burden in *My Ántonia*, a tall woman with wrinkled brown skin who carries a cane for beating snakes when she goes out to hoe potatoes, plasters and whitewashes her kitchen—the plaster laid directly on the earth's walls as it is in dugouts, sets pots of geraniums and wandering Jew in the white-curtained half windows, and takes hampers of food to her neighbors, the Shimerdas.

The experiences of these pioneer women are *meant* to be a contrast to Jim Burden's "romantic" response to the land.[43] Jim is the teller of a tale about Ántonia, not Ántonia—just as Willa Cather is not Jim Burden, though there are autobiographical elements in *My Ántonia*, as well as in *The Song of the Lark*, "The Best Years," "Old Mrs. Harris" and other stories. This is not to say that Cather's landscapes of the imagination are imaginary landscapes. They begin with the real, the everyday, the experienced. At the same time, landscape is for Cather where representation begins; it is the basis for a story. Works of art, Cather's created landscapes, like Thea Kronborg's music, fuse idea, which begins with unconscious memory, with passion, or desire. *Wunsch* is the name of Thea's first teacher, and Thea herself, like Alexandra, like young Lucy Gayheart, has at her core a fierce sense of ecstasy. As long as she lives, she vows to the forces of the city, the things and people lined up against her, "that ecstasy was going to be hers. She would live for it, work for it, die for it; but she was going to have it, time after time, height after height. . . . Nobody could die while they felt like that inside. The springs there were wound so tight that it would be a long while before there was any slack in them."[44] Idea and passion, memory and desire—these are the qualities that characterize Alexandra's relationship to the land. And although memory and desire—of a gentler, more sentimental sort—characterize the pastoral tale Jim Burden tells, it is important to note that violence and death stalk through Cather's stories with the regularity of historical necessity.[45] In *O Pioneers!* a jealous husband kills his wife and her lover beneath the mulberry tree that has been their love-bower; in *My Ántonia* one of the pioneer immigrants tells a story of throwing a bride and groom to the attacking wolves one frozen night in the Russian Ukraine; in *Death Comes for the Archbishop*, Indians enter the fabulous garden of a priest who has been exploiting them and throw him over the cliff. None of this violence is "regenerative." Rather, as in the French Realist paintings, "horror is contained within the fact. . . . It is what it is, when it is, where it is, nothing more."[46] For Cather, the regenerative power comes from the land itself. Indeed, the great fact about these landscapes is the way in which Cather creates, from the vast and empty spaces that give young Jim Burden the feeling of being blotted out, a sense of place.

In order to understand Cather's evocations of place in her western landscape, we must begin, as she did, with what is there. Bernice Slote has observed that in an early story like "The Clemency of the Court" of 1893, "place" means both the "brown, windswept prairies that never lead anywhere" and the plains in the morning where "the sunflowers would shake themselves in the wind, . . . the corn leaves would shine and . . . the cobwebs . . . sparkle all over the grass and the air would be clear and blue." In "On the Divide" of 1896, a half-mad, lonely Norseman lives in a place of "scorching dusty winds that blow up over the bluffs from Kansas [and] seem to dry up the blood in men's veins." The plains are eternally treacherous: every spring they "stretch green and rustle with the promises of Eden, showing long grassy lagoons full of clear water and cattle whose hoofs are stained with wild roses [but] before autumn the lagoons are dried up, and the ground is burnt dry and hard until it blisters and cracks open." Yet "Tommy, the Unsentimental" of the same year is homesick, down East, for "this sky, the old intense blue of it." And if in the mature stories one finds the primitive and natural strength of the West, there are also, in a story like "The Sculptor's Funeral," "disappointed strugglers in a bitter, dead little Western town."[47]

Contemporary reviews in the western newspapers testify to the "realness" of Cather's imagined landscapes.[48] When her story "On the Divide" appeared in the *Overland Monthly* in 1896, for example, another Nebraska writer, Elia W. Peattie, whose own collection of stories, *A Mountain Woman*, had drawn condemnation from Nebraska reviewers for its stark portrayals of poverty, drought and wind "like a blast from a fiery furnace," found Cather's piece "really a story of the plains, and the characters of the people merely inevitable incidents of their surroundings . . . [which] rings true, and seems to be sad because conditions are sad." But when another story, "El Dorado," set in Kansas but drawn from Cather's Nebraska, appeared in the *Overland Review* in 1901, the *Kansas City Journal* called the story "a slander" because Cather had pictured the state "as a howling wilderness," and worst of all, the author was apparently a woman, and "according to the chivalrous code of western Kansas, cannot be killed or scalped."[49]

In Cather's first "novel of the soil," Alexandra Bergson is the "empress of the prairie."[50] She lives in

a big white house that stood on a hill, several miles across the fields. There were so many sheds and outbuildings grouped about it that the place looked not unlike a tiny village. A stranger, approaching it, could not help noticing the beauty and fruitfulness of the outlying fields. There was something individual about the great farm, a most unusual trimness and care for detail. On either side of the road, for a mile before you reached the foot of the hill, stood tall osage orange hedges, their glossy green marking off the yellow fields. South of the hill, in a low, sheltered swale, surrounded by a mulberry hedge, was the orchard, its fruit trees knee-deep in timothy grass. Any one thereabouts would have told you that this was one of the richest farms on the Divide, and that the farmer was a woman, Alexandra Bergson. [83]

In *My Ántonia*, Ántonia Shimerda as earth-mother presides over wheat fields and rye fields; a fruit cave with an abundance of pickled and preserved watermelon rinds, cherries, strawberries, crabapples; cherry and apple orchards, gooseberry, currant and mulberry bushes; and a great crop of children—"big and little, tow heads and gold heads and brown, and flashing little naked legs; a veritable explosion of life out of the dark cave into the sunlight" (382). There is the deepest peace in Ántonia's orchard:

> It was surrounded by a triple enclosure; the wire fence, then the hedge of thorny locusts, then the mulberry hedge which kept out the hot winds of summer and held fast to the protecting snows of winter. The hedges were so tall that we could see nothing but the blue sky above them, neither the barn roof nor the windmill. The afternoon sun poured down . . . through the drying grape leaves. The orchard seemed full of sun, like a cup, and we could smell the ripe apples on the trees. The crabs hung on the branches as thick as beads on a string, purple-red, with a thin silvery glaze over them. [385]

The vast space of the open plain was hardly a place to the Bergsons when they arrived in Nebraska. The complete absence of human landmarks was disheartening and depressing: the little houses on the Divide were tucked away in low places—"you did not see them until you came directly upon them. Most of them were built of the sod itself, and were only the unescapable ground in another form"; the roads were but faint tracks in the grass; the fields were scarcely noticeable. "The record of the plow was insignificant, like the feeble scratches on stone left by prehistoric races, so indeterminate that they may, after all, be only the markings of glaciers, and not a record of human strivings" (19–20). When Alexandra's father lies dying, he looks out over his place and thinks about how small and futile have been his efforts to tame that wild land. John Bergson holds the Old World belief that land in itself is desirable, "but this land was an enigma. It was like a horse that no one knows how to break to harness, that runs wild and kicks things to pieces." It is still a wild thing that has its ugly moods, he muses,

> and no one knew when they were likely to come, or why. Mischance hung over it. Its Genius was unfriendly to man. . . . There it lay outside his door, the same land, the same lead-colored miles. He knew every ridge and draw and gully between him and the horizon. To the south, his plowed fields; to

the east, the sod stables, the cattle corral, the pond,—and then the grass. . . .
One winter his cattle had perished in a blizzard. The next summer one of his
plow horses broke its leg in a prairie-dog hole and had to be shot. Another
summer he lost his hogs from cholera, and a valuable stallion died from a
rattlesnake bite. Time and again his crops had failed. He had lost two
children, . . . and there had been the cost of sickness and death. Now . . . he
was going to die himself. [20–22]

And the Shimerdas come from Bohemia to a sod hut, stuffy and ill-lit;
they wrap their feet in rags and eat potatoes that alternately freeze and rot
because there is no place to keep them. Ántonia's father, a skilled weaver
and musician in the old country, a gentle and intelligent man, sinks into a
deep melancholy. "My papa sad for the old country," Ántonia tells Jim.
"He not look good. He never make music any more. At home he play
violin all the time; . . . here never. When I beg him for play, he shake his
head no. Some days he take his violin out of his box and make with his
fingers on the strings, like this, but he never make the music. He don't like
this kawn-tree" (102). When he takes his own life, he is buried, according
to the Old World superstition, at what are to be the crossroads; but
because, as it happens, one road curves a little to the east just there and the
other a little to the south, the grave with its uncut prairie grass becomes
an island of remembrance.

The strong sense of place evoked in these passages does not make
Cather a "regional" writer.[51] As Bernice Slote insists, not only were Cather's concerns larger than regional; she quite literally drew upon the rich
traditions she found on the Nebraska prairie—of the Poles, Germans,
Swedes, Bohemians—linked together there by allusions to biblical or classical worlds and by folk traditions. In suggesting that the melancholy and
nostalgia for the old ways are really "the elemental core we find in folk
songs and tales, in sagas and legends,"[52] Slote forces us in reading Cather's
stories, to rethink our conceptions of "real," of culture(s), of "American."

Is it the "unrootedness" of Americans that makes us value places
with historical resonances; or to put it another way, do we derive "instinctive pleasure" in reading a novel like *O Pioneers!* "from sharing in that
wish to find such a sheltered place, a refuge carved out of a hostile terrain," as (American male) critics suggest?[53] Why is it, then, that the characters who are the most significant and who give us the most pleasure in
Cather's novels are not the most "American"—shallow and embittered
men like Alexandra's brothers, nomads like Carl Linstrum in *O Pioneers!*
and Jim Burden in *My Ántonia*—but the newest arrived, those who pre-

serve the folkways of their own countries? The most "real" people on Cather's frontier are not English and northern European descendants moving west from Pennsylvania and Virginia, but those whose native language is Czech, Bohemian, Norwegian, Swedish, German, Polish, Russian, Mexican. In *My Ántonia* these immigrants are "a race apart, and out-of-door work had given them a vigour which . . . developed into a positive carriage and freedom of movement" (226). Their children work to help pay for ploughs and reapers, brood sows and steers, and as a result of family solidarity, some of these "displaced" people wind up owning the big prosperous farms. In *O Pioneers!* Marie Shabata is Alexandra's vivacious "arabesque" Bohemian neighbor; she is a dark, curly-haired, laughing-eyed, flirtatious fortune teller, who will be murdered, along with Alexandra's brother Emil, in a scene of Gothic horror. "Crazy" Ivar is a Norwegian hermit who lives in a wild sod hut; from his doorway, where he sits reading his bible, he can see "the rough land, the smiling sky, the curly grass white in the hot sunlight" and hear "the rapturous song of the lark, the drumming of the quail, the burr of the locust against that vast silence" (38). Alexandra herself suggests a kind of geographical vastness: a Swedish farmer who has been brought up on *The Frithjof Saga*, which she knows by heart, she is a woman of classic proportions, perfectly capable of stabbing shabby men who approach her with a "glance of Amazonian fierceness" (8).

Of these characters, only Ivar might be called "rooted," a condition, according to Yi-Fu Tuan, that implies "being at home in an unself-conscious way, . . . that is, unreflectively secure and comfortable in a particular locality," excluding "not only anxiousness and curiosity about what lies beyond the next hill, but also what lies beyond present time."[54] Old Ivar finds contentment in solitude. He dislikes the litter of dwellings, preferring the cleanness and tidiness of wild sod. He shares with the Indians in *Death Comes for the Archbishop* a reverence for the things of the earth, and with Jeanne Le Ber in *Shadows on the Rock* his solitary mysticism. He lives in a clay bank "without defiling the face of nature any more than the coyote that had lived there before him," in direct communication with his own particular God as he sits meditating upon the psalms in his Norwegian bible, or sleeping under the stars in his hand-tied hammock:

> At one end of the pond was an earthen dam, planted with green willow bushes, and above it a door and a single window were set into the hillside. You would not have seen them at all but for the reflection of the sunlight upon the four panes of window-glass. And that was all you saw. Not a shed,

not a corral, not a well, not even a path broken in the curly grass. But for the piece of rusty stovepipe sticking up through the sod, you could have walked over the roof of Ivar's dwelling without dreaming that you were near a human habitation. [36–38, 92]

In the New World he is Crazy Ivar, whose visions come directly from God. From Ivar Alexandra learns the secrets of the land—the words, in his native Norwegian, "No guns, no guns!," the way to cure sick animals, the rhythms and rotations of the cycle of nature. Ivar's instincts and his folk-lore are as important to her as the new scientific methods: his lore is like memory that binds her to the earth.

Marie Shabata is like a caught wild bird of rare and brilliant color, or like a vivid and delicate flower, a surprise in a rather sturdy and practical landscape, a kind of fragrance that lingers in the memory as part of a story. Her very sensuality renders her fragile and vulnerable in the hands of men who would possess her. Desire is in her yellow-brown eyes that glint "like gold-stone, or . . . like that Colorado mineral called tiger-eye," the color of sunflower honey, or of old amber: "In each eye one of these streaks must have been larger than the others, for the effect was that of two dancing points of light, two little yellow bubbles, such as rise in a glass of cham-pagne. Sometimes they seemed like the sparks from a forge" (II, 135–36).

What Marie cares for are fragrances, tastes, touches—things that please her body. She likes her clothes to smell of rosemary leaves; to sit in the shade of the mulberry tree where tufts of wild roses flame in the bunchgrass; to break off branches of the apricot tree so that she can finger its pale yellow, pink-cheeked fruit and blue-green leaves, porous like blot-ting paper, on their waxen stems; to go where the cherries are thick and strip the glittering branches after a rain shower, or have Emil drop "the sweet, insipid fruit,—long ivory-colored berries, tipped with faint pink, like white coral," into her lap (136–37, 153). Marie is a tree worshiper: she believes in the old Bohemian tradition that trees bring good or bad luck. She tells Emil the story of the linden, planted by the old people in the mountains to purify the forest and do away with the spells that come from the old trees that have lasted from heathen times. This tree, she says, referring to the mulberry beneath which she sits, "knows everything I ever think of. . . . When I come back to it, I never have to remind it of any-thing; I begin just where I left off" (152–53).

Indeed, the tree bears witness to the story of Marie, a story that begins with light but ends with the dark staining of its white mulberry leaves with the blood of Emil and Marie:

When he [Emil] reached the orchard the sun was hanging low over the wheatfield. Long fingers of light reached through the apple branches as through a net; the orchard was riddled and shot with gold; light was the reality, the trees were merely interferences that reflected and refracted light. . . . Marie was lying on her side under the white mulberry tree, her face half hidden in the grass, her eyes closed, her hands lying limply where they had happened to fall. . . . The blood came back to her cheeks, her amber eyes opened slowly, and in them Emil saw his own face and the orchard and the sun. "I was dreaming this," she whispered, . . . "don't take my dream away!" [258–59]

It is old Ivar who discovers in the stained and slippery grass, among the darkening mulberries, the two young bodies above which two white butterflies flutter in and out among the interlacing shadows, "diving and soaring, now close together, now far apart" (270). He brings together the pagan story of the forest children and Alexandra's story of Creation.[55]

For Alexandra, the drought and failure of the wild soil that bring her brothers to the brink of despair are a challenge, but not in the sense of mastery and domination. The land is a lover, who will yield up its mysteries in union—distinctly physical and spiritual. Approaching the Divide with a radiant face,

when the road began to climb the first long swells . . . Alexandra hummed an old Swedish hymn. . . . For the first time, perhaps, since that land emerged from the waters of geologic ages, a human face was set toward it with love and yearning. It seemed beautiful to her, rich and strong and glorious. Her eyes drank in the breadth of it, until her tears blinded her. Then the Genius of the Divide, the great, free spirit which breathes across it, must have bent lower than it ever bent to a human will before. The history of every country begins in the heart of a man or a woman.[56]

At the same time, Alexandra understands the *idea* of nature. The kind of order that she projects upon the vastness and distance comes, she believes, from "the great operations of nature, and . . . the law that lay behind them," which give her a sense of personal security. The breadth of the Divide moves her to tears, moves her as a great free spirit, as she begins to understand how its destiny is linked to her own. Through feeling and understanding—Cather's "passion" and "idea"—Alexandra has reached a new consciousness of the country and of her own new relation to it. Notice how "spirit" and "destiny" begin with the particulars of detailed existence: "She had never known before how much the country meant to her. The chirping of the insects down in the long grass had been like the sweetest music. She had felt as if her heart were hiding down there, somewhere, with the quail and the plover and all the little wild things that crooned or buzzed in the sun. Under the long shaggy ridges, she felt the future stirring" (65, 70–71).

Like one of Millet's or Breton's peasants, Alexandra is a woman working on the earth with her hands, a working woman larger than life. She cannot—like Mrs. Shimerda, Grandmother Burden, Old Mrs. Harris or her own mother—be contained or expressed by her "curiously unfinished and uneven" house:

> One room is papered, carpeted, over-furnished; the next is almost bare. The pleasantest rooms in the house are the kitchen—where Alexandra's three young Swedish girls chatter and cook and pickle and preserve all summer long—and the sitting-room, in which Alexandra has brought together the old homely furniture that the Bergsons used in their first log house, the family portraits, and the few things her mother brought from Sweden.
>
> When you go out of the house into the flower garden, there you feel again the order and fine arrangement manifest all over the great farm; in the fencing and hedging, in the windbreaks and sheds, in the symmetrical pasture ponds, planted with scrub willows to give shade to the cattle in fly-time. There is even a white row of beehives in the orchard, under the walnut trees. You feel that, properly, Alexandra's house is the big out-of-doors, and that it is in the soil that she expresses herself best. [83–84]

Together Alexandra and the earth give ungrudgingly, holding nothing back: in each is "the same tonic, puissant quality that is in the tilth, the same strength and resoluteness." The open face of the country rises, like Alexandra's body, like the plains of Lombardy, to meet the sun, and "the air and the earth are curiously mated and intermingled, as if the one were the breath of the other." Alexandra gives to the earth both passion and idea, and the rich soil

> yields heavy harvests; the dry, bracing climate and the smoothness of the land make labor easy. . . . the furrows of a single field often lie a mile in length, and the brown earth, with such a strong, clean smell, and such a power of growth and fertility in it, yields itself eagerly to the plow; rolls away from the shear, not even dimming the brightness of the metal, with a soft, deep sigh of happiness. The wheat-cutting sometimes goes on all night as well as all day, and . . . the grain is so heavy that it bends toward the blade and cuts like velvet. [76–77]

The two stories of *O Pioneers!* are pieced together like the quilts Alexandra and Mrs. Lee make during that neighbor's annual winter visit. The quilt-making is accompanied by storytelling: Mrs. Lee gets so carried away by the plots, taken from the Swedish family paper and from her girlhood in Gottland and narrated in great detail, that she forgets "which were the printed stories and which were the real stories" (189). Like the scraps of material from which the quilts are pieced together, Mrs. Lee's stories are rich in personal evocations of places and times. Like the quilting patterns and like the crochet patterns borrowed from Marie Shabata, their communication binds them together in a design of formal, historical and personal meaning. Their quilts and their stories link these women in a female community, in time, in a place of their own making. Outside, the "variegated fields are all one color now; the pastures, the stubble, the roads, the sky are the same leaden gray. The hedgerows and trees are scarcely perceptible against the bare earth, whose slaty hue they have taken on. The ground is frozen so hard that it bruises the foot to walk in the roads or in the ploughed fields. It is like an iron country, and the spirit is oppressed by its rigor and melancholy" (187–88). As the three women sit and talk in Marie's kitchen, with her windowsills full of blooming fuchsias and geraniums, eating Marie's Bohemian coffee cake and delicate rolls, in the section of the novel called "Winter Memories," they create from the ground of loss and diminution the kind of human—and specifically female—bonding that Sarah Orne Jewett with such delicacy and grace portrayed in her stories of the Maine seacoast villages.[57] Cather's three women are immigrants: they are by definition uprooted, estranged; but together they can make a sense of place.[58]

If rootedness "is an unreflective state of being in which the human personality merges with its milieu," by contrast there are "deliberate acts of creating and maintaining place for which speech, gesture, and the making of things are the common means." Words have great power in creating place: naming, sharing, telling stories. Gestures, either alone or together with words and the making of things, create place: a touch, a ritual dance, movements of the hands. A built object organizes space, transforms it into place: "a jar put on a hill," Wallace Stevens says, "can tame the surrounding space, which rises up to the jar and no longer seems wild."[59] Words, gestures, the making of things transform timeless space into real places, moments of history re-membered.

To argue that Cather re-presents this place, the Divide, as "real" is to insist that her representations encompass the whole range of experience: the fertile prairie land is powerful in its great strength and beauty and also in its brutality, including all of the extremes of freezing cold and blistering heat, raw wind, dust storms, drought and blizzard; the people who live there experience love and death, tenderness and violence, work and relaxation, solitude and companionship through ritual sharing, bliss and every sort of privation. Cather's stories are also "real" as works of art; like real tales they are blends of the everyday and the marvelous. John Bergson on his deathbed recounting his failures, each an episode in the story of his life; the ballads, poems and songs of the Old World which are his children's inheritance, as well as the stories his daughter reads—*Robinson Crusoe*, *The Swiss Family Robinson*, *The Frithjof Saga* and the Swedish bible; old Ivar's bible stories and Marie's Bohemian legends of the "talking tree": all are real. The women piece together bits of material, scraps that remind them of events of their lives, or scraps lovingly handed down like family heirlooms as reminders of times before they were born: their stories are as real and as useful as the warmth their quilts provide; they are engaged not in making ornament, either in their tales or in their work, though both delight the senses and the imagination, but in creating maps of their experience, in preserving and inventing design, in making history.

What if, novelist Margaret Atwood asks, Louisa May Alcott's *Little Women* were elevated to a more important place in the line of ancestral descent, a line that sees the male loner "lighting out for the territory" as the central motif in American fiction? What if *Moby Dick* had been told from the point of view of Ishmael's mother and sisters? It would not have been *Moby Dick* at all, she says, since for them "Captain Ahab and whales and other images of Romanticism have no place except over the mantelpiece."[60] The question is not only what would the story have been like, or what would our American literary tradition be like, but what does a female reader imagine as she reads? What is her response to stories? How do they affect her life?

What if, historian Gerda Lerner has challenged, we were to reperiodize history by studying those documents and events central to *women*'s lives? And from her question the study of women's private papers, familial relationships, work and material culture has begun. Why not study the impact of female bonding, of female friendship and homosexual relations, the experience of women in groups? It is men who have defined women as marginal, but "all history as we know it, is, for women, merely pre-history."[61] Now we need to know: What are the women's stories?

What are their private fantasies, and what stories do they tell to each other, to their children and grandchildren?

Without stories, theologian Carol Christ argues, there is no articulation of experience: "without stories a woman is lost. . . . She does not learn to value her struggles, to celebrate her strengths, to comprehend her pain. Without stories she cannot understand herself. Without stories she is alienated from those deeper experiences of self and world that have been called spiritual or religious. She is closed in silence."[62]

Women often live out inauthentic stories provided by a culture they did not create—that is, they internalize the assumptions of a patriarchal culture. The importance for us as readers of Willa Cather's first novel of the soil, then, is that her story *is* authentic: her hero Alexandra is an ordinary woman working in a particular place and time. In *O Pioneers!* the whole complex range of women's experience and imagination—words, gestures, the making of things—is primary. The great fact is the land: Cather begins there with memory and desire, inventing, re-membering, making, imagining. From her own experience and that of her neighbors, from the stories she has read and listened to, Cather makes a language-scape,[63] rooting her stories in time. "One January day, thirty years ago, the little town of Hanover, anchored on a windy Nebraska tableland," this one begins. Look, listen, and you will find that they all begin with the concrete and particular—the place, the time, the weather, the conditions of the soil, the work being done:

> A mist of fine snowflakes was curling and eddying about the cluster of low drab buildings huddled on the gray prairie, under a gray sky. The dwelling-houses were set about haphazard on the tough prairie sod; some of them looked as if they had been moved in overnight, and others as if they were straying off by themselves, headed straight for the open plain. None of them had any appearance of permanence, and the howling wind blew under them as well as over them. [3]

There is nobody about on this particular January day—the women are all at home, the children in school, the shopkeepers well behind their frosty windows—but a few rough-looking country men in overcoats. Yet this is the beginning of a story, made of memory and desire. The old German song, "Wo bist du, wo bist du, mein geliebtest Land," the graveyard, once prairie, that tells the death of parents and neighbors, the picture carried in a young man's mind of the sun coming up over the country, the young Swedish girl with her milking pails—all are parts of the old story that writes itself on the land. "Isn't it queer," the young man, Carl Linstrum, says to Alexandra, "there are only two or three human stories, and they go on repeating themselves as fiercely as if they had never happened before; like the larks in this country, that have been singing the same five notes over for thousands of years" (4, 126, 118, 119).

It *is* the same: we recognize it as true; but we have not heard it told before in this particular way.

CHAPTER 9

Body, Memory, Architecture

I have been amazed more than once by a description a woman gave me of a world all her own which she had been secretly haunting since early childhood. A world of searching, the elaboration of a knowledge, on the basis of a systematic experimentation with the bodily functions, a passionate and precise interrogation of her erotogeneity. This practice, extraordinarily rich and inventive, . . . is prolonged or accompanied by a production of forms, a veritable aesthetic activity, each stage of rapture inscribing a resonant vision, a composition, something beautiful. . . . I wished that that woman would write and proclaim this unique empire so that other women, other unacknowledged sovereigns, might exclaim: I, too, overflow; my desires have invented new desires. My body knows unheard-of songs. Time and again, I, too, have felt so full of luminous torrents that I could burst—burst with forms much more beautiful than those which are put up in frames.

—Hélène Cixous, "The Laugh of the Medusa"[1]

Body. Bodies come together and move apart. Bodies sweat in the sun, they gleam in the bath, they shiver when the thick snows wrap the wide prairieland in a blanket of forgetfulness. In work their muscles grow taut and hard; in repose they stretch and remember. In youth they move with the energy and grace of a wild bird not yet arrested in flight; in age, nearly bent double but still spry, wrinkled and dry, they remember. The soldiers in the hold of the ship *Anchises* huddle together to keep warm; Ántonia's children huddle together in the haymow like cubs. In the heavy harvest season even the horses have a more sociable existence than usual: they nose the colts of old friends, eat out of strange mangers, drink, or refuse to drink, out of strange troughs.

Alexandra dreams of a man lifting her like a shock of wheat. Jim Burden dreams of a woman with a reaping-hook. The miller takes pleasure in the warmth of old wood and the shine of gleaming copper, but in his lonely mill-house he has learned to live without touching; his wife Sapphira, her legs swollen with dropsy, sits immobile in her chair in lonely splendor, thinking of the slave girl, hatching evil plans. Their little granddaughter, her throat swollen with diphtheria, walks in her sleep to where a bowl of warm chicken broth sits on the kitchen table: she drinks it, it tastes good to her, and she gets well.

Bodies shape themselves against the walls of caves; they sit around a table, their elbows touching; they sit around a fire, their knees touching. One fits her back against the trunk of a mulberry tree, fingers of light filtering through the branches of the tree touching her with gold, waiting. In a grand old house, a woman of tarnished grandeur stands at a table, making pastry: a crude young man enters by the kitchen door, walks up behind her, and carelessly puts both arms around her, his hands meeting over her breasts. Another young man watches at the window, his face shielded by honeysuckle.

A young man lies in a hammock, his body open to the night with longing; an old man lies in a hammock, looking at the stars, meditating.

Bodies are blasted with a shotgun, or crushed by an oncoming train.

Bodies work until their muscles quiver: at night, or on Sunday, the day of repose, they come together and listen to stories, told or read out of a book: the child leans against the mother's knee to listen.

In *O Pioneers!* Alexandra has an illusion of being lifted up bodily and carried lightly by someone very strong:

> It was a man, certainly, who carried her, but he was like no man she knew; he was much larger and stronger and swifter, and he carried her as easily as if she were a sheaf of wheat. She never saw him, but, with eyes closed, she could feel that he was yellow like the sunlight, and there was the smell of ripe cornfields about him. She could feel him approach, bend over her and lift her, and then she could feel herself being carried swiftly off across the fields.[2]

This fancy is strange because Alexandra is self-sufficient; she has little interest in men except as "work-fellows": "she had never been in love, she had never indulged in sentimental reveries" (205), and Carl Linstrum, the friend of her youth whom she marries in middle age, timid and slight as a boy and as a man, is clearly a companion only. The fancy is a familiar one to strong women who carry great weight: they remember a fantasy of youth; they long, when tired or troubled, to be carried by a man of great strength.³ The fancy makes Alexandra angry with herself: as a young woman, after such a reverie she would rise hastily and go down to the bath-house, where she would "prosecute her bath with vigor, finishing it by pouring buckets of cold well-water over her gleaming white body which no man on the Divide could have carried very far." But as she grows older, sometimes she would come in from a day of hard work and go to bed with her body aching with fatigue. It was then, just before sleep, that she would have "the old sensation of being lifted and carried by a strong being who took from her all her bodily weariness" (206–7).

Alexandra is touched by the sun; she is warmed by the earth; she is chilled by the rain as she leans heavily upon her father's gravestone. She looks on with pleasure as her Swedish maids giggle and cluster.

In *The Song of the Lark*, Thea lies in bed, relaxing in warm drowsiness. Her mother comes into her room with a breakfast tray, then sits for a moment's conversation, looking with pleasure at her daughter's well-formed young body. Leaving Thea's room, she stops to put her hand on her daughter's chest. "You're filling out nice," she says, feeling about. "No, I wouldn't bother about the buttons. Leave 'em stay off. This is a good time to harden your chest." Lying still, Thea reflects, there was no sham about her mother; she likes her mother.⁴ Harsanyi, Thea's music teacher, has a hunch. He asks her to sing:

> He kept his right hand on the keyboard and put his left to her throat, placing the tips of his delicate fingers over her larynx. "Again,—until your breath is gone.—Trill between the two tones, always; good! Again; excellent!—Now up,—stay there. . . . Now, once more; carry it up and then down, *ah—ah*." He put his hand back to her throat and sat with his head bent, his one eye closed. He loved to hear a big voice throb in a relaxed, natural throat, and he was thinking that no one had ever felt this voice vibrate before. It was like a wild bird that had flown into his studio. . . . No one knew that it had come, or even that it existed; least of all the strange, crude girl in whose throat it beat its passionate wings. What a simple thing it was, he reflected; why had he never guessed it before? Everything about her indicated it,—the big mouth, the wide jaw and chin, the strong white teeth, the deep laugh. The machine was so simple and strong, seemed to be so easily operated. [187–88]

When Thea visits the cliff dwellings of Panther Canyon, it is through her body that she first begins to understand the ancient people. Climbing the water trail, she feels intuitively the movement of a woman going up and down that path. She finds herself walking with a feeling in her feet

and knees and loins which she has never known before, and she can feel
the weight of an Indian baby hanging on to her own back as she climbs.
Lying on a rock shelf in the sun, she understands certain simple, insistent
and monotonous rhythms, not expressible in words, but translated "into
attitudes of body, into degrees of muscular tension or relaxation; the
naked strength of youth, sharp as the sun-shafts; the crouching timorous-
ness of age, the sullenness of women who waited for their captors." She
imagines herself as an Indian youth, coppery breast and shoulders outlined against the sky, leaning to throw a net to ensnare an unsuspecting
eagle (303).

The later, successful Thea—Kronborg, as she is known—often finds
herself weary in body and spirit, but when she bathes, she becomes her
natural self again, the creature she likes best. She pins her braids about her
head, drops her nightgown and begins her Swedish movements; she
splashes and tumbles about in the tub, using her brushes and sponges like
toys, fairly playing in the water, cheered by the sight of her own body, "the
freshness of her physical self, her long, firm lines, the smoothness of her
skin" (427–28).

The air in the Shimerda's sod dugout is close and stifling. The
Shimerda children huddle together in the cave to keep warm. In the rear
wall is another little cave, a round hole, not much bigger than an oil
barrel, scooped out in the black earth. Inside are some quilts and a pile of
straw. The old man holds a lantern and says in a despairing voice: "Yulka;
my Ántonia!" They sleep there.[5]

Jim Burden likes to dance with the hired girls. Physically they are
almost a race apart: out-of-door work has given them a vigor, a positive
carriage and freedom of movement that makes them conspicuous among
Black Hawk women. The town girls, on the other hand, stay indoors in
winter because of the cold and in summer because of the heat: "When one
danced with them their bodies never moved inside their clothes; their
muscles seemed to ask but one thing—not to be disturbed. . . . [their]
faces . . . , gay and rosy, or listless and dull, [are remembered as] cut off
below the shoulders, like cherubs" (226).

The hired girl Jim likes best is Lena Lingard, but he dreams a dream,
a great many times, always the same:

> I was in a harvest-field full of shocks, and I was lying against one of them.
> Lena Lingard came across the stubble barefoot, in a short skirt, with a
> curved reaping-hook in her hand, and she was flushed like the dawn, with a

kind of luminous rosiness all about her. She sat down beside me, turned to me with a soft sigh and said, Now they are all gone, and I can kiss you as much as I like." [256–57][6]

After an absence of many years, Jim goes back to the prairieland of his youth to visit Ántonia. Her children take him to see the fruit cave: they trace on the glass jars the outline of the cherries and strawberries and crabapples; they point to the barrels of dill pickles, chopped pickles and watermelon rinds, and then they run up the steps together, tumbling out of the cave, "big and little, tow heads and gold heads and brown, and flashing little naked legs; a veritable explosion of life out of the dark cave into the sunlight" (382).

Together Ántonia and her children look at photographs: they speak Bohemian, they tell stories, they crowd together, touching. Murmuring in their rich old language, they are not afraid to touch each other (394).

Jim sleeps that night in the haymow with the boys. Ambrosch and Leo cuddle up in a hay-cave back under the eaves, giggling and whispering, tickling each other, tossing and tumbling in the hay. Jim lies awake thinking of Ántonia, seeing a succession of pictures like old woodcuts: "Ántonia kicking her bare legs against the sides of my pony when we came home in triumph with our snake; Ántonia in her black shawl and fur cap, as she stood by her father's grave in the snowstorm; Ántonia coming in with her work-team along the evening sky-line. . . . All the strong things of her heart came out in her body" (397–98).

We measure and order the world out from our own bodies: the world opens up in front of us and closes behind.[7] Thus a young Jim Burden knows from how tired he is how far he has traveled from Virginia, and he knows the land he is coming to is slightly undulating because he can feel in his body the way the wheels grind against the brake as the wagon goes down into a hollow and lurches up again on the other side. His body-measure tells him that the country he has come to is mostly rough, shaggy red grass: it is as tall as he is and reaches as far as he can see. The glide of the long railway journey he still feels gives him a sense that the country is in motion:

> As I looked about me I felt that the grass was the country, as the water is the sea. The red of the grass made all the great prairie the color of wine-stains, or of certain seaweeds when they are first washed up. And there was so much motion in it; the whole country seemed, somehow, to be running . . . more than anything else I felt motion in the landscape; in the fresh, easy-

blowing morning wind, and in the earth itself, as if the shaggy grass were a sort of loose hide, and underneath it herds of wild buffalo were galloping, galloping.

Sensing the length of the journey in his body, he feels as if has come to the end of the world: "I wanted to walk straight on through the red grass and over the edge of the world, which could not be very far away. The light air about me told me that the world ended here: only the ground and sun and sky were left, and if one went a little farther there would be only sun and sky, and one would float off into them, like the tawny hawks which sailed over our heads making slow shadows on the grass" (16–18).

The earth is known first through the body: the earth delights and sustains, confounds and bruises the body. We make shelter on the earth in the image of our own bodies, shelters for privacy, shelters for coming together. Sheltered, we get on with the telling of stories.[8]

⬚ *Memory.* To tell is to remember, to re-member. Artist Thea Kronborg, in *The Song of the Lark,* working through the idea and the passion to get it "right," depends upon memory: "It's full of the thing every plain creature finds out for himself, but that never gets written down. It's unconscious memory, . . . like folk music" (449).[9] Jim Burden's story of Ántonia is right for him: he calls it *"My Ántonia."* Professor St. Peter reconstructs, from fragments of the past, a history of the Spanish in North America; he sits alone with a piece of turquoise from Tom Outland in order to recover his own lost youth. To re-member is to fit from the shard of pottery, the lump of turquoise, the fragment of the past held in the hand, pen to matter as plough to furrow.

"Some memories are realities, and are better than anything that can ever happen to one again," Jim Burden says (370).

Memory can be triggered by a melody, like the little phrase from the Vinteuil sonata, by a taste, a smell, a touch, a scrap of fabric joined with others to make a quilt, a landscape that recalls another, buried in the unconscious. From a bit of madeleine, Proust has shown us how it is possible to conjure up a re-membered world. Concentrating on the taste of a crumb soaked in tea, the narrator of *Swann's Way* clears a space in his mind: "I place in position before my mind's eye the still recent taste of that first mouthful, and I feel something start within me, something that leaves its resting-place and attempts to rise, something that has been embedded like an anchor at a great depth; I do not know yet what it is, but I can feel it mounting slowly; I can measure the resistance, I can hear the echo of great spaces traversed."[10]

Jim Burden tastes a bit of mushroom: the strangeness recalls the little brown chips, light as feathers, that looked like shavings of some root. His grandmother threw them into the fire. He recalls the penetrating, earthy odor of the dried mushrooms gathered by the Shimerdas in some deep Bohemian forest and brought all the way to Nebraska, preserved as rare treasures in a bag made of bed-ticking. A taste of mushroom and Jim can remember the stifling little dugout cave with its smell of rotting potatoes and the smaller cave within, where Ántonia and Yulka slept; he can hear Mrs. Shimerda's half-phrases, see her take the bag from her wooden chest and stir the contents around with her hand, the crazy child smacking his lips at the sight, see her measure a cupful, tie it up in a bit of sacking and present it ceremoniously to his grandmother; he can smell an odor salty, earthy and pungent, even among the other odors of that cave (88–90).

The scent of a flower gives Ántonia back Bohemia: "It always grew in our yard," she tells Jim, "and my papa had a green bench and a table under the bushes. In summer, when they were in bloom, he used to sit there with his friend. . . . When I was little I used to go down there to hear them talk—beautiful talk, like what I never hear in this country" (269).

The scent of snow in the air gives Jim back Virginia and Nebraska at Christmastime—the cold, fresh-smelling little tree in a corner of the sitting-room:

> We hung it with the gingerbread animals, strings of popcorn, and bits of candle. . . . Its real splendours, however, came from the most unlikely place in the world—from Otto's cowboy trunk. . . . From under the lining he . . . produced a collection of brilliantly coloured paper figures . . . [that] had been sent to him year after year, by his old mother in Austria. There was a bleeding heart, in tufts of paper lace; there were the three kings, gorgeously apparelled, and the ox and the ass and the shepherds; there was the Baby in the manger, and a group of angels, singing; there were camels and leopards, held by the black slaves of the three kings. Our tree became the talking tree of the fairy tale; legends and stories nestled like birds in its branches. Grandmother said it reminded her of the Tree of Knowledge. We put sheets of cotton wool under it for a snow-field, and Jake's pocket-mirror for a frozen lake. [94][11]

Jim hears a story: Pavel is dying; he is afraid of the wolves. When he and Russian Peter were young men, they were asked to be groomsmen for a friend who was to marry the belle of another village. After the wedding ceremony at the church, and a dinner given by the bride's parents that lasted all afternoon, and a supper that continued far into the night with much dancing and drinking, singing and remembering, Pavel and Peter set out with the groom's sledge, the other six sledges with the relatives and friends following behind, the sound of jingling sleighbells marking their progress. As the sledges made their way through the frozen night, the first wolf-howls were heard, taken up and echoed with quickening repetitions. The wolves ran like streaks of shadow; there were hundreds of them. They would get abreast of the horses, and the screams of the horses were more terrible than the cries of the men and women. The horses would go crazy, jump over each other, get tangled up in the harness, and overturn the sledge. As one driver after another lost control, the people who were falling behind shrieked as piteously as those who were already lost. Just before daybreak, the sledge of Pavel and Peter, the only one left, was attacked by the wolves. Pavel called to the groom that they must lighten—and pointed to the bride. The young man cursed them and held her tighter. Pavel tried to drag her away. In the struggle, the groom rose, Pavel knocked him over the side and threw the girl after him; and they drove into their own village, the monastery bells ringing for early prayers. They were run out of town, and everywhere they went, the story followed them, and bad luck followed them. But the story goes on: when Pavel died, their goods in Black Hawk were auctioned off, and when he had kissed the cow good-bye before she was led off, Russian Peter sat down on the bare floor with his clasp-knife and ate all the melons he had put away for winter. He was found with a dripping beard, surrounded by heaps of melon rinds. For Mr. Shimerda, Pavel and Peter's cabin becomes a hermitage. For Ántonia and Jim, the story of the wedding party was never at an end:

> We did not tell Pavel's secret to any one, but guarded it jealously—as if the wolves of the Ukraine had gathered that night long ago, and the wedding party been sacrificed, to give us a painful and peculiar pleasure. At night, before I went to sleep, I often found myself in a sledge drawn by three horses, dashing through a country that looked something like Nebraska and something like Virginia. [63–69]

Committing a story to memory, so that you can tell it again, depends upon *placing* it. Ántonia, her homeland recalled by the scent of a flower, tells Jim that if she were put down there in the middle of the night, "I could find my way all over that little town; and along the river to the next town, where my grandmother lived. My feet remember all the little paths through the woods, and where the big roots stick out to trip you. I ain't never forgot my own country." Jim, when he goes back to the Nebraska prairieland, finds a bit of the first road that went from Black Hawk out to the north country, an old road "which used to run like a wild thing across the open prairie, clinging to the high places and circling and doubling like a rabbit before the hounds" (271, 418). Mlle. Olive de Courcy, in *One of Ours*, stops Claude in their conversation and says, "Describe that to me, minutely, and perhaps I can see the rest." When he has drawn a map in the yellow sand with a stick—the house and the farmyard, the pasture with Lovely Creek flowing through it, the wheatfield and the cornfields, the timber claim, then she allows him to go on.[12]

People who tell stories are distinguished from those who have no stories to tell.[13] In *The Troll Garden*, both trolls and forest children are preferable to people in a little Kansas town who are deader than the sculptor brought home to be buried; to those in Moonstone, Colorado, who would bury Thea Kronborg in funeral song and piano lessons; to those colorless folk in Haverford, Nebraska, who bury Lucy Gayheart. The rich ones are Spanish Johnny, who teaches Thea his native songs and dances; Papa Shimerda, with his stories of Bohemia; Otto Fuchs, who when Papa Shimerda dies, tells Jim stories of the Black Tiger Mine, about violent deaths, casual buryings, and the queer fancies of dying men; the hired girls with their stories of Norway and Sweden; Widow Steavens, "the pioneer woman," who tells Jim the story of *her* Ántonia: "Jimmy, I sat right down on that bank beside her and made lament," she says. "I cried like a young thing. I couldn't help it. I was just about heart-broke. It was one of them lovely warm May days, and the wind was blowing and the colts jumping around in the pastures; but I felt bowed with despair. My Ántonia, that had so much good in her, had come home disgraced" (127, 354).

For those rich in memory and desire, the incidents of daily living are the materials for stories. Crazy Wick Cutter hurries home to carry out an assault on Ántonia, having first put his wife on a train going the wrong way; he later murders his wife just one hour before taking his own life—to prevent her relatives from claiming any part of his property.

Ántonia catches a grasshopper: she makes a nest for him in her hands, then puts him in her hair for safekeeping, tying her kerchief on carefully, and tells Jim the story of Old Hata, a beggar woman in her village at home who sold herbs and roots she had dug up in the forest: "If you took her in and gave her a warm place by the fire, she sang old songs to the children in a cracked voice, like this. Old Hata, she was called, and the children loved to see her coming and saved their cakes and sweets for her" (43–44).

Jim kills a snake: he measures him with his riding quirt—he is about five-and-a-half-feet long—and counts the rattles—twelve, broken off so there might have been twenty-four; he is reminded of "the ancient, eldest Evil, . . . horrible unconscious memories in all warm-blooded life." Jim passes the episode off as a mock-adventure: "the game was fixed for me by chance, as it probably was for many a dragon slayer. I had been adequately armed by Russian Peter; the snake was old and lazy; and I had Ántonia beside me, to appreciate and admire." The colorful storytelling is left to Ántonia: "He fight something awful! He is all over Jimmy's boots. I scream for him to run, but he just hit and hit that snake like he was crazy." And this picture lingers in one's memory: Ántonia riding the pony, slowly, her legs swinging against its sides, Jim following with a spade slung over his shoulder, dragging his snake tied up by a rope, casting furtive glances over his shoulder to make sure no avenging mate, older and wiser, is racing up from the rear (53–55).

Jim and the hired girls see an ordinary plough, left standing on some upland prairie, against the sinking sun:

> We sat looking off across the country, watching the sun go down. The curly grass about us was on fire now. The bark of the oaks turned red as copper. There was a shimmer of gold on the brown river. Out in the stream the sandbars glittered like glass, and the light trembled in the willow thickets as if little flames were leaping among them. . . . The girls sat listless, leaning against each other. The long fingers of the sun touched their foreheads.
>
> Presently we saw a curious thing: . . . the sun was going down in a limpid, gold-washed sky. Just as the lower edge of the red disk rested on the high fields against the horizon, a great black figure suddenly appeared on the face of the sun. We sprang to our feet, straining our eyes toward it. In a moment we realized what it was. On some upland farm, a plough had been left standing in the field. The sun was sinking just behind it. Magnified across the distance by the horizontal light, it stood out against the sun, was exactly contained within the circle of the disk; the handles, the tongue, the share—black against the molten red. There it was, heroic in size, a picture writing on the sun (278–79).

The magical vision—picture writing, in which the image is perfectly contained by the form—occurs in the midst of storytelling, in a place both real and mythic.[14] Ántonia, smelling a flower that makes her homesick for her native land, describes the little village in Czechoslovakia whose paths she knows with her feet; Tiny describes her father's rye fields, planted to keep her mother from being so homesick for the taste of Scandinavian rye; Anna remembers the Norwegian harbor where her grandmother bought fish; and Lena tells of her wild grandfather who married a Lapp. The women are earthbound, placed; Jim, American and educated, speaks in terms of legend, of terrae incognitae:[15] he wants to know if the Lapps really wear skins, if they have "squint eyes, like Chinese." His story comes from a book: he tells of Coronado's dying "in the wilderness, of a broken heart," while Ántonia, thinking of her own father, responds, "More than him has done that" (276, 278).

This Coronado who stirs Jim's imagination was a Spanish explorer who came to the New World in search of the fabled Seven Cities of Gold, basing his pragmatic behavior—the planning of travel routes, the acquiring of supplies and other logistical decisions—on legendary data, a story from Iberian folklore about an archbishop and six bishops who fled westward across the Atlantic after the Moorish invasion of Spain and built seven Christian cities. No one knew just where these cities were located, but by the fourth decade of the sixteenth century, Spanish explorations had made it clear that they were neither in Mexico nor in the Caribbean. Rumor and lore located them somewhere in the western interior of the American Southwest. Speculation led Cabeza de Vaca, Don Hernando de Soto, Fray Marcos and Estevan the Moor, in turn, to wander among Indian villages in what is now New Mexico in search of those cities "seven in number" whose very streets were paved with gold. In the spring of 1540 a company led by Coronado made its way into southeastern Arizona. Expecting towers of gold, they found the adobe pueblos of the Zuñi and Hopi Indians. Coronado's army then moved across the southern reaches of the Rockies, past the Staked Plains of New Mexico and Texas, into the vastness of the Great Plains. Somewhere in Kansas—not in Nebraska, as Jim believes—finding only the poor grass huts of the Wichita Indians, he gave up the attempt to discover the Cities of Gold. Forced to reconcile the discrepancy between preconceived image and observed reality, what Coronado did achieve was a way of negotiating terrae incognitae, reporting the geographical features of his travels with great clarity—"the nature of the pueblo tribes of the Southwest, of the mountains and plateaus of northern Mexico, Arizona, and New Mexico, and of the Great Plains with their nomadic tribes and their endless herds of bison."[16]

It is under the spell of Coronado's story that Jim and the hired girls observe the plough against the sun, and for the moment that this ordinary farm tool becomes something magical, it is as if they reenact the legend of Coronado in the very place where they sit. And because the *story* of Coronado has a continuing life—Jim tells of a farmer in the county just north breaking up his sod and turning up a metal stirrup of fine workmanship and a sword with a Spanish inscription on the blade; the local boys scour the relics and put them on exhibit, the local priest reads the name of the Spanish maker and an abbreviation that stands for Cordova on the sword, and Ántonia has seen it "with my own eyes"—it is as if the thing imagined and the thing seen are the same, mystical and earthly, ephemeral and lasting. As the young people speculate about Coronado and his journey, it is, for the moment, as if he had succeeded in his quest, as if they, themselves, are the explorers in search of the fabled Seven Cities who see in poor Indian villages towers of gold: every tip and edge and surface of the land, the young people themselves, their stories, are touched by the sun with gold. For the moment, a commonplace plough—like the earlier reaper with a cozy seat for little girls from Barbizon to Nebraska—becomes heroic in size, a poetic symbol. This picture writing on the sun invokes reveries—like the flower smell that brings back Ántonia's Bohemia, like a folk song or a story—in which ordinary events take on extraordinary meaning, and in which supernatural events are part of everyday life. Like a photograph, this sun writing is captured briefly and held, as a kernel of memory, and then as suddenly reduced to ordinary and earthbound dimensions:

> Even while we whispered about it, our vision disappeared; the ball dropped and dropped until the red tip went beneath the earth. The fields below us were dark, the sky was growing pale, and that forgotten plough had sunk back to its own littleness somewhere on the prairie. [279]

Architecture. Caves: Ivar's sod hut, in *O Pioneers!*, distinguishable as a human habitation only by its stovepipe sticking out of the ground; the Shimerda's dugout, with a cave in the back where Ántonia and Yulka sleep; Ántonia's fruit cave, from which her children come tumbling out, a veritable explosion of life and color; the cliff dwellings of the Ancient People, the pueblos and hogans, fragments of pottery and ceremonial kivas.

Houses: Mrs. Bergson's farmhouse in *O Pioneers!* and Grandmother Burden's frame house in *My Ántonia*; Mrs. Archie's closed-up and dust-free house in *The Song of the Lark*; *The Professor's House*—his old house with the study at the top, and his new house, from which he retreats; the retreat house of Archbishop Lamy above Santa Fé, New Mexico; the miller's retreat house, with its burnished copper vessels, in *Sapphira and the Slave Girl*.

Rooms: Thea's little attic room in *The Song of the Lark*; Lesley Ferguesson's partitioned room, up under the eaves, in "The Best Years"; the grandmother's room in "Old Mrs. Harris," where the children gather to hear stories and Mandy, the bound-girl, rubs the old woman's swollen feet at the end of the day; the room where Sapphira sits immobile in her lace cap, her feet swollen with dropsy; Grandmother Burden's kitchen in *My Ántonia*, where young Jim Burden takes his first bath in Nebraska while his grandmother bakes gingerbread; the Barbizon kitchen of Mme. Joubert in *One of Ours*, where the smell of flowers from the garden mingles with the smell of fresh bread; the kitchen of Marian Forrester, the *Lost Lady*, where the crude Ivy Peters enters without knocking and stands behind her, his hands on her breasts; the noisy room in which the once-lovely Myra Henshawe lies dying in *My Mortal Enemy*.

Towers: the towers Coronado thought he saw; the towers of the Cliff Palace at Mesa Verde that Tom Outland discovers in *The Professor's House*; the tower of the recluse Jeanne Le Ber and the towerlike house of the Governor of Kebec in *Shadows on the Rock*.

Forms: a Dutch painting with a landscape seen through the window in *The Professor's House*; a musical form in *The Professor's House*; the vessel that one's throat is in singing in *The Song of the Lark*; the epic of Alexander; the epic of Alexandra; Jim Burden's pastoral elegy. Maps: Alexandra's map of the land and Mrs. Lee's quilted landscapes in *O Pioneers!*; Mrs. Wheeler's map of Europe and the map Claude draws in the sand for Mlle. de Courcy in *One of Ours*; Tom Outland's map of Mesa Verde; Coronado's map of the New World. Artifacts: Alexander's bridge; Alexandra's land; ploughs and reapers; pottery vessels for carrying, cooking and serving; houses and barns; quilts and featherbeds; gravestones. Stories, legends, songs: the legend of Coronado; Jim Burden's story of Ántonia; the Pioneer Woman's story of Ántonia; a song about a "yaller gal" named Nancy Till, in *Sapphira and the Slave Girl*, a legend that children not yet born will know about a slave girl who escaped to freedom; the legend, in *Death Comes for the Archbishop*, of Kit Carson; the true story of the discovery of Mesa Verde.

Thea Kronborg, in *The Song of the Lark*, makes a discovery in the land of the Ancient People. Taking her morning bath in a sunny pool at the bottom of the canyon, she thinks about water—that it must have had "sovereign qualities, from having been the object of so much . . . desire." She senses in the stream a continuity of life reaching back from the present moment to the distant past. Suddenly a realization strikes her with such force that she becomes quite still, remaining so until the water dries upon her flushed skin:

> The stream and the broken pottery: what was any art but an effort to make a sheath, a mould in which to imprison for a moment the shining, elusive element which is life itself,—life hurrying past us and running away, too strong to stop, too sweet to lose? The Indian women had held it in their jars. In the sculpture she had seen . . . it had been caught in a flash of arrested motion. In singing, one made a vessel of one's throat and nostrils and held it on one's breath, caught the stream in a scale of natural intervals (304).

The plough against the sun: an earthbound, everyday object, like the people who use it and the land they work, and at the same time, exactly contained within the circle of the disk, it becomes the mould that holds for a moment the shining element that is life itself, picture writing on the sun.

When Jim Burden says in the frame story of *My Ántonia* that his manuscript "hasn't any form," he means that it does not have the usual form: plot, conflict, the development of character, the Aristotelian form of beginning, middle and end. The parts of *My Ántonia* have a semi-independent existence of their own, like separate stories, like the separate squares of hemmed fabric that are pieced together to make a quilt, like the separate rooms of a frame house on a western prairie; together, they do form a whole. The form of the novel is "a triple enclosure," like Ántonia's orchard—"the wire fence, then the hedge of thorny locusts, then the mulberry hedge," (385) which both protect the inner space and screen out everything except the blue sky against which one's vision is projected. Jim's story of Ántonia is written down for a friend he meets on a train, set within his own story of growing up on the Nebraska prairie; and the friend in turn, the other "I," narrates a story of the mature Jim Burden who is a legal counsel for one of the great western railways, whose "romantic disposition" both colors his reminiscence of Ántonia and has made for professional success—and personal disappointment—in his later life. The forms Jim works with—the material for his story—are real things: sod dugouts and frame farmhouses, crops and ploughs, getting cooled off in the river in summer and digging your way out of a snowstorm in winter, children being born and old people dying, mushrooms and snakes, threshing machines and railways; but to Jim, separated from these things by time, by his own choice, by the plate-glass window of his stateroom in a passing train, these things also represent a lost past, and they emerge for him in his present story with the kind of nostalgia typical for those who live in city apartments or in subdivision houses that are no longer institutions, no longer represent anything of permanent significance, have little connection with work, education, birth, death, illness or the land.[17]

For Jim Burden, who spends most of his time in an anonymous stateroom of a moving train and is loosely married to a woman with whom he shares little, these twentieth-century sensibilities are the more poignant because with every trip through the countryside of his youth Jim takes, nostalgia is re-invoked. For Jim, the country is no longer workplace, but landscape.[18] He remembers the real farmhouse in which he grew up, but remembers it through the lens of his own romantic perspective, as representative of a past way of life. The farmstead *is* representative; that is, it is a representation of another time and place, a symbol, like the plough against the sun, and it is also typical of the life that went on in real nineteenth-century farmhouses all across middle America.[19]

The nineteenth-century farmhouse was a place, a workplace, tied for sustenance to the land upon which it stood, a shelter for a family of closely knit individuals. The temporary pioneer shelter was the log house or soddy; the farmhouse was meant for stability—though not to be so permanent as to prevent moving even farther west. Unlike its eastern predecessors, the western pioneer dwelling was not clustered in a village, but set apart from its neighbors and at some distance from the highway, built primarily for use of the family rather than for display or entertaining. This was a house with a flexible plan, a house to which rooms could be added, rooms that could be used for more than one purpose and could be divided by sliding doors—like the parlor, added onto the Kronborg house in *The Song of the Lark*, which serves as Thea's music room, and at night as her sister's bedroom. The house was innovative: in construction it used the latest "balloon" frame—thin plates and studs held together by nails (which the farmer, having been told to do so, would have brought with him), instead of the ancient and expensive method of construction using mortise-and-tenon joints. The nineteenth-century prairie farmhouse was inexpensive, fast to build, large, well-lighted and convenient: it was practical. Unlike a New England hall-and-parlor house with one room for the

family and another for ceremonies, the rooms in this house were thought
of in terms of function: kitchen, milk room, pantry, living room, bedrooms, piazza. The house was designed for social self-sufficiency: it had to
take the place of church, meetinghouse, school, tavern; it was the scene of
weddings, burials, business deals, holidays.[20] In *My Ántonia*, the coffin for
Papa Shimerda's burial is built in the Burden's kitchen; Christmas is in the
sitting room, with the ornaments from Otto's trunk bringing the Old
World to Nebraska "without any help from town" (92); and it is in Grandmother Burden's kitchen that Ántonia learns the niceties of American life.

The Burden and Cuzak farms suggest what we can more clearly see
in Alexandra's farm in *O Pioneers!* and in the increasingly efficient and
impersonal Wheeler farm in *One of Ours*—that the flexible farm plan, with
cash crops instead of those grown for the immediate family needs, repeats
the plan of the house. The pieces of land, loosely connected to each other
and to the house it supports, made also of separate but connected pieces,
are fixed in time and place, but moving, too, across the vision of the man
isolated behind his train window. The land that has become landscape is
not only his past; it is his present. He can get off the train,[21] which he
does; and he can make up stories—sing, tell, write them—about the land,
which he also does, to bring the past into the present. And the form he
chooses for his story—he is, after all, a man of "romantic disposition," one
who is white, American and middle class, and who like Willa Cather was a
classics scholar at the University of Nebraska—is the pastoral. This passage from Virgil's *Georgics*: "*Optima dies . . . prima fugit*," "The best days
are the first to flee," stands as epigraph to a tale in which Jim himself is the
representative shepherd—that is, like the shepherds of Theocritus, Virgil
and Spenser, he describes real *villae*, or farmhouses, and "mean" conditions, and at the same time, as a man of the city, he is, like Shakespeare's
courtiers in the Forest of Arden, *representing* himself as a shepherd.[22]

When Jim Burden and the outer narrator agree that their knowledge
of the past is privileged, "a kind of freemasonry"—no one who had not
grown up in a little prairie town could know anything about "what it is
like to spend one's childhood . . . under stimulating extremes of climate:
burning summers when the world lies green and billowy beneath a brilliant sky, when one is fairly stifled in vegetation, in the color and smell of
strong weeds and heavy harvests; blustery winters with little snow, when
the whole country is stripped bare and grey as sheet-iron"—they recall a
place real enough in its range from lush to barren, in its seasonal changes,
yet one fixed in the past. Jim Burden lives in New York when he writes

down his story, but in his frequent trips across the country by train, like the earlier Bartley Alexander he sees a scene that is both a memory and an emblem of a memory. For Jim the "never-ending miles of ripe wheat, . . . country towns and bright-flowered pastures and oak groves wilting in the sun" (ix), always the same, and associated with Ántonia, correspond to a scene fixed in his imagination and imbued with the magical qualities of the plough against the sun—for example:

> As we walked homeward across the fields, the sun dropped and lay like a great golden globe in the low west. While it hung there, the moon rose in the east, as big as a cartwheel, pale silver and streaked with rose colour, thin as a bubble or a ghost-moon. For five, perhaps ten minutes, the two luminaries confronted each other across the level land, resting on opposite edges of the world. In that singular light every little tree and shock of wheat, every sunflower stalk and clump of snow-on-the-mountain, drew itself up high and pointed; the very clods and furrows in the fields seemed to stand up sharply. I felt the old pull of the earth, the solemn magic that comes out of those fields at nightfall. I wished I could be a little boy again, and that my way could end there. [364]

The scene is fixed in being local and particular—his own spot; at the same time it is a *representative* spot, characteristic of the lost green pasture Leo Marx has traced through American fiction, as when, resting on the riverbank after a swim, looking up at two pretty girls "huddled together . . . and peering down at me like curious deer," Jim, like Virgil's shepherd, is "reluctant to leave that green enclosure where the sunlight flickered so bright through the grapevine leaves" (267).

When Jim begins to study Latin, he likes to commit long passages of Virgil's *Aeneid* and *Georgics* to memory while pacing up and down in his room, "looking off at the distant river bluffs and the roll of the blond pastures between." When he looks out his window and feels the earthy wind blowing in, the landscape he sees becomes the landscape of his text:

> On the edge of the prairie, where the sun had gone down, the sky was turquoise blue, like a lake, with gold light throbbing in it. Higher up, in the utter clarity of the western slope, the evening star hung like a lamp suspended by silver chains—like the lamp engraved upon the title-page of old Latin texts, which is always appearing in the new heavens, and waking new desires in men. [264, 298]

His teacher, Gaston Cleric, has explained that for Virgil "*Primus ego in patriam mecum . . . deducam Musas,*" "for I shall be the first, if I live, to bring the Muse into my country," refers, in the word *patria*, not to a nation or a province, but to "the little rural neighborhood on the Mincio where the poet was born, . . . not to the capital, . . . but to his own little 'country'; to his father's fields, 'sloping down to the river and to the old beech trees with broken tops.'" When Virgil, dying, remembered the perfect utterance in the *Georgics*, "where the pen was fitted to the matter as the plough is to the furrow," then, Cleric said, Virgil must have said to himself with thankfulness, "I was the first to bring the Muse into my country." Jim finds himself wondering, as he studies the *Georgics*, about Cleric's *patria*, a particular rocky strip of New England coast, and he finds himself thinking about his own *patria*, of which he believes himself to be the first to write. The young Jim Burden bringing together in his mind these three landscapes into one repeats the imaginative process of the older Jim Burden bringing together three times—a literary or archetypal time, the past time of his childhood in this *patria* and the present time of his writing—in an autobiographical act that solves for him the problem of form:

> Mental excitement was apt to send me with a rush back to my own naked land and the figures scattered upon it. While I was in the very act of *yearning toward the new forms* that Cleric brought up before me, my mind plunged away from me, and I suddenly found myself thinking of the places and people of my own infinitesimal past. They stood out strengthened and simplified now, like the image of the plough against the sun. They were all I had for an answer to the new appeal. I begrudged the room that Jake and Otto and Russian Peter took up in my memory, which I wanted to crowd with other things. But whenever my consciousness was quickened, all those early friends were quickened within it, and in some strange way they accompanied me through all my new experiences. They were so much alive in me that I scarcely stopped to wonder whether they were alive anywhere else, or how. [296–300, emphasis added]

In this passage, the re-invoking of "the plough against the sun" makes clear the way in which human situations are at the same time real, occurring in a particular and concrete place and time, *and* acts of the imagination, timeless and representative—like Coronado's explorations of the New World, or like the anecdotes in Virgil's *Eclogues* Paul Alpers finds "representative."[23] Virgil's Tityrus is a herdsman who praises an actual god—a powerful young man in Rome—and speaks of real circumstances in his own present time, while Meliboeus, dispossessed and exiled, brings out and intensifies the idyllic. Both, Alpers argues, are "equally . . . representative shepherds, whose differing situations play out different implications of pastoral's central fiction."[24]

The pastoral is, of course, a fiction. Jim Burden creates "his" Ántonia, just as, in the telling of the story, he creates himself. Like the pastoral shepherd, Jim Burden remembers and represents a time and a place in which a great deal of human suffering occurs in an idealized landscape, a moment of *otium* where idyllic bliss of the sort he experiences on the riverbank is possible.[25] Jim Burden's story, like that of Virgil's shepherds, is a kind of "anatomy of nostalgia, which one feels all the more keenly because it responds to a real situation and expresses feelings of concrete, ordinary loss"—which is what makes his story so "representative."[26]

Jim's "My Ántonia," representative of "human singing and a way of life,"[27] is told as it is remembered, beginning with a set of conventions, becoming inventions over a given ground—ground meant here both musically and in its literal, earthy sense. The form of the novel *My Ántonia* is finally Willa Cather's own, arrived at by working backward through given forms, spinning inventions upon them: the clue from *Alexander's Bridge* filled out. Here, in fact, is not one story, but a series of stories, stories within stories. In their interconnectedness they might seem to be without "form," as Jim says, but not only does each of them have very specific form; together they are an increasingly sure experimentation in another way of telling, one perfected in Cather's later works.

My Ántonia is written down, of course, but what the scholarly Jim Burden does in his manuscript is to record and preserve not just his memory of Ántonia, intertwined closely with his personal history and his elegiac sense of loss, but a cultural tradition, or rather, a tradition of cultures, one that is oral, performed, formulaic, and perpetuated by the artist who learns the rhythms and melodies—the craft—and expands, ornaments and varies the tradition in her or his own particular way. This superimposing of classical and folk tradition is not so odd as it might seem. Albert Lord and Milman Parry have compared Yugoslavian epics— observing singers working "in a thriving tradition of unlettered song"— with Homeric epics in order to demonstrate that the latter were composed as they were performed, learning in the process that "the way of life of a people gives rise to a poetry of a given kind."[28] Similarly, Henry Glassie, studying the community of Ballymenone, Ireland, finds that the villagers' tales correspond in structure to those of the great storytellers of our times: Joyce, Beckett, Faulkner. Willa Cather's prairieland is very different from the stable European communities from which her immigrants derive—

places like those Lord and Glassie describe; yet her storytellers, too, begin with the specific and local reference to time and place. This way of situating the story, of insuring its veracity, gives it meaning in a particular culture; what makes the story art is the variation—the ornamentation, decoration, inversion, expansion—invented by the teller.

All good stories, both Lord and Glassie show, depend upon repetition of key words and phrases. Lord explains formulaic expression—the basis of all folk tales—as "a group of words which is regularly employed under the same metrical conditions to express a given essential idea"; in other words, the theme of a tale is expressed in repeated incidents and descriptive passages. But a good storyteller does not simply learn a set of stock phrases and lines and then shuffle them about, mechanically putting together inviolable fixed units; rather, having acquired a feeling for the patterning of lines, the artist learns to create and shape in performance. The artist, in fact, re-creates a tale in each telling: there is no single "pure" form, but rather an ever-changing form because "the theme is in reality protean; in the singer's mind it has many shapes, all the forms in which he has ever sung it, although his latest rendering of it will naturally be freshest in his mind. It is not a static entity, but a living, changing, adaptable artistic creation."[29]

The patterning of words expresses the themes repeated in tales, and words ornament the tale, underlining its basic structure. "Although pace and pricks of silence most exactly demarcate the story's lines, words—conventional words at beginnings and strong, repeated, rhyming and echoing words at ends—further define the story's parts and blend them into the sweep of the whole," Henry Glassie writes. "The repeated key word is a prime decorative feature of spoken narration." Ornaments in a story do more than please the listener: unlike nonsense passages in songs (e.g., "hey-nonny-nonny"), "they lead toward rather than away from meaning. Extract them, and you have the tale's essence"[30]—as in musical ornament (a Bach invention) and architectural ornament (the tracery that accents the structural members of Louis Sullivan's otherwise stark skyscrapers). In Willa Cather's pioneer landscapes, trees function as ornament, punctuating in their rarity the never-ending quality of the shaggy red grass, sun and sky, "the scarcity of detail in that tawny landscape that made detail so precious." Even when the land, through human intervention, changes and becomes more detailed, what one remembers, returning, is "the conformation of the land as one remembers the modeling of human faces" (32–33, 374).

Stories are narratives, Glassie writes, but narrative alone does not make a story:

> Even more deeply, stories are matters of "discourse," of "connecting links" and "line-by-line" ordering—of special diction. . . . Stories begin and end in conversations. During their course they refer to their social situations by returning to the thick, uncadenced sound of chat. In other passages they crack free to arrange themselves in lines. Convolution and embedding yield to grammatical simplicity. . . . in different performances the same teller will locate a different sound between tongue and ear, a different ratio between silence and noise, to suit the pitch of telling.
>
> Two modes make stories. One is full and flat in sound, complex in grammar; it is used to digress informationally, to orient the listener, and it approximates prose. The other is melodic, rhythmically broken, grammatically simple; it is used to advance the narration, to excite the listener, and it approximates poetry. Neither prose nor poetry, thought nor action, stories are both.[31]

This description of the storyteller's discourse and mode is useful in understanding the stories that are the basis of Cather's *writing*, beginning with *My Ántonia*. The reader is invited to compare two of these—the story of Pavel and Peter, already introduced, and the story of The Tramp and the Threshing Machine—with others Cather tells, especially the many wonderful stories in *Death Comes for the Archbishop*.

Ántonia tells Jim the hair-raising story of Pavel and Peter while they are lying close together in the straw on a cold night, traveling home from Pavel's deathbed, where they have been watching with Mr. Shimerda and Peter, the jolting and rattling of their wagon echoing the movement of the troikas in the tale. The journey of Ántonia and Jim could not, however, be more different from the one with which the story begins—Pavel and Peter, the groomsmen, setting off at midnight for a Ukrainian village, traveling through the frozen countryside with the bride and groom in their sledge and the groom's family and friends in six sledges behind them. The introductory theme suggests the well-fed and rather drunken good humor of the wedding party; but there is an almost immediate counterpointing of another theme—the repeated howls of the hungry wolves:

> . . . when they heard the first wolf-cry, the drivers were not much alarmed. They had too much good food and drink inside them. The first howls were taken up and echoed and with quickening repetitions. The wolves were coming together. There was no moon, but the starlight was clear on the snow. A black drove came up over the hill behind the wedding party. The wolves ran like streaks of shadow; they looked no bigger than dogs, but there were hundreds of them.

One by one the drivers lose control, the sledges overturn, and there is the continuous sound of shrieking:

> The screams of the horses were more terrible to hear than the cries of the men and women. Nothing seemed to check the wolves. It was hard to tell what was happening in the rear; the people who were falling behind shrieked as piteously as those who were already lost. . . .
> At length, as they breasted a long hill, Peter rose cautiously and looked back. "There are only three sledges left," he whispered.
> "And the wolves?" Pavel asked.
> "Enough! Enough for all of us."

The sledge with the groom's family overturns: there is just one sledge left following that of Pavel and Peter. Pavel watches as that sledge, too, is overturned. Then—

> When the shrieking behind them died away, Pavel realized that he was alone upon the familiar road. "They still come?" he asked Peter.
> "Yes."
> "How many?"
> "Twenty, thirty—enough."
> Now his middle horse was being almost dragged by the other two. Pavel gave Peter the reins and stepped carefully into the back of the sledge. He called to the groom that they must lighten—and pointed to the bride. The young man cursed him and held her tighter. Pavel tried to drag her away. In the struggle, the groom rose. Pavel knocked him over the side of the sledge and threw the girl after him. He said he never remembered exactly how he did it, or what happened afterward. Peter, crouching in the front seat, saw nothing. The first thing either of them noticed was a new sound that broke into the clear air, louder than they had ever heard it before—the bell of the monastery of their own village, ringing for early prayers. [64–67]

In the silence of the frozen night as Jim and Ántonia travel homeward in a jolting wagon, Ántonia's story is built on a series of sounds: the howls of the wolves, the shrieking of the people and the horses, the monastery bells tolling, as if to tell the village, at once, of Pavel's great sin. And as regularly as the tolling bell, as regularly as the overcoming, one by one, of the horse-drawn sledges by the wolves, is Peter's accompanying counting:

> "There are only three sledges left."
> "And the wolves?"
> "Enough."
> "They still come?"
> "Yes."

"How many?"
"Twenty, thirty—enough."

Pavel and Peter, much as their conversation sounds like Vladimir's and Estragon's in *Waiting for Godot*, are not just the passing time; they are pursued by something terrible, something from which they cannot escape, counting off those who are dead and those who remain to die: there are "enough" wolves for those who yet live. The word "enough" recurs like the repeating sounds—the howls, the shrieks, the bells—and the repeating action—the overturning sledges, the movement of the sledge in front. That single word carries us to the essence of the story—enough wolves; and it is built into a pattern of increasing tension, a series of crescendo-like sentences, simply made, beginning with "the":

> The first howls were taken up . . .
> The wolves ran like streaks of shadow . . .
> The driver lost control . . .
> The sledge was caught in a clump of trees, and overturned . . .
> The occupants rolled out over the snow . . .
> The shrieks that followed . . .
> The people who were falling behind shrieked as piteously as
>   those who were already lost . . .
> The little bride hid her face on the groom's shoulder and
>   sobbed . . .
> The road was clear and white, and the groom's three blacks went
>   like the wind.

What happens in the narrative is one layer of meaning in the story of Pavel and Peter; but this story has another layer of meaning for teller and listener. Ántonia and Jim, riding home in a wagon on a cold and silent winter night, having come from the bedside of a dying man, certainly frightened, *are* passing the time: Ántonia's storytelling binds them, as they huddle together under the straw, one to the other. The story of Pavel and Peter begins and ends with the details of ordinary life: "One afternoon when Ántonia and her father came to our house for buttermilk" is the way it opens, situating this tale of the extraordinary and terrifying in time and place in the known and comfortable, by this contrast making the story itself even more fearful and the known more comforting. The story does not end with Pavel and Peter's exile: the events of that terrible night haunt the pair as relentlessly as the bloodthirsty wolves pursued their troika—and as surely as their European past spiritually and psychologically haunts all of the immigrants on the lonely American frontier, Papa

Shimerda no less than Pavel and Peter. Pavel, burdened with sin, dies; Peter, his beard dripping with juice, moves on, his cabin becomes Papa Shimerda's hermitage, and the story of the wedding party, Jim says, "for Ántonia and me . . . was never at an end . . . as if . . . the wedding party [had] been sacrificed, to give us a painful and peculiar pleasure. At night, before I went to sleep, I often found myself in a sledge drawn by three horses, dashing through a country that looked something like Nebraska and something like Virginia" (69).

If the rhythms of the story of Pavel and Peter are the rhythms of the journey—their journey in the Ukraine, Ántonia and Jim's journey home in a rattling wagon, Jim's remembered journey from Virginia, and his remembered Nebraska as he journeys by rail across the country—the rhythms of the story of The Tramp and the Threshing Machine are those of the daily task.[32] The tramp seems to be a native, but he, too, is a wanderer, even more profoundly alienated than the Europeans. His story is told at the Harlings' on a typical Saturday night—Ántonia sewing while Mrs. Harling tells stories from operas, or Ántonia telling stories in the kitchen with the children grouped around her listening, waiting for cookies to bake or taffy to cool. "We all liked Tony's stories," Jim remembers. "Her voice had a peculiarly engaging quality; it was deep, a little husky, and one always heard the breath vibrating behind it. Everything she said seemed to come right out of her heart." This prologue situates the story in everyday life—"we were picking out kernels for walnut taffy"; and the story grows out of ordinary conversation about the heavy work of threshing wheat. Ántonia, who has been a thresher up at the Norwegian settlement, remembers, "I could shovel just as fast as that fat Andern boy that drove the other wagon. One day it was just awful hot. . . ." And so the story begins, the heat radiating through this story like the howls of the wolves in the story of Pavel and Peter:

> "One day it was just awful hot. When we got back to the field from dinner, we took things kind of easy. The men put in the horses and got the machine going, and Ole Iverson was up on the deck, cutting bands. I was sitting against a straw stack, trying to get some shade. My wagon wasn't going out first, and somehow I felt the heat awful that day. The sun was so hot like it was going to burn the world up. After a while I see a man coming across the stubble, and when he got close I see it was a tramp. His toes stuck out of his shoes, and he hadn't shaved for a long while, and his eyes was awful red and wild, like he had some sickness. He comes right up and begins to talk like he knows me already. He says: 'The ponds in this country is done got so low a man couldn't drownd himself in one of 'em.'

"I told him nobody wanted to drownd themselves, but if we didn't have rain soon we'd have to pump water for the cattle.

"'Oh, cattle,' he says, 'you'll all take care of your cattle! Ain't you got no beer here?' I told him he'd have to go to the Bohemians for beer; the Norwegians didn't have none when they threshed. 'My God!' he says, 'so it's Norwegians now, is it? I thought this was Americy.'

"Then he goes up to the machine and yells out to Ole Iverson, 'Hello, partner, let me up there. I can cut bands, and I'm tired of trampin'. I won't go no farther.'

"I tried to make signs to Ole, 'cause I thought that man was crazy and might get the machine stopped up. But Ole, he was glad to get down out of the sun and chaff—it gets down your neck and sticks to you something awful when it's hot like that. So Ole jumped down and crawled under one of the wagons for shade, and the tramp got on the machine. He cut bands all right for a few minutes, and then . . . he waved his hand to me and jumped head-first into the threshing machine after the wheat.

"I begun to scream, and the men run to stop the horses, but the belt had sucked him down, and by the time they got her stopped he was all beat and cut to pieces. He was wedged in so tight it was a hard job to get him out, and the machine ain't never worked right since." [201–3]

The art of the story lies in its combination of the ordinary and the extraordinary; it is an ordinary tramp who is tired of tramping and over-come with the summer heat that seems, with the repeated emphasis, ex-traordinary: "it was just awful hot," "I felt the heat awful," "the sun was so hot like it was going to burn the world up," "his eyes was awful red and wild." One can feel not only the heat, but the other details of the story as well—the way the tramp's toes stick out of his shoes, the way it feels to lean your back against a straw-stack, the prickliness of chaff down your neck. These are ornaments that lead us back to the single word *heat* and to the main action of the story: an ordinary person, tired of trampin', gone crazy in the heat. The narrative of the story places everyone but the tramp: he is an interruption; he demands that attention be paid to him.

We took things easy . . .
The men put in the horses . . .
Ole Iverson was up on the deck . . .
I was sitting in the shade. . . .

But the tramp is moving, tramping; he looks wild and sick. You ain't got no ponds, he says; you ain't got no beer: I might as well throw myself in the threshing machine.

By this queer logic, he takes over the action of the story—or seems to—and provides the American counterpart to Papa Shimerda by turning the agricultural work he (unlike Mr. Shimerda) knows how to do into self-destruction. Yet the story of the tramp and his violent death is embedded in a context of everyday activity: work, seasonal change, listening to the opera, baking cookies, telling stories—a world of health and life. This is not to domesticate, or diminish, the way in which for all of Cather's misfits—and they are always the ones we pay attention to—America is the land of loss; rather, it is a way of placing the tramp, of situating him in terms of the world the listeners know:

> "Did they never find out where he came from?"
> "Never. . . . He hadn't been seen nowhere except in a little town they call Conway. He tried to get beer there, but there wasn't any saloon. Maybe he came in on a freight, but the brakeman hadn't seen him. They couldn't find no letters nor nothing on him; nothing but an old penknife in his pocket and the wishbone of a chicken wrapped up in a piece of paper, and some poetry. . . cut out of a newspaper."

This is a coda to the tale; it rounds the tale by repeating the geographical information of the introduction, drawing it back toward conversation by raising the issue of the story's veracity.[33] Like the story of Pavel and Peter, this one has a continuing life. "Maybe I'll go home and help you thresh next summer," Mrs. Harling says to Ántonia (205), cementing the tie between mistress and servant, between listeners and teller, between those who journey and those who till the soil, those who leave the land and those who stay. The real meaning of the story, then, is in the community of listeners: they share the work of threshing; they share baking and eating in this warm kitchen where they are together telling and listening to stories.

The story of The Tramp and the Threshing Machine is a kind of paradigm for the story of Jim Burden. Like the tramp, Jim, we learn from the prologue, is always on the move, isolated and uncomfortable in the intense heat—"wilting in the sun, . . . the woodwork . . . hot to the touch and red dust . . . deep over everything." What Jim, like the tramp, longs to do is to get out of the story he is in now, the one of tramping, and get into the other one, "the whole adventure of . . . childhood." He has the memory, and the desire; he only needs the form. "I didn't arrange or rearrange," he says to the narrator to whom he gives his manuscript; "I simply wrote down what of herself and myself and other people Ántonia's name recalls to me" (ix–xiv).

In the epilogue, Jim wanders out by himself and finds the old road, the one he and Ántonia came in on that night when they got off the train at Black Hawk and were bedded down in the straw to be taken to an unknown place. There is only a little piece of that road left, but enough for Jim to find out "what a little circle" one's experience is, thus rounding his tale, giving it form and binding him, at least in his story, before he gets on the train again and heads back in to the city, to himself, to the land, to "the precious, the incommunicable past" (418–19). As he confronts his past, the changes grow less apparent, the identity stronger; mixing memory and desire, Jim unburdens himself in the oldest tale of all.

The Ántonia to whom Jim returns is a stalwart, brown woman with a flat chest and grizzled hair who does not recognize him—but to Jim she is a "miracle." As he confronts her, "the changes grew less apparent to me, her identity stronger. She was there, in the full vigor of her personality, battered but not diminished, looking at me, speaking to me in the husky, breathy voice I remembered so well." It is his imagination that transforms her into a mythic earth-mother. Her body becomes for him a reflection of "all the strong things of her heart"; she is "a rich mine of life, like the founders of early races" (373–74, 398).

Jim's reunion with Ántonia is a return not only to the land, not only to his lost past, but to the telling of stories—stories about the Harlings, about Wick Cutter's murder of his wife, the story Jan tells his mother in Bohemian about his dog, the story told by Ántonia's husband Cuzak about his life. All of the stories come together for Jim and create a series of memory-pictures that make him feel for the moment that he can hold on to them, tied to his past. He is back in the community of storytellers, and the telling of stories is healing. He is placed. In the telling of stories, memory and desire are bridged: you remember a time when you wanted everything, fiercely, and everything was possible in the vast unlimited space before you; now, in the story you can make, everything is still possible. As another Cather storyteller, Godfrey St. Peter in *The Professor's House*, says, "Desire is creation, is the magical element in that process" (29).

Lying in the haymow with Ántonia's sons Ambrosch and Leo, Jim has a moment of clarity in which memory and desire do merge: he sees again that moment when all of Ántonia's children "came tumbling out of the cave into the light, . . . a sight any man might have come far to see." That moment of epiphany gives him his form; he understands that his story of Ántonia is a series of such moments:

Ántonia had always been one to leave images in the mind that did not fade—that grew stronger with time. In my memory there was a succession of such pictures, fixed there like the old woodcuts of one's first primer: Ántonia kicking her bare legs against the sides of my pony when we came home in triumph with our snake; Ántonia in her black shawl and fur cap, as she stood by her father's grave in the snowstorm; Ántonia coming in with her work-team along the evening sky-line. She lent herself to immemorial human attitudes which we recognize by instinct as universal and true. . . . She was a battered woman now, not a lovely girl; but she still had that something which fires the imagination, could still stop one's breath for a moment by a look or a gesture that somehow revealed the meaning in common things. She had only to stand in the orchard, to put her hand on a little crab tree and look up at the apples, to make you feel the goodness of planting and tending and harvesting at last. [397–98]

This "form" is in the stories themselves, just as they occur to Jim as he remembers them and tells them, stories not isolated, but interlocked, making contexts for each other, resonating with each other. Willa Cather's story of Jim Burden, Jim's story "My Ántonia," his stories of "The Shimerdas," "The Hired Girls," "Lena Lingard," "The Pioneer Woman's Story," "Cuzak's Boys" and all of the kernels of tales within those larger stories—all exist in an interlocking context.

In this, Willa Cather's fourth book (fifth, if we count *The Troll Garden*), form becomes "right." As her Professor St. Peter will say of his work, *Spanish Adventurers in North America*, although it does not awaken interest until his fourth volume, or critical attention until his fifth and sixth, "when the whole plan of his narrative was coming clearer and clearer all the time, when he could feel his hand growing easier with his material, when all the foolish conventions about that kind of writing were falling away . . . his relation with his work was becoming every day more simple, natural, and happy."[34]

CHAPTER 10

Felicitous Space

*In the beginning was the prairie: wheat country of southern Wisconsin,
and a farmhouse that looked out upon a yard and six hundred acres of
farmland extending on all sides toward what later . . . [she] would find
again in the Southwest—wind and emptiness. Now, the thing about
emptiness is that one can fill it: an empty landscape, an empty paper.
One can make one's own mark. And in a wide, flat, empty landscape,
one is centered wherever one is.*

—Eleanor Munro,
Originals: American Women Artists[1]

In the beginning was the prairie, for Georgia O'Keeffe, whom these
words describe, and for Willa Cather; both would later find something of
that childhood landscape in the American Southwest. This place seems to
have offered O'Keeffe "a glimpse of that 'something' that seems alive . . .
[and] she would go out to meet it as inevitably as some forms of life seek
light."[2] Sometimes, wandering in the desert, she would pick up a piece of
bone—like the pelvic bones in her paintings—and hold it up in the sun
against the sky "as one is apt to do when one seems to have more sky than
earth in one's world. . . . They were most wonderful against the Blue—
that Blue that will always be there as it is now after all man's destruction is
finished."[3] The image of the artist containing a piece of the sky in a circle
of bone held up against that blue vastness suggests not just what O'Keeffe
sees, but how she sees—or rather, how she experiences.

A Hopi guide says to an Anglo anthropologist: "Close your eyes and
tell me what you see from Hopi House at the Grand Canyon." She describes landscape she has *seen*—the brilliantly colored walls of the canyon,
the trail that winds over the edge of it reappearing and crossing a lower

mesa—and the Hopi responds, "I know what you mean . . . , but your words are wrong." For him the trail does not cross; it does not disappear: it is only that part of the mesa that has been changed by human feet. He says, "The trail is still there even when you do not see it, because *I can see all of it*. My feet have walked on the trail all the way down."[4] He refers to a way of knowing based on a set of cultural assumptions and a relationship with the land different from those of his visitor. The Hopi experiences space with his entire body: information comes from touch, smell, sound; he knows how long the trail is because he has felt it under his feet.[5] For him, space is also a matter of memory, personal and cultural: the trail goes all the way to the Grand Canyon; it is the part of the mesa that feet have worn away. With reference to natural formations, one can make a track in a space that is vast: one envisions the whole in order to understand the trail; or, by envisioning the trail, one understands the whole.

A circle of bone containing a piece of the sky, a trail cutting through a space that is vast—both are physical and spiritual experiences of *felicitous space*;[6] both perceptions rely upon body and memory to understand or create form.

Visual perception limits understanding to background/foreground and perspective;[7] relying on other senses frees the mind and the body from the geometric fixedness of visual structures and makes possible the perception of a world in flux, of connectedness. For Willa Cather's Jean-Marie Latour, a French missionary priest in *Death Comes for the Archbishop*, this freedom comes from the very air of the New Mexican desert. There is in its "dry and aromatic odour" something "soft and wild and free, something that . . . softly, softly picked the lock, slid the bolts, and released the prisoned spirit of man into the wind, into the blue and gold, into the morning, into the morning!"[8] There is something unique to this place—a spatial freedom—that makes possible a sensuous perception so acute that a sound or a smell carries the mind and the body vast distances in time and space. When Father Latour awakens one morning to the ringing of an old bell, installed as a surprise by his friend Father Joseph Vaillant, he is carried back and further back—literally out of his body, as faraway places of the imagination merge, through sound and smell, with landscapes experienced in his young manhood and recalled from childhood:

> He recovered consciousness slowly, unwilling to let go of a pleasing delusion that he was in Rome. . . . Full, clear, with something bland and suave, each note floated through the air like a globe of silver. Before the nine

strokes were done Rome faded, and behind it he sensed something Eastern, with palm trees,—Jerusalem, perhaps, though he had never been there. Keeping his eyes closed, he cherished for a moment this sudden, pervasive sense of the East. Once before he had been carried out of the body thus to a place far away. It had happened in a street in New Orleans. He had turned a corner and come upon an old woman with a basket of yellow flowers; sprays of yellow sending out a honey-sweet perfume. Mimosa—but before he could think of the name he was overcome by a feeling of place, was dropped, cassock and all, into a garden in the south of France where he had been sent one winter in his childhood to recover from an illness. And now this silvery bell note had carried him farther and faster than sound could travel. [42–43][9]

Father Latour experiences this same sense of connectedness when he and an Indian guide take refuge from a storm in a sacred Navajo serpent cave. After carefully filling up a hole in the cavern wall, Jacinto spends the night on his feet, his body stretched against the rock, "his ear over that patch of fresh mud, listening; listening with supersensual ear" for the disturbed spirit within. Father Latour, heedless of the cold, lies with his ear to a crack in the stone floor, listening to "one of the oldest voices of the earth . . . , the sound of a great underground river, flowing through a resounding cavern . . . , a flood moving in utter blackness under ribs of antediluvian rock" (134, 132).

Like Georgia O'Keeffe's holding a circle of bone against the sky, like the Hopi's focusing on a trail dividing and connecting a space he knows with a space he cannot see, in the French priest's letting the sound of a bell bring together the pieces of his geographical memory, and in his listening to the sound of the great river, moving in utter blackness beneath the earth there is a focusing on detail that gives form to space, to understanding, to desire. Gerard Manley Hopkins called this experience *inscape*.[10] It is Jim Burden's experience in *My Ántonia* of images, suddenly apprehended, which become fixed for him against the vastness of the Nebraska prairie—images of Ántonia working, of a tree standing out in the landscape, of the plough inscribed on the molten disk of the setting sun, though Jim describes such visions more prosaically: "It must have been the scarcity of detail in that tawny landscape that made detail so precious."[11] Increasingly, this is Cather's experience as well: concentrating on her inner vision, she pares down language so that words exist as objects—physical things implying spiritual connectedness—as she searches for a form simple and pure enough to express her desire, to contain it exactly.[12] And this is the meaning of Thea Kronborg's discovery in the

Arizona cliff dwellings, when she stands naked in the stream, holding in her hand a fragment of ancient pottery, and suddenly realizes: "The stream and the broken pottery: what was any art but an effort to make a sheath, a mould in which to imprison for a moment the shining, elusive element which is life itself. . . ?"[13]

From her teacher *Wunsch*, Thea learned: "Nothing is far and nothing is near, if one desires. The world is little, people are little, human life is little. There is only one big thing—desire." It is there in the beginning—*"der Geist, die Phantasie, . . . der Rhythmus"*—or it is not (75–76, 78). Desire is what filled the young Thea with an urge "to run and run about those quiet streets until she wore out her shoes, or wore out the streets themselves; when her chest ached and it seemed as if her heart were spreading all over the desert." It kept her awake at night, so that she would drag her low mattress to her open window and lie "vibrating with excitement, as a machine vibrates from speed." It seemed to her at such times that life rushed in upon her through that window, though in reality, "life rushes from within, not from without." No work of art, Cather writes, is "so big or so beautiful that it was not once contained in some youthful body, like this one which lay on the floor in the moonlight, pulsing with ardor and anticipation." And then the phrase that echoes throughout her writings: "It was on such nights that Thea Kronborg learned the thing that old Dumas meant when he told the Romanticists that to make a drama he needed but one passion and four walls" (140).[14]

Desire, in works of art, must be concentrated within form. Form is the envelope and the sheath of the precious element itself—the ancient pottery, for Indian women, in which life-giving water is carried from the stream; the vessel, for Thea Kronborg, that can be made of one's throat and nostrils and held on one's breath; the creation, for Willa Cather, whose own interlude in the Southwest informs Thea's, of four walls to contain one's passion.

"*. . . in a wide, flat, empty landscape, one is centered wherever one is.*" In the wide, flat, empty landscape it is possible to re-experience, to re-enter another space, another time; the wind, the light-hearted mornings of the desert re-create in the imagination of this artist the re-membered landscape of childhood freedom.[15] In the beginning was the prairie—the "moisture of plowed land, the heaviness of labour and growth and grain-bearing," Willa Cather writes, but first there was lightness found "only at the bright edges of the world, on the great grass plains or the sage-brush desert" (*Archbishop*, 276).

Center implies circumference, a place in space. To find the center of one's boundless desire, to give it form, is to begin in a space that is felicitous, one that frees the imagination. For Cather the American Southwest is such a liberating space, one to which she returns as to a touchstone. Both metaphoric and actual, the Southwest becomes her spiritual center, a place that can be both sensed and touched, one that concentrates being within limits that protect.

High up in a canyon in the San Francisco Mountains above Flagstaff, Arizona, Thea Kronborg takes for her own one of the sun-baked, wind-swept rock rooms that smells of the tough little cedars that twist themselves into the very doorways. There she spends whole days hibernating in her sunny, blanket-lined cave, out of the stream of meaningless activity and undirected effort, "undistracted, holding pleasant and incomplete conceptions in her mind—almost in her hands. They were scarcely clear enough to be called ideas. They had something to do with fragrance and color and sound, but almost nothing to do with words" (297–99). Yet physical acuteness and a sense of human connectedness have never been more vivid for Thea: she can dislodge flakes of carbon from the rock room of her cliff dwelling and smell the smoke of the Ancient People; when she walks their paths she discovers "a feeling in her feet and knees and loins that she had never known before—which must have come up to her out of the accustomed dust of that rocky trail"; when she holds a fragment of pottery in her hands, looking from the broad band of white cliff houses painted on a black ground to the cliff houses that appear exactly the same to her, she feels time slide away, as if in the place of the Ancient People, their perceptions have become her own.

Although Thea's days in the cliff dwellings seem to be without form, in fact the ritual of each day is in miniature the ritual of the creative person: the in-dwelling with intensity, the ceremony of purification, the desire for action. Thea re-finds a place in which "everything was simple and definite, as things had been in childhood, . . . [where] the things that were really hers separated themselves from the rest"; she bathes with "ceremonial gravity" in the stream that was the life-giving force and is now the only thing left of "so much . . . desire"; she begins to feel "a livelier movement in her thoughts, . . . a freshening of sensation, . . . a persistent affirmation" (304, 306–7).

The dwelling itself is a form: the cliff dwellings of the Southwest are for Thea houses of secret rooms, abodes of an unforgettable past, with nooks and corners that invite curling up.[16] Protected by the overhanging cliff, Thea's rock room encloses infinite space, like the sky viewed through O'Keeffe's circle of bone, like the house described by Georges Spryidaki in *Mort Lucide*: "My house . . . is diaphanous, but it is not of glass. It is more of the nature of vapor. Its walls contract and expand as I desire. At times, I draw them close about me like protective armor. . . . But at others, I let the walls of my house blossom out in their own space, which is infinitely extensible."[17]

For Thea the relationship between the intimacy of the cliff dwellings and the vastness of the Southwestern desert is analogous to the dialectical relationship between inhabiting and emerging: for the artistic imagination, the more concentrated the repose, the greater the expansion of the emerging being. "Passions simmer and re-simmer in solitude," Gaston Bachelard writes:

> the passionate being prepares his explosions and his exploits in solitude . . . [and] knows instinctively that this space identified with his solitude is creative; that even when it is forever expunged from the present, when, henceforth, it is alien to all the promises of the future, even when we no longer have a garret, when the attic room is lost and gone, there remains the fact that we once loved a garret, once lived in an attic. We return to them in our night dreams. These retreats have the value of a shell. And when we reach the very end of the labyrinths of sleep, . . . we may perhaps experience a type of repose that is pre-human, . . . immemorial . . . in the daydream . . . , the recollection of moments of confined, simple, shut-in space are experiences of heartwarming space, of a space that . . . would like above all still to be possessed. In the past, the attic may have seemed too small, it may have seemed cold in winter and hot in summer. Now, however, in memory recaptured through daydreams, . . . the attic is at once small and large, warm and cool, always comforting.[18]

This pre-human and immemorial repose that Thea finds in the Arizona cliff dwellings is also a re-experiencing of her little attic room in Moonstone, Colorado, and for Willa Cather, a re-imagining of her lost room in Red Cloud, Nebraska—"not plastered, but . . . snugly lined with soft pine," with a low ceiling sloping down on either side and one double window reaching from ceiling to floor. The room is papered, like Cather's own, with "small red and brown roses on a yellowish ground"; it has the same home-made white cheese-cloth curtains hung on a tape, simple walnut furniture, and at the head of the bed a tall round wooden hat-crate standing on end to hold the lantern by which she read at night. This loft room was so bitterly cold on winter nights that Thea would wrap a hot brick from the oven in an old flannel petticoat and put it in her bed. Sometimes the cold would keep her awake for a good while, but "after half an hour or so, a warm wave crept over her body . . . [and] she glowed like a little stove with the warmth of her own blood, and the heavy quilts and red blankets grew warm wherever they touched her, though her breath sometimes froze on the coverlid." The acquisition of this room is the beginning of a new era in Thea's life:

> It was one of the most important things that ever happened to her. Hith-erto, . . . she had lived in constant turmoil. . . . The clamor about her drowned the voice within herself. . . . [Here] her mind worked better. She thought things out more clearly. Pleasant plans and ideas occurred to her which had never come before. She had certain thoughts which were like companions, ideas which were like older and wiser friends. . . . From the time when she moved up into the wing, Thea began to live a double life. During the day, when the hours were full of tasks, she was one of the Kronborg children, but at night she was always a different person. [56–58]

Thea returns to this little room after studying music in Chicago, and she finds it the same and not the same: when she went away, she could just touch the ceiling with the tips of her fingers; now she can touch it with the palm of her hand. The room is "snug and tight, like the cabin of a little boat . . . [and] so little that it was like a sunny cave, with roses running all over the roof." It offers the same quality of protection—from her bed she can watch through the window people going by on the farther side of the street—and yet she senses a hostility in the house and in the town that the room cannot shut out. When she realizes that the time of this little room is over, Thea feels unready to leave her shell and weeps at the sense of being pulled out too soon, of leaving "something that she could never recover; memories of pleasant excitement, of happy adventures in her mind; of warm sleep on howling winter nights, and joyous awakenings on summer mornings. There were certain dreams that might refuse to come to her at all except in a little morning cave, facing the sun—where they came to her so powerfully, where they beat a triumph into her!" (222, 238–39).

All really inhabited space bears the essence of the notion of home, Bachelard writes. We comfort ourselves by reliving memories of protec-tion, by recapturing an image that moves us at an unimaginable depth. This is the chief benefit of the house: it shelters daydreaming, it protects the dreamer, it allows one to dream in peace. Primal images like the cliff dwellings, then, are invitations to begin again to imagine. They re-create

Willa Cather's bedroom in the house at 3rd and Cedar, Red Cloud, Nebraska. (© Lucia Woods 1973)

for Thea in *The Song of the Lark*, and for Willa Cather, "areas of being, houses in which the human being's certainty of being is concentrated." To live in such images as these, in images that are as stabilizing as these are, is to "*start musing on primitiveness*" and to find the life "that would belong to us in our very depths."[19]

Thea goes to the Southwest when she is very tired: she is dissatisfied with herself; she finds the faces around her stupid and the city spent and impotent. Taking little with her, she journeys to a place where she has never been, but she returns "to the earliest sources of gladness"—the brilliant solitudes of sand and sun—where her very personality seems to let go of her: "The high, sparkling air drank it up like blotting-paper. . . . The old, fretted lines which marked one off, which defined her, . . . were all erased," and at night darkness has "once again the sweet wonder that it had in childhood" (296). In the cliff dwellings of Panther Canyon—a dead city carved out of a stratum of rock hollowed out by the action of time until it was like a deep groove running along the sides of the canyon— Thea finds her little morning cave:

> The room was not more than eight by ten feet, and she could touch the stone roof with her finger-tips. This was her old idea: a nest in a high cliff, full of sun. . . . Before her door ran the narrow, winding path that had been the street of the Ancient People. . . . Thea went down to the stream by the Indian water trail. She had found a bathing-pool with a sand bottom, where the creek was dammed by fallen trees. The climb back was long and steep, and when she reached her little house in the cliff she always felt fresh delight in its comfort and inaccessibility. . . . She could lie there hour after hour in the sun and listen to the strident whir of the big locusts, and to the light, ironical laughter of the quaking asps. All her life she had been hurrying and spluttering, as if she had been born behind time and had been trying to catch up. Now, . . . it was as if she were waiting for something to catch up with her. . . . her power to think seemed converted into a power of sustained sensation. She could become a mere receptacle for heat, or become a color, like the bright lizards that darted about on the hot stones outside her door; or she could become a continuous repetition of sound, like the cicadas. [298–300]

Thea's time in the cave is a period of incubation, during which she begins to be aware of "a persistent affirmation . . . going on in her, like the tapping of the woodpecker in one tall pine tree across the chasm." Now musical phrases drive each other rapidly through her mind, the song of the cicada is too long and too sharp, and everything seems suddenly to take form, to demand action. By the time Thea is "waking up every morning with the feeling that your life is your own, . . . that you're all there, and there's no sag in you," she is ready to leave Panther Canyon (307, 317).

The bird imagery—the singing of the lark in the title, the tapping for attention of the woodpecker—suggests the way in which Thea's deep and concentrated repose is to be a prelude to a great soaring. In Panther Canyon, swallows build their nests far above the hollow groove that houses Thea's own rock chamber:

> They seldom ventured above the rim of the canyon, to the flat, wind-swept tableland. Their world was the blue air-river between the canyon walls. In that blue gulf the arrow-shaped birds swam all day long, with only an occasional movement of the wings. The only sad thing about them was their timidity; the way in which they lived their lives between the echoing cliffs and never dared to rise out of the shadow of the canyon walls. As they swam past her door, Thea often felt how easy it would be to dream one's life out in some cleft of the world. [301]

But thinking of nothing at all, her mind and body full of warmth, lassitude, physical comfort, Thea's imagination is suddenly fired by the appearance of an eagle, "tawny and of great size, [which] sailed over the cleft in which she lay, across the arch of sky." She follows his rhythm as he drops for a moment into the gulf between the walls, then wheels and mounts:

> . . . his plumage was so steeped in light that he looked like a golden bird. He swept on, following the course of the canyon a little way and then disappearing beyond the rim. Thea sprang to her feet as if she had been thrown up from the rock by volcanic action. She stood rigid on the edge of the stone shelf, straining her eyes after that strong, tawny flight. O eagle of eagles! Endeavor, achievement, desire, glorious striving of human art! From a cleft in the heart of the world she saluted it. . . . It had come all the way; when men lived in caves, it was there. A vanished race; but along the trails, in the stream, under the spreading cactus, there still glittered in the sun the bits of their frail clay vessels, fragments of their desire. [321]

Thea's salute to the eagle is a moment of epiphany; her linking of the eagle's flight with the vessels that hold the life-giving water is a moment of inscape, or pattern-making, a spiritual, intellectual, physical understanding of form to contain her desire. Like the eagle, Thea has journeyed back, back to a time and space of origins, touching base. Like the journey in the desert or the sea change, this change in space has also been a refinding of that space felicitous for creativity.

This counterpoint of the sky full of motion and change and the desert monotonous and still, of the soaring flight of the eagle and the permanence of the silent and austere cliff dwellings, though it occurs elsewhere in Cather's fiction—in the fixedness of the images of Ántonia working the land against the motion of the train in which Jim Burden travels across the country, for example—is a way of understanding one's world that seems particularly to fit the novels of the Southwest where the land itself is at the center. It seems as if Willa Cather must have discovered this great truth just as Thea Kronborg did—lying on a shelf of rock, motionless, watching the soaring flight of the eagle. Something about this counterpoint of silence and sound, of stillness and motion, must come from the Southwest itself, for in Georgia O'Keeffe's works, Eleanor Munro writes, "there exists motion (in the case of her person: a life of action, self-determination, will; in the case of the world: changing lights, shadows, wind, forms in mutation, music and the breath of life) and . . . there exists a permanent ground (in the case of her person: ritualistic, timeless costume, silence, the austerity of her isolation and manner of life; in the case of the world: stars, earth and bones)."[20] Munro suggests that many women artists, isolated from sources of power in their formative years, take for touchstones not traditional style markers "but primitive archaeological monuments that, in early days, engaged human beings in ritual behavior or afforded them elemental shelter," identifying with primal modes that "continue to align all their later work . . . [with] the 'rhythm of nature.'"[21]

This linking of O'Keeffe's person with her world, and both with her art, and her observation of the importance, for women artists, of the imaginative return to primal sources, suggests another dimension to Thea Kronborg's—and Willa Cather's—experience in the Southwest. I have focused on the imaginative return "to the earliest sources of gladness," but equally important is the way in which Thea physically becomes one with the earth at Panther Canyon—the way in which she fits her body to the shape of the cave, soaking up the warmth of the sun; the feeling of the rock ledge; the sense of the trail of the Ancient People under her feet and in her loins and even the sympathetic feel of the baby on her back and the jug in her arms as she ascends the trail from the stream; the play of the water on her naked body when she bathes in the stream. Even her identification with the eagle is physical: she feels a corresponding soaring in her own body, springing "to her feet as if she had been thrown up from the rock by volcanic action"; when she herself perches on the edge of the cliff, "between sky and the gulf, with that great wash of air and the morning light about her," she radiates a sense of "muscular energy and audacity,—a kind of brilliancy of motion,—of a personality that carried across big spaces and expanded among big things" (320–21).

Look again at what Ellen Moers called "the most thoroughly elaborated female landscape in literature":[22]

> Panther Canyon was . . . one of those abrupt fissures with which the earth in the Southwest is riddled. . . it was accessible only at its head. The canyon walls, for the first two hundred feet below the surface, were perpendicular cliffs, striped with even-running strata of rock. From there on to the bottom the sides were less abrupt, were shelving, and lightly fringed with *piñons* and dwarf cedars. The effect was that of a gentler canyon within a wilder one. The dead city lay at the point where the perpendicular outer wall ceased and the V-shaped inner gorge began. There a stratum of rock, softer than those above, had been hollowed out by the action of time until it was like a deep groove running along the sides of the canyon. In this hollow (like a great fold in the rock) the Ancient People had built their houses. [297]

The land is a textured map of the female body, wild and gentle, with places rocky and fringed and smooth, seemingly inaccessible, yet sheltering life deep within its hollow center. Following the deep groove that runs from the sheltering fold in the rock, one would come to the life-giving source itself: water. All of the ceremonies of the Ancient People, their religion itself, go back to water, Thea learns: the men provided the food, but water was the care of the women. The women mold from the earth itself forms to contain the life-giving source of the earth:

> Their pottery was their most direct appeal to water, the envelope and sheath of the precious element itself. The strongest Indian need was expressed in those graceful jars, fashioned slowly by hand, without the aid of a wheel. . . . Some of them were beautifully decorated. This care, expended upon vessels that could not hold food or water any better for the additional labor put upon them, made her heart go out to those ancient potters. They had not only expressed their desire, but they had expressed it as beautifully as they could. Food, fire, water, and something else—even here, in this crack in the world, so far back in the night of the past! Down here at the beginning that painful thing was already stirring; the seed of sorrow, and of so much delight. [303–5]

What Thea understands as she stands in the stream with a piece of pottery in her hands, as she lies on the rock shelf in the sun, as, watching the eagle soar overhead, her own body tense in affirmation, is the connection between matter and spirit, between form and desire. Her emergence as an artist comes quite literally from the earth: in contact with the earth she learns once again to know and to delight in her body. In fact, to give form to her artistic desire, which is only possible, she says, when there is no "sag" in her physical self, is literally to make of her body—of her throat and nostrils—a vessel in which to hold the life-giving element itself—breath.

The Song of the Lark is the novel that precedes My Ántonia, in which body and memory come together to create form. Willa Cather's first sojourn in the Southwest in 1912, upon which The Song of the Lark is based, shapes the writing of O Pioneers!, Cather's first "novel of the soil." To break away from the "style markers," as Cather clearly did after 1912, was for her to simplify, to purify, to get back to the elemental form, the unfurnished space, as she said in "The Novel Démeublé." The bare rock room at the center of the deep gorge in the perpendicular cliff—like the abstract form of one of Georgia O'Keeffe's desert flowers—is reached by two paths: one tactile, physical, erotic; one spiritual, meditative, mystical.

After The Song of the Lark, where in the enclosed felicitous space the ingathering of the creative person takes place; after the "triple enclosure" of My Ántonia, where the story within the story is form invented, there is a marked falling away from the achieved union of matter and spirit, of body and memory in The Professor's House. Although she called her work "experimental," Cather makes clear in her letter on The Professor's House that this novel is a deliberate reformulation of classical experience. "I wished to try two experiments in form," she wrote:

> The first is the device often used by the early French and Spanish novelists; that of inserting the Nouvelle into the Roman. . . . But the experiment which interested me was something a little more vague, and was very much akin to the arrangement followed in sonatas in which the academic sonata form was handled somewhat freely. Just before I began the book I had seen, in Paris, an exhibition of old and modern Dutch paintings. In many of them the scene presented was a living-room warmly furnished, or a kitchen full of food and coppers. But in most of the interiors, whether drawing-room or kitchen, there was a square window, open, through which one saw the masts of ships, or a stretch of grey sea. The feeling of the sea that one got through those square windows was remarkable, and gave me a sense of the fleets of Dutch ships that ply quietly on all the waters of the globe—to Java, etc.
>
> In my book I tried to make Professor St. Peter's house rather overcrowded and stuffy with new things; American proprieties, clothes, furs, petty ambitions, quivering jealousies—until one got rather stifled. Then I

wanted to open the square window and let in the fresh air that blew off the Blue Mesa, and the fine disregard of trivialities which was in Tom Outland's face and in his behaviour.[23]

If we compare the felicitous space of Thea Kronborg's Southwestern cliff dwelling with that of Tom Outland in *The Professor's House*, we see that in this novel the enclosed form has a precarious vulnerability. Thea has "a superstitious feeling about the potsherds, and she liked better to leave them in the dwellings where she found them" (305). Tom Outland systematically removes the pottery, mummies and other remains from the caves, including "Mother Eve," who seems to him to be the forerunner of the race; he studies, labels and catalogs these artifacts which later, while he is in Washington trying to interest government bureaucrats in his find, are sold off to a foreign collector.[24] Thea's experience in the cliff dwellings is fundamental to her emergence as an artist. Tom becomes a scientist, whose great discovery, a bulkhead vacuum used in aircraft, is directly related to the materialistic decadence that Professor St. Peter finds so disheartening. To name, then, specific forms from the past, forms that embody particular ways of ordering experience, as Cather does in her letter on *The Professor's House*, is to underline a need for clarity about forms in this novel; it is to express a wish to preserve old forms and to reestablish rational ways of perceiving and responding to the world, while at the same time securing the structures that make possible the saving grace of make-believe.

The war in which Tom Outland died left in its wake an especially pronounced need to return to past forms. For Cather, "the world broke in two in 1922 or thereabouts, and the persons and prejudices recalled in these sketches [*Not Under Forty*] slid back into yesterday's seven thousand years."[25] Her war novel, *One of Ours*, written between *My Ántonia* and *The Professor's House*, suggests in her description of the returned heroes the deep pessimism she felt at that time:

> One by one the heroes of that war, the men of dazzling soldiership, leave prematurely the world they have come back to. Airmen whose deeds were tales of wonder, officers whose names made the blood of youth beat faster, survivors of incredible dangers,—one by one they quietly die by their own hand. Some do it in obscure lodging houses, some in their office, where they seemed to be carrying on their business like other men. Some slip over a vessel's side and disappear into the sea.[26]

But Cather's profound alienation and displacement were personal as well as cultural: the marriage of her longtime close friend Isabelle McClung to

Jan Hambourg was a disturbance that meant, among other things, the loss of the little attic sewing-room in the McClung's house where Cather had done so much of her imagining. Like her Professor St. Peter, Cather would find herself unable to write in the splendid new study the Hambourgs furnished for her in their new house, the Ville-d'Avray.[27] In *The Professor's House* and the novels that follow, characters move toward death or toward an extreme rejection of the world. In *My Mortal Enemy*, Cather's "novel démeublé" in extremis, there is no plot; there is no action; there is only Myra Henshawe dying in a rented room, the passion she once felt for her husband now turned inward and focused upon her mortal enemy, time.[28] Like Myra Henshawe, the Professor lives in the negative aspect of time; only in childhood, it seems to him looking back, had he been truly free. It is that freedom he sees, or thinks he sees, through the square window.

Cather's letter on *The Professor's House* describes "old and modern" Dutch paintings. By "old" she must mean preclassical representations of people and events implicated and involved in the natural world—like those in *My Ántonia*. The sixteenth-century paintings of Pieter Brueghel, for example, "tell a story, they are packed with incident and event." The outdoor places where the events of daily life occur are typical and familiar. Place and event are "utterly integrated so that we see peasants and villagers skating or cutting wheat *in* this setting which is the context for their activities."[29] In the seventeenth century, *landscape*—and the very word is new—comes to mean something to be looked at, something that can be arranged and admired for its formal qualities.[30] Paintings explicitly called "landscapes" become impersonal and precise representations of the land as "scene." And this is the vision of landscape in *The Professor's House*: contained and separated from the viewer by a square window, the scene from the Professor's window is like paintings by the seventeenth-century Dutch painter Johannes Vermeer, in which fragments of landscape, isolated for their pictorial qualities, are artistic representations of a prospect seen from a specific standpoint.[31]

The idea of landscape as something separate from life, something to be looked upon and painted, to be admired, modified, explained or interpreted, is part of a new way of looking at the world in the seventeenth century, one which is *rational*, and which in philosophy is represented by René Descartes's influential *Discourse on Method*—written in Amsterdam while Vermeer was painting his landscapes.[32] Descartes's famous proposition, "I think, therefore I am," led him to maintain that although "I could *pretend that I had no body* and that there was no world or place that I was in . . . I could not, for all that, pretend that I did not exist." The mind that reasons is certain, Descartes argued; it is distinct from and superior to the body, world and matter because they do not think. Mind is an indivisible unity, but matter, or nature, is divisible into parts and functions according to the certainties of mathematical laws.[33]

This "rational" division between mind and body, the assertion of human reason over nature symbolized by the vision of landscape framed, contained and separated from the viewer, has a correlative in the reconstruction of actual landscapes: mid-seventeenth-century gardens literally become *spectacles*; the framed landscape Professor St. Peter sees from his attic window has its correlative in his meticulously composed French garden below.[34] With this reconstruction of landscape as a celebration of intellectual and visual perception, "I think, therefore I am" supersedes "I make, therefore I am."[35] The former entails a separation, the latter a unity of matter and spirit, of body and memory—in working the land, as Ántonia does; in making by hand the beautifully formed and decorated pots to hold the life-giving water, as the Indian cliff-dwelling women do; in making music by combining idea (mind) with passion (body), as Thea Kronborg does; in making stories as the immigrants in Cather's fiction do, out of their experiences, out of the earth, out of their bodies. But Professor St. Peter is the Cartesian man who cultivates a dual existence, dividing mind and body and celebrating in this division the supremacy of the rational.

Napoleon Godfrey St. Peter has two houses, two studies, two places of retreat, two lives that he divides with precision:

> Two evenings of the week he spent with his wife and daughters, and one evening he and his wife went out to dinner, or to the theatre or a concert. That left him only four. He had Saturdays and Sundays, . . . and on those two days he worked like a miner under a landslide. . . . All the while that he was working so fiercely by night, he was earning his living during the day; carrying full university work and feeding himself out to hundreds of students in lectures and consultations. But that was another life.[36]

Yet all is not as neat as he would wish. The problem that he is faced with, as the novel opens on the day of moving from one house to another, is that of displacement, or disharmony, both in his world and in his own nature. A product of his time and place—America in the early 1920s—he is, like his contemporaries, expatriated intellectuals and imagined characters who people an increasingly alienating wasteland, out of touch with both. A man who perceives the world of matter as polluted, he withdraws into the world of his own imagining. Unlike Thea Kronborg, however, whose retreat into a felicitous space of physical and spiritual repose is a preparation for emergence, the Professor prefers to remain in the remembered and created space of his imagined world, increasingly oblivious to what goes on beneath and around him. Limiting his existence to a framed and isolated visionary world, his withdrawal becomes a preparation for that final retreat into death.

St. Peter does not exactly deny his body. He is one who enjoys a long, solitary swim, sporting a brightly colored visor to mark his progress through the water; he relishes an exquisitely prepared solitary lunch with a glass of special sherry; when the family is away, he walks to the market to pick out his own fruits and salads, and cooks "a fine leg of lamb, *saignant*, well rubbed with garlic," served with "a dish of steaming asparagus, swathed in a napkin to keep it hot, and a bottle of sparkling Asti." St. Peter has a rather nice body, in fact: he looks well in pajamas, and "the fewer clothes he had on, the better. Anything that clung to his body showed it to be built upon extremely good bones, with the slender hips and springy shoulders of a tireless swimmer." Tellingly, however, his artist daughter finds the best thing about Papa to be "the modelling of his head between the top of his ear and his crown," a moulding "so far from casual, that it was more like a statue's head than a man's." And though his wife admires that very nice body, the St. Peters, once "very much in love," now occupy separate—"more dignified"—bedrooms (176, 12, 13, 31, 34). The body for St. Peter has become a thing to enjoy abstractly, or in solitude— like the dressmakers' dummies stored in his old attic study, abstract forms that express only the sexuality and roles hung upon their frames. One of these dummies has been named by Augusta, the sewing-woman, "the bust": it is a "headless, armless female torso, covered with strong black cotton, . . . richly developed in the part for which it was named," seemingly ample and billowy "(as if you might lay your head upon its deep-breathing softness and rest safe forever), [but] if you touched it you suffered a severe shock. . . . It presented the most unsympathetic surface imaginable. . . . It was a dead, opaque, lumpy solidity, like chunks of putty, or tightly packed sawdust—very disappointing to the tactile sense." The other is a "full-length female figure in a smart wire skirt with a trim metal waist line. It had no legs, as one could see all too well, no viscera behind its glistening ribs, and its bosom resembled a strong wire bird-cage." Up there in the little attic study, St. Peter, isolated with his dummy bodies and insulated from "the engaging drama of daily life," has had only a vague sense of what went on below as it drifted up the narrow stairway. He lives in a fantasy world, imagining scenes like a shipwreck with no one "but himself, and a weather-dried little sea captain from the Hautes-Pyrénées, half a dozen spry seamen, and a line of gleaming snow peaks, agonizingly high and sharp, along the southern coast of Spain"; musing, abstractly, on the erotic passages from the "Song of Songs";[37] dwelling on the memory of Tom Outland's hand, holding a pair of turquoise lumps "the colour of robin's eggs, or of the sea on halcyon days of summer," the hand that held them muscular, the palm many-lined, "the long, strong fingers with soft ends, the straight little finger, the flexible, beautifully shaped thumb that curved back from the rest of the hand as if it were its own master" (17–18, 26, 95, 120–21).

St. Peter's little attic retreat, like Thea Kronborg's, is the spiritual equivalent of the cliff-dweller's cave in the Southwest, a room barely furnished, with a low ceiling sloping down on three sides and a single window affording the only opening for light and air. But if Thea is an eagle, soaring from her canyon nest to the vastness of unlimited space, Professor St. Peter, dreaming his life out in some cleft of the world, is the swallow that lives "between the echoing cliffs and never dared to rise out of the shadow of the canyon walls" (*Song of the Lark*, 301). He admits to himself that "the desk was a shelter one could hide behind, . . . a hole one could creep into"; he muses upon the withdrawal of Euripedes, at the end of his life, into a sea-side cave, all houses having become insupportable to him; and so deep does his solitude become that he experiences "a falling out of all domestic and social relations, out of his place in the human family, indeed" (161, 156, 275).

During the fifteen years St. Peter has spent in that little attic study writing his many-volumed *Spanish Adventurers in North America*, the square window in this room has provided his view of the world. Even his travels to Spain to study records and to Mexico and the southwestern United States with Tom Outland on the trail of his adventurers become memories seen again through that square window. The notes and the records and the ideas "always came back to this room. It was here that they were digested and sorted, and woven into their proper place in his history." When he looks up from his desk, he can also see the framed landscape, "far away, just on the horizon, a long, blue, hazy smear—Lake Michigan, the inland sea of his childhood," a landscape of childhood that St. Peter equates with remembered or re-imagined freedom, one that encourages daydreaming and fosters creativity. This scene is for him the great fact in life: "the always possible escape from dullness, was the lake. The sun rose out of it, the day began there; it was like an open door that nobody could shut. The land and all its dreariness could never close in on you. You had only to look at the lake, and you knew you would soon be free." It is also an echo of the Mediterranean, where once he lay in a boat upon purple waters, looking up at the peaks of the Sierra Nevadas and seeing "the design of his book unfolded in the air above him, just as definitely as the mountain ranges themselves" (25, 29, 30, 106).

The other space of retreat for St. Peter is different in kind, but it shares with the attic study the sense of enclosure and the idea of landscape as vision, as composition. If the inland sea re-invokes the landscape of St. Peter's childhood, the French garden recalls "the happiest years of his youth in a house in Versailles": one represents his natural, the other his rational self. Here in a midwestern university town he creates a walled-in garden that is the comfort of his life—and the one thing his neighbors hold against him. St. Peter has tended this garden for twenty years until he "had got the upper hand of it." There is not a blade of grass: "it was a tidy half-acre of glistening gravel and glistening shrubs and bright flowers. There were trees, of course; a spreading horse-chestnut, a row of slender Lombardy poplars at the back, along the white wall, and in the middle two symmetrical, round-topped linden-trees. Masses of green-brier grew in the corners, the prickly stems interwoven and clipped until they were like great bushes." Like his other sensuous pleasures, St. Peter prefers his garden alone—with one exception. When his family travels, "when he was a bachelor again, he brought down his books and papers and worked in a deck chair under the linden-trees; breakfasted and lunched and had his tea in the garden. And it was there he and Tom Outland used to sit and talk half through the warm, soft nights" (14–15).

The spirit of Tom Outland pervades the attic retreat and the garden retreat. Tom has not only been the one student worth the Professor's trouble; his firsthand knowledge of the Southwest has proved indispensable to St. Peter's great project. It is "Tom Outland's Story," finally, that is the vision seen through the window of the Professor's rather stuffy and overfurnished house; it is the unfurnished room—four walls and one passion—that is the true center of the novel, challenging by contrast the cramped and awkward old house, the decadent materialism of the new house, and the ostentatious oddity of "Outland," the Norwegian manor

Cliff Palace, Mesa Verde, Colorado. (© Lucia Woods 1973)

house designed by a French architect and furnished with all the treasures of ransacked European mansions, built by the Professor's elder daughter, Tom's fiancée, as a tribute to Outland's memory.

"Tom Outland's Story," contained by house and novel, is "true" both in form and in its essence; the Blue Mesa (Mesa Verde), with its spectacularly preserved cliff dwellings, was actually discovered by a cowpuncher named Richard Wetherill in the way Tom recounts to Professor St. Peter:[38]

> The canyon was wide at the water's edge, and though it corkscrewed back into the mesa by abrupt turns, it preserved this open, roomy character. It was, indeed, a very deep valley with gently sloping sides, rugged and rocky, but well grassed. . . . Far up above me, a thousand feet or so, set in a great cavern in the face of the cliff, I saw a little city of stone, asleep. It was as still as sculpture—and something like that. It all hung together, seemed to have a kind of composition: pale little houses of stone nestling close to one another, perched on top of each other, with flat roofs, narrow windows, straight walls, and in the middle of the group, a round tower. . . . It was red in colour, even on that grey day. In sunlight it was the colour of winter oak-leaves. A fringe of cedars grew along the edge of the cavern, like a garden. They were the only living things. Such silence and stillness and repose—immortal repose. That village sat looking down into the canyon with the calmness of eternity. . . . It was more like sculpture than anything else. I knew at once that I had come upon the city of some extinct civilization, hidden away in this inaccessible mesa for centuries, preserved in the dry air and almost perpetual sunlight like a fly in amber, guarded by the cliffs and the river and the desert. [199, 201–2]

"Tom Outland's Story" is now Professor St. Peter's world—the world he has re-created in his many-volumed book, the one he can see through the window of his attic study, the subject of his meditations as he sits alone in his garden. It is a world preserved, like a fly in amber: the vastness of the mesa and the silence of the cliff dwellings suggest "immortal repose." His life's work in the old house is complete; yet he returns to the old space as to a nest.[39] In his silent solitude, spaces and times are compressed: he dreams of the windswept cliff dwellings carved out of bare rock, "fringed with . . . groves of quaking asps and piñons and a few dark cedars, perched upon the air like the hanging gardens of Babylon," beyond which is "a kind of back court-yard, running from end to end of the cavern; a long, low twilit space that had got gradually lower toward the back until the rim rock met the floor of the cavern, exactly like the sloping room of an attic" (192, 208–9). The rock of the Blue Mesa—St. Peter's correlative, as his name suggests—no longer a source of action and creation, is a place of stasis and death.

Sitting in the garden of his old house or in his old attic study, holding in his hands Tom Outland's diary which he intends to edit for publication, retreat suggests to St. Peter permanent withdrawal. In the garden he invites, or becomes again, the boy of his youth, "the original, unmodified Godfrey St. Peter" (263), a primitive like the remembered Tom Outland. In the attic he invites death—and experiences the resurrection of a man in his grave. Like the Archbishop carried by the sound of bells farther and faster than sound could travel, the Professor's retreat carries him literally out of his body.

Death links Professor St. Peter to the cliff dwellers, E. K. Brown suggests: between the life of the midwestern college town and that of the cliff dwellers' village "the common quality is simply that they both end in death," and understanding this, we know how to measure the ugly and insensitive structures of the present against "the beauty of pure and noble design, unspoiled by clutter or ornament."[40] But the real link is the one St. Peter himself makes in one of his lectures when he says that "art and religion (they are the same thing, in the end, of course) have given man the only happiness he has ever had," meaning that the contemplation of pure form in its aesthetic and spiritual sense—for St. Peter the simplicity of Greek sculpture and "the calmness of eternity" (69, 201)—is an end in itself. In the way it frames and shapes St. Peter's vision, then, *The Professor's House* is not only a rite of passage in its consideration "of essential feeling about final issues";[41] it is, unlike Thea Kronborg's fusion of form and desire, an isolation and containment of desire within exact and perfect form, a structure from the past preserved against the fragmentation of the modern world.

"Felicitous space" is not only the space that concentrates being within limits that protect; felicitous also is the space that is *vast*, space that "brings calm and unity . . . [and] teaches us to breathe with the air that rests on the horizon."[42] New space actively imagined is vast space; it is intimate *immensity*. Through a change in space—crossing the water, wandering in the desert—transformation becomes possible. Only in leaving the space of one's usual sensibilities and entering "a space that is psychically innovating"—a change of concrete space that is no mere mental operation, like Professor St. Peter's, but a fundamental change in one's nature, like Thea's—is one able to say, "I am the space where I am."[43]

For Willa Cather, the Southwestern Four Corners area with its vast deserts and distant mountain ranges—the landscape Professor St. Peter saw from the window of his attic study—was this new space actively imagined, and also the old space, the landscape of remembered childhood freedom, re-created here as touchstone. After her first long stay in New Mexico and Arizona in 1912, Cather went back during the next twelve years as often as she could, and although she was working during that period on other material, the Southwest continued to haunt her imagination. She recalls how finding a book printed on a country press—*The Life of the Right Reverend Joseph P. Machebeuf* by Father William Joseph Howlett, the biography and letters of the first French missionary priests in New Mexico, Father Machebeuf and Father Jean Baptiste Lamy—gave her "the tone" from which she could write her story of these "valiant men whose life and work had given me so many hours of pleasant reflection in faraway places"—Joseph Vaillant and Jean Marie Latour in her novel. Then the writing went very quickly "because the book had all been lived many times before it was written, and the happy mood in which I began it never paled." In *Death Comes for the Archbishop* Cather followed the life story of the two bishops presented in Howlett's book, but also used many of her own experiences; writing it, she said, "was like a happy vacation from life, a return to childhood, to early memories."

Readers—once again—found her book "hard to classify." "Then why bother?" she asked. "Myself, I prefer to call it a narrative," whose title "was simply taken from Holbein's *Dance of Death*."[44]

Death Comes for the Archbishop is a "narrative" of a special kind, and the matter is "simple" in a particular way. The work to which Cather refers is a series of woodcuts from the end of the sixteenth century attributed to Hans Holbein the Younger.[45] Based in theme on the mural painted on the cemetery wall of the Church of the Innocents in Paris in the early fifteenth century,[46] in form they go back to the earliest modes of pictorial expression, the woodcarving and the line drawing. Their message, meant for people who could not read, was that death comes to all alike, emperor and peasant, judge and moneylender, physician and lover, new bride and new baby, old woman and worthy bishop. We see Cather, then, journeying back to the oldest forms of representation, where the hand is in direct contact with the material of artistic expression; and we see, too, that death is now the supreme measure of experience. "As a writer I had the satisfaction of working in a special genre which I had long wished to try," Cather wrote, though in fact she had already tried it in *My Ántonia*, where she created a series of "images in the mind that did not fade—that grew stronger with time, . . . a succession of . . . pictures, fixed there like the old woodcuts of one's first primer" (397):

> I had all my life wanted to do something in the style of legend, which is absolutely the reverse of dramatic treatment. Since I first saw the Puvis de Chavannes frescoes of the life of Saint Geneviève in my student days, I have wished that I could try something a little like that in prose; something without accent, with none of the artificial elements of composition. In the Golden Legend the martyrdoms of the saints are no more dwelt upon than are the trivial incidents of their lives; it is as though all human experiences, measured against one supreme spiritual experience, were of about the same importance. The essence of such writing is not to hold the note, not to use an incident for all there is in it—but to touch and pass on. I felt that such writing would be a kind of discipline in these days when the "situation" is made to count for so much in writing, when the general tendency is to force things up. In this kind of writing the mood is the thing—all the little figures and stories are mere improvisations that come out of it.[47]

This is as complete a statement of artisic intention as Cather ever made: the essential elements are the stories, which remain fixed in the mind like a series of primitive woodcuts; the process of invention; the tone, or "mood," that is created in language. "What I got from Father Machebeuf's letters was the mood," she said, "the spirit in which they accepted the accidents and hardships of a desert country, the joyful energy that kept them going. To attempt to convey this hardihood of spirit one must use language a little stiff, a little formal, one must not be afraid of the old trite phraseology of the frontier. Some of those time-worn phrases I used as the note from the piano by which the violinist tunes his instrument."[48]

Language is only for tuning: the impression Cather wished to create was not one of words. The longer she stayed in the Southwest, she wrote, the more she felt drawn to the old mission churches with their "hand-carved beams and joists, the utterly unconventional frescoes, the countless fanciful figures of the saints, no two of them alike," which struck her as "a direct expression of some very real and lively human feeling . . . [—]fresh, individual, first hand. Almost every one of those many remote little adobe churches," she found, had something of its own. "In lonely, sombre villages in the mountains the church decorations were sombre, the martyrdoms bloodier, the grief of the Virgin more agonized, the figure of Death more terrifying. In warm, gentle valleys everything about the churches was milder." No written account of these churches exists, Cather says, "but I soon felt that no record of them could be as real as they are themselves. They are their own story, and it is a foolish convention that we must have everything interpreted for us in written language. There are *other ways of telling* what one feels, and the people who built and decorated those . . . little churches found their way and left their message."⁴⁹

Death Comes for the Archbishop works upon the reader as a series of sensations—of color, of light, of the large become small, as in the monotonous red sand-hills that come to seem as so many hay-cocks to the solitary horseman riding through them, and the small become large, as the cruciform tree that occupies all the space between earth and sky. Light strikes the senses as brilliant and explosive, raw and blinding, full of motion and change, unlike the light of the Old World where objects take on a soft metallic quality in light that is both intense and soft, with a ruddiness of much-multiplied candlelight and splendid finish, light that sends spiral patterns quivering over damask and plate and crystal, over the rectangular caps protecting the heads of churchmen from the sun, over their long black coats and violet vests.

Light hidden strikes the senses, on endless journeys across this vast and strange diocese, as shape and texture, felt as the undercurrent of the great fact of the land itself, in all of its height and depth. In this passage, the two bishops, having ridden through wind and sandstorms, now in the Truchas mountains on their way to Mora ride through rain and sleet, conditions that make it nearly impossible for them to see at all:

> The heavy, lead-coloured drops were driven slantingly through the air by an icy wind from the peak. These raindrops, Father Latour kept thinking, were the shape of tadpoles, and they broke against his nose and cheeks, exploding with a splash, as if they were hollow and full of air. The priests were riding across high mountain meadows, which in a few weeks would be green, though just now they were slate-coloured. On every side lay ridges covered with blue-green fir trees; above them rose the horny backbones of mountains. The sky was very low; purplish lead-coloured clouds let down curtains of mist into the valleys between the pine ridges. There was not a glimmer of white light in the dark vapours working overhead—rather, they took on the cold green of the evergreens. Even the white mules, their coats wet and matted into tufts, had turned a slaty hue, and the faces of the two priests were purple and spotted in that singular light. [64–65]

In the vast space of this southwestern corner of the New World, where no one can even measure the extent of the new diocese, where life is to be "a succession of mountain ranges, pathless deserts, yawning canyons and swollen rivers," where the priests would carry the Cross into territories yet unknown and unnamed, wearing down mules and horses and scouts and stage drivers, the sky was as full of motion and change as the desert beneath it was monotonous and still, —and there was so much sky, more than at sea, more than anywhere else in the world. The plain was there, under one's feet, but what one saw when one looked about was that brilliant blue world of stinging air and moving cloud. Even the mountains were mere ant-hills under it. Elsewhere the sky is the roof of the world; but here the earth was the floor of the sky. The landscape one longed for when one was far away, the thing about one, the world one actually lived in, was the sky, the sky. [41, 234–35]

The land at first seems to Father Latour a kind of geometrical nightmare—every conical hill spotted with smaller cones of juniper, a uniform yellowish green, as the hills were a uniform red, the hills thrust out of the ground so thickly that they seemed to be pushing each other aside, tipping each other over—and he closes his eyes against this intrusive omnipresence. But when he opens his eyes once again, a kind of miracle takes place: he sees one juniper, different in shape from the others, not thick-growing, but a naked, twisted trunk, perhaps ten feet high, which at the top "parted into two lateral, flat-lying branches, with a little crest of green in the centre, just above the cleavage. Living vegetation could not present more faithfully the form of the Cross" (15–16).[50] The tree, anonymous in its objectivity, when invested with the imagination of Latour's inner space, expands until tree and dreamer achieve a kind of oneness, a miracle, like the green thread of verdure and running stream—greener than anything Latour had ever seen in his own greenest corner of the Old World—in the midst of that ocean of wavy sand.

The image of Bishop Latour kneeling before the cruciform tree remains in the mind like one of Holbein's woodcuts: words dissolve; the picture invites meditation. All around Latour, in the background of the novel, political and military events of mid-nineteenth-century America hover: the Mexican-American border disputes, the bloody attacks by dispossessed Indians on caravans moving west, which end only when the United States government forces the Navajos out of their sacred places and onto reservations, the discovery of gold in Colorado, the unmentioned American Civil War—these events are not even the note by which the novel is tuned; they barely matter. The growing city of Santa Fé, seat of the diocese, is scarcely a context.[51] The two great realities are the journey—the endless journeying on mule and horseback through "the alkali deserts [where] the water holes were poisonous, and the vegetation offered nothing to a starving man. Everything was dry, prickly, sharp; Spanish bayonet, juniper, greasewood, cactus; the lizard, the rattlesnake"—and the sense of place. Place is not background, as in the Holbein woodcuts, but the *subject* of meditation. If "the old countries were worn to the shape of human life, made into an investiture, a sort of second body, for man . . . [where] the wild herbs and the wild fruits and the forest fungi were edible [,] . . . the streams were sweet water, the trees afforded shade and shelter," the New World was a hard place "calculated to try the endurance of giants." Missionaries thirsted in its deserts, starved among its rocks, climbed up and down its terrible canyons, broke long fasts by unclean and repugnant food, enduring "*Hunger, Thirst, Cold Nakedness,* of a kind beyond any conception St. Paul and his brethren could have had . . . in that safe little Mediterranean world, amid the old manners, the old landmarks" (279–80).

These things are real: desert, rocks, shelter, legend.

The desert is a place to cross; it can be made to bloom: at the bottom of the world between the towering sandstone walls of the Canyon de Chelly, crops flourish, sheep graze under magnificent cottonwoods and drink at streams of sweet water; it is "like an Indian Garden of Eden." A few miles above Santa Fé, at Tesuque, the Bishop has a garden: "He grew such fruit as was hardly to be found even in the old orchards of California; cherries and apricots, apples and quinces, and the peerless pears of France —even the most delicate varieties." He urges his priests to plant fruit trees wherever they go, and to encourage the Mexicans to add fruit to their starchy diet. Wherever there was a French priest, he said, "there should be a garden of fruit trees and vegetables and flowers," quoting to his students the passage from their countryman Pascal, "Man was lost and saved in a garden" (301, 267–68).

Rocks are sanctuaries. The Pueblos, farming Indians, find sanctuary from the nomadic Navajos and Apaches atop the rock of Ácoma: "It was very different from a mountain fastness; more lonely, more stark and grim, more appealing to the imagination. The rock," Father Latour reflects, "was the utmost expression of human need; even mere feeling yearned for it; it was the highest comparison of loyalty in love and friendship. Christ Himself had used that comparison for the disciple to whom He gave the keys of His Church. And the Hebrews of the Old Testament, always being carried captive into foreign lands,—their rock was an idea of God, the only thing their conquerors could not take from them." North of the Canyon de Chelly is the Shiprock, "a slender crag rising to a dizzy height, all alone out on a flat desert. Seen at a distance of fifty miles or so, that crag presents the figure of a one-masted fishing-boat under full sail, and the white man named it accordingly. But the Indian has another name; he believes that rock was once a ship of the air." Ages ago, according to legend, "that crag had moved through the air, bearing upon its summit the parents of the Navajo race from the place in the far north where all peoples were made,—and wherever it sank to earth was to be their land. It sank in a desert country, where it was hard for men to live. But they had found the Canyon de Chelly, where there was shelter and unfailing water. That canyon and the Shiprock were like kind parents . . . [to the Navajos], places more sacred to them than churches, more sacred than any place is to the white man" (98, 298–99).

Shelters are frail in this place; inside and outside are one. Mexicans use the earth for their adobe structures, mixing earth with water, shaping and packing it with their hands. Navajos also build earth-houses, with tree branches for roofs, like this one Father Latour finds conducive to reflection:

> The hogan was isolated like a ship's cabin on the ocean, with the murmuring of great winds about it. There was no opening except the door, always open, and the air without had the turbid yellow light of sand-storms. All day long the sand came in through the cracks in the walls and formed little ridges on the earth floor. It rattled like sleet upon the dead leaves of the tree-branch roof. This house was so frail a shelter that one seemed to be sitting in the heart of a world made of dusty earth and moving air. [232]

These shelters reflect the Indian manner of vanishing into the landscape rather than standing out against it, as does Father Baltazar, for example, whose hillside garden oasis has been planted with imported fruits and flowers and nurtured by Indian women forced to carry water from their own scarce supply up the steep cliff to satisfy the epicurean tastes of the foreign priest—and who is finally flung over the cliff by the Indian men. These Navajos, who lavish exhaustless patience upon their blankets, belts and ceremonial robes, have no wish to decorate or master nature in the European tradition, to arrange and re-create. Instead, they accommodate themselves to the place where they are, not so much from indolence, Father Latour understands, as from inherited caution and respect:

> When they left the rock or tree or sand dune that had sheltered them for the night, the Navajo was careful to obliterate every trace of their temporary occupation. He buried the embers of the fire and the remnants of food, unpiled any stones he had piled together, filled up the holes he had scooped in the sand. . . . Just as it was the white man's way to assert himself in any

landscape, to change it, make it over a little (at least to leave some mark or memorial of his sojourn), it was the Indian's way to pass through a country without disturbing anything; to pass and leave no trace, like fish through the water, or birds through the air. . . . It was as if the great country were asleep, and they wished to carry on their lives without awakening it; or as if the spirits of earth and air and water were things not to antagonize and arouse. [235–37]

Legends are based on real stories: the legend of Kit Carson, Indian scout; the legend of Ácoma Pueblo, the sanctuary built on a rock with its holy picture of St. Joseph that miraculously produces rain; the legend of Doña Olivares, who refused to tell her age; the legend of the mutinous Mexican priests, the gluttonous Padre Martínez and the miserly Padre Lucero, who died with over twenty thousand dollars in coin buried beneath the floor of his house; the passion of Christ. All are invitations to reverie.

Father Latour, a legend himself, makes no division between body and memory, between matter and spirit. He savors a glass of fine wine, the taste of a peach; he enjoys the fragrance and coolness of his garden with the same physical intensity that characterizes his difficult journeys across this vast diocese, journeys also spiritual in nature. The walled garden, as foreign to the New Mexico landscape as the priest who created it, is at the same time a place of sensuous delight, a cloister of contemplation and a spiritual symbol. Like the garden, the great cathedral Father Latour envisions is a place not so much seen as experienced totally. This Midi-Romanesque structure that is to be built out of the earth itself—made of New Mexican sandstone—is for him a re-creation of the kind of structure that marked the landscape of his childhood.[52] Riding one day through a ridge covered with cone-shaped, rocky hills all of a curious shade of green, something between sea-green and olive, he has a vision that recalls his experience years earlier with the cruciform tree. He sees one hill, quite high and alone, which is not green like the surrounding hills, but yellow, a strong golden ochre, very much like the gold of the sunlight beating about it. He picks up a chip of the yellow rock, holds it in his palm with his very special way of handling objects sacred and beautiful, and looks up at the rugged wall, gleaming gold above him. "That hill," he says, "is my Cathedral" (242).

In building his Cathedral upon the Rock, in planting his garden with the purple verbena that mats the hills of New Mexico "like a great violet velvet mantle thrown down in the sun; of all the shades that the dyers and weavers of Italy and France strove for through centuries, the violet that is full of rose colour and is yet not lavender; the blue that becomes almost pink and then retreats again into sea-dark purple—the true Episcopal colour and countless variations of it" (268), Father Latour has achieved a kind of synthesis between the vastness of the landscape and the intimacy of inner space that is for him felicitous. Well might he say, "Space, vast space, is the friend of being," or "I am the space where I am," for here "every object invested with intimate space becomes the center of all space. For each object, distance is the present, the horizon exists as much as the center."[53] Here in the vast desert spaces of the Southwest, journey and place meet to become legend.

CHAPTER II

The Flowering of Desire

Out of her own body she pushed
silver thread, light, air
and carried it carefully on the dark, flying
where nothing moved.

Out of her body she extruded
shining wire, life, and wove the light
on the void.

—From "Grandmother" by Paula Gunn Allen

This long journey brings us back, at the end of all our exploring, to the place where we started, to the image of Jeanne Le Ber, the recluse in her tower at the center of Willa Cather's *Shadows on the Rock*. The woman in the tower is silent; but the absence of speech suggests a presence, insists upon an understanding of experience that supersedes language.

"They are their own story," Cather had said of the hand-carved beams and joists, the utterly unconventional frescoes, the countless fanciful figures of the saints that became the material of *Death Comes for the Archbishop* and about which she insisted, "it is a foolish convention that we must have everything interpreted for us in written language. There are other ways of telling." In the Quebec of *Shadows on the Rock*, she described a mood "hard to state . . . in language; it was more like an old song, incomplete but uncorrupted, than like a legend. The text was mainly anacoluthon, so to speak, but the meaning was clear. I took the incomplete air and tried to give it what would correspond to a sympathetic musical setting; tried to develop it into a prose composition not too conclusive, not too definite: a series of pictures remembered rather than experienced."[2]

It is indeed another way of telling that turns our attention away from words, replacing words with images distantly perceived, locating meaning in the incomplete pieces of memory. Cather invites the reader to indulge in reverie, to take the cue—the fragment of a song, the old photograph—and to invent upon that ground, to re-member.

Words obfuscate; but other forms of representation are not in themselves complete: it is the compelling *suggestion* Cather had found in the nearly faceless forms of Millet's peasants that evokes deep memory. A drawing by Millet "of a well in front of a house with geese and chickens and a woman" elicits a similar response from John Berger, who writes at length about images. For Berger, the "realistic" drawing was also "the site of every fairy story which begins with an old woman's cottage. I saw it as a hundred times familiar, although I knew I had not seen it before; the 'memory' was inexplicably in the drawing itself"—Berger's memory and Millet's memory. Millet re-created the scene visible in front of the house where he was born, consciously or unconsciously enlarging the proportions of the well to coincide with his childhood perception;[3] Berger re-creates a scene associated with fairy tales and with complete freedom (it would be possible in the world of the Millet picture to escape from danger via the well or on the back of a goose)—freedom associated with the dreaming and reverie experienced in a re-membered childhood landscape.[4]

This is what Cather is after in *Shadows on the Rock*: an intersection of two kinds of memory for both writer and reader—or, for artist and viewer, listener, perceiver, since Cather explicitly states that her creation goes beyond words. When she says that her text is *anacoluthon*—not following, lacking sequence—she means that less is given even than in *Death Comes for the Archbishop*, where fragments are based on legend, legend that is to some extent known—passed down like stories of miracles, re-enacted in pageant, written. She had named two visual images as cues to *Death Comes for the Archbishop*: Holbein's *Dance of Death* and Puvis de Chavannes's mural of Sainte Geneviève in the Panthéon. A given theme connects and gives sequence to the Holbein woodcuts; the Chavannes mural, however, is a series of pictorial fragments of the life of the patron saint of Paris, each an invitation to meditation—pictures "remembered rather than experienced." And in *Shadows on the Rock*, only the barest hints would be given: a fragrance, a bit of an old song; the rest to be puzzled out, remembered, invented.

"*The thing that teases the mind over and over for years, and at last gets itself put down rightly on paper—whether little or great, it belongs to Literature*," Sarah Orne Jewett had written to Cather.[5] And it is finally in *Shadows on the Rock* that we get something like the "pale, primeval shades" of Puvis de Chavannes, whose frescoes, Cather said, had teased her mind since her student days.[6] Meditating on this late novel, "inconclusive" though it may be, we understand that there is nothing "indefinite" about it at all, that its difference from *Death Comes for the Archbishop* is most of all one of tone and timbre—the frosty clearness of Quebec as against the somber and fierce shades of New Mexico;[7] the rituals and rites of French culture as distinct from those of Indian and Mexican cultures. *Death Comes for the Archbishop* is, in fact, one of the way stations for *Shadows on the Rock*. We can trace the twin strands of memory and desire in Cather's fictions: one most clearly sounded in *My Ántonia*, where stories are carefully crafted as things to be shared with a circle of listeners, part of the ritual of daily life and seasonal change that includes eating, planting, building, loving, and in *Death Comes for the Archbishop*, where Bishop Latour cultivates and preserves the treasured amenities of his culture in the New Mexican desert; the other present in all of Cather's stories about artists, and especially in *The Professor's House*, where St. Peter in his attic haven or his enclosed garden meditates on the lost civilization of the Mesa Verde, and in *Death Comes for the Archbishop*, where Bishop Latour meditates in an Indian hogan, in a Mexican adobe church, in his cloistered garden, which has to do with a withdrawal from the world and especially from its infected language.

These "shapes and scenes that have 'teased' the mind for years, when they do at last get themselves rightly put down, make a very much higher order of writing, and a much more costly, than the most vivid and vigorous transfer of immediate impressions," Cather wrote in her essay on Jewett. She means "costly" in Emily Dickinson's sense: "'Tis just the price of Breath"; in Thoreau's sense: "A written word is . . . carved out of the breath of life itself."[8] Thus Thea Kronborg's discovery, in *The Song of the Lark*, of the need to create "a mould to imprison for a moment the shining elusive element which is life itself" is for singer and writer both a need to mould breath (304). Thus Professor St. Peter's discovery that the "price" of absolute dedication to the life of the imagination is that other life—romance, all domestic and social relations, "the human family, indeed"; thus his discovery of the seeming impossibility of finding language to express the things that haunt the mind—language, so long as one *is* a member of the human family, that is pure, that is one's own, that is faithful to the vision; and thus his longing for the silent, seaside cave.[9]

"You must find your own quiet centre of life, and write from that," Sarah Orne Jewett had told Cather. "To work in silence and with all one's heart, that is the writer's lot."[10] It is this fidelity to one's own vision that Cather values in Jewett's work; and it is her sense of this vision as *alternative* that inspires her search for nonlinguistic equivalents in which to describe it. Citing Walter Pater's notion that "every truly great drama must, in the end, linger in the reader's mind as a sort of ballad," Cather says that stories "must leave in the mind of the sensitive reader an intangible residuum of pleasure; a cadence, a quality of voice that is exclusively the writer's own, individual, unique. A quality that one can remember without the volume at hand, can experience over and over again in the mind but can never absolutely define, as one can experience in memory a melody, or the summer perfume of a garden." Memory, again—a quality of voice remembered—and something else: a writer who begins with "subject-matter," using "imagination" upon it and twisting it to suit one's purpose, can at best produce "only a brilliant sham, which, like a badly built and pretentious house, looks poor and shabby in a few years." It is rather the "gift of sympathy" that is the artist's greatest gift, the fine thing that alone can make one's work fine[11]—the "sympathy" that Cather has for her heroine Ántonia, that Thea Kronborg has for the operatic characters she portrays, that the Professor has for Tom Outland, and that Tom comes to feel for the mesa when he gives up trying to "know" the ancient civilization and begins to let the place he is in possess *him*:

> I lay down on a solitary rock that was like an island in the bottom of the valley, and looked up. The grey sage-brush and the blue-grey rock around me were already in shadow, but high above me the canyon walls were dyed flame-colour with the sunset, and the Cliff City lay in a gold haze against its dark cavern. In a few minutes it, too, was grey, and only the rim rock at the top held the red light. When that was gone, I could still see the copper glow in the piñons along the edge of the top ledges. The arc of sky over the canyon was silvery blue, with its pale yellow moon, and presently stars shivered into it, like crystals dropped into perfectly clear water.
>
> I remember these things, because, in a sense, that was the first night I was ever really on the mesa at all—the first night that all of me was there. This was the first time I ever saw it as a whole. It all came together in my

understanding, as a series of experiments do when you begin to see where they are leading. Something had happened in me that made it possible for me to co-ordinate and simplify, and that process, going on in my mind, brought with it great happiness. It was possession. The excitement of my first discovery was a very pale feeling compared to this one. For me the mesa was no longer an adventure, but a religious emotion. [250–51][12]

Vision, then, like the design that came to St. Peter as he lay in a little boat in the purple water, and the "gift of sympathy"—these are given to the artist; it is the *process* of creation that is so painfully difficult. Art is not thought or emotion, Cather had written as a young critic, "but expression, expression, always expression"—the finding of which, the journey from brain to hand, she called "the voyage perilous."[13] "The artist spends a lifetime in loving the things that haunt him, in having his mind 'teased' by them, in trying to get these conceptions down on paper exactly as they are," she would later write, "and he emerges at the end of a lifetime with much that is more or less happy experimenting, and comparatively little that is the very flower of himself and his genius."[14]

Cather's books are, of course, written in *words*. Professor St. Peter, though he withdraws to the silence of attic retreat or walled garden, finds the words to express his vision in his many-volumed *Spanish Adventurers in North America*. But the words found, created, invented, remembered are, Cather suggests, a different language. "Outland," for example, means one thing to Professor St. Peter—a vision, a sense of recaptured youth, of the world of childhood dreaming; it means something else to his family— personal threat (to his wife), money and something unattainable (to his son-in-law), an extravagant country house (to his elder daughter). In *My Ántonia*, the Bohemian and Scandinavian storytellers give up their own language and learn to speak the language of the New World. For Thea Kronborg in *The Song of the Lark*, music is her own language, one not understood by the townsfolk in Moonstone, Colorado, but spoken by her German music teacher, Wunsch, and her friend Spanish Johnny. In *Death Comes for the Archbishop*, the French missionaries must learn the language of their new country, but at the end of his life, in retreat, Father Latour reverts to his "mother tongue." This is no mere semantic cavil, for in speaking the mother tongue, Father Latour ceases to speak the official languages of Rome and of his mission in the New World. In other words, he gives up what anthropologist Mary Douglas calls "restricted speech"— the official and public language—for "elaborated speech," a private and creative language.[15] Similarly, there are two languages in *Shadows on the*

Rock; all the stories and songs and Jeanne Le Ber's description of her cloister are in the mother tongue: "*ma chambre est mon paradis terrestre; c'est mon centre; c'est mon élément. Il n'y a pas de lieu plus délicieux, ni plus salutaire pour moi; point de Louvre, point de palais, qui me soit plus agréable. Je préfère ma cellule à tout le reste de l'univers.*"[16]

The two languages are not separate; they overlap and coexist. Professor St. Peter has a professional and a domestic life in which he speaks both languages, more often the restricted, official language in conducting university business and in conversing with his sons-in-law at the family dinner table; but he speaks more intimately with his daughter Kathleen, and in the lecture we (and his wife) overhear, he presents his own elaborated discourse as public discourse. In this case, not only does he speak in the elaborate structure of his privately worked-out thought, but he opposes the art/religion equation to the foundations of public discourse—rationality itself:

> I don't myself think much of science as a phase of human development. It has given us a lot of ingenious toys; they take our attention away from the real problems, of course, and since the problems are insoluble, I suppose we ought to be grateful for distraction. But the fact is, the human mind, the individual mind, has always been made more interesting by dwelling on the old riddles, even if it makes nothing of them. Science hasn't given us any new amazements, except of the superficial kind we get from witnessing dexterity and sleight-of-hand. It hasn't given us any richer pleasures, as the Renaissance did. . . . I don't think you help people by making their conduct of no importance—you impoverish them. As long as every man and woman who crowded into the cathedrals on Easter Sunday was a principal in a gorgeous drama with God, glittering angels on one side and the shadows of evil coming and going on the other, life was a rich thing. The king and the beggar had the same chance at miracles and great temptations and revelations. And that's what makes men happy, believing in the mystery and importance of their own little individual lives. It makes us happy to surround our creature needs and bodily instincts with as much pomp and circumstance as possible. Art and religion (they are the same thing in the end, of course) have given man the only happiness he has ever had. [67–69][17]

When St. Peter's wife tells him at the end of the lecture, "It's hardly dignified to think aloud in such company. It's in rather bad taste," he responds, "I won't do it again"; and less and less does he think aloud. Although we have located him in his Renaissance structures—the framed landscape, the formal garden, we see in the Professor a retreat from what George Steiner has called "the primacy of the word"—the classic and the

Christian sense of reality as ordered within the governance of language. "Literature, philosophy, theology, law, the arts of history, are endeavors to enclose within the bounds of rational discourse the sum of human experience, its recorded past, its present condition and future expectations," Steiner writes. "They bear solemn witness to the belief that all truth and realness—with the exception of a small, queer margin at the very top—can be housed inside the walls of language."[18] The small, queer place at the top is, of course, where St. Peter houses himself, his attic retreat now not only separated from the rest of the house, but in a separate house, just as his French garden is not an extension of his house, but a separate, cloistered space—both spaces used not for communication, but for solitary contemplation.

Although we live inside the act of discourse, Steiner says, "we should not assume that a verbal matrix is the only one in which the articulations and conduct of the mind are conceivable. There are modes of intellectual and sensuous reality founded not on language, but on other communicative energies such as the icon or musical note. And there are actions of the spirit rooted in silence." Steiner is interested primarily in the way in which, after the middle of the seventeenth century, the moment Professor St. Peter in his lecture posits as the high point of Western civilization, "significant areas of truth, reality, and action recede from the sphere of the verbal statement." The natural sciences, and even mathematics, with its long history of symbolic notation, were meaningful within the framework of linguistic description, tied to the material conditions of experience, ordered and ruled by language. But with the formulation of analytic geometry and the theory of algebraic functions, with the development by Newton and Leibniz of calculus, mathematics ceases to be a dependent notation, an instrument of the empirical, and becomes "a fantastically rich, complex, and dynamic language. *And the history of that language is one of progressive untranslatability.*"[19] It is this untranslatability to which Professor St. Peter objects in his lecture—to modernism, to the tenor of Western life, which since the seventeenth century subsumes successively larger areas of knowledge to the modes and proceedings of mathematics.

The other kind of "retreat from the word" is more germane to our interests, for what St. Peter experiences in this novel is a retreat into the "actions of the spirit rooted in silence." Models for this perception of reality come from Oriental metaphysics—Buddhism and Taoism, for example, where "the soul is envisioned as ascending from the gross impediments of the material, through domains of insight that can be rendered by lofty and precise language, toward ever deepening silence," where "the highest, purest reach of the contemplative act is that which has learned to leave language behind it"—and in Western culture from the abandonment of speech by the Trappist monks and by the Desert Fathers. It is only by breaking through the walls of language that, freed from the impurities and fragmentation that speech necessarily entails, one can attain total understanding. It is language, Steiner says, that artificially separates past, present and future; "in ultimate truth they are simultaneously comprised."[20] Like the holy recluse who withdraws not only from the temptations of worldly action but from speech, for whom the retreat into the cave or the monastic cell is the outward gesture of silence, St. Peter in his attic study or his walled garden seeks to separate himself from restricted language.[21]

When Cather says, then, that she had in mind for *The Professor's House* the sonata form,[22] or the landscape seen through the window of the house in a Dutch painting; when she says that Holbein's *Dance of Death* inspired the title of *Death Comes for the Archbishop* or that Puvis de Chavannes's mural of the life of Sainte Geneviève teased her mind for years until, finally, she tried something like that, she offers more than a cue that informs a particular novel: like St. Peter, she retreats from the word in order to free herself from restricted language.

Shadows on the Rock, Cather had said, was drawn from "a series of pictures remembered rather than experienced; a kind of thinking . . . left over from the past."[23] The title suggests a focus on the "muted" part of experience, on the things in the shadow. In painting, the shadows are the corners traditionally reserved for scenes of low life, "glimpsed in passing, indulgently even enviously, by the traveller on the high road where there is space and light." In the early genre paintings of Cather's beloved Millet, the shadows contain shepherd girls in the shade of trees, a woman churning butter, a cooper in his workshop, but after 1853, as John Berger points out, these shadowy characters "moved to the forefront and become the centre of the world assumed by the painting. And from now on, this is true in all of Millet's major works which include figures. Far from presenting these figures as something marginal seen in passing, he does his utmost to make them central and monumental."[24]

As the title suggests, Cather's novel is about things in the shadow:

the villagers of Kebec live in the shadow of the rock; the apothecary Auclair lives under the protection of the Count de Frontenac, his patron; the Lower Town is "so directly underneath the Upper Town that one could stand on the terrace of the Château Saint-Louis and throw a stone down into the narrow streets below"; and the whole little colonial outpost is in the shadow of France, and of Louis XIV, the Sun-King.[25] In exploring the way in which the French colonists in the New World live simultaneously inside two traditions, and in focusing on the experiences of a "muted" culture, Cather undertakes here the task that Gerda Lerner would later suggest of "light[ing] up areas of historical darkness." The focus of the novel is a woman-centered inquiry, a kind of answer to Lerner's question, "What would history be like if it were seen through the eyes of women and ordered by values they define?"[26] If we consider the novel in this way, we see "meaning in what has previously been empty space. The orthodox plot recedes, and another plot, hitherto submerged in the anonymity of the background, stands out in bold relief like a thumbprint."[27]

Like the horizontal plane in the paintings of Millet, which, juxtaposed with the continual struggle to encourage the vertical, claims everything;[28] like the image of Professor St. Peter transcending, in his attic retreat, the domestic life beneath him, and transcending, too, the horizontal plane of vision that he sees through the window of his room; like the endless journeys across the horizontal plane of the Southwestern desert undertaken by the bishop whose name is *La Tour*; like the twin images of the seasonal and daily ritual life of Cécile Auclair and that of the recluse Jeanne Le Ber in her tower, the novel *Shadows on the Rock* can be diagrammed in the shape of a cross. The horizontal line represents chronological, historical time: the past and the future, the temporal, seasonal changes and cycles, Cécile Auclair's experience. The vertical line represents the moving present, now, Jeanne Le Ber's experience. This diagram is a representation of the space-time of the Carmelite nuns,[29] the order founded by Saint Teresa of Avila, whose "Interior Castle" would be located toward the upper end of the vertical line.[30] The horizontal line is "'natural' or physical space-time, the line on which we might express physical birth and death, on which we might count the passage of years or reckon age[,] . . . ecological space-time." The vertical line represents "liturgical space-time," connected in the Carmelite cosmology "with higher and lower states of being, . . . and with constant inner efforts towards greater self-awareness." It is as if the Carmelite has two "maps," "one which locates her in ordinary geographical space-time, another consisting of an interior 'territory' of a spiritual and psychological nature in which she is located at the same time."[31]

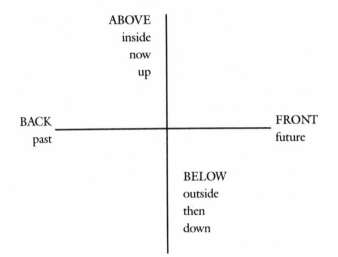

ABOVE
inside
now
up

BACK   FRONT
past   future

BELOW
outside
then
down

Space-time continuum of the Carmelite nuns.

The tone of *Shadows on the Rock* is set by the epigraph, a line from a letter written by Marie de l'Incarnation to one of her Sisters, dated "Québec, 1653"—the time, the beginning of the modern world, the place, a timeless medieval refuge: *"Vous me demandez des graines de fleurs de ce pays. Nous en faisons venir de France pour notre jardin, n'y en ayant pas ici de fort rares ni de fort belles. Tout y est sauvage, les fleurs aussi bien que les hommes."* But the novel proper begins in the fall of 1697, when the last ships are returning to France, marking the beginning of the isolation that will seal off the colony of Kebec through the long winter, and ends one year later, in the fall of 1698. The sailors take their pleasure with the women of the streets; the apothecary Euclide Auclair selects his wood doves, his fruits and vegetables from the market to put down for the winter, and measures out the powders and syrups of his trade; the trappers return from their long treks in the wilderness and set out again; the villagers light candles in the Lady Chapel and celebrate the round of holidays with special seasonal rituals; the Count de Frontenac dies an old man. For a moment in the summer the rock of Kebec stands "gleaming above the river like an altar with many candles, or like a holy city in an old legend, shriven, sinless, washed in gold" (169).

Along this horizontal space-time line we follow Cécile Auclair. She is a tradition-bound and imaginative child, with a glow of rapture about her that is not self-abnegation, but rather sensuous delight. We learn a great deal about her from her visit to Mother Juschereau. The two women delight in the stories the older one tells to the younger, but when Mother Juschereau would end the story with an explanation, Cécile takes her hand and implores her, "*N'expliquez pas!*" (39). We see Cécile feeding the deformed and disfigured Blinker because her mother has always done so, knitting stockings for a neglected litle boy who becomes her special friend; we see her preparing and serving her father's dinners in the old French way and getting up in the middle of a cold winter night to cover the parsley so that it will not freeze; we see her lying ill in bed, swaddled in layers and layers of shelter, "the dripping grey roofs and spires, the lighted windows along the crooked streets, the great grey river choked with ice and frozen snow, the never-ending, merciless forest beyond, . . . with this one flickering, shadowy room at the core" (157–58). Cécile's mother has bequeathed to her daughter a sense of "our way"; she has made sure that "life would go on almost unchanged in this room with its dear . . . objects; that the proprieties would be observed, all the little shades of feeling which make the common fine. The individuality, the character, of M. Auclair's house, though it appeared to be made up of wood and cloth and glass and a little silver, was really made of very fine moral qualities in two women: the mother's unswerving fidelity to certain traditions, and the daughter's loyalty to her mother's wish" (25–26). Cécile's sense of the permanence and orderliness of this world as she knows it even shapes her idea of heaven. Her favorite church is the Lady Chapel of the Lower Town, where she and her little friend Jacques love to go and gaze at the paintings of Sainte Geneviève as a little girl, and at the altar, a very simple, but definite representation of a feudal castle, all stone walls and towers—layers and layers of shelter, like the town itself:

> The outer wall was low and thick, with many battlements; the second was higher, with fewer battlements; the third seemed to be the wall of the palace itself, with towers and many windows. Within the arched gateway . . . the Host was kept. Cécile had always taken it for granted that the Kingdom of Heaven looked exactly like this from the outside and was surrounded by just such walls; that this altar was a reproduction of it, made in France by people

who knew; just as the statues of saints and of the Holy Family were portraits. She had taught Jacques to believe the same thing, and it was very comforting to them both to know just what Heaven looked like,—strong and unassailable, wherever it was set among the stars. [64–65]

The vertical line is the "moving present" of Jeanne Le Ber, the recluse from Montreal who dwells in an Interior Castle, an earthly symbol of which is the little house she has built for herself, a vertical three-room cell attached to a chapel. The bottom room looks onto a garden; through one of its little windows she receives her food, and by means of the other, which has a grille, she can attend mass without being seen. She sleeps in the middle room, and the top room is her atelier where she weaves and embroiders beautiful altar cloths and vestments, spins yarn and knits stockings for the poor.

Jeanne Le Ber takes up very little space in the novel; yet her story lingers in the reader's mind like a fragment of a melody, something remembered rather than experienced. Positioned as her story is at the center of *Shadows on the Rock*, it intersects the story of Cécile in an important way. Just as Cécile is literally and figuratively at the nexus of her world, located on the one street that connects the upper and lower towns, the house where she tends tradition like a sacred fire a kind of center of warmth in the frozen village, so Jeanne Le Ber is centered in her world—unlike the solitary Count de Frontenac. While Jeanne Le Ber lives in a kind of rock garden—something like the sand garden of Father Latour in *Death Comes for the Archbishop*, a sacred space, a cloister of contemplation—the Governor-General of the province lives in a château at the very top of the Rock, seeming to dominate not only the lower town spread out beneath him, but the very forces of the earth. These dwelling places are not only universal responses to nature, as Yi-Fu Tuan has demonstrated; they are also perceptions, enfigured images of the self.[32] The lonely Count returns in his dreams to the warmth of his childhood home, but the dream becomes nightmare as the child struggles to defend the house from a giant intruder, and the man wakes in his château drenched with sweat, wishing to die. Jeanne Le Ber's room, on the other hand, is her earthly paradise: it is my center, she says, my element. There is nothing more delicious, and I prefer my cell to all the rest of the universe (233–34, 136). The Count's gift to Cécile is a bowl of glass fruit, "lovelier than real fruit" (60). Jeanne Le Ber's gift is a legend.

Jeanne Le Ber *is* a legend. During the severe Canadian winters, people love to tell the story of how when the recluse, as she is called, broke

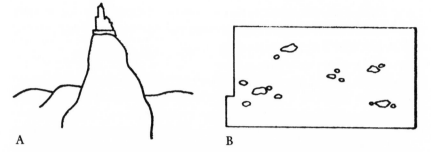

A: St. Michel, Le Puy, France. B: Rock and sand garden of contemplation. (Yi-Fu Tuan, *Topophilia: A Study of Environmental Perceptions, Attitudes, and Values,* © 1974, pp. 144–45; courtesy, Prentice-Hall)

her spinning wheel, two angels descended to her workroom and repaired it for her, how she saw the light in the room, and when she entered it, the angels spoke with her. The story is told and re-told with loving exaggeration, bringing pleasure with each repetition, "as if the recluse herself had sent to all those families . . . some living beauty,—a blooming rose-tree, or a shapely fruit-tree in fruit," an incomparable gift indeed, for in the long evenings, when the tales of Indian massacres and lost hunters had been told, "someone would speak the name of Jeanne Le Ber, and it again gave out fragrance." And stories are miracles, loved "for so many hundred years, not as proof or evidence, but because they are the actual flowering of desire. In them the vague worship and devotion of the simple-hearted assumes a form. From being a shapeless longing, it becomes a beautiful image; a dumb rapture becomes a melody that can be remembered and repeated; and the experience of a moment, which might have been a lost ecstasy, is made an actual possession and can be bequeathed to another" (136–37).

This is, of course, a description of the process of writing: moments of epiphany are seized, written down so that they can be remembered and repeated, and bequeathed to another—the flowering of desire. Jeanne Le Ber's first moments of self-knowledge, of the sense that she is destined to transcend the horizontal space-time line in order to serve some higher purpose, are like Thea's in *The Song of the Lark* and like the young Willa Cather's: kneeling beside the casement of her upstairs window after the rest of the family is asleep and gazing at the red spark of the sanctuary lamp showing in the dark church, Thea would whisper, *"I will be that lamp; that shall be my life"* (131). Clearly Cather—unlike some of the characters in her novel, and some readers—values the necessary and creative solitude of Jeanne Le Ber. But she also values the necessary and creative work of Cécile: "A new society begins with the salad dressing more than with the destruction of Indian villages," she had said of this culture kept alive, sheltered and tended on this rock "as if it really were a sacred fire."[33] The worth of Cécile is in the "graces, traditions, riches of the mind and spirit," in a history that "shine[s] with bright incidents, slight, perhaps, but precious, as in life itself, where the great matters are often as worthless as astronomical distances, and the trifles dear as the heart's blood" (98).

Cécile Auclair, mediating between Cap Diamant at the top of the mountain and the Basse Ville spread out below, between the Old World and the savage Canadian wilderness, and Jeanne Le Ber, in her Interior Castle, her cloister of contemplation: they keep alive traditions much older and more important than wars and colonization, political and industrial revolutions, and all of the contextual appurtenances of modernization scarcely mentioned in the novel. Both Cécile Auclair and Jeanne Le Ber offer an alternative version to the "reality" of the Indian massacres and destruction of Indian villages,[34] to the power of the lonely Count, to the perception of Pierre Charron, husband of one and disappointed suitor of the other, that Jeanne's life is one of resignation and despair. Cécile Auclair makes a version of life that is good: "These coppers, big and little, these brooms and clouts and brushes, were [her] tools; and with them one made, not shoes or cabinet-work, but life itself. One made a climate within a climate; one made the days,—the complexion, the special flavour, the special happiness of each day as it passed; one made life" (198). Jeanne Le Ber spins and weaves: she makes altar cloths and vestments that adorn churches all over the province; she knits stockings for the poor; she weaves the tapestry of the world, spinning out of herself her own filaments of light. Willa Cather, with her gift of sympathy for trifles, dear as the heart's blood, makes stories from what has hitherto been consigned to the shadows.

Shadows on the Rock, medieval in its setting, is an extraordinarily modern, filmic novel.[35] It is as if conventional narration would prevent us from getting back to the story of Cécile, back to the story of Jeanne Le Ber. Seeking out the shadows, the camera eye moves from a view of the ships departing for France, in the opening scene, to the great cliff, from the rock-set town all the way up to Cap Diamant, then scans again the grey buildings, monasteries and churches, "steep-pitched and dormered, with spires and slated roofs," down to the St. Lawrence River, "rolling north toward the purple line of the Laurentian mountains, toward frowning Cap Tourmente which rose dark against the soft blue of the October sky," out in the middle of the river to the Île d'Orléans, "like a hilly map, with downs and fields and pastures lying in folds above the naked tree-tops," across the river to the black pine forest that came down to the water's edge, stretching no living person knew how far, "the dead, sealed world of the vegetable kingdom, an uncharted continent choked with interlocking trees, living, dead, half-dead, their roots in bogs and swamps, strangling each other in a slow agony that had lasted for centuries," then scans the moving, glittering surface of the river once again, all the way to the open sea, and finally sweeps back to the town, to the winding street called Mountain Hill, following the path of Euclide Auclair as he makes his way through the garden of the Récollet friars past the new Bishop's Palace, and down to his own house (6–8).

The mountain rock, "cunningly built over with churches, convents, fortifications, gardens, . . . some high, some low, some thrust up on a spur, some nesting in a hollow, some sprawling unevenly along a declivity," resembles, except for its "Oriental colour," one of those little artificial mountains that were made in the old churches to present a theatric scene of the Nativity:

> The Château Saint-Louis, grey stone with steep dormer roofs, on the very edge of the cliff overlooking the river, sat level; but just beside it the convent and the church of the Récollet friars ran downhill, as if it were sliding backwards. To landward, in a low, well-sheltered spot, lay the Convent of the Ursulines . . . lower still stood the massive foundation of the Jesuits, facing the Cathedral. Immediately behind the Cathedral the cliff ran up sheer again, shot out into a jutting spur, and there, high in the blue air, between heaven and earth, rose old Bishop Laval's Seminary. Beneath it the rock fell away in a succession of terraces like a circular stair-case; on one of these was the new Bishop's new Palace, its gardens on the terraces below. [5–6][36]

In the shadow of the rock, at the center, is Cécile's house, not an unfurnished room, but a series of connecting rooms, a set of those haunting interiors filled with meaning for Cather, like those of Tolstoi's old Moscow houses, where "the clothes, the dishes . . . are always so much a part of the emotions of the people that they are perfectly synthesized; they seem to exist, not so much in the author's mind, as in the emotional penumbra of the characters themselves." Fused like this, she said, the literalness of one's personal space "ceases to be literalness—it is merely part of the experience."[37] The house is built of wood in the earliest Quebec manner—"double walls, with sawdust and ashes filling in the space between the two frames, making a protection nearly four feet thick against the winter cold." One journeys horizontally through the spaces of this house, following Auclair through the shop, lit by a single candle; to the living room, behind and partly concealed by a partition made of shelves and cabinets, drawn to the warmth of the fireplace and the round dining-table set with a white cloth, silver candlesticks, glasses and decanters of red and white wine; to the small, low-roofed, stone kitchen. This is Cécile's domain: there is the rich odor of roasting fowl, and a child's voice singing, then calling, "Is it you, Papa?" (9).

At the center of the novel, *Shadows on the Rock*, is Jeanne Le Ber's tower, a series of three rooms connected to one another and joining heaven and earth—a fabulous vertical structure. The tower is silent, like a place in a dream: Jeanne Le Ber is not seen nor heard directly. The story of the angels' visit to her is "the news from Montreal"; the sound of her voice, once gay and musical, now "harsh and hollow like an old crow's" to Pierre Charron's ear, accompanies Pierre on his solitary wilderness journeys; the legend of the recluse, like the pictures of Sainte Geneviève in the Lady Chapel, becomes the material of Cécile's reveries while her father reads aloud from Plutarch's *Lives*, the material for stories told to little Jacques, and of stories told and retold with loving exaggeration in the remote parishes all over snow-burdened Canada (128, 180, 129, 136).

Silently spinning and weaving to her own rhythm, Jeanne Le Ber makes there, with Cécile in her shelter, a counterpoint to the great Rock in whose shadow they both live. The novel is that simple: a series of pictures, like old woodcuts, engraved upon the memory. We see these pictures, and we experience them: we have been there. We know the shadows, but until now what takes place in the shadows has not been the subject of stories told.

Cécile loves stories. When Father Hector Saint-Cyr, the missionary priest, visits the Auclairs and tells his story—"Listen," he says to the father and daughter, "No man can give himself heart and soul to one thing while in the back of his mind he cherishes a desire, a secret hope, for something very different. . . . nothing worth while is accomplished except by that last sacrifice, the giving of oneself altogether and finally"—Cécile, listening, "had almost ceased to breathe in her excitement; . . . her eyes, in the

candlelight, were no longer blue, but black." As Mother Juschereau realizes when she tells Cécile stories of the saints and martyrs, although Cécile
is utterly unself-conscious and without vanity, the eagerness with which
she responds to these stories is less the rapture of self-abnegation than the
flow of worldly pleasure (149–50, 39–40). Such moments of rapture come
to Cécile from the simple things that make up her life: a row of clean and
shining copper pots in her kitchen, the smell of roasting fowl and the
sweet taste of gooseberry preserves, the rows of filled glass jars and bottles
in her father's shop, the magic of the missionary's story and of the legend
of Jeanne Le Ber.

Each object—a beautiful harp-shaped elm in the middle of a waving
green hayfield (193), the Count's bowl of glass fruit, the story of Marie the
pécheresse—is named and given concrete existence as object; then its objec-
tiveness dissolves as it enters the boundaries of Cécile's inner world as
subject. Objects seen and named are then felt. For example, in the scene in
which Cécile dresses for a sailor's party—the highlight of which is to be
the captain's talking parrot—the progression, characteristic of movement
in the novel as a whole, is from the objective to the subjective, a montage
of sensations that leads us into the fantasy-making world of Cécile:

> Cécile had no looking-glass upstairs—the only one in the house was in the
> salon—so she always dressed by feeling rather than by sight. This afternoon
> she put on the blue silk dress with black velvet bands, walked about in it,
> then took it off and spread it out on her bed, where she smoothed it and
> admired it. It was too different from anything she had ever worn before, too
> long and too grand—quite right to wear to mass or to a wedding, perhaps,
> but not for tonight. She slipped on one of her new jerseys and felt like
> herself again. The coral beads she would wear; they seemed appropriate for
> a sailor's party. She left the beautiful dress lying on her bed and went down
> to see that her father had brushed his Sunday coat, and to give Jacques's
> hands a scrubbing. She and the little boy sat down on the sofa to wait for
> Pierre, while Auclair was arranging his shop for the night. To Cécile the
> time dragged very slowly. She was thinking, not about the novelty of having
> supper by moonlight, or of the *tête de veau* they were promised, or of the
> celebrated Captain Pondaven, but of his parrot.
>
> All her life she longed to possess a parrot. The idea of a talking bird was
> fascinating to her—seemed to belong with especially rare and wonderful
> things, like orange-trees and peacocks and gold crowns and the Count's
> glass fruit. Her mother, she whispered to Jacques, had often told her about
> a parrot kept in one of the great houses at home, which saw a servant steal
> silver spoons and told the master. Then there was the imprisoned princess
> who taught her parrot to say her lover's name, and her cruel brothers cut
> out the bird's tongue. [214–15]

There is in this world, where language belongs to a fabulous bird and sensation is rendered through the consciousness, or unconscious fantasy-making mind of a female child, a radical alteration of vision—what Adrienne Rich calls "re-vision."[38] It is this woman-centered view of historical experience that Cather would explore in her last novel, *Sapphira and the Slave Girl*, where mistress and servant are joined in their confinement, the one paralyzed by illness, the other enslaved by her mistress, and where the escape from confinement, made possible through the bonding of women, is literally the story—not only the plot of the novel, but the legend told and retold as story and remembered as the significant event in the childhood of the storyteller.

The themes of *Sapphira and the Slave Girl*, set in the Virginia of Cather's childhood, are in fact first sounded in *Shadows on the Rock*, the novel begun just after the death of Cather's father and written during the long period of her mother's illness, necessitating repeated cross-country traveling and finally, toward the end of the two-and-a-half-year period, a long stay with her dying mother in Pasadena, California. During this time Cather suffered "a troubling inner division of her powers," as she told her friend Elizabeth Shepley Sergeant. "She kept her new book (figuratively speaking), in a kind of underground place, to which she could retire for a few hours of concentrated work." Sergeant likens Cather in this period to the Pueblo Indian who "retired from the teeming village to the kiva or underground chamber" in order to "find herself as an artist in her hidden imaginary retreat on the rock of Quebec, and emerge from it with the power to bring something vital to the life that clung to hers."[39] Cather was unable to work on *Shadows on the Rock* in California—that writing took place in her "attic" at Grand Manan, an island off the coast of New Brunswick, where she summered with Edith Lewis; in her apartment at the Grosvenor in New York, where she hung full-size copies of the *Lady and Unicorn* tapestries at the foot of her bed; and at Jaffrey, New Hampshire. Near her mother she worked on *Obscure Destinies*, its title suggesting stories culled from the shadows, completing "Two Friends" and beginning "Old Mrs. Harris," a story about mothers and daughters, about the bonding of women.[40]

Cather had speculated as early as 1895 about the nature of woman's experience and wondered whether the writing that describes that experience, when it is so "highly subjective, . . . self-centered, self-absorbed, centrifugal," has any place in literature at all. In other words, she understood from the beginning that "literature" describes the experience of the dominant culture, for whose members the experience of muted cultures takes place literally in a "no-man's land." Comparing Christina Rossetti with her brother, Cather decided that

> it must have taken considerable individuality of thought and inspiration to withstand the constant influences of so winning a personality and so enchanting a style as Gabriel Rossetti's. Her themes and her treatment of them are in most cases diametrically opposite from his. . . . She wrote the best sacred poetry of this century, of that there can be no doubt. Never sinking to moralizing, never yielding to accepted forms, she wrote with the mystic, enraptured faith of Cassandra, which is a sort of spiritual ecstasy, and which is to the soul what passion is to the heart.[41]

Significantly, Cather would use Christina Rossetti's "one perfect poem," "Goblin Market," as the epigraph to her own collection of stories, *The Troll Garden*, in 1905. "Goblin Market" contrasts two sisters: Lizzie, who stops her ears to the goblin song, and Laura, who crouches in the reeds and gazes longingly at the goblin fruit, which she buys with one of her golden curls, and from then on "goes hungering and thirsting for the goblin fruits, dreaming of them, longing for them." Like Father Hector, the missionary priest in *Shadows on the Rock*, however, Laura finds that "the goblin fruit gives only hunger, not satisfaction; only desire, not fulfillment."[42]

In linking "the wild" (the goblin fruits) with "spiritual ecstasy," and religion with art, Cather drew upon a very ancient tradition in mythology and folklore of women "speaking in tongues," from the mysterious cults of Eleusis and Corinth to the witch covens of western Europe to various ecstatic religions.[43] Her Cassandra-like characters (including her priests, with their ambiguous middle status between civilized and wild, between male and female, and her reclusive Professor St. Peter)[44] are quasi-acceptable models for a retreat into "the wild."

In *Shadows on the Rock* Jeanne Le Ber secludes and encloses herself within the tower of her own design in order to clear a space for moments of spiritual ecstasy; hers is what Susan Sontag has called in another context, "a full void, an enriching emptiness, a resonating . . . eloquent silence."[45] But so is Cécile's inner life along the horizontal space-time line an orderly progression of moments of rapture, pleasure felt in the simple things that make up her life. This ecstasy is the novel's real theme, "the secret treasure at its heart, the thing that gave it its reason for being": the "primary ecstasy"—like that Bishop Latour experiences in his encounter with landscape and sky, like that Willa Cather experienced observing her rock from above, "in wonderful vistas of weather and sea and forest—the whole citadel, stuck over with churches, nunneries, spires, and bishops' and governors' residences, ringing with bells, . . . [with] the feel and look of a single religious and noble house of prayer and obeisance"—is the very foundation stone of the story.[46]

Like the towering stone upon which it stands, and appropriate to the primary ecstasy that she teaches us to value, Jeanne Le Ber's house seems to coexist sensuously with its surroundings, confirming the human need to touch, to shape. As Lucy Lippard has written of the towering standing stones of ancient sites, "something seems to flow back to us through these places—which we see perhaps as symbols of lost symbols."[47]

In all cultures, the tower—the pillar, pole or tree in the center of sacred space—has been seen as a religious symbol for passage from one cosmic level to another. From the ladder in Jacob's dream to the sacred pillar worshiped by the Celts and Germans before their conversion to Christianity, "the vertical upright was an almost universal symbol for the passage to the worlds of the gods above and below the earth."[48] The religious person of fixed settlements "wanted his own house to be at the Center and to be an *imago mundi*," Mircea Eliade writes. He "could only live in a space opening upward, where the break in place was symbolically assured and hence communication with the *other world*, the transcendental world, was ritually possible."[49]

As an artistic symbol, Jeanne Le Ber's tower is a fantasy environment imagined to express "earthly paradise," her "center," her "element"—or as Jung says of his tower, the place where "I am in the midst of my true life, I am most deeply myself."[50] Jung's vertical structure, however, like the Count de Frontenac's in *Shadows on the Rock*, is a statement of self-assertion, cast in stone, and a return to the sheltering womb. Jeanne Le Ber's structure expresses "transcendence, abolition of the cosmos, absolute freedom."[51]

As one of the most complete descriptions we have of tower building, Jung's is a useful text for understanding the very different legend of Jeanne Le Ber. He describes the tower at Bollingen on Lake Zurich as his wish to make manifest in stone the symbol of his self. At first, he writes in his *Autobiography*, he planned merely a primitive one-story dwelling, a round structure with a hearth at the center, but he felt compelled to add another story to make it into "a suitable dwelling tower." This tower gave him a feeling of repose and renewal "intense from the start," he writes; "it represented for me the maternal hearth." Later Jung added another building with a towerlike annex, and then after another interval he built onto the tower a retiring room for meditation and seclusion where no one could enter; it was his own retreat for spiritual concentration. Still later, he felt the need for another area, open to nature and the sky, and so added a courtyard and adjoining loggia. Finally, realizing that the small central section of the house "which crouched so low and hidden was myself! I could no longer hide behind the 'maternal' and 'spiritual' towers," he added another story to this section "which represents myself or my ego-personality. Earlier, I would not have been able to do this; I would have regarded it as presumptuous self-emphasis. Now it signified an extension of consciousness achieved in old age." From the beginning, Jung says, "I felt the Tower as in some way a place of maturation—a maternal womb or a maternal figure in which I could become what I was, what I am and will be. It gave me a feeling as if I were being reborn in stone. It is thus a concretisation of the individuation process."[52]

Where Jung, then, builds in stone a mythic structure in order to learn to inhabit a world made of words and symbols to which he belongs by right, the stone of his structure expressing the power and permanence of that tradition, Jeanne Le Ber chooses silence in order to *create* a world. Rather than an image of her physical self, Jeanne Le Ber's house on the Rock is, as in archaic times, a repository for the soul, intended not to offer a likeness but to evoke a living presence. The stone, as Lippard points out, "*represented* nothing; it *was* both spirit and spirit's dwelling place." The stone, invulnerable and irreducible, was the image and symbol of being:

> Stones touch human beings because they suggest immortality, because they have so patently *survived*. . . . Earth and stone are two forms of the same material, symbolizing the same forces. Both are the sources of the world as we know it. The alchemical *petra genetrix*, or generative stone, is an incarnation of *prima materia*—the beginning, the bedrock, the Old European Great Goddess who was both earth and sky—"unmated mother"—sole creator of everything.[53]

Jeanne Le Ber's tower on the Rock, like her cloistered garden, is open to the sky, to the visits of angels. Her tower of transcendence, where like the women in the triptych by Remedios Varo she spins and weaves the tapestries of the world, rises from the small womblike space, the empowering cave, Thea's cave of the Ancient People in the Southwestern cliff dwellings, "the place of female power, the *umbilicus mundi*, one of the great antechambers of the mysteries of transformation."[54] In *Shadows on the Rock*, however, we must add to Thea's experience that of Marie the *pécheresse*, considered a sinner by the townsfolk in Normandy, "driven out by the good people of the town, shunned by men and women alike, [until] she fell lower and lower, and at last hid herself in a solitary cave. There she dragged out her shameful life, destitute and consumed by a loathsome disease. And there she died; without human aid and without the sacraments of the Church. After her death her body was thrown into a ditch and buried like that of some unclean animal" (37). The cave, then, has been imprisoning as well as empowering for women, "a house of earth, secret and often sacred . . . to . . . [which] the initiate comes to hear the voices of darkness, the wisdom of inwardness"—Plato's cave of half-blindness and immoblization, Freud's womb-tomb, Simone de Beauvoir's place of "immanence with no hope of transcendence"—and also the dwelling place of Sibyl, or Cybele, "the primordial prophetess who mythically conceived all women artists."[55]

The story of Jeanne Le Ber is the story of the Sibyl, of "the woman artist who enters the cavern of her own mind and finds there the scattered leaves not only of her own power but of the tradition which might have generated that power." In this version of the parable, the Sibyl's cave becomes a place of vision and power: the female arts to which Beauvoir's cave-dwelling seamstresses were condemned become transfigured into the powerful arts of the underground Weaver Woman.[56] And preserved in the cliff dwellings of Mesa Verde, the reader will recall, are the mummified remains of "Mother Eve," whom the Indians of the Southwest would have called "Spider Woman," the Great Weaver, powerful underground Earth Mother who possesses the powers of creation,[57] like the spinning and weaving women of antiquity, the mother goddesses who in their concealed workshops "weave veins, fibers, and nerve strands into the miraculous substance of the live body, . . . weave the world tapestry out of genesis and demise."[58]

Jeanne Le Ber is related not only to the underground Weaver Woman; her tower gives focus to the Rock of Quebec in the same way as the tower at Mesa Verde defines the pale little houses built into the side of a cliff. In *The Professor's House*, the tower Tom Outland saw when he looked across the cavern at the little city of stone, asleep,

> was beautifully proportioned, . . . swelling out to a larger girth a little above the base, then growing slender again. There was something symmetrical and powerful about the swell of the masonry. The tower was the fine thing that

held all the jumble of houses together and made them mean something. . . .
I wondered how many Christmases had come and gone since that round
tower was built. I had been to Ácoma and the Hopi villages, but I'd never
seen a tower like that one. It seemed to me to mark a difference. I felt that
only a strong and aspiring people would have built it, and a people with a
feeling for design. That cluster of buildings, in its arch, with the dizzy drop
into empty air from its doorways and the wall of cliff above, was as clear in
my mind as a picture. By closing my eyes I could see it against the dark, like
a magic-lantern slide. [201, 203–4]

Jeanne Le Ber in her tower, a version of the sacred tree once brought
to the sanctuary of Cybele in celebration of the season of creation,[59] suggests that the ancient rhythms of Mother Eve, of Spider Woman, of the
mother goddesses can be re-membered, that, as Adrienne Rich insists in
"Cartographies of Silence," the choice of silence "can be a plan / rigor-
ously executed / the blueprint to a life / It is a presence / it has a history a
form"—that, having discovered the Eleusinian mysteries of the self, it is
possible to map out our own consciousness, to learn to speak in words we
have invented of the place that we know, to understand our experience
there as history, to dream a common language.[60] A world in which the
immanent rhythm of women is sacrified to the transcendence of men,
where things in the shadows are not seen or heard, where the muted zone
is feared and shunned as wild, where the rituals of art and religion become
separated from the rituals of daily life, is a world in which stories are lost.
A world in which there is no more spinning and weaving is one in which
the art of storytelling becomes "unraveled at all its ends after being woven
thousands of years ago in the ambience of the oldest forms of craftsman-
ship." The ancient and essential rhythm of spinning and weaving must
seize the listener "in such a way that the gift of retelling . . . [stories]
comes . . . all by itself. This . . . is the nature of the web in which the gift
of storytelling is cradled."[61]

Withdrawn from the world, spinning and weaving in solitude, joining together the horizontal and vertical strands of experience, creating
living forms out of her own substance, Jeanne Le Ber communicates with
a world beyond herself through her gifts—the altar cloths, the knitted
stockings for the poor, the legend that people all over the province take
for their own as a kind of miracle, spinning their own stories about her at
their firesides—and in the continuous prayer that links her to a religious
tradition of contemplative mystics. She remains—deliberately—a shadowy fictional construct, a legend.

To project an imaginative structure, as Willa Cather does in this novel with the legend of Jeanne Le Ber in her tower, and at the same time to acknowledge it *as an imaginative structure* is to proceed "as if," in the most fundamentally radical utopian mode—as if there were another possibility in response to the double bind of muteness, on the one hand, and the restricted language of the dominant culture, on the other, as if there were a possibility of transcendence, of the re-creation, from memory and desire, of living forms that retain all their primary ecstasy.

NOTES

PROLOGUE

1. See Octavio Paz and Roger Caillois [eds.], *Remedios Varo 1913–1963* (Mexico: Ediciones Era, 1969).
2. Thomas Pynchon, *The Crying of Lot 49* (Philadelphia: Lippincott, 1966), pp. 21–22.

CHAPTER I

1. Virginia Woolf, *A Room of One's Own* (New York: Harcourt, Brace & World, 1929), pp. 23–24.
2. Erik H. Erikson, "Inner and Outer Space: Reflections on Womanhood," *Daedalus* 93 (Spring 1964): 588–89.
3. Gwendolyn Wright, *Building the Dream* (New York: Pantheon, 1981), p. 198.
4. Edith Wharton, "The Valley of Childish Things," in R. W. B. Lewis, ed., *The Collected Short Stories of Edith Wharton* (New York: Scribner's, 1968), 1:58–59.
5. Erving Goffman, *The Presentation of Self in Everyday Life* (Garden City, N.Y.: Doubleday, Anchor Books, 1959), pp. 35–36.
6. Edward T. Hall argues in *The Silent Language* (Garden City, N.Y.: Doubleday, Anchor Books, 1973), on the other hand, that "silent language"—nonverbal communication—is very much social.
7. See Nathaniel Hawthorne's letter to Henry W. Longfellow of June 4, 1837, cited in Malcolm Cowley, ed., *The Portable Hawthorne* (New York: Viking, 1948), pp. 607–8.
8. The phrase is Henry Adams's, in *The Education of Henry Adams* (1918; reprint, Boston: Houghton Mifflin, Sentry ed., 1961), p. 381.
9. Ibid., p. 388.
10. George Santayana, "The Genteel Tradition in American Philosophy," in *Winds of Doctrine: Studies in Contemporary Opinion* (New York: Scribner's, 1913), reprinted in Richard Colton Lyon, ed., *Santayana on America* (New York: Harcourt, Brace & World, 1968), pp. 37–38.
11. Edith Wharton and Ogden Codman, Jr., *The Decoration of Houses* (New York: Scribner's, 1897; reprint, New York: Norton, 1978), pp. 122, 123, 124, 129.

12. Ibid., pp. 20, 125.

13. Ibid., p. 67, emphasis original. In Wharton's *Italian Villas and Their Gardens* (1904), landscapes become outdoor rooms.

14. Wharton and Codman, *The Decoration of Houses*, p. 198.

15. William A. Coles, "The Genesis of a Classic," introduction to *The Decoration of Houses*, p. xxxvii.

16. Louis Sullivan, *Kindergarten Chats*, rev. 1918 ed. (New York: Dover, 1979), p. 229.

17. Ibid., p. 51.

18. Ibid., p. 23.

19. Cited in Alan Trachtenberg, *The Incorporation of America: Culture and Society in the Gilded Age* (New York: Hill and Wang, 1982), p. 120.

20. Sullivan, *Kindergarten Chats*, pp. 23, 29.

21. Thorstein Veblen, *The Theory of the Leisure Class* (New York: Macmillan, 1899), pp. 22–23.

22. B. F. Skinner, a contemporary of Erik H. Erikson, expands upon these "progressive" notions about the relationship between space and behavior in *Walden Two* (New York: Macmillan, 1948) and other works.

23. Frederick Jackson Turner, "The Significance of the Frontier," in *The Frontier in American History* (New York: Henry Holt, 1920), pp. 2–3, 12, 15, 37.

24. David M. Potter, "American Women and the American Character" (1959), in John A. Hague, ed., *American Character and Culture in a Changing World: Some Twentieth-Century Perspectives* (Westport, Conn.: Greenwood Press, 1979), pp. 209–25. Also of interest is Alice Kessler-Harris's "American Women and the American Character: A Feminist Perspective" in the same volume, pp. 227–42.

25. See, for example, Elizabeth Hampsten, *Read This Only to Yourself: The Private Writings of Midwestern Women, 1880–1910* (Bloomington: Indiana University Press, 1982); Lillian Schlissel, *Women's Diaries of the Westward Journey* (New York: Schocken, 1982); Joanna L. Stratton, *Pioneer Women: Voices from the Kansas Frontier* (New York: Simon & Schuster, 1981).

26. *The Notebooks of Henry James*, ed. F. O. Matthiessen and Kenneth B. Murdock (New York: Oxford University Press, 1947), pp. 47, 129.

27. Henry James, *The American Scene* (1907; reprint, Bloomington: Indiana University Press, 1968), pp. 15–16, 166–67.

28. Ann Douglas, *The Feminization of American Culture* (New York: Knopf, 1977), pp. 12, 8.

29. John Winthrop's "A Modell of Christian Charity," for example, written aboard the ship *Arabella* in 1629 as it approached the shores of Massachusetts, states, "Wee shall be as a Citty upon a Hill, the eies of all people are upon us." Cited in Trachtenberg, *Incorporation of America*, p. 102.

30. Ibid., pp. 209, 215.

31. Adams, *Education*, p. 341.

32. Cited in Trachtenberg, *Incorporation of America*, pp. 219, 215.

33. Cited in Gwendolyn Wright, *Moralism and the Model Home: Domestic Architecture and Cultural Conflict, 1873–1913* (Chicago: University of Chicago Press, 1980), p. 209.

34. Cited in Trachtenberg, *Incorporation of America*, pp. 218–19.

35. Ibid., pp. 221–22.

36. Cited in Jeanne Madeline Weimann, *The Fair Women* (Chicago: Academy Chicago, 1981), p. 262.

37. G. Wright, *Moralism*, pp. 151–52.

38. Ibid., p. 210.

39. Cited in ibid., p. 235.

40. Ibid., p. 123. See also Sophia P. Breckinridge, "The Activities of Women Outside the Home," in *Recent Social Trends in the United States: Report of the President's* [Hoover's] *Committee on Social Trends* (New York: McGraw-Hill, 1932), reprinted in Stanley Coben, ed., *Reform, War, and Reaction: 1912–1932* (Columbia: University of South Carolina Press, 1972), and Elaine Tyler May, *Great Expectations: Marriage and Divorce in Post-Victorian America* (Chicago: University of Chicago Press, 1980).

41. G. Wright, *Moralism*, p. 115.

42. Dolores Hayden, *The Grand Domestic Revolution: A History of Feminist Designs for American Homes, Neighborhoods, and Cities* (Cambridge, Mass.: MIT Press, 1981), pp. 209–10.

43. G. Wright, *Moralism*, pp. 1–2.

44. Ibid., p. 293.

45. John Ruskin, *The Seven Lamps of Architecture* (New York: Wiley, 1849), pp. 165, 172–73, 188), cited in G. Wright, *Moralism*, pp. 12–13.

46. Clifford E. Clark, Jr., "Domestic Architecture as an Index to Social History: The Romantic Revival and the Cult of Domesticity in America, 1840–1870," *Journal of Interdisciplinary History* 7 (Summer 1976): 42.

47. Cited in Ethel Puffer Howes, "The Meaning of Progress in the Woman Movement," *The Annals of the American Academy of Political and Social Science* 143 (May 1929): 14–20, reprinted in Coben, ed., *Reform, War, and Reaction*, p. 327.

48. Cited in G. Wright, *Moralism*, p. 199.

49. Ibid., pp. 233–34, 275–77.

50. Ibid., pp. 137–38. Gwendolyn Wright points out that in the year of Frank Lloyd Wright's Fricke House, pattern books featured inexpensive cottages "in which all of the living space flowed around a central double-sided fireplace and staircase" with no partitions in the living and dining area. With fewer walls, these small houses could still seem spacious (p. 246).

51. George L. Hersey, "Godey's Choice," *Society of Architectural Historians Journal* 18 (Oct. 1959): 104.

52. Cited in G. Wright, *Moralism*, p. 247.

53. Ibid., pp. 234–35, 33–34.

54. Cited in ibid., p. 239.

55. Charlotte Perkins Gilman, *Women and Economics: A Study of the Economic Relation between Men and Women as a Factor in Social Evolution* (Boston: Small, Maynard, 1898; reprint, New York: Harper & Row, 1966), p. 246, cited in Hayden, *Revolution*, p. 195. An earlier version of Hayden's chapter on Gilman and her influence appears in *Radical History Review* 21 (Fall 1979): 225–47, as "Charlotte Perkins Gilman and the Kitchenless House." The following summary of the work

of Gilman, Melusina Fay Peirce and Marie Stevens Howland is drawn from Hayden's brilliant analysis of domestic and environmental space.

56. Gilman, "Why Cooperative Housekeeping Fails," *Harper's Bazar* 41 (July 1907): 629, cited in Hayden, *Revolution*, p. 195.

57. Gilman, "What Diantha Did," *The Forerunner*, pt. 14 (Dec. 1910): 9–11, cited in Hayden, *Revolution*, pp. 196–97.

58. Marie Stevens Howland, *The Familistère*, originally published in 1874 as *Papa's Own Girl* (Philadelphia: Porcupine Press, 1975), cited in Hayden, *Revolution*, p. 91.

59. "Over the Draughting Board: Opinions Official and Unofficial," *Architectural Record* 13 (Jan. 1903): 89–91, cited in Hayden, *Revolution*, p. 194.

60. Hayden, "Gilman and the Kitchenless House," p. 241.

61. Ibid., p. 245.

62. This information is drawn from Weimann's *The Fair Women*, pp. 353–92.

63. James D. Hart, *The Popular Book: A History of America's Literary Taste* (New York: Oxford University Press, 1950), p. 199.

64. Ibid., p. 212.

65. Kate Chopin, *The Awakening* (1899; reprint, New York: Putnam's, Capricorn ed., 1964), pp. 166, 204, 217, 289, 122.

66. Charlotte Perkins Gilman, *The Yellow Wallpaper* (1899; reprint, Old Westbury, N.Y.: The Feminist Press, 1973), pp. 17–18, 16.

67. Edith Cobb, "The Ecology of Imagination in Childhood," *Daedalus* 88 (Summer 1959): 540.

68. Charlotte Perkins Gilman, *Herland*, ed. Ann J. Lane (New York: Pantheon, 1979), pp. 19, 130.

69. Cited in Trachtenberg, *Incorporation of America*, pp. 140–41.

70. Cited in Kent C. Bloomer and Charles W. Moore, *Body, Memory, and Architecture* (New Haven: Yale University Press, 1977), p. 58.

71. Cited in Suzanne Langer, *Feeling and Form: A Theory of Art* (New York: Scribner's, 1953), p. 91.

72. Yi-Fu Tuan, *Space and Place* (Minneapolis: University of Minnesota Press, 1977), p. 6.

73. Edward T. Hall, *The Hidden Dimension* (Garden City, N.Y.: Doubleday, 1966), pp. 99–100.

74. Shirley Ardener, "Ground Rules and Social Maps for Women: An Introduction," in Shirley Ardener, ed., *Women and Space: Ground Rules and Social Maps* (New York: St. Martin's Press, 1981), p. 12, emphasis original.

75. Tuan, *Space and Place*, p. 54.

76. G. Wright, *Moralism*, p. 99.

77. Kevin Lynch, "The Openness of Open Space," in Gyorgy Kepes, ed., *Arts of the Environment* (New York: Braziller, 1972), p. 108.

78. Willa Cather, *Shadows on the Rock* (New York: Knopf, 1931), pp. 136–37.

79. Susan Griffin, *Woman and Nature: The Roaring Inside Her* (New York: Harper & Row, 1978), pp. 169–71.

CHAPTER 2

1. Stéphane Mallarmé, "Considérations sûr l'art du Ballet et la Loïe Fuller," *National Observer* (March 1893), in Margaret Haille Harris, *Loïe Fuller: Magician of Light* (Richmond: The Virginia Museum, 1979), pp. 28–29.

2. Richard Guy Wilson, "The Great Civilization," in *American Renaissance, 1876–1917* [Brooklyn Museum catalog] (New York: Pantheon, 1979), p. 46; "Augustus Saint Gaudens," *The Century Magazine* 35 (Nov. 1887), cited in *American Renaissance*, p. 162; Chandler Christy, *The American Girl* (1906), cited in *American Renaissance*, p. 51.

3. Mario Praz, *An Illustrated History of Furnishing*, trans. William Weaver (New York: Braziller, 1964), p. 66. As Edna Carter Southard points out in her exhibition catalog, *George Bottini: Painter of Montmartre* (Oxford, Ohio: Miami University Art Museum, 1983), Bottini's women also "hold flowers, arrange flowers in their hair, or have flowers in their clothing or rooms. The spaces they inhabit enclose or trap them and the use of space underlines a sense of disorientation and disquiet." Southard cites one reviewer's "from flowers to women is only a step. But what strange and perverse flowers are the work of Mr. George Bottini" (p. 22).

4. See, for example, Petr Wittlich, *Art Nouveau Drawings* (London: Octopus Books, 1974). Cynthia Griffin Wolff has pointed out that the American painter John Singer Sargent becomes a kind of bridge between the American and European movements. In a painting such as *The Wyndham Sisters* of 1899, for example, "the figures are elongated, with the central figure extended and languid. . . . The ruffling of the dress fabric is suggestive almost of sea foam, and the attenuated fingers of the central figure trail off the right side of the canvas, framed by what appear to be massive groups of flowers, only the edges of which are seen in the picture." *A Feast of Words: The Triumph of Edith Wharton* (New York: Oxford University Press, 1977), p. 114n. Wolff also notes, in connection with *The House of Mirth*, the fascination of Art Nouveau artists with lilies.

5. Harris, *Loïe Fuller*, pp. 23–25.

6. "The Dynamo and the Virgin," in *The Education of Henry Adams* (1918; reprint, Boston: Houghton Mifflin, Sentry ed., 1961), pp. 379–88.

7. *The Venetian Painters*, cited in *American Renaissance*, p. 12. According to Richard Guy Wilson, the term "American Renaissance" came into usage in 1880. See Talbot F. Hamlin, "The American Spirit in Architecture," in Ralph Henry Gabriel, ed., *The Pageant of America* (New Haven: Yale University Press, 1926), 13:165; Oliver W. Larkin, *Art and Life in America*, rev. ed. (New York: Holt, Rinehart, Winston, 1960), p. 293; Howard Mumford Jones, "The Renaissance and American Origins," *Ideas in America* (Cambridge, Mass.: Harvard University Press, 1945), pp. 140–51, cited in *American Renaissance*, p. 11n.

8. Robin Evans, "Figures, Doors and Passages," *Architectural Design* 48 (1978): 272. In painting, Evans argues, the fascination with the human body had centered on physiological detail. It was only in the sixteenth century that bodies were "brought together in peculiarly intense, carnal, even lascivious poses by Leonardo, Michaelangelo, Raphael and their followers." The fifteenth-century Virgin and Child, for example, were traditionally enthroned and *separated* figures,

raised above the rest of the world, staring fixedly out into nothing, in holy and untouchable tranquility. In a painting like Raphael's *Madonna dell'Impannata* (1514), on the other hand, however spiritual in origin, the mutual adorations of the characters are distinctly sensual: "the figures are not so much composed in space as joined together despite it. They look closely on one another, stare myopically into eyes and at flesh, grasp, embrace, hold and finger each other's bodies as if their recognition rested more firmly on touch than on sight" (p. 268).

9. Ibid., p. 277. Evans's examples here are the compartmentalized floor plan of William Morris's Red House of 1859 and Morris's painting of Queen Guinevere of 1858, which depicts two physically separate figures, neither recognizing the presence of the other. One is the setting for, the other a representation of, his new wife, Jane—who, "tall and thin, endowed with sensuous lips, drooping eyelids and a profusion of hair," was the very prototype of the Pre-Raphaelite woman who was the source of the Art Nouveau woman. Jan Thompson, "The Role of Woman in the Iconography of Art Nouveau," *Art Journal* 30 1/2 (Winter 1971–72): 160–61.

10. Evans shows that in the case of the Villa Madama, contrary to an 1809 reconstruction of the plans, Raphael's original scheme for the villa near Rome submitted to Cardinal Giulio de' Medici was not one of classical symmetry. In fact, the way in which the latent structure of inhabited space bursts through the confines of classical planning here has its parallel in the way "carnality shone through the vacuous signalling of gestures in . . . [Raphael's] figure compositions." "Figures," p. 268.

11. The favored alternative of the terminal room with one door opening onto a corridor was opposite to that of Italian theorists, who following ancient precedent, recommended "a door wherever there was an adjoining room, making the house a matrix of discrete but thoroughly interconnected chambers." Ibid., pp. 268–70. Edith Wharton also found Kerr an important source. See Edith Wharton and Ogden Codman, Jr., *The Decoration of Houses* (New York: Scribner's, 1897; reprint, New York: Norton, 1978), p. 132.

12. Evans, "Figures," pp. 270, 273, 276. The modern definition of privacy is also to be found in late seventeenth-century America: the puritan "armouring" of the soul, Evans points out, has to do with the sequestering of the body from the "impertinent" interruptions of others (pp. 272–73). See also Edward T. Hall, *The Hidden Dimension* (Garden City, N.Y.: Doubleday, 1966).

13. The successful and important connection to the business world that such structures announce belies the protest against the tyranny of the new technology to be found in their interior decoration. Walter Benjamin sees in such interiors not only an "escapist" art that is the apotheosis of the individual, but also the foreshadowings of Art Nouveau. The minutely conceived rooms of the bourgeois nineteenth century, he believes, are a direct contrast to the world of business: "The interior represents the universe for the private individual. He collects there whatever is distant, whatever is of the past. His living room is a box in the theatre of the world." Cited in Mario Praz, *An Illustrated History of Furnishing*, p. 25.

14. Henry James, *The American Scene* (1907; reprint, Bloomington: Indiana University Press, 1968), pp. 40, 167, 249–51.

15. In *The Decoration of Houses* Wharton described the ideal bedroom as a

suite of rooms. Separated from the rest of the house by an antechamber with only two entrances from the main corridor, one for the occupant, leading to the antechamber, the other for servants, leading to the bathroom, this suite becomes the most private of retreats within the house (pp. 169–70).

16. Wharton and Codman's introduction to *The Decoration of Houses*, unpaged, emphasis original.

17. *Decoration of Houses*, p. 13.

18. Ibid., pp. 103, 115, 117, 35. The servants' quarters were apparently not spacious enough, however, for in 1907 Hoppin drew up a set of plans for a major expansion of the servants' wing (never completed).

19. "Charming as the Italian Villa is, it can hardly be used in our Northern States without certain modifications," Wharton noted in *The Decoration of Houses*, "whereas the average French or English country house built after 1600 is perfectly suited to our climate and habits" (p. 4n).

20. There is no conflict between originality and tradition, Wharton believed. Originality, she said, "lies not in discarding the necessary laws of thought, but in using them to express new intellectual conceptions; in poetry, originality consists not in discarding the necessary laws of rhythm, but in finding new rhythms within the limits of those laws." Ibid., pp. 33, 9–10.

21. Ibid., pp. 61, 35.

22. Ibid., pp. 66–67, emphasis original.

23. Ibid., pp. 22, 112.

24. Edith Wharton, *A Backward Glance* (New York: Appleton-Century, 1934), pp. 125, 207–9.

25. Edith Wharton, *The Writing of Fiction* (New York: Scribner's, 1925), p. 117.

26. Ibid., p. 112, emphasis original. Multiple points of view, on the other hand, she would have learned from *The Wings of the Dove*, where the "coigns of vantage" are the "windows and balconies" of other people's interest in Milly Theale, or from Conrad's "hall of mirrors," as he called his series of reflecting consciousnesses, a method that originated with Balzac, who caused a tale "to be reflected, in fractions, in the minds of a series of accidental participants or mere lookers-on." Ibid., pp. 91–92. Henry James, *The Art of the Novel* (New York: Scribner's, 1934), p. 306; *Writing of Fiction*, pp. 91–92.

27. The thesis of Ecclesiastes is that *all* worldly experience is fleeting and insubstantial, "a breath," for example: "I made great works; I built houses . . . ; I made myself gardens . . . and planted in them all kinds of . . . trees. . . . Then I considered all that my hands had done . . . and behold, all was vanity and striving after wind" (2:12). The titles of both *The House of Mirth* and *The Golden Bowl* come from Ecclesiastes: "The heart of the wise is in the house of mourning; but the heart of fools is in the house of mirth" (7:4), and "Remember . . . your Creator . . . before the evil days come, . . . and the mourners go about the streets; before the silver cord is snapped, . . . or the golden bowl is broken, or the pitcher is broken at the fountain, or the wheel [cup] broken at the cistern. . . . Vanity of Vanities . . . all is vanity" (12:1–9).

28. Henry James, *Art of the Novel*, p. 46.

29. The protagonist, whose name links her both to the lilies-of-the-valley (the "valley of childish things," the "valley of decision") that are an appropriate adornment for her luncheon table, and to the decorative lilies of Art Nouveau, is a gilded woman of Junoesque proportions with masses of abundant hair.

30. Edith Wharton, *The House of Mirth* (1905; reprint, New York: Scribner's, 1969), p. 5. Further references to the 1969 edition are cited parenthetically in the text.

31. The painting, from a private collection, is reproduced in Ellis K. Waterhouse, *Reynolds* (London: Kegan Paul, Trench Trubner, 1941).

32. "Gardening, as far as Gardening is an Art, or entitled to that appellation, is a deviation from nature; for if the true taste consists, as many hold, in banishing every appearance of Art, or any traces of the footsteps of man, it would then be no longer a Garden." Sir Joshua Reynolds, thirteenth *Discourse*, cited in John Dixon Hunt, *The Figure in the Landscape: Poetry, Painting, and Gardening during the Eighteenth Century* (Baltimore: Johns Hopkins University Press, 1976), p. 188.

33. One is reminded of Wharton's mother's greeting the young author's first attempt at creative writing, which reproduces a bit of drawing-room conversation, with the chilling phrase, "Drawing-rooms are always tidy." *A Backward Glance*, p. 73.

34. Ibid., p. 207.

35. Cf. Lore Segal's description of the person who can say, "I hold a landscape in my head as old and personal as the geography of my childhood bedroom" as one who can understand the Ur-time of fairy tales as *true*, who enters into a world imaginatively, and who creates out of a sense of self. See "Grimm under the American Skin," *New York Times Book Review*, Feb. 27, 1983, special supplement, p. 3.

36. Edith Wharton, *Hudson River Bracketed* (New York: Appleton, 1929), p. 498.

37. The work of Edvard Munch comes to mind, for example, *The Shout* (1893), reproduced in Wittlich, *Art Nouveau Drawings*, frontispiece.

38. See Erving Goffman, *The Presentation of Self in Everyday Life* (Garden City, N.Y.: Doubleday, Anchor Books, 1959).

39. This image will be repeated in Wharton's *The Custom of the Country*, where Ralph Marvell sees himself as Perseus and Undine as Andromeda.

40. This is the meaning of the ironic reference to Marvell's "Coy Mistress" at the end of the novel: like Eliot's Prufrock, Selden hastens to Lily's door when it is too late; by the time he arrives to drain "their last moment to its lees," she has purchased her own freedom in her own way (pp. 326, 329).

CHAPTER 3

1. Edgar Allan Poe, "The Philosophy of Composition," in James A. Harrison, ed., *Complete Works* (New York: Crowell, 1902), 14:201. Wharton critics, noting that the death of Lily Bart is viewed through the eyes of the bereaved lover,

have compared *The House of Mirth* to *Daisy Miller*. Blake Nevius, for example, has written that like Winterbourne in the James novella, "betrayed by his aloofness, his hesitations, his careful discriminations," Selden "is the least attractive ambassador of his 'republic of the spirit,' and Mrs. Wharton knows this as well as her readers." *Edith Wharton: A Study of Her Fiction* (Berkeley: University of California Press, 1961), p. 59. For whatever reason, "this situation—the death of a beautiful woman as seen through the eyes of her lover—had become a set piece in American literature," but no one before Wharton, Cynthia Griffin Wolff writes of Lily Bart's "Beautiful Death," "had troubled to detail what it would be like to be the woman thus exalted and objectified." Noting Henry James's praise of John Singer Sargent's work—that he "handles . . . [the delicate feminine] elements with a special feeling for them, and they borrow a kind of noble intensity from his brush"— Wolff suggests that "Wharton's own portrait of a lady must lead us to wonder how well any real or realistically conceived woman could tolerate the compliment of being thus ennobled." *A Feast of Words: The Triumph of Edith Wharton* (New York: Oxford University Press, 1977), pp. 132–33. Henry James, "John S. Sargent," in *The Painter's Eye*, ed. John L. Sweeney (Cambridge, Mass.: Harvard University Press, 1956), p. 226, cited in Wolff, *Feast of Words*, p. 133.

2. Guy Davenport, *The Geography of the Imagination* (San Francisco: North Point Press, 1981), p. 3.

3. Ibid., pp. 6, 9–10.

4. Poe, "The Philosophy of Furniture," in Harrison, ed., *Complete Works*, 14:107–9; "The Masque of the Red Death," in ibid., 4:250.

5. Mario Praz, *An Illustrated History of Furnishing*, trans. William Weaver (New York: Braziller, 1964), pp. 28, 25, 344. A recent review of this book suggests that these are the keyhole visions of a voyeur, reproducing as evidence a photograph of Praz's own *salone* in the Via Giulia in Rome with a piano surrounded by a huge display of military paraphernalia. Hugh Honour, "From the House of Life," *New York Review of Books*, March 3, 1983, p. 6.

6. Juliet Blair, "Private Parts in Public Places: The Case of Actresses," in Shirley Ardener, ed., *Women and Space: Ground Rules and Social Maps* (New York: St. Martin's, 1981), p. 217.

7. John Berger, *Ways of Seeing* (Harmondsworth, England: Penguin, 1972), pp. 46–47.

8. R. W. B. Lewis, ed., *The Collected Short Stories of Edith Wharton*, 2 vols. (New York: Scribner's, 1968), 1:14.

9. Ibid., 2:23.

10. Poe, "The Masque of the Red Death," in Harrison, ed., *Complete Works*, 4:250–51.

11. Wharton even made Poe a character in her novella *False Dawn*.

12. Cited in R. W. B. Lewis, *Edith Wharton: A Biography* (New York: Harper & Row, 1975), pp. 154, 236. The Wharton-Brownell correspondence is in the Firestone Library, Princeton University, Princeton, N.J.

13. Wharton, "The Bolted Door," in Lewis, ed., *Collected Short Stories of Edith Wharton*, 2:33.

14. Aubrey Beardsley, one of the Art Nouveau painters discussed in the last chapter, did four drawings for the ten-volume American edition of the works of Poe.

15. The things about modern civilization that fascinated Whitman could, however, enrage Wharton. "It is bad enough to break with all that charms life, as one does in leaving Europe," she wrote in 1907, hearing that Harvard was instituting a course on business, "but to come back to business courses and skyscrapers! 'Alas, alas!'" Cited in Lewis, *Edith Wharton*, p. 180.

16. See R. W. B. Lewis, *Edith Wharton: A Biography*, and Cynthia Griffin Wolff, *A Feast of Words: The Triumph of Edith Wharton*, for a description of Wharton's love affair with Morton Fullerton. *The Custom of the Country* was written in the year of her own divorce, when Wharton would have felt both an attachment to expressive rituals of civilization and a need to assert her own power.

17. "A Passage to India," in James E. Miller, Jr., ed., *Walt Whitman: Complete Poetry and Selected Prose* (Boston: Houghton Mifflin, 1959), p. 288.

18. Edith Wharton, *A Backward Glance* (New York: Appleton-Century, 1934), p. 224.

19. "To a Common Prostitute," "The City Dead-House," "You Felons on Trial in Courts," "Sparkles from the Wheel," in Miller, ed., *Walt Whitman*, pp. 273, 260, 272, 275.

20. Ferdinand Tönnies, *Community & Society* (1887), trans. Charles P. Loomis (East Lansing: Michigan State University Press, 1957).

21. John Berryman, Afterword to Theodore Dreiser's *The Titan* (New York: New American Library, 1965), pp. 503–11, emphasis added.

22. Charlotte Perkins Gilman, *Women and Economics: A Study in the Economic Relation between Men and Women as a Factor in Social Evolution* (Boston: Small, Maynard, 1898).

23. *The Atlantic Monthly* 83 (June 1899): 771–85, 760–71.

24. Richard Guy Wilson, "Cultural Conditions," in *American Renaissance, 1876–1917* [Brooklyn Museum catalog] (New York: Pantheon, 1979), p. 27. See also Daniel J. Boorstin, *The Americans: The Democratic Experience* (New York: Random House, 1973); H. Wayne Morgan, *Unity and Culture: The United States, 1877–1900* (Baltimore: Penguin, 1971); Robert H. Wiebe, *The Search for Order, 1877–1920* (New York: Hill and Wang, 1967).

25. Wharton, *A Backward Glance*, pp. 126–27.

26. Lewis, *Edith Wharton*, p. 104.

27. *A Backward Glance*, p. 137.

28. In *The Custom of the Country*, Leota Spragg is called "Loot" by her husband when she tries to get money out of him, and an American heiress who marries into the French aristocracy is named "Looty" Arlington.

29. Edith Wharton, *The Custom of the Country* (New York: Scribner's, 1913), p. 370. Further references to this edition are cited parenthetically in the text.

30. Blair, "Private Parts," pp. 206–7.

31. The kind of split woman such a culture produces is the subject of Woody Allen's film *Interiors* (1978), in which a woman who is an interior decorator—that is, one who designs interiors according to externally imposed rules—cannot pro-

vide an interior structure for the lives of her daughters and is succeeded by an uncouth, uneducated stepmother, who lives according to instinctual insights. Blair, "Private Parts," p. 214.

32. Letter from Marilyn Monroe to Norman Rosten in Norman Mailer, *Marilyn* (New York: Grosset & Dunlap, 1973; reprint, London: Millington, 1974), p. 77, cited in Blair, "Private Parts," p. 219.

33. In Wharton's time, Sarah Bernhardt (mentioned in *The Custom of the Country* and much portrayed in posters by Art Nouveau artist Alphons Mucha) versus her Lily Bart, for example. Whitman, in "Song of Myself," strips himself down to his "gross, mystical, nude" Self, assumes himself, the androgynous Walt, "the Me myself." In "Crossing Brooklyn Ferry," the crossing from country to city is to "play the part." Unlike Poe, whose "Man of the Crowd" wanders the city all night in solitary isolation, Whitman announces in "Salut au Monde!":

> I see the cities of the earth and make myself at random a part of them,
> I am a real Parisian,
> I am a habitan of Vienna, St. Petersburg, Berlin, Constantinople,
> I am of Adelaide, Sidney, Melbourne,
> I am of London, Manchester, Bristol, Edinburgh, Limerick,
> I am of Madrid, Cadiz, Barcelona, Oporto, Lyons, Brussels, Berne,
>   Frankfort, Stuttgart, Turin, Florence,
> I belong in Moscow, Cracow, Warsaw, or northward in Christiania or
>   Stockholm, or in Siberian Irkutsk, or in some street in Iceland,
> I descend upon all those cities, and rise from them again.
>   [Miller, ed., *Walt Whitman*, pp. 38, 27, 119, 104]

34. Blair, "Private Parts," p. 219.

35. The pastoral tradition in literature has been defined as "a double longing after innocence and happiness" (Renato Poggioli, *The Oaten Flute*), as an idea of the Golden Age (W. W. Greg, *Pastoral Poetry and Pastoral Drama*), or of the antithesis of Art and Nature (Frank Kermode, ed., *English Pastoral Poetry*, and Leo Marx, *The Machine in the Garden*), as one whose fundamental motive is hostility to urban life or a celebration of rural life (K. W. Gransden, "The Pastoral Alternative," *Arethusa* 3 [1970]: 103–21, 177–96, and Raymond Williams, *The Country and the City*), as one whose central tenet is "the pathetic fallacy" (E. W. Tayler, *Nature and Art in Renaissance Literature*), as *otium* or irresponsible erotic bliss (Hallett Smith, *Elizabethan Poetry*), as "the poetic expression of the cult of aesthetic Platonism" in the Renaissance or of Epicureanism in the Hellenistic world (Richard Cody, *The Landscape of the Mind*, and Thomas G. Rosenmeyer, *The Green Cabinet*), as "the mode of viewing common experience through the medium of the rural world" (John Lynen, *The Pastoral Art of Robert Frost*). See Paul Alpers, "What Is Pastoral?," *Critical Inquiry* 8 (Spring 1982): 437–38n.

36. See, for example:

> Meanwhile the mind, from pleasure less,
> Withdraws into its happiness;
> The mind, that ocean where each kind
> Does straight its own resemblance find;

Yet it creates, transcending these,
Far other worlds and other seas,
Annihilating all that's made
To a green thought in a green shade.

[Andrew Marvell, "The Garden," in Alexander Allison et al., eds., *The Norton Anthology of Poetry* (New York: Norton, 1970), pp. 374–75]

37. In fact, in the play the emphasis is on the courtiers who *represent* themselves as shepherds: "It is the courtiers who play out the possibilities represented by the shepherd-singers of traditional pastoral." Alpers does not claim that pastoral representations are "realistic" in the way novelistic and some dramatic representations are; he distinguishes between depiction, which is potentially realistic, and the claim to be humanly *typical*, which would seem to resist novelistic particularity. But pastoral *is* realistic, he concludes, in the sense that "the central fictions and conventions of the mode have as their motive certain views of and recognitions about human life, its nature, powers, and pleasures" which we call "plausible"; "the pastoral representation of human life is such that realistic claims and modes are part of its repertoire." Alpers, "What Is Pastoral?," pp. 457–60; emphasis on "literary, social and political world" is added.

38. Wharton, *A Backward Glance*, p. 5.

39. Claud Walsingham Popple in the novel is probably another portrait (in addition to that in *The House of Mirth*) of John Singer Sargent.

40. Alexis de Tocqueville, *Democracy in America* (1840), trans. Henry Reeve, ed. Thomas Bender (New York: Modern Library, 1981), p. 431.

41. A rather similar criticism was made of Wharton by Janet Flanner (Gênet), an expatriate American journalist who spent most of her life in Paris. See "Edith Wharton (1862–1937)," reprinted from *The New Yorker* in *Paris Was Yesterday* (New York: Viking, 1972), pp. 171–78.

42. Richard Sennett, *The Uses of Disorder: Personal Identity and City Life* (New York: Knopf, 1970), p. 8.

43. Ibid., pp. 6–10.

44. Rollo May, *Power and Innocence: A Search for the Sources of Violence* (New York: Norton, 1972), p. 49. Melville's Billy Budd, for example, is rendered impotent by Claggart's foul charges: because he is *unable to speak*, he unintentionally kills the offender with a blow. What did Billy Budd mean, May asks, when he said, as he was being tried by the ship's officers for murder, that he would not have killed Claggart if he could have spoken? Melville must have meant not meaningless chatter, but "a kind of communication that overcomes the impulse to violence and that binds persons to each other" (p. 246).

45. Ibid., pp. 247–48.

46. "Signs of the Times" (1829), cited in Leo Marx, *The Machine in the Garden: Technology and the Pastoral Ideal in America* (New York: Oxford University Press, 1964), p. 176.

CHAPTER 4

1. Fernand Braudel, *The Structures of Everyday Life: The Limits of the Possible*, trans. Sian Reynolds (New York: Harper & Row, 1981), pp. 312, 323.

2. Ibid., p. 313.

3. See Dolores Hayden and Peter Marris's discussion of American women's patchwork quilts as an elaborate design language based on the natural and built environments, and a search for a satisfying balance between formal design and personal meaning, in "The Quiltmaker's Landscape," *Landscape* 25, no. 3 (1981): 39–47.

4. Edith Wharton, *The Age of Innocence* (New York: Appleton, 1920), pp. 45, 356. Further references to this addition are cited parenthetically in the text.

5. Edith Wharton and Ogden Codman, Jr., *The Decoration of Houses* (New York: Scribner's, 1897; reprint, New York: Norton, 1978), p. 5.

6. Anzia Yezierska, "The Lost Beautifulness," originally published in *Hungry Hearts* (1920), in Alice Kessler-Harris, ed., *The Open Cage: An Anzia Yezierska Collection* (New York: Persea Books, 1979), p. 105. I thank Alice Kessler-Harris for introducing me to Yezierska's work.

7. Edith Wharton, "Mrs. Manstey's View," originally published in *Scribner's Magazine* 10 (July 1891), in R. W. B. Lewis, ed., *The Collected Short Stories of Edith Wharton*, 2 vols. (New York: Scribner's, 1968), 1:3–11; *Ethan Frome* (New York: Scribner's, 1911, with 1922 introduction by Edith Wharton), pp. 134–35; *Hudson River Bracketed* (New York: Appleton, 1929), p. 506.

8. Anzia Yezierska, *The Bread Givers* (New York: Grosset & Dunlap, 1925), pp. 34, 13.

9. Ibid., pp. 157, 158, 159, 277.

10. R. W. B. Lewis, *Edith Wharton: A Biography* (New York: Harper & Row, 1975), pp. 419, 427.

11. Dianne H. Pilgrim points out that books like Eastlake's, aimed not at master carpenters, like earlier pattern books, but at middle-class homeowners, became extremely popular in the 1870s and 1880s. Though these books differed in their stylistic points of view, Pilgrim writes, they share strong moralistic overtones and the conviction that there was no longer any excuse for the bad taste they saw in the household art of the 1840s to 1860s. Among the more important pattern books were Clarence Cook's *The House Beautiful* (1877); Harriet Prescott Spofford, *Art Decoration Applied to Furniture* (1878); Henry Hudson Holly, *Modern Dwellings in Town and Country Adapted to American Wants and Climate. With a Treatise of Furniture and Decoration* (1878); Jakob von Falke, *Art in the House* (1879); Constance Cary Harrison, *Woman's Handiwork in Modern Homes* (1881); Maria Reynolds Oakey Dewing, *Beauty in the Household* (1882); Henry T. Williams and Mrs. C. S. Jones, *Beautiful Homes* (1885); Arnold Brunner and Thomas Tyron, *Interior Decoration* (1887); Frederick Bartlett Goddard, *Furniture and the Art of Furnishing* (1887). "Decorative Art: The Domestic Environment," in *American Renaissance, 1876–1917* [Brooklyn Museum catalog] (New York: Pantheon, 1979), p. 114.

12. Charles C. Perkins, Editor's Preface to Charles Locke Eastlake, *Hints on Household Taste* (Boston: James R. Osgood, 1872), pp. x, viii.

13. William A. Coles, "The Genesis of a Classic," introduction to *The Decoration of Houses*, p. xxxviii.

14. Eastlake comes close, Gowans argues, to describing what Louis Sullivan would call "reality in the architectural art." He assumes "the criteria of good architecture to be honest use of materials, direct expression of structure, and function dictating the nature of ornament and the relationships of mass to void." His standard is thirteenth-century cathedrals "because they of all medieval buildings used materials most honestly, expressed structure most directly, were ornamented most naturally." Gowans believes this aspect of Eastlake's thought is so entirely "modern" that it goes unnoticed; it has become a commonplace, an assumption of architects like H. H. Richardson, who worked through the Gothic in order to arrive at sound modern concepts of design.

Unlike Henry Adams, who also took thirteenth-century cathedrals as his standard, Eastlake explains building styles only in terms of aesthetic taste. The different styles of the Victorian era—Greek Revival, Roman Revival, Gothic Revival—have as a common denominator a borrowing of past forms associated with certain *ideas*: "Roman building types were revived primarily because of their association with ideas of republicanism and civic virtue, Greek for associations with liberty, Egyptian for associations with permanence and wisdom, Moorish for exoticism, and so on—the choice in any given case being determined by what sort of symbolic imagery social circumstances seemed to call for."

Eastlake "does not see that if the Gothic Revival was not primarily a matter of aesthetic tastes but depended on the dominance of certain social and political convictions, it must fade if ever those convictions weakened," Gowans argues. Neither does he seem to realize that by his criteria of "good architecture," the Crystal Palace of 1851—a "charming vision of glass-and-iron"—must be a "better" building than anything the Gothic Revival could produce. "For once assume that direct expression of structure and honest use of materials are the supreme qualities to be sought, and you must inevitably follow some such path as H. H. Richardson and Louis Sullivan." Alan Gowans, Introduction to Charles Locke Eastlake's *A History of the Gothic Revival* (1872; reprint, New York: American Life Foundation and Study Institute, 1975), pp. vii–xxi passim.

15. "So both 'traditional' and 'modern' easel painters look down upon comic-strips or movies or advertising as inferior . . . without seeing that forms which fulfil social needs are alive no matter how 'crude' or 'tasteless,' whereas forms that do not are dead, no matter how glorious their pedigree or how glamorous their rationale." Gowans, Introduction, p. xx.

16. *Decoration of Houses*, pp. 198, 64n.

17. Granny Mingott, whom Ellen resembles in character, says, "Ah, these Mingotts—all alike! Born in a rut, and you can't root 'em out of it. When I built this house you'd have thought I was moving to California! Nobody ever *had* built above Fortieth Street—no, says I, nor above the Battery, either, before Christopher Columbus discovered America" (pp. 153–54).

18. I owe this insight to my friend Herwig Friedl, a Wharton scholar in Heidelberg, Germany.

19. Henry James, "The Jolly Corner" (1909), in Clifton Fadiman, ed., *The*

Short Stories of Henry James (New York: Modern Library, 1945), pp. 618, 620, 613, 631–32.

20. "The Jolly Corner," pp. 619–20, 633, 635, 634, 623.

21. Edith Wharton, *Fighting France: From Dunkerque to Belfort* (New York: Scribner's, 1915), pp. 98–99.

22. Edith Wharton, *A Backward Glance* (New York: Appleton-Century, 1934), pp. 364, 368–69.

23. This is the position taken by Cynthia Griffin Wolff in *A Feast of Words: The Triumph of Edith Wharton* (New York: Oxford University Press, 1977).

24. Lee R. Edwards, "War and Roses: The Politics of Mrs. Dalloway," in Arlyn Diamond and Lee R. Edwards, eds., *The Authority of Experience: Essays in Feminist Criticism* (Amherst: University of Massachusetts Press, 1977), pp. 161–62.

25. *Fighting France*, pp. 58, 152–53.

26. Ibid., pp. 157, 104.

27. Sherry B. Ortner, "Is Female to Male as Nature Is to Culture?," in Michelle Zimbalist Rosaldo and Louise Lamphere, eds., *Woman, Culture & Society* (Stanford, Calif.: Stanford University Press, 1974), pp. 73–75.

28. Michelle Zimbalist Rosaldo, "Woman, Culture, and Society: A Theoretical Overview," in ibid., pp. 38–39.

29. *A Backward Glance*, p. 94.

30. Dion Boucicault, *The Shaughraun*, in David Krause, ed., *The Dolmen Boucicault* (Dublin: Dolmen Press, 1964).

31. Edith Wharton, *The Fruit of the Tree* (New York: Scribner's, 1907), pp. 304, 633.

32. *Hudson River Bracketed*, p. 336.

33. Leon Edel, ed., *Henry James: Letters* (Cambridge, Mass.: Harvard University Press, 1974), 1:249. Chadwick Hansen brought this to my attention.

34. Wharton tried other versions of *The Age of Innocence* in which Newland and Ellen marry, only to separate because of their difference from each other.

35. On deviant behavior and American communities see Kai T. Erikson, *Wayward Puritans: A Study in the Sociology of Deviance* (New York: Wiley, 1966).

36. Mary Douglas, *Purity and Danger: An Analysis of the Concepts of Pollution and Taboo* (London: Routledge & Kegan Paul, 1966), p. 113.

37. Wharton, in fact, disparaged communities of women of the sort to be found in the fiction of Mary E. Wilkins Freeman. See *A Backward Glance*, p. 293.

38. See Nina Auerbach, *Communities of Women: An Idea in Fiction* (Cambridge, Mass.: Harvard University Press, 1978).

39. Joan Bamberger, "The Myth of Matriarchy," in Rosaldo and Lamphere, *Woman, Culture & Society*, p. 265.

40. Edith Wharton, *French Ways and Their Meanings* (New York: Appleton, 1919), p. 130.

CHAPTER 5

1. Susan Griffin, *Woman and Nature: The Roaring Inside Her* (New York: Harper & Row, 1978), pp. 155–58.

2. John Barrington Bayley, "The Decoration of Houses as a Practical Handbook," introduction to Edith Wharton and Ogden Codman, Jr., *The Decoration of Houses* (New York: Appleton, 1897; reprint, New York: Norton, 1978), pp. vii, ix; *Decoration of Houses*, pp. 22–23.

3. Edith Wharton, "A Further Glance," Wharton Archives, Beinecke Library, Yale University, New Haven, Conn., pp. 2–3.

4. Ibid., pp. 24–28.

5. Edith Wharton, *A Backward Glance* (New York: Appleton-Century, 1934), p. 203.

6. "A Further Glance," pp. 3–4, 6–7.

7. Ibid., pp. 7–10.

8. Ibid., p. 21.

9. Walt Whitman, "A Backward Glance O'er Travel'd Roads," in *Leaves of Grass*, ed. Sculley Bradley and Harold W. Blodgett (New York: Norton Critical Edition, 1973), pp. 571, 573–74, emphasis original.

10. Barrett J. Mandel, "Full of Life Now," in James Olney, ed., *Autobiography: Essays Theoretical and Critical* (Princeton: Princeton University Press, 1980), p. 72, emphasis original.

11. Erving Goffman, *The Presentation of Self in Everyday Life* (Garden City, N.Y.: Doubleday, Anchor Books, 1959), pp. 35, 22.

12. *A Backward Glance*, p. 5.

13. Simone de Beauvoir, *The Second Sex*, trans. H. M. Parshley (New York: Knopf, 1952), p. 533.

14. "A Further Glance," p. 1.

15. *A Backward Glance*, pp. vii, 1.

16. See James Olney, "Autobiography and the Cultural Moment," in *Autobiography: Essays Theoretical and Critical*, p. 19.

17. Mandel, "Full of Life Now," pp. 50–52, 62. Mandel refers to Wolfgang Iser, "The Reading Process: A Phenomenological Approach," *New Literary History* 3 (1972): 279–99.

18. *A Backward Glance*, pp. 1–2.

19. Leon Edel uses these words to describe Henry James's venture in his introduction to *The American Scene* (1907; reprint, Bloomington: Indiana University Press, 1968), p. xxi. Cf. James's stated purpose: "The very *donnée* of the piece could be given, the subject formulated: the great adventure of a society reaching out into the apparent void for the amenities, the consummations, after earnestly having gathered in so many of the preparations and necessities" (p. 12).

20. Edith Wharton, "Life and I," Wharton Archives, Beinecke Library, Yale University, New Haven, Conn., pp. 1–2.

21. Nancy K. Miller, "Women's Autobiography in France: For a Dialectics of Identification," in Sally McConnell-Ginet, Ruth Borker and Nelly Furman,

eds., *Women and Language in Literature and Society* (New York: Praeger, 1980), p. 263.

22. Georges Gusdorf, "Conditions and Limits of Autobiography," trans. James Olney, in *Autobiography: Essays Theoretical and Critical*, p. 39.

23. Germaine Brée, "The Fictions of Autobiography," *Nineteenth-Century French Studies* 4 (Summer 1976): 446, cited in Miller, "Women's Autobiography," p. 270.

24. Italo Calvino makes this point in the introduction (trans. Catherine Hill) to his *Italian Folk Tales*, trans. George Martin (New York: Harcourt Brace Jovanovich, 1980).

25. *A Backward Glance*, pp. 1, 6–7. The epigraph from Goethe is "Gute Gesellschaft hab ich gesehen; man nennt sie die gute Wenn sie zum kleinsten Gedicht nicht die Gelegenheit giebt."

26. *A Backward Glance*, pp. 33–35.

27. "Memories," p. 1, Wharton MSS, Lilly Library, Indiana University, Bloomington, Ind. This typed manuscript is also at Beinecke Library in handwritten form.

28. Washington Irving, *The Alhambra* (New York: Putnam's, 1891), Preface to the revised edition, p. vii. Given Wharton's lifelong fascination with this book, she probably knew of the sumptuous Darrow and Holly editions; the former especially, of 1891, is enough like her own *Italian Backgrounds* in format and delicacy of illustration to have served as model.

29. "Memories," pp. 1–2, emphasis original.

30. Wharton may have been punning upon the words "gob[e]lin," thinking perhaps of Christina Rossetti's "Goblin Market." The heroine of Wharton's last, unfinished novel, *The Buccaneers*, written about the same time as *A Backward Glance*, is a distant relation of the Rossettis, for one thing; also, the young Willa Cather, who acknowledged Wharton as one of her teachers, used part of "Goblin Market" as epigraph for her first collection of stories, *The Troll Garden*, in 1905.

31. *A Backward Glance*, pp. 197–205.

32. Edith Wharton, *The Custom of the Country* (New York: Scribner's, 1913), p. 76.

33. Edith Wharton, *The Age of Innocence* (New York: Appleton, 1920), p. 262.

34. Edith Wharton, *Hudson River Bracketed* (New York: Appleton, 1929), pp. 506, 515.

35. "Life and I," p. 10.

36. Edith Wharton, Preface to *Ghosts* (New York: Appleton-Century, 1937), pp. vii, x, xii.

37. *A Backward Glance*, p. 198.

38. Ibid., pp. 202–4.

39. "Life and I," pp. 17–18.

40. *A Backward Glance*, pp. 69–70.

41. Critics and biographers have made much of the fact that Lucretia Rhinelander Jones was a negative influence on her daughter—taking as evidence *A*

Backward Glance as *factual* document of Edith Wharton's life. In this text, however, we have the contradictory examples of the mother's icy rigidity in these incidents and an earlier spiritedness when, for example, she allowed herself to be carried away at age nineteen by her suitor—later Wharton's father—in a boat with a bed-quilt rigged to an oar for a sail. The image of the repressive mother is the daughter's *creation*—negative, perhaps, because of the role model the mother presented for emulation—beautiful, slim, elegant, "the best-dressed woman in New York" (pp. 18–20).

42. Cynthia Griffin Wolff, *A Feast of Words: The Triumph of Edith Wharton* (New York: Oxford University Press, 1977), p. 307, emphasis added. For the text of "Beatrice Palmato" and an outline of the story accompanying the "unpublishable fragment" (from the Wharton Archives, Beinecke Library, Yale University, New Haven, Conn.), as well as a note on the dating of the fragment, see Wolff, *Feast of Words*, pp. 301–5.

43. For other versions of *The Age of Innocence* in which Newland and Ellen flee to Florida for a few weeks of sexual abandon only to have their love destroyed by guilt, see "Old New York" and "1st Plan" (of "The Age of Innocence") in Wharton Archives, Beinecke Library, Yale University, New Haven, Conn.

44. Cited in Wolff, *Feast of Words*, pp. 303–4. This Victorian domination by a satanic father has its counterparts in the popular Svengali story in George du Maurier's *Trilby* (1894), in Bram Stoker's *Dracula* (1897) and in Freud's study of Dora K. (1905). See Nina Auerbach, *Woman and the Demon: The Life of a Victorian Myth* (Cambridge, Mass.: Harvard University Press, 1982).

45. Gaston Bachelard, *The Poetics of Reverie: Childhood, Language, and the Cosmos*, trans. Daniel Russell (Boston: Beacon, 1971), pp. 102, 99.

46. *A Backward Glance*, pp. 80–82.

47. Ibid., pp. 143–44.

48. Gusdorf, "Autobiography," p. 32.

49. Robert F. Sayre uses this story in his discussion of American autobiography. He says that modern society forces upon us emulations of others and that exceptional people choose exceptional models. "Autobiography and the Making of America," in *Autobiography: Essays Theoretical and Critical*, pp. 154–55.

50. Henry Adams, *The Education of Henry Adams* (1918; reprint, Boston: Houghton Mifflin, Sentry ed., 1961), p. 4, emphasis added.

51. The term is Erving Goffman's, in *The Presentation of Self in Everyday Life*. He means by it a "performance" that is a rejuvenation and affirmation of the moral values of the community. "In so far as the expressive bias of performances comes to be accepted as reality," he writes, "it will have some of the characteristics of a celebration. "To stay in one's room away from the place where the party is given . . . is to stay away from where reality is being performed" (pp. 35–36).

52. Sayre writes, "'The American book' . . . builds an ideal house (like Thoreau's), a house of fiction (like James's) that is an improvement on the . . . mundane houses in which we are born. The autobiography is . . . that second house into which we are reborn, carried by our own creative power. We make it ourselves, then remake it—make it new." "Autobiography," p. 148.

53. *Decoration of Houses*, p. 20; *A Backward Glance*, pp. 144, 263, 151, 224.

54. Henry James, Preface to *The Portrait of a Lady*, in *The Art of the Novel* (New York: Scribner's, 1934), pp. 48, 51.

55. Henry James, *The Portrait of a Lady* (1881; New York: Modern Library, 1951), p. 200.

56. Mandel, "Full of Life Now," p. 63; Olney, "Autobiography," p. 21.

57. *Decoration of Houses*, p. 198.

58. *A Backward Glance*, p. 379.

59. "A Further Glance," pp. 1–3.

CHAPTER 6

1. Edith Wharton, *Italian Villas and Their Gardens* (New York: Century, 1904; reprint, New York: Da Capo, 1976), pp. 7–8, 11–12, emphasis original.

2. John Brinckerhoff Jackson, "Gardens to Decipher and Gardens to Admire," *The Necessity for Ruins and Other Topics* (Amherst: University of Massachusetts Press, 1980), p. 45.

3. Ibid., pp. 37, 49–51. Theater—meaning the building, stage, scenery, the whole illusion of space achieved by the skillful use of light and color and form, the space of a make-believe world that revolves around the presence of actors, and landscape painting—either as depictions of everyday life or as settings for subjects inspired by myth and philosophy—began to assume importance at the end of the sixteenth century as part of a conscious attempt to impose order and design on surroundings, to spell out a particular relationship between human beings and nature. The word *theater*, for example, was much used in the new field of descriptive geography—*The Theater of Geography*, a popular textbook; *The Theater of Cities*, a picture book; the *Theater of Agriculture*, *Theater of the Garden*, *Theater of the World* emphasizing the visual, spectacular aspect of the environment and suggesting "a spectacle in the sense of a dramatic production with a well-defined space, an organization of place and time, and coherent action." *Landscape* in this period meant "both the *background* of a picture, and a stage set—that element in a composition which gave it form and suggested location but which was not of the main body of the argument."

But toward the middle of the seventeenth century the metaphor of landscape as theater began quite abruptly and radically to change. Theater ceased to mean spectacle and came to mean drama, the analysis and solution of a problem. At the same time, landscape painting acquired a formal, almost abstract quality. As the plan or the detailed map replaced the panorama of countryside and city, as geographers abandoned their exclusive interest in description based on observation and personal experience for "earth sciences," "vision itself demanded a new, scientific perspective." John Brinckerhoff Jackson, "Landscape as Theater," *The Necessity for Ruins*, pp. 69–73.

4. Geoffrey Grigson, *Gardenage* (1952), emphasis original. Edmund Gosse, observing that well into the seventeenth century almost all urban and suburban gardens paid less attention to flowers than to herbs and trees and vegetables, noted that "even the famous gardens of Vauquelin des Yveteaux close to Paris were said

to contain more melons than tulips, and more cabbages than hyacinths." Both cited in Jackson, "Gardens," p. 39.

5. Olivier de Serres, a sixteenth-century writer on agriculture, for example, described "herbs shaped into letters, designs, ciphers, coats of arms; arranged to imitate buildings, ships, boats, and other things . . . with a marvelous industry and patience." Cited in Jackson, "Gardens," pp. 42−43.

6. Ibid., pp. 43, 44.

7. See John Dixon Hunt, *The Figure in the Landscape: Poetry, Painting, and Gardening during the Eighteenth Century* (Baltimore: Johns Hopkins University Press, 1976), especially Chapter 1 on "the old hieroglyphic landscape."

8. Jackson, "Gardens," pp. 45−46; Foucault cited in Jackson, *Necessity for Ruins*, p. 47.

9. Edith Wharton, *A Backward Glance* (New York: Appleton-Century, 1934), p. 363.

10. Wharton named Scott, along with Poe and Hawthorne, as belonging "to that peculiar category of the eerie," in *The Writing of Fiction* (New York: Scribner's, 1925), p. 34.

11. *A Backward Glance*, p. 198.

12. These can be studied in Beinecke Library, Yale University, New Haven, Conn.

13. Wharton would have agreed with Bacon that it would be nearly as fitting "to harness a polar bear to the gardener's mowing-machine as seek to appropriate the eerie phenomena of Nature in her untamed moods for the ornamental purposes of a garden," but, Bacon concludes, because the true gardener is in touch with both the wild and the ornamental in nature, "Nature in a garden and Nature in the wild are at unity." Cited in Geoffrey Grigson, "The Room Outdoors," *Landscape* 4, no. 2 (Winter 1954−55): 28.

14. June 5, 1903, Wharton Archives, Beinecke Library, Yale University, New Haven, Conn.

15. Edith Wharton, *The Hermit and the Wild Woman and Other Stories* (New York: Scribner's, 1908), p. 15.

16. Cited in R. W. B. Lewis, *Edith Wharton: A Biography* (New York: Harper & Row, 1975), p. 487.

17. "Gardening in France," n.d., p. 1, Wharton Archives, Beinecke Library, Yale University, New Haven, Conn.

18. Ibid., pp. 2−3.

19. Geoffrey Grigson uses this term in "The Room Outdoors," p. 28.

20. Henry James, *The American Scene* (1907; reprint, Bloomington: Indiana University Press, 1968), pp. 8−12, 15; Harvard MS, cited by Edel in his Notes to this edition, p. 469.

21. Letter from Edith Wharton to Bernard Berenson, Jan. 4, 1911, Villa I Tatti, cited in Lewis, *Edith Wharton*, p. 297.

22. *A Backward Glance*, p. 293.

23. Cited in Lewis, *Edith Wharton*, p. 396; *A Backward Glance*, p. 356.

24. *A Backward Glance*, p. 356.

25. Wharton worked simultaneously on placing herself—her plans for The

Mount—and on her creation of a displaced person. "There was no place in the world that she (Lily) loved more than any other," she noted; "her memories had no roots in the soil, her wandering impulses no hearth by which to rest." Notes for "A Moment's Ornament," Wharton Archives, Beinecke Library, Yale University, New Haven, Conn.

26. *The Writing of Fiction*, pp. 131–33, 126.

27. *A Backward Glance*, pp. 293–94.

28. Elizabeth Shepley Sergeant reports in her memoir of Willa Cather a conversation the two had about Wharton's *Ethan Frome*. They contrast it with Sarah Orne Jewett's *The Country of the Pointed Firs* where "Poor Joanna," a woman who has had a misadventure in love and to expiate goes to live alone on an island, is protected there by the community—"nobody was allowed to laugh at her or hinder her queer way of life." Mrs. Wharton could never have written "Poor Joanna," they decide, nor Miss Jewett *Ethan Frome*. "The brilliant outsider, a New York summer visitor for a mere six years, had levelled her cold lorgnette relentlessly and with a kind of bang, snapped up New England curtains that William Dean Howells had been nervous about raising, even as much as an inch." *Willa Cather: A Memoir* (Lincoln: University of Nebraska Press, 1963), p. 73.

29. *A Backward Glance*, pp. 296, 294.

30. Ibid., p. 294.

31. In 1799 Robert Fulton, the American inventor, brought to Paris the first large diorama, a grandiose, circular panorama of New World scenery, accurate in every detail, a landscape without the disturbing presence of a single actor. The diorama was an immediate success. Soon a theater opened, devoted exclusively to dioramas, dedicated "to the reproduction on a theatrical scale of those views which are most worthy of exciting public curiosity from the historical and picturesque point of view," and organized by, among others, a young Frenchman who would soon make a name for himself as a pioneer photographer, Louis Daguerre. This first theater without actors, devoted to a display of landscapes without people, marks a shift from the Renaissance notion that "all the world's a stage" to one that would increasingly set scenes in domestic interiors and present private and psychological problems hidden from the public world. Jackson, "Landscape as Theater," pp. 74–75.

32. Nathaniel Hawthorne, *Tales and Sketches* (New York: Library of America, 1982), pp. 1065, 1063. Wharton uses the name Brand for her characters Sylvester and Ora Brand, a father and ghost of a dead daughter, in her story "Bewitched." As in her *Ethan Frome*, this tale is set in Starkfield, a snowbound and silent winter landscape.

33. Edith Wharton, *Ethan Frome* (New York: Scribner's, 1911, with 1922 introduction by Edith Wharton), p. 181. Further references to this edition are cited parenthetically in the text.

34. Hawthorne, *Tales*, p. 1064; *The Blithedale Romance* (1852) (New York: Library of America, 1983), p. 645.

35. Henry James, *Hawthorne* (New York: Harper, 1879), pp. 131, 130.

36. Newton Arvin, ed., *The Heart of Hawthorne's Journals* (Boston: Houghton Mifflin, 1929), p. 272.

37. Jan. 31, 1936, Wharton Archives, Beinecke Library, Yale University, New Haven, Conn.

38. Wharton's introduction to *Ethan Frome*, pp. vi–vii, emphasis original. See John Stilgoe's essay, "Winter as Landscape," *Orion Nature Quarterly* 3 (Winter 1984): 5–11, for a description of harsh New England winters in the writings of William Bradford, Cotton Mather, Henry D. Thoreau, John Greenleaf Whittier, Robert Frost and various popular sources. Insulated as we are from the older experience of winter, Stilgoe writes, "blue shadows and white silence, . . . raw winter threatens to congeal the voluptuous warmth of contemporary metropolitan civilization. Old Man Winter now stalks ever more fragile defenses" (p. 5).

39. *A Backward Glance*, p. 209.

40. *The Writing of Fiction*, p. 133, emphasis original. There is, of course, a class distinction to be made between Wharton and her narrator on the one hand and Ethan Frome on the other, and this consciousness of class underlies—in a way I find disturbing—her "principles" of gardening and decor.

41. Cynthia Griffin Wolff dates the first version as about 1906 or 1907, based on Wharton's meeting her French tutor in 1905 and publishing a story in proficient French in 1908. *A Feast of Words: The Triumph of Edith Wharton* (New York: Oxford University Press, 1977), pp. 161, 426, n. 124.

42. *A Backward Glance*, pp. 295–96. The "black book" is in the Wharton Archives, Beinecke Library, Yale University, New Haven, Conn.

43. See R. W. B. Lewis, *Edith Wharton*, and Cynthia Griffin Wolff, *Feast of Words*, for accounts of Wharton's affair with Morton Fullerton and of her reading.

44. *A Backward Glance*, p. 296.

45. For information on New England house plans, see Henry Glassie, *Pattern in the Material Culture of the Eastern United States* (Philadelphia: University of Pennsylvania Press, 1968), pp. 124–31; Abbott Lowell Cummings, *The Framed Houses of Massachusetts Bay, 1625–1725* (Cambridge, Mass.: Harvard University Press, 1979), Chapter 3; J. Frederick Kelly, *The Early Domestic Architecture of Connecticut* (New Haven: Yale University Press, 1924), Chapter 5.

46. The complete entry reads: "I am secretly afraid of animals—of *all* animals except dogs, & even of some dogs. I think it is because of the *usness* in their eyes, with the underlying *not-usness* which belies it, & is so tragic a reminder of the lost life when we human beings branched off and left them: left them to eternal inarticulateness & slavery. *Why?* their eyes seem to ask us." Wharton Archives, Beinecke Library, Yale University, New Haven, Conn., emphasis original. Cf. this passage from "Kerfol": "It was as if they [the dogs] had lived a long time with people who never spoke to them or looked at them: as though the silence of the place had gradually benumbed their busy inquisitive natures. And this strange passivity, this almost human lassitude, seemed to me sadder than the misery of starved and beaten animals." *The Ghost Stories of Edith Wharton* (New York: Scribner's, 1973), p. 84.

47. In the earlier version, although Mattie does open the door for Hart, this repeated vision is imagined before it occurs. As W. D. MacCallan suggests, Hart represses his feelings here in a way that Ethan does not. "The French Draft of

Ethan Frome," *The Yale University Library Gazette* 27 (July 1952): 40. This article reprints the French draft (the "black book").

48. Edith Wharton, *Hudson River Bracketed* (New York: Appleton, 1929), p. 511. Cf. this passage from *The Glimpses of the Moon*: ". . . she saw bits of moon-flooded sky incrusted like silver in a sharp black patterning of plane-boughs." (New York: Appleton, 1922), p. 5.

49. The setting of *Ethan Frome* is like a recurring dream in Wharton's fiction: most of the ghost stories are set in large country estates like Wharton's where one "feel[s] all the place had to communicate," especially the quality of silence, as in "Kerfol"; in deserted spaces and wastes of snow, as in "The Lady's Maid's Bell"; in the winter silence and entrapment of Starkfield in "Bewitched"; "day after day, winter after winter, year after year . . . [the] speechless, soundless," loneliness of "Mr. Jones"; the empty, silent winterhouse of "All Souls'." *Ghost Stories*, pp. 81, 193.

50. *A Backward Glance*, pp. 355–58.

51. Sandra Gilbert, "Soldier's Heart: Literary Men, Literary Women and the Great War," *Signs* 8 (Spring 1983): 424. The letter from the young man at the front is cited from Vera Brittain's *Testament of Youth* (London: Fontana/Virago, 1979), p. 143, in Gilbert, p. 427. "From now on, their only land was No Man's Land, a land that was *not*, a country of the impossible and the paradoxical," Gilbert writes. In our literature, to experience war, from D. H. Lawrence's paralyzed Clifford Chatterley to Hemingway's sadly emasculated Jake Barnes to T. S. Eliot's mysteriously sterile Fisher King—modern antiheroes churned out by the war who suffer specifically sexual wounds—has been to travel "literally or figuratively through No Man's Land, . . . [to] become not just No Men, nobodies, but *not* men, *un*men" (p. 423, emphasis original).

52. Ibid., p. 425.

53. *A Backward Glance*, p. 356.

54. Edith Wharton, "My Work Among the Women Workers of Paris," *New York Times Magazine*, Nov. 20, 1915, Wharton Archives, Beinecke Library, Yale University, New Haven, Conn. Along with photographs of children in the day nursery of the American hostels and of the Children of Flanders making lace, a rather incongruous one of the ladylike Edith Wharton seated in her garden—which Wharton must have selected—accompanies this article.

55. Virginia Woolf, for example, wrote in *Three Guineas*: "So profound was [the] unconscious loathing" of women for "the education" in oppression which all women had received that while most "consciously desired [the advancement of] 'our splendid Empire,'" many "unconsciously desired" the apocalypse of "our splendid war." Cited in "Soldier's Heart," pp. 425–26. Gilbert, in this provocative essay, finds evidence of such unconscious desire in Wharton's *A Son at the Front* and Willa Cather's *One of Ours*—and here, I think, her argument breaks down, for the former is among the weakest of Wharton's novels and the latter is Cather's only weak novel. The evidence of Gilbert's argument is to be found not in the war novels written by women—for as she herself points out, their experience of the war was very different from that of men—but in war*time* novels that turn away from the war.

56. The themes of "Beatrice Palmato" are, as I have indicated, incest, madness and death: the sexual intercourse between father and daughter is not only incestuous and irregular (in its explicit description of fellatio, in its placement in the drawing-room, the space for the most formal of activities); it is an activity of a sort to undermine the very foundations of social order. Its time of composition suggests a relationship between this piece and events like the rape in Gerbéviller of both town and old woman described in *Fighting France*.

57. This theme is present even in Wharton's great novel of manners, *The Age of Innocence*. In an earlier version (the "1st plan" of what she was then calling "Old New York"), Wharton has Newland Archer and Ellen Olenska marry but then separate because of the "European corruption" that has "tainted" Ellen's soul. Returning from their honeymoon and realizing the monotony of the life she will be expected to lead as Newland's wife, Ellen's "whole soul recoils, & she knows at once that she has eaten of the Pomegranate Seed & can never never live without it" (p. 2). Wharton Archives, Beinecke Library, Yale University, New Haven, Conn.

58. Edith Wharton, *Summer* (New York: Appleton, 1917), pp. 21, 53-54. Further references to this edition are cited parenthetically in the text.

59. Here, as is the case with Undine Spragg in *The Custom of the Country* and May Welland in *The Age of Innocence*, the world of books separates men and women. Just as the library makes clear the difference between Charity and Lucius Harney, Undine's entrance into the book-lined room of the Marvells and May's visit to Newland's library underscore the existence of a domain open to men that is not accessible to certain kinds of women—though clearly Charity and Undine, even in a different sense May, "know" in spite of the deprivation of books.

60. Cf. Wharton's description of her own "sensuous rapture produced by the sound and sight of . . . words" in "Life and I," cited here in Chapter 5.

61. Cf. Wharton's (deliberate?) use of the words of the funeral service for Newland Archer's marriage to May Welland in the first edition of *The Age of Innocence*.

CHAPTER 7

1. Henry James, *The Golden Bowl*, 2 vols. (New York: Scribner's, 1909), 2:3-4.

2. Ibid., 2:237, 189.

3. Willa Cather, "My First Novels [There Were Two]," *The Colophon* (1931), reprinted in Stephen Tennant, ed., *Willa Cather on Writing* (New York: Knopf, 1949), p. 93. In 1895 Cather had written of James that "one could read him forever for the mere beauty of his sentences" which she found always "as correct, as classical, as calm and as subtle as the music of Mozart." In 1905 she waited in trepidation—knowing of his expressed abhorrence of the "promiscuous fiction" of "young American females"—for James's verdict (never forthcoming) on her collection of stories, *The Troll Garden*, sent to him by Witter Bynner. *Lincoln Courier*, Nov. 16, 1895, p. 6, cited in Bernice Slote, ed., *The Kingdom of Art: Willa Cather's*

First Principles and Critical Statements, 1893–1896 (Lincoln: University of Nebraska Press, 1966), p. 361. Letter from Henry James to Witter Bynner in Elizabeth Shepley Sergeant, *Willa Cather: A Memoir* (Lincoln: University of Nebraska Press, 1963), pp. 68–69.

4. "My First Novels," pp. 92–93.

5. Cather in her own "reportorial" days had reviewed Zola's books for the *Nebraska State Journal* and the *Pittsburgh Leader.* "The fourteenth rejection of M. Zola from the Academy of France is another landmark in the gradual waning of the realistic school," she wrote in 1894. "Taken as an indication of the feeling of the world toward a school of art which is perhaps more painful than useful, it is a most hopeful symptom. . . . While the greater part of Zola's work arouses only sensations of distaste and offense for the man himself, it is hard to find any feeling more hostile than profound pity . . . for a man who is great, misguided, miserable and who has the supreme misfortune of making others as miserable as himself." And in 1898 she made a similar judgment: "Once again the foremost novelist of France has written a book full of repulsive odors, about another kind of unhappiness. . . . he has the searching eye and the strong hand of his generation. No burden of detail is too heavy for him, no type of distorted, misshapen humanity baffles his keen penetration. . . . I suppose in his time this man has described, analyzed and catalogued every color, scent, sound, sensation; and yet out of them all he has never created one effect of absolute beauty. He is like a miser who has gathered together all the delights of the world, but who has lost the capacity to enjoy. That delicate fiber, lurking somewhere in the brain, which responds to beauty, has in him been paralyzed from birth." In an omitted paragraph from an earlier version of this piece, Cather's scorn rose to passionate eloquence: "You may heap the details of beauty together forever, but they are not beauty until one human soul feels and knows. That is what Zola's books lack from first to last, the awakening of the spirit. An artist may be clever when he answers you, he may be skilful when he pleases your senses, but when he speaks to the living soul within you, then and then only is he great. Only a diamond can cut a diamond, only a soul can touch a soul." *Nebraska State Journal*, Dec. 30, 1894, p. 13, cited in William M. Curtin, ed., *The World and the Parish: Willa Cather's Articles and Reviews, 1893–1902*, 2 vols. (Lincoln: University of Nebraska Press, 1970), 1:139–42. *Pittsburgh Leader*, May 24, 1898, p. 5, cited in Curtin, ed., *The World and the Parish*, 2:591–94. *Nebraska State Journal*, Feb. 16, 1896, p. 9, cited in Slote, ed., *The Kingdom of Art*, pp. 367–71.

6. Willa Cather, "On the Art of Fiction," in *The Borzoi, 1920* (New York: Knopf, 1920), reprinted in Tennant, ed., *Willa Cather on Writing*, p. 102.

7. *Oxford English Dictionary* (New York: Oxford University Press, 1971), pp. 1476–77.

8. Cited in Randolph Runyon, *Fowles/Irving/Barthes: Canonical Variations on an Apocryphal Theme* (Columbus: Ohio State University Press, 1981), pp. xi–xii. Runyon's musical information is not entirely correct.

9. *The Golden Bowl*, 1:138.

10. Edith Wharton, *The Writing of Fiction* (New York: Scribner's, 1925), p. 112.

11. *The Golden Bowl*, 2:232, 235–36.

12. Preface to *The Golden Bowl*, 1:x.

13. Ibid., 1:x–xii.

14. Sergeant, *Willa Cather*, p. 139.

15. Preface to *The Golden Bowl*, 1:xiv–xvi; Preface to *The American Scene* (1907; reprint, Bloomington: Indiana University Press, 1968), unpaged.

16. *The American Scene*, pp. 74–75, emphasis original.

17. Ralph Waldo Emerson, "The Poet," in Stephen E. Whicher, ed., *Selections from Ralph Waldo Emerson* (Boston: Houghton Mifflin, 1957), p. 230.

18. Robert Plant Armstrong, *The Affecting Presence: An Essay in Humanistic Anthropology* (Urbana: University of Illinois Press, 1971). Henry Glassie introduced me to Armstrong's work. See Glassie's "Meaningful Things and Appropriate Myths: The Artifact's Place in American Studies," *Prospects: The Annual of American Cultural Studies* 3 (1978): 1–49.

19. Bernice Slote, Introduction to *Alexander's Bridge* (Lincoln: University of Nebraska Press, 1977), pp. xv–xvi. See also John P. Hinz, "The Real Alexander's Bridge," *American Literature* 21 (Jan. 1950): 473–76, and E. K. Brown, *Willa Cather: A Critical Biography*, completed by Leon Edel (New York: Knopf, 1953), pp. 157–59.

20. Alan Trachtenberg, *Brooklyn Bridge: Fact and Symbol*, rev. ed. (Chicago: University of Chicago Press, 1979).

21. Willa Cather, *Alexander's Bridge* (Boston: Houghton Mifflin, 1912; reprint, Lincoln: University of Nebraska Press, 1977), pp. 37, 38, 36. Further references to this edition are cited parenthetically in the text.

22. Cited in Trachtenberg, *Brooklyn Bridge*, p. 16.

23. Ibid., pp. 16, 18.

24. See Slote, Introduction to *Alexander's Bridge*, pp. xvii–xviii.

25. This is Newland Archer's pattern in alternate versions of *The Age of Innocence*. Wharton Archives, Beinecke Library, Yale University, New Haven, Conn.

26. Even here, however, there is no necessary connection between Wharton and Cather. As Bernice Slote points out in her introduction to *Alexander's Bridge*, imagery associated with the moon goddess appears frequently in Cather's fiction, and in her collection of stories of 1905, *The Troll Garden*, Cather contrasts "trolls" with "forest children," the palace/garden with the wood/country.

27. See Burton Rascoe's 1922 comparison of Wharton and Cather in *Shadowland*, "Mrs. Wharton and Others": "The difference between Mrs. Wharton and Miss Cather is largely a difference between fine workmanship and genius, talent and passion, good taste and ecstasy. . . . Cather is a poet in her intensity and . . . Wharton is not. . . . Wharton gives us correct pictures; . . . Cather gives us life." Cited in Slote, ed., *Kingdom of Art*, pp. 50–51.

28. See Slote, ed., *Kingdom of Art*, p. 39.

29. In an essay called "148 Charles Street," Cather describes the drawing-room of Mrs. Annie Fields—a real salon, where all the great men and women of letters were frequent visitors—as a place, like Winifred Alexander's, where the past was cherished. At tea-time, she wrote, "the long room was dimly lighted, the fire

bright, and through the wide windows the sunset was flaming, or softly brooding, upon the Charles River and the Cambridge shore beyond. The ugliness of the world, all possibility of wrenches and jars and wounding contacts, seemed securely shut out. It was indeed the peace of the past, where the tawdry and cheap have been eliminated and the enduring things have taken their proper, happy places." *Not Under Forty* (New York: Knopf, 1936), p. 63. It was at 148 Charles Street that Cather met Sarah Orne Jewett, who was to have so important an influence on her development as a writer.

30. *The Master Builder* (1892) in *Henrik Ibsen: The Complete Major Prose Plays*, trans. Rolf Fjelde (New York: New American Library, 1965), pp. 847, 833.

31. The performance is based on one of several by the Irish actress Maire O'Neill, whom Cather would have seen in the plays of Synge and Lady Gregory when she was in London in 1909 as arts critic for *McClure's*. See Slote, Introduction to *Alexander's Bridge*, pp. xiii–xiv.

32. *Nebraska State Journal*, Jan. 18, 1896, and *Lincoln Courier*, Nov. 16, 1895, cited in Slote, ed., *Kingdom of Art*, p. 75.

33. "The Wife," *Lincoln Courier*, Sept. 28, 1895, p. 8, cited in ibid., p. 282n.

34. Bernice Slote suggests that an early exploration of the divided self, and one that is relevant to *Alexander's Bridge*, is Cather's story-cycle, *The Troll Garden* (1905), with its paired stories suggesting "the basic contrasts . . . [of] the Trolls inside and the Forest Children outside, the Romans and the Barbarians, Palace-Garden and Wood-Country, and the cyclic movements of decaying civilization and reconquering nature." Cather's title comes from Christina Rossetti's "The Goblin Market," part of which is used as epigraph for the book—"We must not look at goblin men, / We must not buy their fruits; / Who knows upon what soil they fed / Their hungry thirsty roots?"—and from Charles Kingsley's lectures, "The Roman and the Teuton" (1891). "Fancy to yourself a great Troll-garden," Kingsley had said,

> a fairy palace, with a fairy garden; and all around the primaeval wood. Inside the Trolls dwell, cunning and wicked, watching their fairy treasures, working at their magic forges, making and making always things rare and strange; and outside, the forest is full of children. . . , frank . . . [,] pure . . . and [in] devout awe of the unseen; . . . in . . . love of excitement and adventure, and the mere sport of overflowing animal health. They play unharmed among the forest beasts . . . ; but the forest is too dull and too poor for them; and they wander to the walls of the Troll-garden and wonder what is inside. . . . Some of the more adventurous clamber in. Some, too, the Trolls steal and carry off into their palace. Most never return: but here and there one escapes out again, and tells how the Trolls killed all his comrades: but tells too, of the wonders he has seen inside, of shoes of swiftness, and swords of sharpness, and caps of darkness; of charmed harps, charmed jewels, and above all of the charmed wine: and after all, the Trolls were very kind to him—see what fine clothes they have given him—and he struts about awhile among his companions; and then returns, and not alone. The Trolls have bewitched him, as they will bewitch more. So the fame of the

Troll-garden spreads; and more and more steal in, boys and maidens, and tempt their comrades over the wall. [Ibid., pp. 95–97, 442–43]

35. Ibid., pp. 83–84. Willa Cather, "The Novel Démeublé," in *Not Under Forty* (New York: Knopf, 1936).

36. Slote, ed., *Kingdom of Art*, p. 87.

37. Cited in Trachtenberg, *Brooklyn Bridge*, p. 190.

38. Ibid., pp. 190–92, emphasis original.

39. Edith Lewis, *Willa Cather Living: A Personal Record* (New York: Knopf, 1953; reprint, Lincoln: University of Nebraska Press, 1976), pp. 78–79.

40. Walter Benjamin defines these as the two kinds of storytellers: one has come from afar; the other is the resident tiller of the soil. An interpenetration of their stories occurred in the Middle Ages when "the resident master craftsman and the traveling journeyman worked together in the same rooms; and every master had been a traveling journeyman before he settled down in his home town or somewhere else. If peasants and seamen were past masters of storytelling, the artisan class was its university." "The Storyteller," in *Illuminations*, trans. Harry Zohn (New York: Schocken, 1969), pp. 84–85.

41. John Berger, *Another Way of Telling* (New York: Pantheon, 1982), p. 122. Berger cites Hegel's *Philosophy of Right* here: "Every self-consciousness knows itself (1) as universal, as the potentiality of abstracting from everything determinate, and (2) as particular, with a determinate object, content and aim. Still, both these moments are only abstractions; what is concrete and true (and everything true is concrete) is the universality which has the particular as its opposite, but the particular which by its reflection into itself has been equalised with the universal. This unity is individuality." In every expressive photograph, Berger concludes, "the particular, by way of a general idea, has been *equalised with the universal,*" emphasis original.

42. Marcel Proust, *Swann's Way* (1913) from *Remembrance of Things Past*, trans. C. K. Scott Moncrieff and Terence Kilmartin (New York: Random House, 1981), 1:227–28, 230–31.

43. Henry James, Preface to *The Golden Bowl*, 1:vi, emphasis original.

44. As Walter Benjamin writes, "the most extraordinary things, marvelous things, are related with the greatest accuracy, but the psychological connection of the events is not forced on the reader," who is free to interpret things in the way she or he understands them. "The Storyteller," p. 89. One thinks of Hawthorne introducing his magical tale with a parody of verifiability—the documents found in the Custom House—or of Melville interleaving Ishmael's tale with chapters on cetology.

45. Storytelling "is always *the art of repeating stories,*" Benjamin writes, an art lost when stories are no longer remembered. Ibid., p. 91, emphasis original.

46. Mary McCarthy, in a recent essay, "Novel, Tale, Romance," shows that the etymology of our English word "tale" is "count": in French the word is *conte*, in Italian *conto*, in Spanish *cuento*; in German it is *Erzählung*, in Dutch *vertelling*— all words, even though they stem from different roots, that have to do with adding up, with numbers. "The counting, the addition of particulars implicit in those

words for tale in so many different tongues must refer to the piling up of incident," McCarthy suggests, in which "the anticipation of the listeners is keyed to a spoken narrative where incidents are doled out, . . . one after another, like haricot beans, each having equal weight, without the increasing pressure of 'building' toward one or more climaxes that is typical of the novel. In a tale we wait to hear what will come next, but the waiting is less suspenseful than it tends to be in the novel; from long practice in listening, we can afford to be patient while our teller counts out the bills that are our due reward." *New York Review of Books*, May 12, 1983, p. 49.

47. Benjamin, "The Storyteller," pp. 100–101, 98, 102. This insistence upon memory—the listener's memory, the reader's memory—as a fundamental part of the story must be at the root of Cather's refusal to permit her works to be dramatized or filmed. She was right. A recent production of "Paul's Case" (now in the public domain), as part of the PBS television series of American short stories, was rich in information—the viewer is given the exact details of the Waldorf lobby, of what Paul orders to eat from the hotel menu, of what he buys at Brooks Brothers—but meager in imaginative value; there is nothing to envision, to ponder, reflect upon, meditate about what has been completely presented. And the version thus presented is finished; there is no need to tell it again, to another.

48. Cited in ibid., pp. 107–8.

49. Reprinted in Tennant, ed., *Willa Cather on Writing*, p. 93.

50. "A Mighty Craft," *Nebraska State Journal*, Mar. 1, 1896, p. 9, cited in Slote, ed., *Kingdom of Art*, p. 417.

51. James Joyce, *Stephen Hero* (1904), in Chester G. Anderson, ed., *Portrait of the Artist as a Young Man: Text, Criticism, and Notes* (New York: Viking, 1968), p. 289.

52. Glassie, "The Artifact's Place," p. 39.

53. Berger, *Another Way of Telling*, p. 118, emphasis original.

54. Ibid., p. 280.

55. Ibid., pp. 285–86, emphasis original.

CHAPTER 8

1. Cited in Linda Nochlin, ed., *Realism and Tradition in Art, 1848–1900: Sources and Documents* (Englewood Cliffs, N.J.: Prentice-Hall, 1966), p. 35, emphasis original.

2. Yi-Fu Tuan, *Landscapes of Fear* (New York: Pantheon, 1979), p. 11.

3. Cited in Ellen Moers, *Literary Women* (Garden City, N.Y.: Doubleday, 1976), p. 238. For a brief discussion of the way in which critics have misread and misunderstood Cather, see David Stineback, "No Stone Unturned: Popular versus Professional Evaluations of Willa Cather," *Prospects: The Annual of American Cultural Studies* 7 (1982): 167–76. Stineback's debunking of scholarly criticism is somewhat amusing, but his assessment of discussions of Cather's work in the popular press is misleading.

4. Moers, *Literary Women*, pp. 238–39.

5. Annette Kolodny, *The Lay of the Land: Metaphor as Experience and History in American Life and Letters* (Chapel Hill: University of North Carolina Press, 1975), pp. 8–9. In her survey of sermons, travel pieces, political tracts, novels, histories and folk songs, Kolodny finds a growing sense of frustration and aggression toward an Arcadia that refuses to stay intact in the face of an encroaching technology that is at once the instrument of wealth and of penetration into nature's darkest and most hidden precincts. The very structure of this literature is regressive, she argues; in novels heroes resort to a compensatory infantilism in order to escape the guilt of incest or the accusation of rape, "and the pastoral figure who had attempted to inhabit those spaces remains fixed in our fiction as a perennial outsider, standing both as our society's lost ideal and as its critic" (pp. 134–35).

6. Ibid., pp. 153–56.

7. "Melodramas of Beset Manhood: How Theories of American Fiction Exclude Women Authors," *American Quarterly* 33 (Summer 1981): 139. Baym considers in this provocative piece the criticism of Marius Bewley, F. O. Matthiessen, Robert Spiller, Joel Porte, Sacvan Bercovitch, Jay Hubbell, Richard Poirier, Lionel Trilling, Leslie Fiedler, Richard Chase, Donald Kartiganer, Malcolm Griffith and Eric Sundquist.

8. Ibid., pp. 131–35.

9. Joel Kovel, *White Racism: A Psychohistory* (New York: Pantheon, 1970), p. 260, cited in Kolodny, *Lay of the Land*, p. 153.

10. Leo Marx, *The Machine in the Garden: Technology and the Pastoral Ideal* (New York: Oxford University Press, 1976), p. 10.

11. Richard Slotkin, *Regeneration through Violence* (Middletown, Conn.: Wesleyan University Press, 1973), pp. 551–54. "True myths are generated on a subliterary level by the historical experience of a people and thus constitute part of that inner reality which the work of the artist draws on, illuminates, and explains," Slotkin writes. "In American mythogenesis the founding fathers . . . tore violently a nation from the implacable and opulent wilderness—the rogues, adventurers, and land-boomers; the Indian fighters, traders, missionaries, explorers, and hunters who killed and were killed until they had mastered the wilderness; the settlers who came after, suffering hardship and Indian warfare for the sake of a sacred mission or a simple desire for land; and the Indians themselves, both as they were and as they appeared to the settlers, for whom they were the special demonic personification of the American wilderness. Their concerns, their hopes, their terrors, their violence, and their justifications of themselves . . . are the foundation stones of the mythology that informs our history" (p. 4).

12. Marx, *Machine in the Garden*, p. 228. Marx distinguishes between "simple" pastoralism—"a romantic perversion of thought and feeling," and "complex" pastoralism—a mode which "call[s] into question, or bring[s] irony to bear against the illusion of peace and harmony in a green pasture" (pp. 10, 25).

13. Baym, "Melodramas of Beset Manhood," p. 135.

14. This is the subject of Annette Kolodny's *The Land Before Her: Fantasy and Experience of the American Frontiers, 1630–1860* (Chapel Hill: University of

North Carolina Press, 1984). For women going west, she argues, "paradisal images became inextricably associated with images of home, and images of home embraced not only the cabin and landscape at the end of the trail but also the elements of former houses and former gardens that could be introduced there" (p. 237).

15. Marx, *Machine in the Garden*, p. 70. This, as I have shown in earlier chapters, was Edith Wharton's position.

16. Baym, "Melodramas of Beset Manhood," p. 131.

17. Gabriel P. Weisberg, *The Realist Tradition: French Painting and Drawing, 1830–1900* (Bloomington: The Cleveland Museum of Art and Indiana University Press, 1980), Foreword, p. xiii.

18. Willa Cather, *The Song of the Lark* (Boston: Houghton Mifflin, 1915; reprint, Lincoln: University of Nebraska Press, 1978), p. 197. Further references to this edition, which is different from the better-known version that Cather edited in 1932, are cited parenthetically in the text.

19. *Lincoln Courier*, Aug. 10, 1901, p. 2, cited in William M. Curtin, ed., *The World and the Parish: Willa Cather's Articles and Reviews, 1893–1902*, 2 vols. (Lincoln: University of Nebraska Press, 1970), 2:843.

20. *Nebraska State Journal*, Jan. 6, 1895, p. 13, cited in Bernice Slote, ed., *The Kingdom of Art: Willa Cather's First Principles and Critical Statements, 1893–1896* (Lincoln: University of Nebraska Press, 1966), p. 218. Cather's affinity for French art was not confined to painting. In 1895 she wrote in the *Journal*: "In these days it is as necessary for a literary man to have a wide knowledge of the French masterpieces [Daudet, Maupassant, Hugo, George Sand] as it is for him to have read Shakespeare or the Bible." Cited in Slote, ed., *Kingdom of Art*, p. 60. Slote also mentions Dorothy Canfield Fisher's recollection of Cather's passionate interest in French writers during their university years; Helen and George Seibel's descriptions of reading aloud from Alfred de Musset, Verlaine and Flaubert with the young Willa Cather in Pittsburgh from 1896 on; and Elizabeth Shepley Sergeant's memory of the portrait of George Sand by Coutoure that hung in Cather's New York living room. Cather's *My Ántonia* owes something to Sand's *Antonia*; two novels, *Shadows on the Rock* and *One of Ours*, evoke Cather's passion for French culture; and her last, unfinished novel was set in Avignon.

21. See Edith Lewis, *Willa Cather Living: A Personal Record* (New York: Knopf, 1953; reprint, Lincoln: University of Nebraska Press, 1976), p. 55.

22. *Nebraska State Journal*, Sept. 21, 1902, p. 18, cited in Curtin, ed., *World and the Parish*, 2:931.

23. "Willa Cather Talks of Work," *Philadelphia Record*, Aug. 9, 1913, cited in Slote, ed., *Kingdom of Art*, p. 447.

24. Henry Glassie, *Passing the Time in Ballymenone: Culture and History of an Ulster Community* (Philadelphia: University of Pennsylvania Press, 1982), p. 468.

25. Cather recalls Jewett's advice—"One must know the world *so well* before one can know the parish"—in her preface to the 1922 edition of *Alexander's Bridge* (Boston: Houghton Mifflin), p. vii, emphasis original.

26. Linda Nochlin, *Realism* (New York: Penguin, 1971), p. 112.

27. Cited in ibid., p. 113.

28. *Nebraska State Journal*, Sept. 21, 1902, p. 18, cited in Curtin, ed., *World and the Parish*, 2:931.

29. "Old Mrs. Harris," in *Obscure Destinies* (New York: Knopf, 1932), pp. 81, 190, 92–93.

30. Letter to Théophile Thoré, ca. Feb. 18, 1862, cited in Nochlin, *Documents*, pp. 56–57.

31. Timothy J. Clark, *The Absolute Bourgeois: Artists and Politics in France, 1848–1851* (Greenwich, Conn.: New York Graphic Society, 1973), pp. 95–96.

32. Charles Rosen and Henri Zerner, "What Is, and Is Not, Realism?," *New York Review of Books*, Feb. 18. 1982, p. 26.

33. Cited in ibid., p. 24. The authors add, "'*Écrire bien*' has a strong meaning for Flaubert which 'to write well' would not convey, and '*écrire bien le mediocre*' is a peculiar turn of phrase. 'To write the *mediocre* beautifully' is the best we can do, but it is not very satisfactory."

34. "A Chance Meeting," in *Not Under Forty* (New York: Knopf, 1936), p. 25.

35. Willa Cather, *O Pioneers!* (Boston: Houghton Mifflin, 1913), pp. 14–15. Further references to this edition are cited parenthetically in the text.

36. Baym, "Melodramas of Beset Manhood," p. 136.

37. *The Song of the Lark*, p. 297, cited in Moers, *Literary Women*, pp. 258–59.

38. Willa Cather, *My Ántonia* (Boston: Houghton Mifflin, 1918), pp. 7–8. Further references to this edition (in which the introduction is longer than in the 1926 edition) are cited parenthetically in the text.

39. Elizabeth Hampsten, *Read This Only to Yourself: The Private Writings of Midwestern Women, 1880–1910* (Bloomington: Indiana University Press, 1982), pp. 33–36. Hampsten cites as an example of language and interests typical of frontier working-class women this letter from a Norwegian woman named Caroline to her cousin Christine:

> Me and mother are well and lead a good life under the circumstances since there are fairly tough times now that the timber froze over large parts of this country.... if we get a bad year this year again, it will be best to leave Dakota.
>
> You say aunt wonders whether I still own land. Well I have it mainly because as long as I keep it we have a home.... You know I cannot take care of the land like a man. All I can do is to live there as much as I can and to plow what I can so that no one can take it away from me because I hope in time to sell ... if we get railway over here....
>
> I wish you were here today so I could talk to you for a while. I am very lonely here as my work is not much. I crochet and knit and sew. Right now I am making a skirt for myself. Here you can see a sample of the material of it. It is simple, but good enough for the Dakota prairie because there isn't enough money for lots of fine dresses for me who is farming. But when I come to Norway again I am going to have a silk skirt I have been kind of thinking to myself. [Trans. from Norwegian by Marianne Mathies, pp. 34–35]

40. There is a vast new literature on this subject, but see especially Lillian Schlissel, *Women's Diaries of the Westward Journey* (New York: Schocken, 1982); Elizabeth Hampsten, *Read This Only to Yourself: The Private Writings of Midwestern Women*; and Annette Kolodny, "To Render Home a Paradise: Women on the New World Landscape," in E. L. Epstein, ed., *Women's Language and Style* (Akron: University of Akron Press, 1978).

41. "The Quiltmaker's Landscape," *Landscape* 25, no. 3 (1981): 39–47.

42. Willa Cather, *One of Ours* (New York: Knopf, 1922), p. 161.

43. See *My Ántonia*, Introduction, p. xi.

44. *The Song of the Lark*, pp. 201, 218.

45. Death is the sanction of everything that the storyteller can tell, Walter Benjamin writes, citing the way in which Johann Peter Hebel made a long period of years graphic in his story "Unexpected Reunion": "In the meantime the city of Lisbon was destroyed by an earthquake, and the Seven Years' War came and went, and Emperor Francis I died, and the Jesuit Order was abolished, and Poland was partitioned, and Empress Maria Theresa died, and Struensee was executed. America became independent, and the united French and Spanish forces were unable to capture Gibraltar. The Turks locked up General Stein in the Veteraner Cave in Hungary, and Emperor Joseph died also. King Gustavus of Sweden conquered Russian Finland, and the French Revolution and the long war began, and Emperor Leopold II went to his grave too. Napoleon captured Prussia, and the English bombarded Copenhagen, and the peasants sowed and harvested. The millers ground, the smiths hammered, and the miners dug for veins of ore in their underground workshops. But when in 1809 the miners at Falun. . . ." Never, Benjamin writes, "has a storyteller embedded his report deeper in natural history than Hebel manages to do in this chronology. Read it carefully. Death appears in it with the same regularity as the Reaper does in the processions that pass around the cathedral clock at noon. "The Storyteller," in *Illuminations*, trans. Harry Zohn (New York: Schocken, 1968), pp. 94–95.

46. Nochlin, *Realism*, pp. 32–33.

47. Bernice Slote, "Willa Cather as a Regional Writer," *Kansas Quarterly* 2 (1970): 10, 11. Good Transcendentalist that she is (i.e., not bothered by contradictions), Slote elsewhere has argued that Cather (at least the early Cather) was a Romantic; she points out, however, that Cather must be seen not as pastoral, but as primitive, that her language is elegiac not in theme, but in *tone*. See *Kingdom of Art*, pp. 33–34, 61–66.

48. Cather was well known in the West quite early on: her fiction was serialized in the local press, and her columns and reviews appeared continuously in the Lincoln papers from 1893 to 1902. These reviews have been collected in Curtin, ed., *World and the Parish*.

49. Slote, "Willa Cather as a Regional Writer," pp. 12–13.

50. Moers, *Literary Women*, p. 231.

51. Elizabeth Hampsten believes that the term "regional" applies more to men than to women. In her examination of thousands of letters written by immigrant women coming from and living in a variety of places, she found the differences to be of degree rather than of kind, and based more on class than on region.

Settings are unimportant; minute domestic detail and expressions of friendship and female bonding are what stand out (pp. 29–36).

52. Slote, "Willa Cather as a Regional Writer," p. 14. David Stouck, on the other hand, argues that Cather's stories are not folk tales because "they are the product of an individual imagination rather than [of] a group." *Willa Cather's Imagination* (Lincoln: University of Nebraska Press, 1975), p. 38.

53. Ibid., p. 30.

54. Yi-Fu Tuan, "Rootedness versus Sense of Place," *Landscape* 24, no. 1 (1980): 4–5.

55. David Stouck suggests further associations for the two stories: "Alexandra's heroic character and actions are enriched by her connection with the old Swedish legends. Emil and Marie's story acquires a universal pathos by its association with classical tales of lovers who die. When old Ivar comes to the despoiled orchard at dawn he sees two white butterflies fluttering over the dead bodies, like metamorphosed lovers in Ovid's tales. The staining of the white mulberries with the lovers' blood recalls specifically the story of Pyramus and Thisbe. . . . The innocent, domestic love of Baucis and Philemon is . . . remembered [in Marie's love for the trees] and . . . the Endymion story when Marie resolves in the moonlight that to dream of her love will henceforward be enough" (p. 31). For Cather's reading in Homer, Virgil, the Grimms' *Fairy Tales*, *The Arabian Nights* and Greek, Roman and Germanic-Norse mythology, see Slote, ed., *Kingdom of Art*, pp. 35–36.

56. No wonder critics have seen the landscape both as male and as an emblem of the female body: clearly, in such a passage, the land is Alexandra's lover. Without digressing into a discussion of lesbian love, I would suggest that loving the land, as Willa Cather who loved women did, is for women a different experience from the dominance and mastery suggested by critics like Richard Slotkin.

57. *O Pioneers!* is dedicated to Jewett, Cather's early mentor, "in whose beautiful and delicate work there is the perfection that endures."

58. It is this sort of scene that leads male critics to see Cather as a "pastoral" writer. David Stouck, for example, attributes to Alexandra all of the qualities of the epic hero; yet he values her most of all for her "feminine" ability to create a sense of place. In this cozy scene of domesticity, he writes, although the men are far away, "the scene is imaginatively complete, as the refuge desired is a maternal and innocent one." In a note, Stouck admits that the question of "identification" between the reader and a fictional character "is always a thorny one, for it depends on the reader's particular nature," unlike that of the artist, whose imaginative involvement with the epic protagonist is possible because "like the artist, he is a figure set apart from other men and his values are those of individual creativity." *Willa Cather's Imagination*, p. 30; p. 34, n. 14. Stouck's concern is whether his writers and readers are "active" or "passive"; the problems of "identification," for him, have little to do with gender.

59. Cited in Tuan, "Rootedness," p. 6.

60. Margaret Atwood, "Romantic Idealism, Barnyard Realism," *New York Times Book Review*, June 12, 1983, p. 9.

61. Gerda Lerner, "Placing Women in History," in *The Majority Finds Its Past* (New York: Oxford University Press, 1979), pp. 145–59.

62. Carol P. Christ, *Diving Deep and Surfacing: Women Writers on Spiritual Quest* (Boston: Beacon, 1980), p. 1.

63. The term is Annette Kolodny's in "Honing a Habitable Languagescape: Women's Images for the New World Frontiers," in Sally McConnell-Ginet, Ruth Borker and Nelly Furman, eds., *Women and Language in Literature and Society* (New York: Praeger, 1980), pp. 188–204. The experiential is equally at the core of Willa Cather's real and imagined life: work—as journalist, teacher, editor, writer; friendship—with her brothers Roscoe and Douglas, with Isabelle McClung, Sarah Orne Jewett, Edith Lewis; and the great fact of the land itself—Virginia, Nebraska, the American Southwest, the Northeast (particularly New Hampshire), Canada and France.

CHAPTER 9

1. Hélène Cixous, "The Laugh of the Medusa," trans. Keith and Paula Cohen, *Signs* (Summer 1976), reprinted in Elaine Marks and Isabelle de Courtivron, eds., *New French Feminisms* (Amherst: University of Massachusetts Press, 1980), p. 246. I borrow the chapter title from Kent C. Bloomer and Charles W. Moore's *Body, Memory, and Architecture* (New Haven: Yale University Press, 1977).

2. Willa Cather, *O Pioneers!* (Boston: Houghton Mifflin, 1913), p. 206. Further references to this edition are cited parenthetically in the text.

3. Think, for example, of Zenobia, the strong woman of Hawthorne's *The Blithedale Romance*, who longs for a godlike man, which Hollingsworth clearly is not.

4. Willa Cather, *The Song of the Lark* (Boston: Houghton Mifflin, 1915; reprint, Lincoln: University of Nebraska Press, 1978), p. 225. Further references to this edition are cited parenthetically in the text.

5. Willa Cather, *My Ántonia* (Boston: Houghton Mifflin, 1918), p. 85. Further references to this edition are cited parenthetically in the text.

6. The dream invites psychological speculation. Jim has been discouraged from intimacy with the hired girls: when he goes to their dances, his grandmother weeps; when he attempts to kiss Ántonia, she tells him not to be like the others. Presumably, the issue is class, but for "Willie" Cather, who in real life and in this story assumed the persona of a young man, the issue might also be sex—attraction to the lively immigrant *girls*. In the story, someone with a reaping-hook, i.e., a penis, says to Jim, "Now they are all gone, and I can kiss you as much as I like." The dream suggests an encoded story within the story, making more sense of Jim's usually discredited later remark that he was once "very much in love with" Ántonia. See also "Paul's Case" and *Lucy Gayheart* as similarly encoded stories.

7. Bloomer and Moore, *Body, Memory, and Architecture*, p. 1.

8. Henry Glassie, *Passing the Time in Ballymenone: Culture and History of an Ulster Community* (Philadelphia: University of Pennsylvania Press, 1982), p. 651.

9. "Right" means more than "correct," Henry Glassie suggests; it means to produce an object of delight that is wholly original, true, complete, in perfect tune with conditions. Ibid., p. 460.

10. This is the memory triggered by the tea-soaked bit of madeleine:

[I]mmediately the old grey house upon the street, where her room was, rose up like a stage set to attach itself to the little pavilion opening on to the garden which had been built out behind it . . . and with the house the town, from morning to night in all weathers, the Square where I used to be sent before lunch, the streets along which I used to run errands, the country roads we took when it was fine. And as in the game wherein the Japanese amuse themselves by filling a porcelain bowl with water and steeping in it little pieces of paper which until then are without character or form, but, the moment they become wet, stretch and twist and take on colour and distinctive shape, become flowers or houses or people, solid and recognisable, so in that moment all the flowers in our garden and M. Swann's park, and the water-lilies on the Vivonne and the good folk of the village and their little dwellings and the parish church and the whole of Combray and its surroundings, taking shape and solidity, sprang into being, town and gardens alike, from my cup of tea. [Marcel Proust, *Swann's Way* (1913) from *Remembrance of Things Past*, trans. C. K. Scott Moncrieff and Terence Kilmartin (New York: Random House, 1981), 1:49–51]

Ellen Moers believes that Proust learned this technique from George Sand. He recalls in *Swann's Way*, listening to his mother read Sand's fables, "his mind wandering, his fantasy embroidering everything that was faded and old-fashioned in a country tale like *François le Champi*. In Sand's prose and in her moral idealism, Proust writes, he would ever after hear the maternal and grandmaternal accent." *Literary Women* (Garden City, N.Y.: Doubleday, 1976), p. 224n.

11. Bernice Slote points out the relationship between this tree and Carlyle's Ygdrasil, a subject of interest to Cather since her student days at the University of Nebraska. *The Kingdom of Art: Willa Cather's First Principles and Critical Statements, 1893–1896* (Lincoln: University of Nebraska Press, 1966), p. 36. This talking tree is also related to the legendary mulberry tree in *O Pioneers!*

12. Willa Cather, *One of Ours* (New York: Knopf, 1922), p. 389. "Think of the past as space expanding infinitely beyond our vision," Henry Glassie writes of another place, another time. "It is not a record of progress or regress, stasis or change; uncharted, it simply, smugly, vastly is. Then we choose a prospect. The higher it is, the wider and hazier our view. Now we map what we see, marking some features, ignoring others, altering an unknown territory, absurd in its unity, into a finite collection of landmarks made meaningful through their connections. History is not the past, but a map of the past drawn from a particular point of view to be useful to the modern traveler. . . . history does not begin with a raid to snatch scraps to add color or flesh or nobility. . . . It begins when the observer adopts the local prospect, then brings the local landmarks into visibility, giving the creations of the community's people—the artifacts in which their past is entombed, the texts in which their past lives—complete presence." *Passing the Time in Ballymenone*, p. 621.

13. Henry Glassie writes of Ballymenone's storytellers: "Their stories exist within two intersecting categories of action that compel the creative person into

social responsibility. As a heightened kind of speech, the story lifts above the 'silence' through which individuals sicken into themselves. Stories rise above 'talk' where words are idle, unconnected, or potentially harmful. Stories rise above 'chat,' where words bring people into engagement, above 'crack,' where engagement becomes amusing. Aloft, stories seek the beauty and benign power of music. As 'entertainment,' stories are like food, gifts designed to please other people and carry them on. 'Stories of history,' since they are stories, are more than factual. They provide nourishment. Indirectly but truthfully, artistically but generously, historical narratives give their listeners 'information' they must know and 'warnings' they must heed as they endure the present and go to meet the future. Stories of history are at once beautiful and useful. As 'stories' and 'entertainment' they bring people into engagement and urge them to accord." *Passing the Time in Ballymenone*, p. 155.

14. On the "empirical" and "imaginative" knowledge of place, see John Kirtland Wright, *Human Nature in Geography* (Cambridge, Mass.: Harvard University Press, 1966), John L. Allen, "Lands of Myth, Waters of Wonder: The Place of the Imagination in the History of Geographical Exploration," and other essays in David Lowenthal and Martyn J. Bowden, eds., *Geographies of the Mind* (New York: Oxford University Press, 1976).

15. See John Kirtland Wright, "*Terrae Incognitae*: The Place of the Imagination in Geography," Presidential Address to the Association of American Geographers (1946), *Annals of the Association of American Geographers* 37 (1947): 1–15. Wright came from a family rich in the creation of imaginary countries, including his own; the most famous is his brother Austin Tappan Wright's *Islandia*.

16. For a description of the uses of imagination in geographical exploration, and of Coronado's explorations in particular, see Allen, "Lands of Myth, Waters of Wonder," pp. 48–52, from which this summary of Coronado's explorations is drawn.

17. See John Brinckerhoff Jackson, "The Westward Moving House," in *Landscapes* (Amherst: University of Massachusetts Press, 1970), pp. 30, 34, 36. The modern house, Jackson writes, is a "transformer"; it neither increases nor decreases the energy in question but merely changes its form. "There is no use inquiring what this house will retain from the lives of its inhabitants, or what it will contribute to them. It imposes no distinct code of behavior or set of standards; it demands no loyalty which might be in conflict with loyalty to the outside world." No one will associate this house with repression or wax sentimental about days spent in it; it represents a transient society, filtering the crudities of nature, the lawlessness of society and producing an atmosphere of temporary well-being (p. 36).

18. See John R. Stilgoe, *Common Landscape of America: 1580–1845* (New Haven: Yale University Press, 1982), for a discussion of the changing meanings of the word "landscape" and a description of the things upon the land in rural America.

19. The similarity of houses in America to each other makes them remarkably good "cultural spoor," Peirce F. Lewis argues in "Common Houses, Cultural Spoor," *Landscape* 29, no. 2 (Jan. 1975): 1–22. Form does not follow function, as some architectural historians would have us think; rather, Lewis argues, most

domestic house types spring from the past. See also Ronald Rees and Carl J. Tracie, "The Prairie House," *Landscape* 22, no. 3 (Spring 1978): 3–8, who argue that westward-moving migrants copied housing patterns of the dominant culture; and Thomas Harvey on mail-order architecture: "Mail-Order Architecture in the Twenties," *Landscape* 25, no. 3 (1981): 1–9. Gwendolyn Wright and Dolores Hayden are cited on housing types in Chapter 1. See also Henry Glassie, *Pattern in the Material Culture of the Eastern United States* (Philadelphia: University of Pennsylvania Press, 1968), *Folk Housing in Middle Virginia* (Knoxville: University of Tennessee Press, 1975), and *Passing the Time in Ballymenone* on the transformation of house plans.

20. Jackson, "Westward Moving House," pp. 20–30.

21. It is still possible to do this. I stopped, not from a train, but from a car, in Red Cloud, Nebraska. I drove out into the country and saw the real fruit cave of Annie Pavelka (Ántonia in the novel) and spent a delightful evening talking with Emil Pavelka (Jan Cuzak in the novel, Ántonia's shy son). For a vicarious visit to Red Cloud (and other places), see Lucia Woods's photographic evocations of the landscapes and people of the Divide in *Willa Cather: A Pictorial Memoir* (Lincoln: University of Nebraska Press, 1973).

22. For these observations on "pastoral," I draw once again on the insights of Paul Alpers, in "What Is Pastoral?," *Critical Inquiry* 8 (Spring 1982): 437–60. Alpers argues that shepherds are representative of "real men" and that pastoral landscapes are those in which shepherds lead their lives. He frees the term "pastoral" from the overtones of Romantic poetry and aesthetics, "which give a privileged status to nature and states of innocence and assume that poetry is essentially a matter of individual sensibility and spiritual experience. It makes far more sense," he suggests, "to say that the representative anecdote of pastoral is in the lives of shepherds" (p. 449). See my discussion of Edith Wharton's "urban pastoral" in Chapter 3.

23. William Empson makes the same point when he observes that "you can say everything about complex people by a complete consideration of simple people"—though I would challenge his assumption that "simple" people are not "complex." *Some Versions of Pastoral* (London: Chatto & Windus, 1935), p. 137, cited in Alpers, "What Is Pastoral?," p. 451.

24. Ibid., pp. 451–52.

25. See Renato Poggioli, *The Oaten Flute: Essays on Pastoral Poetry and the Pastoral Ideal* (Cambridge, Mass.: Harvard University Press, 1975) for a discussion of *otium*, and see Erwin Panofsky, "*Et in Arcadia Ego*: Poussin and the Elegiac Tradition," in *Meaning and the Visual Arts* (Garden City, N.Y.: Doubleday, Anchor Books, 1955), pp. 295–320, for a discussion of death in the pastoral landscape.

26. Alpers, "What Is Pastoral?," pp. 452–54. As I point out in Chapter 8, the American pastoral narrative is more representative for (white, middle-class) men than for women, and this, I think, is the reason for the frame story—to remind us that Jim Burden's pastoral romance is a fiction. The "triple enclosure" is more complicated than that, however. Willa Cather's female role models would have been her mother, a Virginia lady with many of the qualities of Victoria Templeton in "Old Mrs. Harris," or conventional and unimaginative women like Lucy Gay-

heart's sister Pauline (in *Lucy Gayheart*) and girls like Lily Fisher in *The Song of the Lark*. Growing up in Red Cloud, Nebraska, she chose to name and to represent herself as male, in dress, hairstyle and signature. What would be more logical, then, in this representation of growing up on the Divide than to create a male alter ego? The triple enclosure allows her to do so with detachment and irony.

27. Alpers, referring to Virgil's *Eclogues*, ibid., p. 451.

28. Albert B. Lord, *The Singer of Tales* (Cambridge, Mass.: Harvard University Press, 1960), p. 3. Milman Parry was a classics scholar at Harvard when he began this study, recording in 1934 and 1935 over 12,500 texts of Yugoslavian epic and lyric songs and conversations with singers about their lives and art (the collection is now housed at Harvard). He had completed but a few pages of this study when he died; the book based on the work of Parry was written by Lord (p. 279, nn. 1 and 2).

29. Ibid., pp. 4, 37, 94. Lord's detailing of the way in which the young person learns to become a singer of tales is worth noting. The first stage is listening—absorbing the names of heroes, the faraway places and habits of long ago, and also the oft-repeated phrases and formulas of the tale's pattern. The second stage is one of imitation: elements of structure, rhythm and melody learned, the singer begins to sing for a critical audience. In the third stage the singer begins to experiment with ornamentation and expansion, moving within the tradition with freedom and adding to the repertory of songs. Finally the singer embarks upon the never-ending process of accumulating, recombining and remodeling formulas and themes according to individual desire (pp. 21–26). In just this way does Willa Cather work to transform the *act* of writing into storytelling, fitting pen to matter as plough to furrow.

30. *Passing the Time in Ballymenone*, pp. 519–20. For Glassie, ornament in tales is like ornament in Irish metalwork and manuscript illumination: "ornament contains and converges with meaning, writhing around, penetrating sacred texts, housing holy relics, springing from mathematics to reference as a graceful line swells into a bird's head or repetitive embedded jewels become staring, eternal eyes. The trapped eye is led in. The mind follows" (p. 520).

31. Ibid., pp. 39–40. It is worth noting that, like Cather, Glassie *writes these stories down* and is concerned that the story on the page be "right."

32. Walter Benjamin maintains that the two sources of stories are the traveler and the tiller of the soil; we feel their rhythms in all stories, he writes, along with the rhythms of the listeners. "The Storyteller," in *Illuminations*, trans. Harry Zohn (New York: Shocken, 1969), pp. 84–85.

33. See Glassie, *Passing the Time in Ballymenone*, p. 519.

34. Willa Cather, *The Professor's House* (New York: Knopf, 1925), p. 32.

CHAPTER 10

1. (New York: Simon & Schuster, 1979), p. 78.

2. Ibid., pp. 90–91.

3. Georgia O'Keeffe, *Georgia O'Keeffe* (New York: Viking, 1976), unpaged,

#74, *Pelvis III* (1944), reprinted from *An American Place* (1944) [exhibition catalog].

4. *Hopi Dreams*, cited in Yi-Fu Tuan, *Topophilia: A Study of Environmental Perceptions, Attitudes, and Values* (Englewood Cliffs, N.J.: Prentice-Hall, 1974), p. 61, emphasis original.

5. Cf. Kent C. Bloomer and Charles W. Moore's discussion of the importance of *haptic* perception in relation to architectural form in *Body, Memory, and Architecture* (New Haven: Yale University Press, 1977): "To sense haptically is to experience objects in the environment by actually touching them (by climbing a mountain rather than staring at it). Treated as a perceptual system the haptic incorporates all those sensations (pressure, warmth, cold, pain, and kinesthetics) which previously divided up the sense of touch, and thus it includes all those aspects of sensual detection which involve physical contact both inside and outside the body" (p. 34).

6. Gaston Bachelard defines "felicitous space" as that which "concentrates being within limits that protect" and also as that which is vast, opening up unlimited space, or what he calls "intimate immensity." *The Poetics of Space*, trans. Maria Jolas (Boston: Beacon, 1969), pp. xxxii, 183–210.

7. Tuan, *Topophilia*, p. 51.

8. Willa Cather, *Death Comes for the Archbishop* (New York: Knopf, 1927), pp. 276–77. Further references to this edition are cited parenthetically in the text.

9. Heightened consciousness that comes with the acuteness of sensuous perception is not, of course, particular to this landscape, to those trained in religious meditation exercises, or to women writers; but certain landscapes seem to re-create, in imaginative persons, the spatial freedom of landscapes recalled from childhood. Experiences similar to those of Father Latour occur in the chapter "Sounds" in Thoreau's *Walden*, for example, and in Book 2, Chapter 9, in Virginia Woolf's *To The Lighthouse*. On the way in which imaginative persons travel vast geographical distances in the process of artistic creation, see Guy Davenport, "The Geography of the Imagination," in *The Geography of the Imagination* (San Francisco: North Point Press, 1981).

10. Hopkins in his *Notebooks* described *inscape* as "the 'whatness' of a thing, suddenly apprehended like an electrical impulse, a divine spark." Cited in Richard Ellmann and Robert O'Clair, *Norton Anthology of Modern Poetry* (New York: Norton, 1973), p. 68. The best-known critical definition of *inscape* is Austin Warren's "the unique configuration of the sensuously transient"; the one I find most helpful in understanding Cather's search for form is poet Josephine Miles's description of Hopkins's "word-making force" as a way of catching "the inner landscape in the outer." Austin Warren, "Gerard Manley Hopkins" and "Instress of Inscape"; Josephine Miles, "The Sweet and Lovely Language," in The Kenyon Critics, *Gerard Manley Hopkins* (New York: New Directions, 1945; reprinted from *The Kenyon Review*, 1944), pp. 4, 76–77, 67.

11. Willa Cather, *My Ántonia* (Boston: Houghton Mifflin, 1918), pp. 32–33.

12. I cannot prove that Cather knew Hopkins's work, which was first published posthumously in 1918, but there is a remarkable similarity in Hopkins's fascination with cloud formations as objects of meditation and in such passages as

this in Cather's *Death Comes for the Archbishop*: "Coming along the Santa Fé trail, . . . Father Latour had found the sky more a desert than the land; a hard, empty blue, very monotonous to the eyes of a Frenchman. But west of the Pecos all that changed; here there was always activity overhead, clouds forming and moving all day long. Whether they were dark and full of violence, or soft and white with luxurious idleness, they powerfully affected the world beneath them. The desert, the mountains and mesas, were continually re-formed and re-coloured by the cloud shadows. The whole country seemed fluid to the eye under this constant change of accent, this ever-varying distribution of light" (pp. 96–97). There is a similarity, too, in Hopkins's noting of linguistic habits—an observed laborer, for example, when he began to speak "quickly and descriptively, . . . dropped or slurred the article" (cited in Warren, "Instress of Inscape," p. 79)—and Cather's noting of Indian speech patterns: "Jacinto usually dropped the article in speaking Spanish, just as he did in speaking English, though the Bishop had noticed that when he did give a noun its article, he used the right one. The customary omission, therefore, seemed to be a matter of taste, not ignorance. In the Indian conception of language, such attachments were superfluous and un-pleasing, perhaps" (*Archbishop*, p. 91). Hopkins's celebrations in poems like "Pied Beauty" and "Hurrahing in Harvest" of sudden recognitions of forms that express meaning and order in God's universe are based on a religious training in contem-plation—like Cather's Father Latour's and like her religious mystic Ivar's in *O Pioneers!*. Latour's life she studied (he was Jean Baptiste Lamy, Archbishop of the diocese of New Mexico), and Ivar might have had an original in her Nebraska childhood, but she came to her own preference for solitary meditation by another route than that of Hopkins—though both shared a reading of Walter Pater, John Ruskin and William Morris.

13. Willa Cather, *The Song of the Lark* (Boston: Houghton Mifflin, 1915; reprint, Lincoln: University of Nebraska Press, 1978), p. 304. Further references to this edition are cited parenthetically in the text.

14. The phrase recurs, for example, in a review of the plays of Dumas *père* and *fils* for the *Nebraska State Journal* of 1896: "All ye young writers of plays, there is a precept for you. 'I needed only four walls, four boards, two characters and one passion'"; in the *Pittsburgh Leader* of 1897: "Once, when the elder Dumas was asked what were the materials he required to make a play, he replied: 'A stage, four walls, two characters and one passion'"; in the *Courier* of 1901: "Old Dumas said that to make a play he needed but four walls, two people and one passion"; and in "The Novel Démeublé": "The elder Dumas enunciated a great principle when he said that to make a drama, a man needed one passion, and four walls." Bernice Slote, ed., *The Kingdom of Art: Willa Cather's First Principles and Critical State-ments, 1893–1896* (Lincoln: University of Nebraska Press, 1966), p. 249; William M. Curtin, ed., *The World and the Parish: Willa Cather's Articles and Reviews, 1893–1902*, 2 vols. (Lincoln: University of Nebraska Press, 1970), 1:479, 2:848; *Not Under Forty* (New York: Knopf, 1936), p. 51.

15. "I find that I have painted my life—things happening in my life—with-out knowing," writes Georgia O'Keeffe. "After painting the shell and the shingle many times, I did a misty landscape of the mountain . . . , and the mountain

became the shape of the shingle—the mountain I saw out my window, the shingle on the table in my room. I did not notice that they were alike for a long time after they were painted." *Georgia O'Keeffe*, #52, *Shell and Old Shingle VII* (*Last of Shell and Old Shingle Series*), (1926).

16. This activity, Bachelard suggests, belongs to the phenomenology of the verb "to inhabit": only those who curl up can *inhabit* with intensity. *The Poetics of Space*, p. xxxiv. The old German word for "to build" was *buan* [*sic*] and means "to dwell," Heidegger reminds us, "that is, to stay, to remain. . . . The word 'bin' (am) came from the old word to build, so that 'I am', 'you are' means: I dwell, you dwell. The way that you are and I am, . . . is 'Buan' [*sic*], dwelling. . . . Dwelling is the basic principle of existence." Cited in Christian Norberg-Schulz, *Existence, Space and Architecture* (London: Studio Vista, 1971), p. 31.

17. Cited in Bachelard, *Poetics of Space*, p. 51.

18. Ibid., pp. 9–10.

19. Ibid., pp. 6, 33, emphasis original.

20. Munro, *Originals*, p. 91.

21. Ibid., pp. 57, 472. Munro's speculations are based on a study of the works of twentieth-century American women artists, beginning with Mary Cassatt. For a radical feminist perspective on the relationship of women to nature see Susan Griffin, *Woman and Nature: The Roaring Inside Her* (New York: Harper & Row, 1978), and Mary Daly, *Gyn/Ecology: The Metaethics of Radical Feminism* (Boston: Beacon, 1978); for the viewpoint of an environmental scientist see Carolyn Merchant, *The Death of Nature: Women, Ecology, and the Scientific Revolution* (New York: Harper & Row, 1980); for the connection of women's artistic expression to primal sources see Lucy Lippard, *Overlay: Contemporary Art and the Art of Prehistory* (New York: Pantheon, 1983).

22. Ellen Moers, *Literary Women* (Garden City, N.Y.: Doubleday, 1976), p. 258.

23. *News Letter*, Dec. 12, 1938, in Stephen Tennant, ed., *Willa Cather on Writing* (New York: Knopf, 1949), pp. 30–32. According to Cather's friend Elizabeth Shepley Sergeant, the sonata form was meant literally: "There were to be three parts, every one with Italian musical nomenclature," the first *molto moderato*, "Tom Outland's Story" *molto appassionata*, though one might question exactly how "free" was Cather's handling of this form. Oddly enough, in describing the most self-conscious of Cather's novels, Sergeant notes in the same passage Cather's belief that " 'writing' should be so lost in the object that it doesn't exist for the reader. Self-consciousness was a mistake—the writer should be just an eye and an ear." Elizabeth Shepley Sergeant, *Willa Cather: A Memoir* (1953; reprint, Lincoln: University of Nebraska Press, 1963), pp. 203–4. I think Cather meant the *sonata allegro*—ABA—form of the first movement of a classical sonata. For further discussion of this point see Richard Giannone, *Music in Willa Cather's Fiction* (Lincoln: University of Nebraska Press, 1968), pp. 153–54. This appears to be one of those Emersonian contradictions (or correspondences) of the sort that is to be found in the landscapes of nineteenth-century luminist painters Fitz Hugh Lane and Martin Johnson Heade, where precise classical structure coexists with an

attempt to eliminate all reminders of paint and painter, all intermediaries between viewer and nature. See Barbara Novak, *American Painting of the Nineteenth Century* (New York: Praeger, 1969; rev. ed., Harper & Row, 1979), Chapters 5, 6, 7.

24. Wetherill displayed some of these artifacts in a booth at the World's Columbian Exposition. Had Cather gone to Chicago in 1893, she might have first seen the Indian pottery in a setting far different from the Southwest!

25. *Not Under Forty*, p. v.

26. Willa Cather, *One of Ours* (New York: Knopf, 1922), p. 458.

27. E. K. Brown, *Willa Cather*, completed by Leon Edel (New York: Knopf, 1953), p. 236.

28. It is because man's love has been for her body, Simone Weil wrote, that woman's "most mortal enemy then is time—time our torture." Rather than constantly measure up to the ever-triumphant monster, Weil preferred to deny it, to short-circuit it. Perhaps this is what she meant, in *Waiting for God*, by "accepting the void." Cited by Claudine Hermann, "Women in Space and Time," in Marks and Courtivron, *New French Feminisms*, pp. 171, 169.

29. E. Relph, *Rational Landscapes and Humanistic Geography* (London: Croom Helm, 1981), p. 24, emphasis original.

30. *Landscape* entered the English language in the last years of the sixteenth century along with Dutch scenery, or *landschap*, in painting, John Stilgoe writes. By *landschap* the Dutch understood "the traditional territorial *landschaft*, the houses surrounded by common fields and encircled by wildernesses of ocean or swamps. The English garbled the meaning, however, and *landschap* entered the language as *landskip* and meant at first only the Dutch paintings." By 1630, the word, now spelled *landscape*, had come to mean large-scale rural vistas and also large-scale ornamental gardens objectifying ideals of beauty and still paintings of rural vistas. *Common Landscape of America: 1580–1845* (New Haven: Yale University Press, 1982), pp. 24–25.

31. Like landscape as background for an official portrait, the "scene" of a "pose," such visions become fully integrated with the world of make believe, Yi-Fu Tuan suggests in *Topophilia*, p. 133. See also John Brinckerhoff Jackson, "Landscape as Theater," in *The Necessity for Ruins and Other Topics* (Amherst: University of Massachusetts Press, 1980).

32. There is "a remarkable similarity between the detached clarity of the landscape paintings and Descartes's argument for adopting a detached attitude for an understanding of the world and man's [*sic*] place in it," Relph points out. "If Johannes Vermeer and others painted for the fashion of their times, Descartes formulated and focused its philosophical character. This character rested above all on faith in the capacity of disinterested human reason to describe and to account for the order of things." *Rational Landscapes*, pp. 27–28.

33. *Discourse 4*, cited by Relph, ibid., emphasis added. This is "the Cartesian dualism which is at the basis of all detached and objective science—the human mind has the role not only of disclosing the mechanical and mathematical character of nature, but also of dominating its surroundings" (p. 28). This is also the basis of the patriarchal domination of nature that is at the root of our current

ecological crisis. See Annette Kolodny, *The Lay of the Land: Metaphor as Experience and History in American Life and Letters* (Chapel Hill: University of North Carolina Press, 1975), and Merchant, *The Death of Nature*.

34. As we have seen in Chapter 6, these formal gardens impose a visual geometry on the landscape; their plan is an extension of the plan of the house, movement in which is now controlled by a floor plan that separates and compartmentalizes, creating conditions of harmony and proportion, as Edith Wharton had argued. The straight lines separating the spaces of the garden, as extensions of the spaces of the house, not only control movement, but create long vistas for the eye to follow. Intellectually and physically, the garden becomes a series of outdoor rooms, a transitional zone between the planned and orderly pattern of the house and the random, uncontrolled and disorderly expanse of nature.

35. Cf. Raymond Williams: "A working country is hardly ever a landscape. The very idea of landscape implies separation and observation." *The Country and the City* (New York: Oxford University Press, 1973), p. 120.

36. Willa Cather, *The Professor's House* (New York: Knopf, 1925), p. 28. Further references to this edition are cited parenthetically in the text.

37. See the Professor's exchange with Augusta (*The Professor's House*, p. 99.) It is not possible to tell which version of the "Song of Songs" inspires the Professor's musings; his fascination is with the images themselves—the Rose, the Lily, the Tower of Ivory.

38. Cather heard the story from Richard Wetherill's brother. She also read the account of Mesa Verde by the Swedish anthropologist Nordenskjöld. See the Letter on *The Professor's House* in Tennant, ed., *Willa Cather on Writing*, p. 32. For an account of Richard Wetherill, see Frank McNitt, *Richard Wetherill: Anasazi*, rev. ed. (Albuquerque: University of New Mexico Press, 1966).

39. "Memories are dreams, because the home of other days has become a great image of lost intimacy," Bachelard suggests; and "human returning takes place in the great rhythm of human life, a rhythm that reaches back across the years and, through the dream, combats all absence." *The Poetics of Space*, pp. 100, 99.

40. Brown, *Willa Cather*, p. 241.

41. Ibid., p. 247.

42. Bachelard, *Poetics of Space*, p. 197, emphasis original.

43. Ibid., p. 206; Noël Arnaud, cited in Bachelard, *Poetics of Space*, p. 137. See also Chapter 13, "Intimate Immensity."

44. Letter on *Death Comes for the Archbishop*, *The Commonweal*, Nov. 23, 1927, reprinted in Tennant, ed., *Willa Cather on Writing*, pp. 6-12.

45. See *The Dance of Death*, designed by Hans Holbein and cut in wood by Hans Lutzelburger, with introductory essays by Philip Hofer and Amy Turner Montague (Boston: The Cygnet Press, 1974). Hofer discusses the dating and authorship in his essay. "The frequent meditation on death and physical decay was not a superficial exercise resulting in a happy end," Montague writes. "Rather, it was one portion of late medieval devotional practice intended to help men in their daily lives to place in the larger context of eternity the things which concerned them" (unpaged).

46. Montague points out that the earliest recorded instance of the Dance of Death theme is in dramatic form; performed in a church in Normandy in 1393, it was "none other than the famous *danse macabre*." The first known pictorial representation was painted in 1424–25 on the southern wall of the cemetery of the Church of the Holy Innocents. "Inside the wall was a cloister; above the cloister, charnel houses were built. The cemetery doubled as a marketplace, and the cloister and charnel houses were frequented by Parisians *en promenade*. In such a location, the mural was a familiar sight to the people of Paris." In 1485, the Paris printer Guyot Marchant published the *Danse Macabre* in book form, with four figures to a page, the whole a rendition of the processional on the cemetery wall. Holbein's representation is different: he abandoned the idea of a procession, meaning his work as a *book*, which the reader can study only one page at a time. Each of Holbein's pages contains—like Cather's scenes in *Death Comes for the Archbishop*— a single detailed scene that stands meaningfully alone.

47. Letter on *Death Comes for the Archbishop*, in Tennant, ed., *Willa Cather on Writing*, pp. 9–10. The frescoes of Puvis de Chavannes were also the inspiration of Mary Fairchild MacMonnies's mural *Primitive Woman* in the Woman's Building of the World's Columbian Exposition in 1893. See Chapter 1. The "situation" might be a direct reference to the novels of Edith Wharton, with whom Cather was often compared. See Burton Rascoe, e.g., "Mrs. Wharton and Some Others," *Shadowland* (Oct. 1922): 35–36, 68.

48. Letter on *Death Comes for the Archbishop*, in Tennant, ed., *Willa Cather on Writing*, p. 10.

49. Ibid., pp. 5–6, emphasis added.

50. This is Hopkins's "inscape"—projecting one's inner space upon the outer landscape through meditation. Rainer Maria Rilke described a similar experience:

> Space, outside ourselves, invades and ravishes things:
> If you want to achieve the existence of a tree,
> Invest it with inner space, this space
> That has being in you. Surround it with compulsions,
> It knows no bounds, and only really becomes a tree
> If it takes its place in the heart of your renunciation.
> [Cited in Bachelard, *Poetics of Space*, p. 200]

51. For descriptions of these "real" events and places, see Paul Horgan, *Lamy of Santa Fé* (New York: Farrar, Straus & Giroux, 1975).

52. In fact, Lamy's cathedral, and his other French buildings in Santa Fé— hospital, chapel, school—are not so well suited to the landscape as the adobe buildings he found "primitive." In the novel, however, I think Cather intends no disharmony between structure and place.

53. Bachelard, *Poetics of Space*, pp. 208, 137, 203.

CHAPTER 11

1. Willa Cather, Letter on *Death Comes for the Archbishop*, *The Commonweal*, Nov. 23, 1927, reprinted in Stephen Tennant, ed., *Willa Cather on Writing* (New York: Knopf, 1949), pp. 5–6.

2. Willa Cather, Letter on *Shadows on the Rock*, *Saturday Review*, Oct. 17, 1931, reprinted in Tennant, ed., *Willa Cather on Writing*, p. 15.

3. John Berger, "Millet and the Peasant," in *About Looking* (New York: Pantheon, 1980), pp. 73–74.

4. On fairy tales see Walter Benjamin, "The Storyteller," in *Illuminations*, trans. Harry Zohn (New York: Schocken, 1968), p. 102. On childhood reveries, see Gaston Bachelard, *The Poetics of Reverie: Childhood, Language, and the Cosmos*, trans. Daniel Russell (Boston: Beacon, 1969). See also Thoreau: ". . . the pond . . . is one of the oldest scenes stamped on my memory. . . . Almost the same johnswort springs from the same perennial root in this pasture, and even I have at length helped to clothe that fabulous landscape of my infant dreams." "The Bean-field," *Walden* (Princeton: Princeton University Press, 1973), pp. 155–56. Further references are to this edition.

5. Willa Cather, "Miss Jewett," in *Not Under Forty* (New York: Knopf, 1936), p. 76.

6. The phrase comes from Cather's review of an exhibit at the Carnegie Gallery in Pittsburgh for a weekly called *The Library*: "A Philistine in the Gallery," Apr. 21, 1900, reprinted in William M. Curtin, ed., *The World and the Parish: Willa Cather's Articles and Reviews, 1893–1902*, 2 vols. (Lincoln: University of Nebraska Press, 1970), 2:764. Curtin points out that although Cather saw other work by Puvis (in the Boston Public Library and the Carnegie Gallery), she probably first saw the Ste. Geneviève murals when she traveled to Paris in 1902 with Isabelle McClung; the journey included a pilgrimage to Barbizon to see the landscape of Millet, Courbet and Breton (2:760, n. 13).

7. Cf. Georgia O'Keeffe's *Cross by the Sea, Canada* (1932), and *Black Cross, New Mexico* (1929). "The Canadian crosses were singing in the sunlight," O'Keeffe wrote of the first painting; and of the second, the crosses were like "a thin dark veil of the Catholic Church spread over the New Mexico landscape. . . . Large enough to crucify a man," they stood out dark against the sky, and against the grey hills, "all the same size and shape with once in a while a hot-colored brown hill." Georgia O'Keeffe, *Georgia O'Keeffe* (New York: Viking, 1976), unpaged, #68 and #64, reprinted from *An American Place* (1944) [exhibition catalog].

8. Dickinson's poem, #234 in Thomas H. Johnson, ed., *The Complete Poems of Emily Dickinson* (Boston: Little, Brown, 1960), is as follows:

> You're right—"the way *is* narrow"—
> And "difficult the Gate"—
> And "few there be"—Correct again—
> That "enter in—thereat"—
>
> 'Tis Costly—So are *purples*!
> 'Tis just the price of *Breath*—

With but the "Discount" of the *Grave*—
Termed by the *Brokers*—"*Death!*"

And after *that* — there's Heaven—
The *Good* Man's—"*Dividend*"—
And *Bad* Men—"go to Jail"—
I guess—

Thoreau's statement comes from "Reading" in *Walden*: "A written word is the choicest of relics. It is something at once more intimate . . . and more universal than any other work of art. It is the work of art nearest to life itself. It may be translated into every language, and not only be read but actually breathed from all human lips;—not be represented on canvas or in marble only, but be carved out of the breath of life itself" (p. 102).

    9. Willa Cather, *The Professor's House* (New York: Knopf, 1925), pp. 69, 106, 258, 275. Further references to this edition are cited parenthetically in the text. As early as 1896 Cather had announced her dedication to the "mighty craft" of literature, when as a young reporter she affirmed her own inward vision and, like Dickinson, described her artistic vocation as religious. "In the kingdom of art there is no God, but one God," she wrote, "and his service is so exacting that there are few men born of woman who are strong enough to take the vows. There is no paradise offered for a reward to the faithful, no celestial bowers, no houris, no scented wines; only death and the truth." It is likely that Cather knew the Dickinson poems beginning to be published in the 1890s. "Certainly somebody on the *Courier* liked Emily," Bernice Slote suggests, "for while Willa Cather helped to edit the paper in the fall of 1895 'Success is Counted Sweetest' appeared in two issues," though the choice could have been made by the co-editor, Sarah B. Harris, who had written an article on Dickinson for the April 6, 1895, issue. *The Kingdom of Art: Willa Cather's First Principles and Critical Statements, 1893–1896* (Lincoln: University of Nebraska Press, 1966), pp. 417, 345.

    10. Letter from Sarah Orne Jewett to Willa Cather, Dec. 13, 1908, in Annie Fields, ed., *Letters of Sarah Orne Jewett* (Boston: Houghton Mifflin, 1911), pp. 249, 250.

    11. "Miss Jewett," in *Not Under Forty*, pp. 78–80.

    12. Tom does not mean "possession" as male possession of the female landscape; rather, he experiences Thoreau's sense of center: "Wherever I sat, there I might live, and the landscape radiated from me accordingly," or "Sometimes, . . . I sat in my sunny doorway from sunrise till noon, rapt in a revery, amidst the pines and hickories and sumachs, in undisturbed solitude and stillness, while the birds sang around or flitted noiseless through the house, until by the sun falling in at my west window, or the noise of some traveller's wagon on the distant highway, I was reminded of the lapse of time. I grew in those seasons like corn in the night, and they were far better than any work of the hands would have been. They were not time subtracted from my life, but so much over and above my usual allowance. I realized what the Orientals meant by contemplation and the forsaking of works." "Where I Lived and What I Lived For" and "Sounds" in *Walden*, pp. 81, 111–12.

    13. "A Mighty Craft," in Slote, ed. *Kingdom of Art*, p. 417.

14. "Miss Jewett," in *Not Under Forty*, p. 80.

15. Mary Douglas, *Natural Symbols: Explorations in Cosmology*, 2d ed. (London: Barrie and Jenkins, 1973). Douglas applies the work of linguist Basil Bernstein to a study of restricted and elaborated rituals, for example: ". . . the differences between the two coding systems [restricted and elaborated] depend entirely on the relation of each to the social context. The restricted code is deeply enmeshed in the immediate social structure, utterances have a double purpose: they convey information, yes, but they also express the social structure, embellish and reinforce it. The second function is the dominant one, whereas the elaborated code emerges as a form of speech which is progressively more and more free of the second function. Its primary function is to organize thought processes, distinguish and combine ideas. In its more extreme, elaborate form it is so much disengaged from the normal social structure that it may even come to dominate the latter and require the social group to be structured around the speech, as in the case of a university lecture" (p. 44). Cf. Thoreau on "Visitors": "If we are merely loquacious and loud talkers, then we can afford to stand very near together, . . . but if we want to speak reservedly and thoughtfully, we want to be farther apart. . . . If we would enjoy the most intimate society with that in each of us which is without, or above, being spoken to, we must not only be silent, but commonly so far apart bodily that we cannot possibly hear each other's voice in any case." *Walden*, p. 141.

16. Willa Cather, *Shadows on the Rock* (New York: Knopf, 1931), p. 136. Further references to this edition are cited parenthetically in the text.

17. Cf. art historian Lucy Lippard: "I realized . . . that I was exploring the collective components of the origins of art—which lay, of course, in religion. . . . I understood that if art is for some people a substitute for religion, it is a pathetically inadequate one because of its rupture from social life and from the heterogeneous value systems that exist below the surface of a homogenized dominant culture." *Overlay: Contemporary Art and the Art of Prehistory* (New York: Pantheon, 1983), p. 7.

18. George Steiner, "The Retreat from the Word," in *Language and Silence* (New York: Atheneum, 1977), pp. 13–14.

19. Ibid., pp. 12–14, emphasis original.

20. Ibid., pp. 12–13.

21. In a sense, Professor St. Peter's walled garden is his *Walden*, Thoreau's "walled-in pond."

22. "Music has always had its own syntax, its own vocabulary and symbolic means," Steiner writes. With mathematics, it is "the principal language of the mind when the mind is in a condition of non-verbal feeling. . . . A classical sonata . . . is not in any way a verbal statement. . . . *Nevertheless*, there is in classical forms of musical organization a certain grammar or articulation in time which does have analogies with the processes of language. Language cannot translate into itself the binary structure of a sonata, but the statement of successive subjects, the fact of variation on them, and the closing recapitulation do convey an ordering of experience to which language has valid parallels." "Retreat from the Word," p. 23, emphasis original.

23. Letter on *Shadows on the Rock*, in Tennant, ed., *Willa Cather on Writing*, p. 15.

24. "Millet and the Peasant," pp. 75–76. Millet failed in these paintings, Berger believes, because the language of traditional oil painting could not accommodate this subject. Imagine "a peasant suddenly appearing at work between the table and the *view*, and the social/human contradiction becomes obvious. . . . The visitor or solitary onlooker who surveys the scene [is] an *alter ego* for the spectator himself. But there was no formula for representing the close, harsh, patient physicality of a peasant's labor *on*, instead of *in front of*, the land. And to invent one would mean destroying the traditional language for depicting scenic landscape" (pp. 76–77; emphasis added on view, otherwise original). This, as I have shown, is exactly Cather's experiment.

25. Louis XIV as the "Sun King" is a literal symbol of man in the center of his universe, replacing an older concept of the Ptolemaic *primum mobile* encircling the female earth in the time of Elizabeth I. See Carolyn Merchant, *The Death of Nature: Women, Ecology, and the Scientific Revolution* (New York: Harper & Row, 1980). Merchant traces the growing concern with "the sense of sickness and decay in the organic order of nature" in the late sixteenth and early seventeenth centuries. Among the new scientific discoveries that disrupted the old hierarchical structure of the macrocosm was the new cosmology of Copernicus, which advanced the heliocentric hypothesis and challenged the Ptolemaic geocentric model of the universe. As Bernard Fontenelle later perceived in his *Plurality of Worlds* (1686), Copernicus displaced the female earth from the center of the cosmos and replaced it with the masculine sun: "He snatches up the earth from the center of the universe, sends her packing, and places the sun in the center, to which it did more justly belong. . . . All now goes round the sun, even the earth itself; and Copernicus to punish the earth for her former laziness, makes her contribute all she can to the motion of the planets and heavens; and now deprived of all the heavenly equipage with which she was so gloriously attended, she has nothing left her but the moon, which still turns round her." Cited in ibid., p. 128.

26. Gerda Lerner, "The Challenge of Women's History," in *The Majority Finds Its Past* (New York: Oxford University Press, 1979), p. 178. See Edwin Ardener, "Belief and the Problem of Women" (1972) and "The Problem Revisited" (1975) in Shirley Ardener, ed., *Perceiving Women* (London: Malaby Press, 1975), for an investigation of the perceptions of "dominant" and "muted" groups. Studying women as a "muted" group, Ardener argues that female experience not shared by men is perceived by males as "wild."

27. Elaine Showalter, "Feminist Criticism in the Wilderness," in Elizabeth Abel, ed., *Writing and Sexual Difference, Critical Inquiry* 8 (Winter 1981): 204. Cf. Annette Kolodny, who in examining the familiar captivity narrative finds that by asking two new questions of the text—how do women's concerns constitute part of the historical context for this work? and what is the symbolic significance of gender in this text?—a submerged plot does indeed stand out in bold relief. See "Turning the Lens on 'The Panther Captivity': A Feminist Exercise in Practical Criticism," in ibid., pp. 329–45, and *The Land Before Her: Metaphor as Experience*

and History in American Life and Letters (Chapel Hill: University of North Carolina Press, 1975).

28. "In 1862 Millet painted *Winter with Crows*. It is nothing but a sky, a distant copse, and a vast deserted plain of inert earth, on which have been left a wooden plough and a harrow. Crows comb the ground whilst waiting, as they will all winter. A painting of the starkest simplicity. Scarcely a landscape but a portrait in November of a plain. The horizontality of that plain claims everything. To cultivate its soil is a continual struggle to encourage the vertical. This struggle, the painting declares, is back-breaking." Berger, "Millet and the Peasant," p. 69.

29. Drid Williams, "The Brides of Christ," in Ardener, *Perceiving Women*, pp. 105–25. This is the simplest of Williams's diagrams. She goes on to show that the horizontal "life-track" of the nuns is actually a continuous spiral.

30. Cf. St. Teresa's "I began to think of the soul as if it were a castle made of a single diamond or of very clear crystal in which there are many rooms," in *The Complete Works of St. John of the Cross*, vol. 2, trans. A. Peers, p. 201, cited in Williams, "The Brides of Christ," p. 114.

31. The Carmelite Order belongs to one of the contemplative monastic orders of the Roman Catholic church which originated with hermits living on the slopes of Mount Carmel in North Palestine in the twelfth century. The particular order with which Williams is concerned is the Discalced (unshod) Order founded by St. Teresa of Avila in the mid-sixteenth century, which in 1975 had a total membership of 13,643 women living in monasteries—that is, as hermits, not collectively in convents. Williams warns against considering our twentieth-century desires for solitude and privacy as of the same nature as the conviction of the contemplative nuns, who "isolate themselves in virtue of a submission to a cosmology, to a whole view of the world, to a conceptual structure which involves notions of mankind's and womankind's relation to nature, to time, to ultimate questions about life and death, and . . . to God." Speaking only in prayer, their very language, though English (in the group she examines) is different from the language we speak. The Carmelites' rejection of the notion of "usefulness"—that is, biological, economic, political "use"—and the notion of human male partnership is not, according to Williams, a negative conception, but rather an expression of a connection with an interior life; they, themselves, are living, though hidden, symbols of that way of life. The diagram used here indicates that "inside" and "above" are connected, and the Carmelites' commitment to ceaseless prayer is a constant striving upwards, for self-transcendence—in St. Teresa's words: "Each of us in an Interior Castle . . . the innermost Mansion, the central point is 'in-dwelt' by God. Let us imagine that there are many rooms in this castle, of which some are above, some below, others at the side. In the centre, in the very midst of them all is the principal chamber in which God and the soul hold their most secret exchanges." "The Brides of Christ," pp. 105–10, 117–18. I do not know that Cather had the Carmelites in mind in creating her Jeanne Le Ber, but she would have at least known of the order from Henry James's *The American*, in which Claire de Cintré becomes a Carmelite nun.

32. Yi-Fu Tuan, *Topophilia: A Study of Environmental Perceptions, Attitudes, and Values* (Englewood Cliffs, N.J.: Prentice-Hall, 1974), pp. 133–34.

33. Letter on *Shadows on the Rock*, in Tennant, ed., *Willa Cather on Writing*, p. 16.

34. Cf. the response of Edith Wharton to the First World War as a violation by men of all that gives life meaning, and the meaningful encounter, in the midst of the destruction of Gerbéviller, with a nun in hob-nailed boots, working in the fields, who seems to leave pink peonies "flowering in the very prints of her sturdy boots!" *Fighting France: From Dunkerque to Belfort* (New York: Scribner's, 1915), p. 104. See Chapter 4.

35. On the relationship between film and the modern novel see Alan Spiegel, *Fiction and the Camera Eye: Consciousness in Film and the Modern Novel* (Charlottesville: University of Virginia Press, 1976).

36. Cf. William Butler Yeats's "Thoor Ballylee," in Ireland, with its winding stair which appears in so many of his poems and gives title to one of his books.

37. Willa Cather, "The Novel Démeublé," in *Not Under Forty*, p. 48.

38. Adrienne Rich, "When We Dead Awaken: Writing as Re-Vision" (1971), in *On Lies, Secrets, and Silence: Selected Prose, 1966–1978* (New York: Norton, 1979), pp. 33–49. See also "Vesuvius at Home: The Power of Emily Dickinson" in the same volume, pp. 157–84.

39. Elizabeth Shepley Sergeant, *Willa Cather: A Memoir* (1953; reprint, Lincoln: University of Nebraska Press, 1963), pp. 240–41.

40. Edith Lewis, *Willa Cather Living: A Personal Record* (New York: Knopf, 1953; reprint, Lincoln: University of Nebraska Press, 1976), pp. 153–60.

41. *Nebraska State Journal*, Jan. 13, 1895, p. 13, in Slote, ed., *Kingdom of Art*, pp. 346–47.

42. Ibid., pp. 347–48.

43. Showalter, "Feminist Criticism," p. 192. See also I. M. Lewis, *Ecstatic Religion* (Harmondsworth, England: Penguin, 1971) and Evelyn Underhill, *Mysticism* (London: Methuen, 1942). Emily Dickinson also linked "the wild" with spiritual ecstasy in her poetry. Nathaniel Hawthorne, withdrawn into his own "owl's nest," created Hester Prynne as an expression of his isolation: consigned to an ambiguous middle status between the wildness of the forest and the culture of the town, living as an outcast between them, assigned polarized and contradictory meanings within the same symbolic system, Hester civilized is mostly silent; the warning of the enforced cap that confines her luxuriant hair is a memory of the way in which our own wildness has been confined, for, says Hawthorne, linking Hester to Anne Hutchinson, "Woman when she feels the impulse of genius like a command of Heaven within her, should be aware that she is relinquishing a part of the loveliness of her sex, and obey the inward voice with sorrowing reluctance, like the Arabian maid who bewailed the gift of prophecy." "Mrs. Hutchinson," in *Biographical Sketches of Nathaniel Hawthorne* (Boston: Houghton Mifflin, 1883), 12:217–19. Cf. also Edith Wharton's description of withdrawing into the strange, secluded, supernatural world of the imagination in the unpublished fragment of her autobiography, "Life and I," cited in Chapter 5.

44. Cf. Cather's priests, with their ambiguous middle status between civilized and wild, between male and female (photographs in the Horgan and Howlett books show them in elegantly embroidered surplice and gown), between language

and silence. See Ann Douglas, *The Feminization of American Culture* (New York: Knopf, 1977), on the "femininity" of the clergy.

45. Susan Sontag, "The Aesthetics of Silence," in *Styles of Radical Will* (Farrar, Straus & Giroux, Delta ed., 1966), p. 11. Cf. contemporary French feminists like Monique Wittig, who writes in *Les Guérillères*: "The women say, the language you speak poisons your glottis tongue palate lips. They say, the language you speak is made up of words that are killing you. They say, the language you speak is made up of signs that rightly speaking designate what men have appropriated." Annie Leclerc calls on women "to invent a language that is not oppressive, a language that does not leave speechless but that loosens the tongue." Shoshana Felman sees "the challenge facing the woman today [as] ... nothing less than to 'reinvent' language, ... to speak not only against, but outside of the specular phallogocentric structure, to establish a discourse the status of which would no longer be defined by the phallacy of masculine meaning." *Parole de femme*, trans. Isabelle de Courtivron, in Elaine Marks and Isabelle de Courtivron, eds., *New French Feminisms* (Amherst: University of Massachusetts Press, 1980), p. 179; "Woman and Madness: The Critical Phallacy," *Diacritics* 5 (Winter 1975): 10, all cited in Showalter, "Feminist Criticism," pp. 20–21.

46. Lewis, *Willa Cather Living*, p. 155; Sergeant, *Willa Cather*, pp. 228–30, 241–42.

47. Lippard, *Overlay*, p. 8.

48. Claire Cooper, "The House as Symbol of the Self," in John Lang, Charles Burnette, Walter Moleski and David Zachon, eds., *Designing for Human Behavior* (Stroudsburg, Pa.: Dowden, Hutchinson & Ross, 1974), p. 445. Cf. John Stilgoe's discussion of the *roland*—a tree or staff suggesting the once-potent efficacy of the Old Religion of unhewn trees—in *Common Landscape of America* (New Haven: Yale University Press, 1982). The roland predated Christianity, Stilgoe writes, but came to epitomize "Christian order, for it marked the landschaft hierophany, the place where Christian Heaven touched the wilderness-slaying Christian place made by agriculture and artifice. It objectified the 'peace of the market,' the rule of holy law, and it objectified too a centripetal view of things. ... The roland was indeed an *axis mundi*, a shaft about which a small, almost self-sufficient world continuously revolved" (pp. 18–19).

49. Mircea Eliade, *The Sacred and Profane: The Nature of Religion*, trans. Willard R. Trask (New York: Harcourt, Brace, 1959; Harper Torchbook, 1961), pp. 26, 43, emphasis original. Cf. Dolores Hayden, *Seven American Utopias: The Architecture of Communitarian Socialism, 1790–1975* (Cambridge, Mass.: MIT Press, 1981), pp. 42–43, on the boundaries and vantage points of intentional communities.

50. Cited in Cooper, "House as Symbol," p. 444.

51. Eliade, *Sacred and Profane*, p. 177.

52. Carl Gustav Jung, *Autobiography*, pp. 250–53, cited in Cooper, "House as Symbol," p. 444.

53. Lippard, *Overlay*, p. 18; Mircea Eliade, *The Forge and the Crucible: The Origins and Structures of Alchemy*, trans. Stephen Corrin (New York: Harper, 1962), p. 44; Lippard, *Overlay*, p. 15, emphasis original.

54. Sandra M. Gilbert and Susan Gubar, *The Madwoman in the Attic: The*

Woman Writer and the Nineteenth-Century Literary Imagination (New Haven: Yale University Press, 1979), p. 95.

55. Ibid., pp. 93–94, 97. How, Gilbert and Gubar ask, do we reconcile such negative metaphoric potential with the cave's positive mythic possibilities? How does a woman "distinguish what she is from what she sees, her real creative essence from the unreal cutpaper shadows the cavern-master claims as reality" if she is "Reading the Parable of the Cave / while living in the cave?" In the discovery of the Sibyl's "dim hypaethric cavern" in Mary Wollstonecraft Shelley's introduction to *The Last Man* they find an answer. This cave is a female space that belonged to the female hierophant who received "divine intuitions" through an aperture in the roof of her sea-cave which "let in the light of heaven" and inscribed them on tender leaves and fragments of delicate bark. The way to the Sibyl's cave has been forgotten, and the coherent truth of her leaves shattered and scattered; the way can be "remembered" by accident, but "the whole meaning of the sibylline leaves can only be re-membered through painstaking labor: translation, transcription, and stitchery, re-vision and re-creation" (pp. 102, 95–97).

56. Ibid., pp. 98, 102.

57. In Gladys A. Reichard's *Spider Woman: A Story of Navajo Weavers and Chanters* (1934; reprint, Glorieta, N.M.: Rio Grande Press, 1983), an anthropologist writes of living among the Navajo in order to learn to weave. She records the story of Marie, her Indian teacher/friend/sister, whose difficulty in learning to weave and in being accepted as a weaver—her parents had designated her older sister as the weaving woman in their family and Marie as the tender of the sheep—could be the familiar story of the woman artist's struggle for time and space to learn her craft and for acceptance. Weaving-Woman, as the Indians call their visitor, is given her own hogan—a cave-like "shade" of each Navajo weaving woman open on the sides, with her own loom inside—a place both private and communal, for Marie and the other members of her "family" visit her there. Indeed, the communal is at the core of the author's experience: the encouragement and support of the other women are as important as the pieces of weaving she completes. She finds that women have time and space here to make in solitude beautiful and useful things valued by the entire community; the rhythm of the weaving is at one with the rhythm of communal life. See also Marta Weigle, *Spiders & Spinsters: Women and Mythology* (Albuquerque: University of New Mexico Press, 1982).

58. Helen Diner, *Mothers and Amazons* (New York: Julian Press, 1965), p. 22.

59. Sir James George Frazer, *The Golden Bough: A Study in Magic and Religion* (1922; abridged ed., London: Macmillan, 1957), p. 459.

60. Adrienne Rich, "Cartographies of Silence," in *The Dream of a Common Language* (New York: Norton, 1978), pp. 16–20.

61. Walter Benjamin, "The Storyteller," in *Illuminations*, p. 91. Cf. Penelope's weaving and unweaving her husband's shroud during the telling of the *Odyssey*.

INDEX